MEDIATION AND
CONFLICT RESOLUTION

D0621744

MEDIATION AND CONFLICT RESOLUTION IN SOCIAL WORK AND THE HUMAN SERVICES

Edward Kruk, Editor

University of British Columbia

Nelson-Hall Publishers/Chicago

Project Editors: Libby Rubenstein and Dorothy Anderson
Compositor: E.T. Lowe
Text Designer: Keata Brewer
Manufacturer: Integrated Book Technology
Cover Painting: "The Couple" by Christina Haglid

Library of Congress Cataloging-in-Publication Data
Mediation and conflict resolution in social work and the human services / Edward Kruk
    editor.
      p.   cm.
    Includes bibliographical references and index.
    ISBN 0–8304–1468–1 (pbk).
    1. Social service.   2. Conflict management.   3. Mediation.
    4. Interpersonal conflict.   I. Kruk, Edward.
361.3'2'0684--dc21   97-2283
                                                       CIP

Copyright © 1997 by Nelson-Hall Inc.
Reprinted 1998
All rights reserved. No part of this book may be reproduced in any form without permission in writing from the publisher, except by a reviewer who wishes to quote brief passages in connection with a review written for broadcast or for inclusion in a magazine or newspaper. For information address Nelson-Hall Inc., 111 N. Canal Street, Chicago, Illinois 60606.

Manufactured in the United States of America

10 9 8 7 6 5 4 3 2

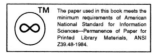

TM The paper used in this book meets the minimum requirements of American National Standard for Information Sciences—Permanence of Paper for Printed Library Materials, ANSI Z39.48-1984.

CONTENTS

ACKNOWLEDGMENTS

Thanks to all the people who devoted extraordinary time and effort to this project—the contributors for their hard work and persistence, the reviewers for their unflinching eyes for detail and instructive commentary, and the many others involved in the mediation endeavor for their enthusiasm and encouragement to see this book through to completion.

This book is a testament to the passion that those in the field of mediation and conflict resolution—practitoners, policymakers and researchers—share in the endeavor. I have been extremely fortunate to work in settings and locales where this passion has made itself manifest in many different ways.

Thank you to my clients and students over the years who have contributed in the largest measure to my growth as a professional and academic in the fields of social work and conflict resolution, and to whom I owe a huge debt. Thanks also to my professional and academic colleagues, especially fellow board members of the British Columbia Mediation Development Association, associates at Family Mediation Canada, and fellow faculty members at the School of Social Work, University of British Columbia, for your stimulation and challenge, sharing of expertise, and continued strong support of this project.

In particular, I would like to recognize the contributions of the following who acted as reviewers of the chapter manuscripts: Doug and Angie Chalke, Marje Burdine, Peggy English, Tom Kalpatoo, Anne O'Mahony-May, David Gustafson, Kathleen Gibson, Carole McKnight, Jean Hannon and her "team" at Family Services of Greater Vancouver, Mark Morissette, Susan Gamache, Lynda Lougheed, and Lucinda Ferndon. Your considered, thoughtful, and detailed commentary contributed in large measure to the final outcome. Paul Young of Family Mediation Canada was instrumental in getting the research project on mediation practice methods and models, which was the stimulus to this project, off the ground, and Jay Lees, my graduate assistant, helped toward its completion. Bernie Mayer and Peter Maida were of immense help in the beginning stages of work on the book as I struggled with the apparent enormity of the task.

And finally thanks to Nelson-Hall Publishers, who saw the potential in taking on this project and provided encouragement and support throughout.

1

INTRODUCTION

Mediation and Conflict Resolution in Social Work and the Human Services: Issues, Debates, and Trends

by Edward Kruk

In virtually all of the fields of practice in which they work, settings in which they locate themselves, and client populations that they serve, social workers and human service professionals are routinely called upon to deal with conflict. Yet for most conflict produces discomfort, and conflict resolution presents numerous challenges on both a personal and professional level. Most of us tend to respond to conflict in fairly patterned ways, often reflecting styles established in our families of origin. Although few of us can be said to adhere rigidly to a single style of dealing with the variety of conflict situations that present themselves in our personal and professional lives, we rely on certain modes more than others as we are not always aware of what other modes may be at our disposal.

Conflict is not inherently destructive; indeed, it can present us with an opportunity to strengthen relationships and achieve personal growth. Our attitude and reaction to conflict is a critical factor: unresolved conflict is destructive; addressing, even welcoming, the conflict in our lives can transform an adversarial situation into something constructive.

The purpose of this book is to explore a method of conflict resolution that has been associated with positive outcomes related to not only settling disputes, but also to personal development and restoration of important relationships in a range of diverse fields of practice, professional practice settings, and client populations relevant to social work and the human services. Mediation, defined most simply as "negotiation assistance," has been demonstrated effective in a wide range of interpersonal conflicts and disputes. The book focuses on the theory, process, and skills of mediation, and attempts to integrate conceptual frameworks that guide mediation and conflict resolution with generalist social work theory and practice. It is unique in two respects: it covers a broad range of fields of practice and applications, and it is specifically directed toward social work students and practitioners as well as allied human service professionals.

Given that conflict resolution is a central theme in social work practice and mediation is an integral part of social workers' repertoire of practice methods, it is surprising that this is the first mediation practice text written from a social work perspective. Social workers interface with systems in conflict and regularly assume the mediation role, acting as intermediaries and emphasizing collaborative and consensual processes when dealing with conflict. Yet during the past twenty years, as the application of mediation has been extended to a wide array of settings and issues, social work education and the social work profession have not kept pace with the rapid development of mediation as both a conceptual framework and a practice approach to conflict resolution in diverse settings. Although there has been significant growth in the number of social workers who identify themselves as mediators, either specializing in conflict resolution or including the mediation role as an integral part of their practice, the field of mediation is gradually being appropriated by the legal profession which, as Umbreit (1995) notes, does not offer a strong foundation to serve as an alternative to itself. The opportunity still exists for social workers and other human service professionals to have a far greater impact on the developing field of mediation.

It is hoped that this book will provide a new tool for social work and human service educators to institutionalize the mediation role and mediation as a practice model in their curricula and for practitioners to apply mediation in a wide range of settings and fields of practice. Historically, social work is a tradition rich in mediation and conflict resolution. It has affected the development of mediation theory and practice in an important way, both as a formal practice model and via a set of interventive techniques that can be used (with other roles) to meet the unique circumstances of particular conflicts and client systems. As Mayer (1995) notes, mediation is the natural outgrowth of social work practice because its goal is to help empower people in conflict to solve their own problems, and because it builds on core social work theory and skills such as problem analysis, communication, and systems intervention. Not only are the theory and skill sets of mediation and generalist social work practice highly compatible, but each embraces a set of core values to which practitioners are expected to adhere, including client self-determination, empowerment, and professional competence.

Conflict, Conflict Resolution, and Mediation

Conflict can be defined as a state that occurs when "two or more parties believe they have incompatible objectives" (Kriesberg, 1982). This definition implies that there are two essential elements of conflict: people's perception that they are in conflict and their attendant feelings, and the objective differences in the outcomes they are seeking. Moore (1986) identifies five causal elements in social conflict: relationship issues, value conflicts, inconsistencies in data, structural problems, and conflicts about interests. It is important to understand which aspects of the conflict the parties are struggling with at any one time (Mayer, 1995).

Conflict is unavoidable in daily life; what is important is how we respond to it. According to Thomas and Kilmann (1974), conflict can be viewed as having two dimensions: assertiveness and cooperativeness. The assertiveness dimension reflects the extent to which we seek to satisfy our own concerns and promote our own needs and interests; the cooperativeness dimension reflects the degree to which we focus on satisfying others' concerns, needs, and interests. Using these two basic dimensions as a foundation, Thomas and Kilmann have delineated five distinct styles of conflict management: competition, accommodation, avoidance, compromise, and collaboration. Each of these modes represents a useful set of social skills as each is useful in certain situations; the effectiveness of a given mode depends on the requirements of a specific conflict situation. Most people are capable of using all five modes; however, most of us tend to rely on certain modes more heavily than others.

As mediators it is crucial that we know four things: our dominant mode(s) of handling conflict (and conversely the mode(s) we tend not to use); what other modes exist as alternative ways to deal with conflict; in what types of situations our conflict mode works well; and when we might consider other methods of conflict management.

Competitive individuals are high on assertiveness and low on cooperation, able to stand up for their rights, defending positions they believe are correct, or simply trying to "win." This power-oriented mode can be useful when quick and decisive action is vital, where unpopular courses of action need implementing, and when one is defending a position one believes to be correct. The drawback of relying on this mode is that others may be unwilling to disagree with or influence you, closing you off from other perspectives and the opportunity to learn.

Accommodators, on the other hand, are high on cooperation but low on assertiveness, neglecting their own needs to satisfy those of the other. Accommodation may take the form of selfless generosity or charity, or yielding to another's point of view. When you realize you may be wrong, when the issue is more important to the other than to you, and when preserving harmony is important, accommodation is a helpful strategy. But the costs of relying on such a mode include your own ideas and concerns not getting the attention, respect, and recognition they deserve, and the likelihood of others taking advantage of you.

One who avoids or withdraws from conflict, pursuing neither his or her own nor the other's concerns, scores low on both cooperation and assertiveness. Avoidance may be beneficial when an issue is trivial, when one perceives no chance of satisfying one's concerns, when the potential for damage if a conflict is confronted is high, and when one wants to let people and tensions cool before directly dealing with conflict. But a pattern of denial or avoidance of conflict results in one's influence suffering and decisions being made by default. And sometimes an inordinate amount of energy can be devoted to the avoidance of issues.

Compromise is somewhere between assertiveness and cooperation, where the objective is to find an expedient solution that partially satisfies both parties. Seeking a middle ground, each side gains and gives up something. Such a strategy is useful to arrive at expedient solutions when under time pressure, when the issues in dispute are moderately important, or when people are locked into mutually exclusive positions. However, within such a mode one can sometimes lose sight of larger issues underlying conflicts and an overemphasis on bargaining and trade-offs might undermine interpersonal trust and deflect attention away from the merits of each person's position.

Mediation is based on the collaborative style of conflict management, which is high on both assertiveness and cooperativeness and involves a mutual problem-solving process to resolve conflicts, seeking a solution that will fully satisfy the concerns and interests of all parties. Collaboration is critical when important relationships are at stake, the issues in dispute are significant to both parties, and a commitment can be made to spend the time required in a problem-solving process. Like other conflict resolution modes, however, there are potential drawbacks even to collaboration: trivial problems do not require optimal solutions and it is hard to justify the time and energy that collaboration requires for such issues.

Mediation is a collaborative conflict resolution process in which two or more parties in dispute are assisted in their negotiation by a neutral and impartial third party and empowered to voluntarily reach their own mutually acceptable settlement of the issues in dispute. The mediator structures and facilitates the process by which the parties make their own decisions and determine the outcome, in a way that satisfies the interests of all parties in the dispute.

This definition reveals a number of core components of mediation. First, it is a distinct *process* and practice model, with an internal structure and clearly defined stages. The mediator is responsible for establishing the framework and controlling the negotiation process. Second, what is mediated is the *conflict* or dispute, usually reframed as "issues" to resolve; mediation is a model that is used in situations where there is a conflict, dispute, or disagreement between two or more parties. Third, it is a method of conflict resolution that emphasizes *collaboration* as the preferred mode, calling for a high degree of both assertiveness and cooperation from the parties, searching for solutions that will benefit everyone involved. This approach presumes the potential for balanced negotiation between the parties and containment of hostility. Fourth, the mediator facilitates or *assists negotiation* between the parties, helping them in areas such as communication, solving problems, exploring options, and evaluating options that can lead to decision making and agreement. Fifth, the mediator remains *neutral and impartial,* neither biased toward any one of the parties nor invested in any particular outcome. Sixth, *empowerment* is seen as the cornerstone of mediation: the parties are empowered to make their own decisions and are responsible for determining the outcome. Being responsible for the process of mediation, the mediator can assist the parties in developing options and evaluating alternatives and can guide in the decision making, but he or she does not have the power to make decisions or even recommendations. Finally, the parties determine and enter into a *voluntary, mutually acceptable agreement,* one that is made without any form of coercion or control.

Essentially, mediation is negotiation assistance. The mediator is a manager of other people's negotiations. Whereas the mediator controls the process, the parties determine the outcome. The primary outcome of mediation is an agreement, that is, the settlement of issues in dispute. The goal of the mediator is to assist the parties' negotiations in a neutral and impartial manner so that they can reach that agreement.

Mediation is thus an alternative form of dispute resolution that falls on a continuum of dispute resolution processes, between negotiation and arbitration-adjudication. Negotiation consists of direct discussions between two or more parties toward the goal of reaching a mutually satisfactory agreement. Arbitration is a system of deciding issues in dispute by presenting them to a neutral third party who is empowered to make either a recommendation or a decision on the issues. The process is more formal than negotiation and mediation but less formal than adjudication. Adjudication is a system of deciding issues in dispute by presenting them to a neutral third party who is empowered to make a binding decision on the issues. Adjudication involves a more formal process of rules of evidence and precedents and takes place within an adversarial or competitive framework of conflict resolution—frequently a courtroom.

Mediation is also a distinct practice model that differs from other social work practice theories and approaches. As mediators, we no longer have the luxury of approaching our clients entirely from a social work perspective since mediation draws heavily not only from the human service professions but also from the fields of law and labor negotiation. Some of the key defining features of mediation are summarized by Kelly (1983), who distinguishes it from other practice models. First, the *goal* of mediation is distinct and usually limited to a negotiated settlement of issues; the mediation *process* is relatively time-limited, task and goal oriented, focusing on the future and containing psychological exploration; the *role* of the mediator is that of a neutral facilitator, but one who is highly active and directive: the mediator structures the process, manages conflict, educates, organizes information, facilitates communication, helps the parties develop bargaining proposals, suggests options, helps the parties evaluate alternatives, and produces a written agreement; *assessment* in mediation is limited as mediation is future oriented; and *interventions* are not only adapted from social work and the human service professions but from the fields of law and labor negotiation, including conflict management, negotiation strategies, and bargaining techniques.

Mediation is not a panacea. Mediation as a conflict resolution process and a social work practice model is most likely to be useful when there are issues in dispute that are clear and when the parties agree to what these are. The parties must be assertive enough to be able to represent their interests in the negotiations and must be able to influence one another; and parties are interdependent and their relationship will be ongoing, cooperation between them will be required, and they must have at least the potential to cooperate with each other; there is some commonality of needs and interests; and collaboration is seen as preferable to adversarial methods. Conversely, mediation may not be useful where there is insufficient time or energy to complete the process, when one of the parties clings to a particular position (and appears more interested in "winning" or revenge), when there is a high degree of hostility between the parties, when one of the parties is submissive or the other dominant (to the point that the weaker party is unable to represent her or his interests in the negotiations), and when one of the parties is in danger of abuse.

Values, Theory, and Skills

In 1991 the National Association of Social Workers, in recognition of the centrality of conflict resolution in the professional activities of social workers and the importance of mediation as a social work practice role and practice theory, approved its *Standards of Practice for Social Work Mediators*. These standards were developed to complement the NASW Code of Ethics and are consistent with the standards of the major North American mediation organizations. Their purpose is to promote the practice of mediation among social workers, provide a set of ethical directives for social work mediators, and furnish consumers, employers, and referral sources with a set of standards for ethical mediation practice. Six core principles and twelve standards of practice are delineated, which together provide a set of ethical guidelines for social work mediators (see appendix).

A number of conceptual frameworks have informed the development of mediation as a distinct practice theory. Foremost among these is the negotiation theory of Fisher and Ury (1991). In their classic work, *Getting to Yes,* Fisher and Ury define a number of key aspects of "principled negotiation": separate the people from the problem; focus on interests, not positions; invent options for mutual gain; insist on objective criteria. Of particular importance to the field of mediation is the concept of shifting the parties from position-based bargaining to interest-based negotiation. Interests may be defined as the concerns and needs of the parties that must be met if they are to be satisfied with the outcome of the negotiations. Interest-based negotiation focuses on interests, rather than positions, outcomes, solutions, or proposals. In practice, this involves eliciting from stated positions the underlying interests that they represent, and then seeking out and using the common interests between and among parties in the dispute. Conflict resolution is then advanced by reframing the conflict in such a way that all parties' interests are taken into account: "How can we meet x's interests while at the same time meeting y's interests?" Identifying the interests underlying positions and reframing the conflict accordingly result in new options for conflict resolution becoming apparent, advancing the process of conflict resolution. The generation of criteria, or core values, around which options are evaluated is the final element of the Fisher and Ury framework.

Communication theory, the problem-solving framework, and systems theory also underpin the mediation approach. The strategic use of neutral and neutralizing language, metaphor, questioning, and reflection are core communication principles essential to effective mediation. The problem-solving model provides mediation with a staged process applicable to the wide range of settings, fields of practice, client populations, and issues of concern relevant to mediation. Systems theory posits that each system has a unique integrated character in which the whole of the system is greater than the sum of its parts, and mediation focuses on the system as a whole in determining the parties to a conflict resolution process.

The mainstream settlement-oriented model of mediation is comprised of three basic phases: a beginning stage, where issues in dispute and the parties' positions are elicited; a middle phase, where the interests underlying stated positions are identified and commonalties in interests sought; and an ending stage involving the generation of options for settlement, evaluation of options, and settlement of the dispute (Haynes, 1994). Breaking the process down further, seven distinct stages (with corresponding skills) of the mediation process can be identified:

1. *Intake, orientation, and screening:* The parties are interviewed separately or jointly, basic information is sought, and the parties are oriented to the mediation process. The ability of the parties to negotiate, represent their

interests, and make decisions is carefully assessed. An agreement to mediate is made, including a commitment on the part of both parties to make responsible use of the process, and procedural guidelines are negotiated.

2. *Defining the issues:* Each party is asked to identify salient issues and their positions on the issues; the mediator's task at this stage is to develop an agenda that frames the issues in dispute in a neutral manner.
3. *Data gathering:* Information relevant to the issues in dispute is sought.
4. *Exploring needs and interests:* Concerns, needs, and interests underlying stated positions are brought to the surface, and the parties are moved away from position-based bargaining. Once a focus on interests underlying the positions is established, the mediator identifies commonalties in interests and reframes the issues in a way that incorporates these interests.
5. *Generating options for settlement:* The mediator assists the parties in developing options addressing their needs and interests. Brainstorming and other option-generating techniques are introduced, including discussion of the "best alternative to a negotiated agreement" when parties are at an impasse.
6. *Evaluating options and problem solving:* Decisions are made on the options in relation to resolving each issue in dispute and agreements are recorded.
7. *Settlement:* A written agreement is formulated and the parties take the mediated agreement to their lawyers, where appropriate, to be formed into a legally binding agreement.

Generic social work practice skills of attending and focusing in the beginning stages, including using questions, partializing, summarizing, reflecting, and intervening more actively in the negotiation phase—such as helping the parties to explore and evaluate options—serve as the foundation for effective mediation. A number of specialized skills, however, are critical to the mediation endeavor, including normalizing, reframing, shifting the parties from position- to interest-based negotiation, mutualizing and emphasizing the common connectedness between the parties, future focus, task focus, conflict management, establishing and maintaining ground rules, preempting, confrontation, reality testing, and caucusing.

Issues, Debates, and Trends

In recent years, the assumptions underpinning the mainstream settlement-driven model of mediation have come under a great deal of scrutiny and challenge. The short-term, task-oriented, sequentially structured and future-focused nature of settlement-driven mediation, it is argued, provides a blunt instrument for the resolution of disputes in which unresolved emotional issues are preventing one or both parties from effectively negotiating. Mediation is often considered inappropriate in these situations; other mechanisms for resolving such disputes, however, are limited.

A second concern relates to the issue of mediator neutrality and impartiality (Rifkin, Millen, & Cobb, 1991). The settlement-driven model assumes that the parties not only have the ability to articulate their needs and interests and the skills to negotiate and problem solve but will be able to do so in a balanced way, arriving at a fair and equitable agreement. The reality is that most conflict situations in which social workers intervene contain an imbalance of power, knowledge, or functioning between parties in dispute. The presumption of mediator neutrality is perhaps most problematic in situations of spousal abuse in family conflict. The inherent and marked imbalance of power in abuse situations not only renders abused parties powerless to represent their interests in mediation, but seriously compromises their safety.

These and other issues in the field of mediation have sparked a number of lively debates (Elwork & Smucker, 1988). The result is that the field is beginning to embrace a number of emergent models of practice that provide alternatives to the mainstream approach. This diversifying trend stands in sharp contrast to the emphasis on a unitary unifying approach in the earlier days of mediation as a distinct field.

Some current debates in mediation policy and practice are worth noting.

- Does mediation privatize social conflict? Does mediation serve to deflect attention away from structural factors contributing to social conflict and human oppression?
- Should mediators be certified? Should they be certified within their particular field of practice or should a generic form of certification be established? Will formulating and monitoring quality standards diminish the expansion of mediation and the creation of innovative approaches?
- Should the mediator's role be that of structuring negotiation between the parties, or should mediation adopt a more therapeutic or educative approach, focusing on the emotional aspects of the conflict or dispute, or teaching communication, negotiation, and problem-solving skills?
- Should mediation be limited to the settlement of disputes or should it seek to transform the parties through empowerment and recognition? Should mediation aim toward healing, restoring, or restructuring relationships and restoring harmony between parties?
- Should the mediator assume a neutralist or interventionist stance in regard to the process of mediation or to the outcome? Should the mediator avoid taking sides throughout the mediation process or actively intervene in situations where there are imbalances of power, knowledge, or functioning? To what extent should mediators actively shape the outcome of an agreement? Is mediator neutrality an illusory concept?

- What is the place of mediation in situations of marked imbalances of power, knowledge, and functioning? Can such imbalances be overcome in mediation, or will the weaker party continue to be disadvantaged within the mediation context? Can mediation effectively address such imbalances and provide an opportunity for empowering the disadvantaged party to identify needs and interests and have these acknowledged and dealt with in a safe environment? How can mediators strive for "fairness" when dealing with such imbalances, and can they effectively counter the problem of inequitable bargaining positions?
- Should mediation be mandatory/legislated in certain contexts or voluntary? In which specific instances is mandatory mediation contraindicated?
- Is mediation better situated in a court-based or independent facility? Should mediation be an adjunct or an alternative to the legal process?
- In regard to confidentiality, should mediation be open or closed? Should communications made during mediation sessions be considered privileged, or should mediators be able to give evidence regarding the mediation in subsequent court proceedings?
- Should third parties be allowed into the mediation process? To what degree should attorneys, advocates, and experts participate in the process? What about the role of support persons to parties in dispute? What about affected third parties in a dispute?
- In regard to the delivery of mediation services to culturally diverse clients and communities, can a generic mediation model be adapted to fit cross-cultural contexts, or should new culturally-sensitive and culturally-specific models be developed, building on the traditional dispute resolution processes within the culture of the clients with whom mediators work?

These and other issues pertaining to the process and practice of mediation remain largely unresolved. However, a number of alternative approaches to the mainstream settlement-driven, structured negotiation model have emerged in recent years that reflect a variety of positions in relation to these debates. Today, the strength of mediation lies in the richness and diversity of mediators' approaches to parties in conflict, as the complexity and diversity of the fields of practice in which we work, the client populations we serve, and the types of conflicts we encounter call for a range of mediation options.

There have been a number of attempts to categorize existing and emerging mediation models, particularly in the family arena (Brown, 1985; Irving & Benjamin, 1987; Schwebel, Gately, Renner, & Milburn, 1994). Kruk (1995) examined the use of various models from the perspective of a sample of two hundred fifty Canadian family mediators, exploring the utility of different models of practice to diverse client and dispute characteristics, including the nature and level of the conflict, balance of power between the participants,

communication skill level, problem-solving ability, negotiation skill level, nature of preconflict relationships, and potential for future cooperation. This study
found that although the structured negotiation model continues to serve as the
foundation of most mediators' practice, three models in particular are emerging
as adjuncts or alternatives to the mainstream approach: the therapeutic model,
emphasizing the emotional and relational elements of disputes; a feminist-
informed approach, focusing on the reality of gender-based power inequities in
dispute resolution; and culturally specific models, which build on the traditional dispute resolution processes of diverse cultures. Current mediation practice may thus be conceptualized as falling on different points along several
continua, from structured to therapeutic, neutralist to interventionist, directive
to nondirective, depending on how mediators align themselves in relation to the
current debates in the field and to various client and dispute characteristics.
This particularly applies to social workers and human service professionals,
who were more likely to make frequent use of these models than mediators
from other professional backgrounds, who tended to rely on the structured negotiation approach. Social workers and human service professionals are clearly
leading the way in the development of new mediation approaches.

Therapeutic approaches have been advanced by several social work and
human service scholars, and three in particular are worth noting: Irving and Benjamin's (1987) "Therapeutic Family Mediation," Kruk's (1997) therapeutic-
interventionist approach, and Johnston and Campbell's (1988) trilevel model
of high conflict mediation. These models share a number of common elements: the primary focus of mediation is underlying emotional issues and relational processes blocking agreement, and the goal of mediation is not only
settlement of the dispute, but restructured relationships, enhanced communication and problem-solving skills, and increased cooperation or at least reduction of conflict between and among the parties. The mediator's role is not only
that of facilitator of negotiations but also that of therapist and educator. The
mediation process is longer than the structured negotiation approach, with an
emphasis on assessment and premediation preparation, and postmediation
follow-up. Irving and Benjamin's "Therapeutic Family Mediation" model encompasses four phases—assessment, premediation, negotiation, and follow-
up—and is presented as an alternative to the structured negotiation approach
in family mediation. Kruk's therapeutic-interventionist approach is designed
specifically for social workers and human service professionals to facilitate
the development of postdivorce parenting plans, and positions the mediator in
the additional role of advocate for children's interests in the mediation process.
Johnston and Campbell's trilevel model of high-conflict mediation, simultaneously focusing on the external, interactional, and intrapsychic levels of the
conflict, is directed at family mediation parties exhibiting a high level of conflict or at an impasse in their dispute, and provides for mediation and counseling by the same professional, a lengthy period of premediation assessment

and counseling, the option of individual and group counseling as an adjunct to the mediation process, and a lengthier implementation stage that assists the parties in following through on their agreement.

Quite distinct from yet related to the therapeutic approach is the feminist-informed model, a highly interventionist process that highlights the reality of gender-based power imbalances in mediation and provides a strong counter-point to the neutralist-structured negotiation model (Irving & Benjamin, 1995). The primary focus of feminist-informed mediation is power imbalances blocking a fair and equitable agreement, and the goals of mediation are twofold: a settlement of the dispute that is equitable and fair, and the empow-erment of the disadvantaged party in the dispute. Mediator neutrality is seen as potentially dangerous to women who are viewed as disadvantaged within the settlement-driven approach, particularly those at risk of abuse, and the role of the mediator is interventionist in process and outcome. The mediation process places a strong emphasis on screening of the nature of the parties' prior relationship, particularly in regard to abuse and power imbalances, and provides a variety of safety measures during the negotiation, including the op-tion of caucusing or a "shuttle diplomacy" format.

The structured negotiation "one size fits all" mediation model has also come under a lot of scrutiny because it is grounded in the values of white Anglo-American culture and disregards significant cultural variations regard-ing dispute resolution. Despite its emphasis on cooperation and informal dis-pute resolution, which appears to resonate more with the collectivist orientation of many minority cultures and less with the individualist and more competi-tive orientation of the dominant culture, mediation in the United States and Canada has largely failed to engage members of racial and ethnocultural minorities and remains largely a white middle-class phenomenon.

Duryea and Grundison (1993) point out that mediation has been prac-ticed in a variety of cultural contexts for centuries, but in vastly different forms. One illustration of these differences is a comparison of mediation processes used in North American aboriginal and traditional Chinese societies. Native peoples are consensus oriented, and elders are not unilateral decision makers; the primary emphasis is on peacemaking, healing, and rebuilding relationships in dispute resolution. Chinese mediators, on the other hand, explain laws and government policies and attempt to persuade disputants to comply to a resolution that they deem appropriate to the situation; as promot-ers of a harmonious agreement, they educate, criticize, and effectively woo disputants toward certain outcomes.

The North American structured negotiation mediation model rests on a number of culture-bound values and assumptions: (1) communication should be direct and forthright, with confrontation seen as a sign of strength in nego-tiation; (2) there should be full and open disclosure of relevant facts and feel-ings; (3) individual rights and interests are paramount; and (4) the process should be short term, task focused and future oriented. Duryea and Grundison (1993) caution that these values stand in sharp contrast to those of more collectivist cultures in which family, group, and community norms and goals prevail in conflict situations; where longer-term harmony takes precedence over immediate resolution of a dispute; where attitudes toward conflict and confrontation are markedly different, including an intolerance or avoidance of direct expressions of conflict in the interests of harmony, diplomacy, or saving face; and in which attitudes toward self-disclosure may be contrary to dominant cultural norms.

The culturally competent mediator begins by reflecting on his or her own culture and the culturally-based values, assumptions, and biases that are brought to one's mediation practice. At the same time, it is important to develop an understanding of the worldview of culturally diverse clients, and to draw upon the resources of diverse cultures in conflict resolution. The primary emphasis of culturally-specific mediation approaches is the provision of conflict resolution services that are grounded in the traditional dispute resolution processes of the disputants' culture. This is not to say that there is a single recipe for mediating with people from a given culture; every person is an individual who may be a member of a number of cultures and subcultures and who can exercise choices that take him or her beyond the norms of any of these groups (Este & Barsky, 1995). A culturally-specific approach to mediation is above all an elicitive or consultative approach, as opposed to prescriptive, in which the process preferences of culturally diverse clients are carefully assessed and a dispute resolution process is custom-designed and built from the bottom up, rather than being imposed from the top down.

Apart from the emerging mediation models described above, a great deal of discussion in mediation circles in recent years has focused on the transformative mediation approach outlined by Bush and Folger (1994) as an alternative to the settlement-driven structured negotiations model (referred to by Bush and Folger as the "problem-solving" orientation). Proponents of transformative mediation emphasize the capacity of mediation for engendering moral growth through empowerment and recognition, with attention focused on change for mediation participants at both the individual and relational levels (Docking & Pries, 1995). The primary focus of the transformative approach is the emotional and psychological needs of the participants, along with the nature of the relationship between the parties. Within the transformative approach, the mediator's role is first to encourage the empowerment of the parties through the exercise of their self-determination in deciding whether and how to resolve their dispute; and second to promote the parties' mutual recognition of each other as human beings with a need for validation of their needs and interests, as well as recognition of their own contribution to the conflict. The goal of reaching agreement on issues in dispute becomes secondary to the objectives of empowerment and recognition (Bush & Folger,

1994). Such a mediation process orients the parties toward dialogue, empathy, and mutual aid, which may or may not conclude with a formal written agreement.

Bush and Folger's humanistic approach to mediation is echoed by others in the field who emphasize the potential of mediation for repairing relationships, restoring harmony, and promoting healing. Gold (1993) focuses on the healing and peacemaking aspects of mediation in an approach that acknowledges brokenness, affirms common humanity, and embraces a "preference for peace." As Gold and others (Zumeta, 1993; Huber, 1993) note, the paradigm of healing taps into the spiritual dimension of conflict resolution, in which the parties are helped to listen to their innate wisdom and their deeper needs and interests. Umbreit (1995) proposes a humanistic mediation model, a nondirective, empowering, and therapeutic approach that emphasizes mediation's transformative and healing powers. Such a mediation process, the antithesis of the directive and bargaining emphasis of the settlement-driven approach, orients the parties toward dialogue, empathy, and mutual aid, and places much less emphasis on formal written agreements. It works toward laying the foundation for a heightened sense of community and social harmony, and thus a more complete resolution of conflict.

Application of Mediation in Social Work and the Human Services: Diverse Fields of Practice

From its early emphasis on a unitary approach to practice to unify the field, mediation has developed to the point where it now embraces a range of mediation structures, working methods, and theoretical and practice models. The range of models currently in use is reflective of a wide diversity of client and dispute characteristics. The field has now reached the stage where it can begin to isolate which practice approaches are best suited to which client and dispute characteristics.

Given the diversity of mediation models at their disposal, individual mediators must carefully assess where on the various continua—settlement-driven versus therapeutic, neutralist versus interventionist, generic versus culturally specific—they should locate themselves in working with particular parties in dispute. Such an assessment would consider client styles and preferences (the task becomes particularly challenging when the parties choose opposite extremes on the continuum to resolve their conflict), the type and nature of the dispute, and the field of practice in which one is practicing. While mediator styles and preferences also inevitably enter the mix, mediators should exercise caution not to take the right of choice away from the parties, not to allow their commitment to a particular model to supersede client self-determination.

An increasing number of mediation practitioners find themselves comfortable conceptualizing a continuum of mediation approaches from which they practice. Rigid adherence to a particular framework dramatically limits the potential application of mediation; freeing oneself to move along the continuum of models allows one to work with a much broader array of client and dispute characteristics, and to adopt a client-directed approach to mediation (Docking & Pries, 1995).

Given the wide range of fields of practice presented here, this book represents an attempt to portray the full richness of mediation and its broad range of applications to the practice of social workers and human service professionals. The book is also a testament to the fact that that there is ample room for a diversity of mediation models and approaches to flourish; it tells us that there is no single approach to mediation that is normative. Each field of practice, with its unique constellation of dispute and client characteristics, necessitates a particular approach to the practice of mediation and conflict resolution. While the models presented in this volume locate themselves at very different points along a number of continua—structured-therapeutic, neutralist-interventionist, settlement-driven transformative—they share one important commonality: each is tailored to the unique characteristics of the disputes and conflicts that arise within that field of practice and the unique needs of the parties involved in the dispute. In this respect they are all fundamentally client-directed approaches.

The chapters are written by leading figures in their respective fields of practice. Each begins with a description of the field of practice and the utility of mediation for that field, and is followed by the two main parts of the chapter: an overview of salient *theory,* research, current controversies and debates, and emerging trends in conflict resolution in that field; and a detailed outline of the actual process of mediation *practice* in the field. Alternatives to mediation as a conflict resolution mechanism are also discussed.

The application of mediation in areas that have traditionally been associated with the practice of social workers and human service professionals has in recent years developed apace, and the applications are continuing to grow. Although the centrality of mediation and conflict resolution in social work and the human services is well established, there is still considerable application potential, both in the use of mediation as a formal practice model and in an informal manner, incorporating mediation methods into one's generic practice, applying them liberally to meet the particular circumstances of client systems in conflict. Expertise in formal mediation and flexibility in the use of mediation strategies offer the practitioner the widest range of options to effectively intervene and work toward the resolution of an array of conflicts and disputes.

References

Baruch Bush, R. A. & J. P. Folger. 1994. *The Promise of Mediation: Responding to Conflict through Empowerment and Recognition*. San Francisco: Jossey-Bass.

Brown, S. M. 1985. Models of Mediation. In J. C. Hansen & S. C. Grebe, eds., *Divorce and Family Mediation*. Rockville, MD: Aspen Publishers.

Docking, B. & B. Pries. 1995. Transformative Mediation and Settlement-Driven Mediation: Examining the Divide. *Manitoba Social Worker* 27 (5): 1–11.

Duryea, M. L., & B. Grundison. 1993. *Conflict and Culture: Research in Five Communities in Vancouver, British Columbia*. Victoria, BC: University of Victoria Institute of Dispute Resolution, Multiculturalism and Dispute Resolution Project.

Elwork, A. & M. R. Smucker. 1988. Developing Training and Practice Standards for Custody Mediators. *Conciliation Courts Review* 26: 21–31.

Este, D. & A. E. Barsky. 1995. Cultural Competence in Family Mediation: Examples from Work with the Vietnamese and Ismaili Communities. Unpublished paper.

Fisher, R., & W. Ury. 1991. *Getting to Yes: Negotiating Agreement Without Giving In*. New York: Penguin.

Gold, L. 1993. Influencing Unconscious Influences: The Healing Dimension of Mediation. *Mediation Quarterly* 11 (1): 55–65.

Haynes, J. M. 1994. *The Fundamentals of Family Mediation*. Albany: State University of New York Press.

Huber, M. 1993. Mediation and the Medicine Wheel. *Mediation Quarterly* 10 (4): 355–65.

Irving, H. H. & M. Benjamin. 1995. *Family Mediation: Contemporary Issues*. Toronto: Carswell.

Irving, H. H. & M. Benjamin. 1987. *Family Mediation: Theory and Practice of Dispute Resolution*. Thousand Oaks, CA: Sage.

Johnston, J. R. & L. E. G. Campbell. 1988. *Impasses of Divorce: The Dynamics and Resolution of Family Conflict*. New York: Free Press.

Kelly, J. B. 1983. Mediation and Psychotherapy: Distinguishing the Differences. *Mediation Quarterly* 1: 33–44.

Kriesberg, L. 1982. *Social Conflicts*. Englewood Cliffs, NJ: Prentice-Hall.

Kruk, E. 1997. Parenting Disputes in Divorce: Facilitating the Development of Parenting Plans through Parent Education and Therapeutic Family Mediation. In E. Kruk, ed., *Mediation and Conflict Resolution in Social Work and the Human Services*. Chicago: Nelson-Hall.

Kruk, E. 1995. *Working Methods of Canadian Family Mediators: Implications for Practice*. Paper presented at the ninth annual conference of Family Mediation Canada, Victoria, BC (October).

Mayer, B. 1995. Conflict Resolution. In National Association of Social Workers, *Encyclopedia of Social Work*. Washington, DC: NASW Press.

Moore, C. W. 1986. *The Mediation Process: Practical Strategies for Resolving Conflict*. San Francisco: Jossey-Bass.

National Association of Social Workers. 1991. *Standards of Practice for Social Work Mediators*. Washington, DC: NASW Press.

Schwebel, A. I., D. W. Gately, M. A. Renner, & T. W. Milburn. 1994. Divorce Mediation: Four Models and Their Assumptions about Change in Parties' Positions. *Mediation Quarterly* 11 (3): 211–27.

Rifkin, J., J. Millen, & C. Cobb. 1991. Toward a New Discourse for Mediation: A Critique of Neutrality. *Mediation Quarterly* 9 (2): 151–64.

Thomas, K. W. & R. H. Kilmann. 1974. *Thomas-Kilmann Conflict Mode Instrument*. Tuxedo, NY: Xicom.

Umbreit, M. S. 1995. *Mediating Interpersonal Conflicts: A Pathway to Peace*. West Concord, MN: CPI Publishing.

Zumeta, Z. D. 1993. Spirituality and Mediation. *Mediation Quarterly* 11 (1): 25–38.

2

MARRIAGE AND FAMILY

Mediation of Couple and Family Disputes

by Lois Gold

There has always been a cross-fertilization of ideas, strategies, and models of practice in the human services. Family mediation, a unique synthesis of practice and theory drawn from the fields of labor negotiation, law, and the social and behavioral sciences, is no exception in this regard. In its nascence mediation had to clearly differentiate itself from other disciplines, including social work, counseling, and psychotherapy in order to define and establish itself as a distinct profession. Over time, boundaries have become blurred with the advancement of models of mediation that incorporate a focus on goals such as improved communication and interparty cooperation, reduced anger and hostility, and healing. At this point, the field of mediation embraces a diversity of models and approaches, although discussion and debate remain with respect to whether mediation should be settlement driven or also oriented toward therapeutic outcomes.

The mediation spectrum runs from the work of Haynes (1981), whose formulations emerged from labor mediation and whose approach is highly task oriented and settlement focused, to Ricci's (1980) "Confluent Mediation," a model that emphasizes psychoeducational objectives and improved coparental functioning, to Wiseman's (1990) "Mediation Therapy," a structured decision-making approach toward family restructuring, Irving and Benjamin's (1995) therapeutic family mediation, Kruk's (1993) therapeutic-interventionist model, and Gold's (1993) healing-focused paradigm.

Family mediation is gradually becoming reshaped as a practice model that goes beyond merely settling disputes between and among family members. As mediators have become more adept at dealing with the complex interpersonal and psychological dynamics that underlie family disputes, there has been greater utilization of strategies from the field of family therapy, particularly the brief systemic therapies. Gold (1990), for example, has promoted the use of embedded suggestions, hypothetical questioning, and other techniques drawn from Ericksonian hypnotherapy for their effectiveness in dealing with situations of high conflict and impasse; Gadlin and Ouellette (1986) describe an approach to parent-child mediation based on the Milan family systems model in which positive connotation, circular questioning, and prescription are used; Saposnek (1983) has addressed the use of preemption, paradox, and other techniques from the brief strategic therapies; Maida (1986) has discussed the application of Bowenian family theory, particularly the concepts of fusion and differentiation; and Amundson and Fong (1986) have proposed a family systems approach based on Haynes' (1981) earlier work.

Given that mediation has drawn from the fields of marital and family therapy, particularly the brief systemic approaches, it is interesting that the fertilization has not gone the other way. There has yet to be a defined application of mediation techniques or a model of conflict resolution for working with marital and family disputes within a therapeutic context. This chapter will turn to that inquiry, focusing on how mediation as a model of practice, mediative strategies, and conflict resolution theory can be used in couple and family dispute resolution in clinical settings.

Family Mediation and Therapy: Contrasts and Comparisons

While mediation is clearly distinguished from marital and family therapy by its settlement objectives, it shares certain fundamental assumptions and interventive strategies with brief solution-oriented therapy and family systems theory. The focus in mediation on identifying specific problems to be solved, containing troublesome interactions by concentrating on future behavior, a call for action rather than insight, and generating solutions rather than understanding etiology is similar to the principles defining brief solution-oriented therapies. Its focus on the impact of conflict on the entire family system and its subsystems, and consideration of the interests of all family members in problem resolution, echoes fundamental precepts of family systems theory.

At the same time, the structure and methods of mediation are largely antithetical to an expressive, psychodynamic approach to family therapy. According to Wallerstein (1986), mediation is effective precisely because it is designed to discourage and "undo" the ego regression that occurs in crisis. The highly structured approach of mediation and the ground rules guiding the process are designed to strengthen ego controls and participants' capacity for rational decision making. The "voice of reason" is strengthened by the very structure of mediation.

Mediation, like family therapy, operates fundamentally on a systemic level. The escalation of disputes and conflict can be viewed as a systemic process, whether the dispute is over the division of household tasks in an intact marriage or the division of assets in a disintegrating one. Like family systems theory, mediation theory is based on the recognition of the reciprocal impact of the parties' interactions and the effect the system they create has on the behaviors of the individuals within that system. The principles and operating rules of mediation are designed to change the system from a competitive orientation to conflict to a cooperative one. Mediation is effective precisely because it acts on factors affecting the systemic relationship between cooperation and competition.

Whether the course of conflict takes a competitive or cooperative course, according to an early formulation by Deutsch (1973), largely depends on the parties' ability to see conflict as a mutual problem to be solved rather than a "win-lose" proposition. Marital and family conflict coming to the attention of professional helpers has almost invariably followed a competitive course. As spouses or family members have to defend their feelings against attack, positions become more rigid, differences polarize, and interactions become increasingly adversarial. As each feels that their concerns and needs are not acknowledged or validated, mutual acceptance diminishes, as does trust. Often the parties do not even realize that their relationship is no longer a partnership and that they are in the grip of a power struggle. Because mediation reframes disputes as interconnected problems requiring collaborative, mutually acceptable agreements, it places the parties in a side-by-side search for solutions. The mediation process induces the effects of cooperation into the system, generating an increasing cycle of cooperation. When couple and family relationships have become adversarial, a mediation frame is one of the most powerful and efficient interventions to change parties' stances toward each other and systemically alter family interaction.

A family therapist is also interested in restructuring the family system, but is not necessarily going to focus on how the dynamics of dispute escalation have affected the couple or family. He or she is likely to be more interested in changing power relationships, triangulation, or the family's regulation of intimacy and distance. The unique contribution of mediation is that it can undo the impact of adversarial conflict on the system and allow it to reorganize itself on the basis of recognition, mutuality, and cooperation.

Central to the adaptation of mediation to couple or family conflict is the fact that it operates primarily on the basis of a conflict resolution paradigm, rather than, for example, a psychodynamic approach to conflict. This assumes that family problems and conflict are defined in terms of a competitive approach to differences, and the focus of work is on identifying the underlying concerns and interconnected needs and goals of the parties, narrowing differences, confronting the "right-wrong" polarization and invalidation that ensues from such a stance, and correcting perceptual distortion, attribution of negative motives, and fault-based assumptions. The mediation practitioner encourages behaviors consistent with cooperation and curbs competitive or destructive behaviors without delving into the underlying etiology.

In contrast, a psychodynamic orientation would focus on the underlying causes of conflict. It might examine the need for excessive external validation, threats to self-esteem, problems with trust, and the historic roots of the need to be "right" or to "win." It might explore unrealistic expectations and demands, the personalizing of differences, or the attendant difficulties associated with the fundamental inability to individuate or differentiate oneself from one's family of origin. A systemic approach might see conflict in terms of its functions to maintain stability in the system, rigidity of boundaries, and regulation of intimacy and distance.

One's theoretical model determines what issues will be considered, what information will be sought, and the interventions utilized. A conflict resolution paradigm is interested in methods of responding to conflict, not psychological contributors to conflict. Mediation, which narrows the focus of intervention and contains the exploration of historic emotional issues, allows solutions to be more directly addressed.

This chapter will explore how mediation strategies and techniques may be used in marital and family dispute resolution, the types of marital and family issues that lend themselves to a mediation approach, and the process of integrating these strategies within a therapeutic context. I am not proposing a model of family therapy based on mediation, but exploring how mediation as a practice model and mediation strategies can be used in the realm of couple and family disputes. Central to this approach is that negotiation, not self-understanding, is the main instrument of conflict resolution.

Theory, Debates, and Trends

While there is no existing model of therapeutic intervention in marital and family disputes based on mediation in the professional literature, there are defined areas of practice such as divorce, parent-child interactions, child protection, permanency planning, and adoption mediation. There are a number of issues to be considered in the use of mediation in couple and family disputes, including the types of disputes that can be addressed by a formal mediation process or the use of selected mediation strategies; neutrality and the problem of dual roles; and defining the balance between solution- and process-oriented interventions in emotionally complex disputes.

Types of Couple and Family Disputes That Can Be Mediated

Many people see negotiation as the antithesis of love. The myth of, "If you loved me you would automatically do what I need . . ." (usually without my asking, let alone negotiating), runs deep in the psyche of mainstream North American culture. While generosity is an expression of love, the art of marriage is the art of negotiation of "fit"; that is, how we are going to meet each other's needs, and how our joined life is going to meet our individual expectations and dreams. Most couples in trouble do not understand the kind of negotiation that marriage and family life require. Their usual response is fight or flight until the conflict or unhappy accommodations wear away the very fabric of the marriage.

Any dispute in a relationship that can be defined as a failure to achieve an acceptable "fit" lends itself to a mediation approach in which each person is helped to identify his or her underlying needs and interests, options to address those needs are generated, and agreements based on compromise, trade-offs, and creativity are sought. Disputes over money, allocation of free time, sharing of child-rearing responsibilities, division of family work tasks, relationships with in-laws, job changes or relocation—areas in which negotiation is called for and thriving relationships negotiate successfully—can be approached from a conflict resolution paradigm. The primary focus of a mediation approach, as in brief solution-oriented family therapy models, is on solutions, not increased insight and understanding.

A problem in using a conflict resolution paradigm in the marital and family context is that many couples do not seek help until the inability to resolve differences has resulted in a pattern of either avoidance and withdrawal, or protracted arguing and power struggles, to the point of eroding the foundation of their relationship. By the time many couples seek professional help, the estranged or battered relationship is usually the presenting issue and any mediation of differences can only be addressed within the context of repairing the marital rupture and generating hope that the marriage can be healed. Thus more time must be devoted to dealing with angry feelings and emotional wounds than with disputes that do not have such an emotional overlay.

Particularly in the beginning stages of therapy, mediation and conflict resolution theory provide an effective way to address marital and family deterioration by reframing it as the result of a competitive approach to differences, or an inability to effectively negotiate. By reframing the presenting complaints in terms of undeveloped negotiation skills, and by reviewing the impact of conflict escalation and polarization on the relationship, couples and family members can move from feeling hurt, betrayed, and faulting each other to a more benign view of their problems. This recasts many levels of blame into shared responsibility, and diminishes feelings of failure and inadequacy. As in any formal mediation process, neutralizing, mutualizing, and externalizing the problem definition is a critical first step; stored anger, hurts, and resentments begin to dissipate within a broader perspective in which no one person is seen to be at fault or to blame for the couple's or family's difficulties.

Another issue to consider is using mediation in couple and family disputes is the need to carefully assess the presence of individual psychopathology underlying the escalation and polarization of the dispute. For example, a young couple wanted help negotiating the terms of their relationship with the husband's parents, who were perceived by the wife as intrusive and excessively demanding of their time. As a couple they had been unable to come to an agreement about an acceptable amount of time they would spend with his parents, and this tension was felt by all concerned. After an altercation at a family event, the wife and the husband's family refused to have further contact with each other. Asked by his wife to choose between her and his family, the husband felt "caught in the middle." The issue of negotiating time with his parents was approached using a conflict resolution model, which involved reframing the marital conflict as a problem all young couples face in needing to establish themselves as a separate unit from their families of origin while still maintaining a relationship with them. Within this paradigm, each spouse was helped to identify his and her needs and desires regarding independence and contact with extended family, develop options for addressing those needs, and evaluate those options and negotiate a specific agreement. This took place within the context of the husband's struggle to psychologically separate himself from his family: he was still the accommodating child, deeply fearful of abandonment if he asserted his needs or opposed his parents' requests. Subsequently, it became necessary to use a family of origin therapeutic approach to help him establish autonomy in relation to his family. Toward the end of counseling, we considered whether to have a mediation session with the couple and the husband's parents to deal with the issue of the breakdown in communication, but the couple decided that the husband was now equipped to directly negotiate with his parents and repair the damage between his wife and his family. Thus in this situation a model of negotiation was successfully used in combination with a multigenerational family therapy approach.

Other family issues and disputes that lend themselves to a conflict resolution orientation or a formal mediation process occur during periods of life transition in which there has been a failure to adapt to change. This category includes adolescents striving for more independence, children moving out or an adult child returning home, remarriage and stepfamily formation, care of elderly parents, serious illness, and retirement. All of these are situations in which family members need help renegotiating the terms of their relationship subsequent to an anticipated or unexpected life transition. If problems attendant to family transition have become acute, there is often a symptomatic member of the family whose difficulties warrant therapeutic intervention. Because of the potentially serious underlying psychopathology in families with symptomatic members, more traditional psychotherapeutic interventions are usually indicated in these situations. However, if the family's concerns can be reframed in terms of a failure to recognize and adapt to change, then creative exploration of ways to address these needs and concerns could be the focus of a mediation approach.

The other major category where mediation can be used in a couple or family context is when there is an identified dispute and communication has broken down, specific issues need to be resolved, or a decision needs to be made. Interfamilial or intergenerational disputes where legal action may be involved, such as the division of an estate, how family land should be allocated, or disputes within a family business are examples. When there is an identified dispute and the parties are specifically seeking a resolution of the dispute, a therapeutically-oriented model of mediation can be used from the outset, with the process clearly defined as mediation, and the practitioner's role that of mediator. Because the parties usually identify the repair of relationships as a stated goal, it is important that restoration of goodwill and healing be explicitly targeted as mediation objectives. However, the dynamics leading to family estrangement are complex and the mediator must be careful that in allowing expression of emotions or exploration of historic issues associated with the dispute, he or she is not opening a field of inquiry better served within a family therapy setting. In the context of family mediation, the focus on settlement of the dispute must be maintained. Clients' feelings are acknowledged and validated in order to diffuse the dispute; it is not within mediation's purview to resolve historic emotional issues.

Neutrality and the Problem of Dual Roles

In integrating mediation strategies in couple and family therapy, or therapeutic strategies in family mediation, there is potential confusion over the roles of both practitioner and client. It has always been important for mediators to clearly define their role, and for the parties to understand exactly what mediation is and what it is not. The Code of Ethics of the Academy of Family Mediators prohibits the use of dual roles; that is, one may not provide mediation services to former therapy clients, or therapy to former mediation clients, not only because of conflict of interest concerns but because the two roles are fundamentally different. While facilitating negotiation between and among family members in conflict is a common therapeutic strategy, the therapist is not seen as having a central or critical role in resolving the dispute; whereas a mediator is a third-party neutral whose primary purpose is to bring the parties to an agreement.

When a practice includes both marriage and family therapy and mediation services, it is extremely important for the practitioner's role as either mediator or therapist to be defined in the initial consultation. Because the mediation and therapeutic contracts are based on different assumptions and expectations, it is inadvisable for the practitioner to shift between roles with the same clients. Moving from a therapeutic alliance to the position of neutrality and impartiality required of a mediator can leave clients feeling confused and emotionally abandoned. Therefore, in working to resolve a dispute in couple and family therapy, the practitioner should remain in the role of therapist; in using therapeutically-oriented interventions in mediation, she or he should sustain the role of mediator.

Another reason the practitioner must exercise caution vis-à-vis dual roles relates to the fact that a request for mediation can sometimes be a "back door" to therapy in situations where one of the parties objects to the personal exploration involved within the therapeutic process and perceives mediation as a less threatening, solution-oriented approach. A family with an acting-out adolescent who will not participate in family therapy but would see a mediator, or a married couple where the husband will only consult a mediator about conflicts over money while his wife's desire is for counseling to address the power balance in the marriage, are two common examples.

Because of the potential confusion over the family therapist-mediator's role and consumers' limited knowledge about the differences between mediation and therapy, the initial development of a clear contract is extremely important in working with family disputes, particularly in a dual practice.

Defining the Relationship between Solution- and Process-Oriented Interventions in Emotionally Complex Disputes

In introducing mediation strategies within couple and family therapy, or in using a formal mediation process in the realm of family disputes, the balance between solution and process-oriented interventions, between obtaining agreement on issues in dispute and generating insight or behavioral change, is an important consideration.

Mediation has long been distinguished from therapy by its settlement goals, task focus, and highly structured format. The psychological and emotional benefits accrued from mediation have usually been considered secondary goals or by-products of a cooperative process. It has been generally held that the mediator should intervene in the interaction between the parties to the extent that their behaviors or attitudes interfere with or stalemate the negotiation process.

Mediation of couple and family disputes requires more behavioral and relationship-oriented interventions than other forms of mediation because of the emotional complexity and history of family disputes. Focusing on the settlement of the dispute alone is unlikely to achieve behavioral change in long-established patterns of family interaction. Unlike other disputants, family members develop patterns of emotionally responding to each other that can be highly resistant to change. Two sisters who had established a business together making and selling garden sculpture came to mediation to renegotiate their respective roles in the business. Communication had broken down between them, and the younger sister had fallen back into a childhood pattern of being intimidated by her sister's "controlling" style. While mediation centered on developing a business plan and defining the responsibilities of each sister, one sister's feelings of inadequacy and the other's need for control interfered with their decision making. Thus the process also focused on changing the pattern of dominance and subassertion within their relationship.

In working with couple and family disputes, the practitioner will often be using multiple paradigms. It is difficult to envision adapting mediation strategies to family conflict without inclusion of other therapeutic objectives, or combining conflict resolution techniques with other therapeutic strategies. It is important that there be a clear delineation of objectives, jointly negotiated between practitioner and clients. Clearly stated objectives can help clients make decisions about where to focus at critical choice points in the therapeutic mediation process.

The Mediation Process

There are a number of essential differences between couple and family dispute resolution and mediation in other fields of practice. The interdependence of the parties, the existence of continuing relationships, and the fact that they draw on each other for approval, validation, and support make family members emotionally vulnerable with one another. Conflict has a high degree of emotional overlay and becomes invested with messages about caring, love, and respect. In family disputes, the feelings about how people have been treated may be more important than any material differences between them. Parties are more likely to become defensive and polarized in relation to underlying hurt feelings or power struggles, which need to be acknowledged, especially if the negotiation process stalls.

It can be difficult for family members to separate the issues in dispute from their feelings about each other; it is extremely difficult, in Ury and Fisher's (1983) terms, to "separate the people from the problem," as they are likely to see each other as "the problem." Perceived lack of respect, support, and acknowledgment can result in a painful level of rejection and diminished self-worth, and this is often what the conflict is really about. Therefore, it is particularly important in working with family disputes to probe to identify feelings and concerns underlying the presenting difficulties and to bring to the surface any symbolic issues in the conflict.

It also important to keep in mind that while family disputes tend to involve high levels of emotional enmeshment and intensity, underlying the hurt is the desire to heal and restore the relationship. This desire, when surfaced and acknowledged, can become highly instrumental in the process of conflict resolution. Drawing on the universal desire for wellness and healing is an underutilized aspect of the family mediation process. Gold (1993) outlines a number of strategies to augment the potential for healing inherent in a cooperative process. Framing mediation in terms of its potential to lay the groundwork for healing by describing how a cooperative process allows people to draw on the deeper and wiser parts of self, lay aside old grievances, understand each other's wounds, build trust, and begin to forgive each other stimulates that part of the psyche that Jampolsky (1983) describes as a "preference for peace." Within families, the yearning for love can remain alive even in the most devastated relationships. When the mediator acknowledges how painful current difficulties are, while speaking to the potential for future healing, parties begin, consciously or unconsciously, to think in terms of these possibilities. The mediator can also weave in the language of healing, which speaks to a different part of the psyche than the language of problem solving. This is done by using phrases like "mend" or "heal" the family rather than "resolve" the dispute; create "harmony" in the family rather than "reach a decision;" "wound" rather than "conflict;" "make peace" rather than "settle a grievance." It is also helpful to elicit the parties' highest purpose, the ideal or wished-for outcome in choosing to mediate their conflict so that the unspoken hopes and desires for healing ruptured relationships can become more concrete, visible, and attainable. These strategies essentially stimulate the desire for self-healing and allow the mediator to draw on the universal wish for wellness.

In working with family disputes within a formal mediation process or using mediative strategies in couple and family therapy, a structured, four-stage process is used, as follows.

Stage 1: Problem Definition and Issue Identification

The first stage in the mediation of marital and family disputes is establishing the context for dispute resolution and reframing the presenting problem in neutral, mutual terms. It is helpful to preemptively describe the natural course of a competitive style of conflict resolution: how disputes escalate and take on a life of their own, people lose sight of each other's needs and cling to their initial stated position, and disputants see their own hurts and disappointments but overlook those of others. This places the presenting problems in a normalizing context—the nature of dispute escalation, preempts the justifications parties are likely to use to promote their position, and provides a descriptive set of behavioral norms associated with positive results. This can be a particularly effective method to deal with stored hurts, resentment, and blame, as family members begin to realize, often for the first time, that no one person is responsible for the escalation of the family's difficulties. The task, then, is to begin to engage the couple or family in a side-by-side search for solutions to their conflicts and to begin to change the system from one that is based on competition to one based on cooperation.

The way in which the presenting problem is framed will determine the solutions that will be sought. For example, in the case of the couple with conflict over money, the problem could be framed in terms of the wife's inability to control her spending, the lack of agreement about how financial decisions affecting the family are made, or the couple's differences in values and ideas about financial matters. Each of these problem definitions lead to the exploration of different aspects of the dynamics around money in the family, and to very different solutions.

The manner in which problems and disputes are framed for negotiation is particularly important if one family member is labeled as the identified "problem." In the case of an adolescent whose angry and disrespectful behavior has been identified as the problem and who sees the parents as intrusive, controlling, and critical, the problem can be reframed in terms of the need to identify mutually respectful behaviors and negotiate mutually acceptable expectations appropriate to the growing independence of an adolescent. The focus then becomes the interconnected reciprocal dynamic of the parent-child interaction rather than the teenager's unmanageable behavior.

Neutralizing the problem definition in terms of *differences* in needs, expectations, and desires gives the parties in couple and family mediation a way to depersonalize the dispute and preserve self-esteem. Since the underlying dynamic in many family disputes relates to the need for validation and the inability to recognize differences without one person having to be wrong, the reframing eloquently acknowledges and legitimizes differences, and preempts the pattern of arguing over who is "right."

Stage 2: Identification of Needs, Interests, and Fears That Underlie Positions

While the positions of the parties in dispute may be clear, their underlying concerns may be intangible, vague, or inconsistent. Many people in families have difficulty identifying and asking for what they actually want; most can more readily speak to their complaints. The mediator should thus probe to clarify why a particular position is important, what the person is most concerned or fearful about, and what it is that he or she most wants. The focus in this stage is to help each person clarify his or her needs and goals and to express them in concrete behavioral terms, and for family members to better understand each other's needs and vulnerabilities. Such probing is not for the purpose of increasing historical insight, but is designed to clearly identify *current* needs and interests. It allows family members to "hear each other's thinking," in order to dispel assumptions and misinterpretations, increase empathy, and generate the desire to develop collaborative solutions.

The goal of this stage of mediation is to rebuild a willingness to meet each other's needs. Couples or families in trouble have almost invariably stopped listening to each other. Their interaction is characterized by criticism, complaint, and defensiveness. The desire for love and acceptance, however, is a powerful force in couple and family disputes. Structured, open-ended questions addressed to each party and limiting dialog between the parties allows each to express their anger, hurt, and hopes for the future without being interrupted or sidetracked. Structured questions enable people to access and express their true feelings and allows family members to see each other in their vulnerability and humanness, which is fundamental to forgiveness.

It is important for the mediator to focus on the concrete things that each person does that make the others feel the way they do, and to assist the parties to negotiate for changes regarding those specific behaviors. Clarifying questions should be asked in behavioral rather than emotional terms, from "How do you feel?" to "What do you want? What are the specific changes that will address your needs?" The mediator attempts to get at the bedrock concern, the basic human need reflected in a position.

A couple was referred to marital counseling because they were unable to get along in the family business. The husband wanted the wife to leave the business, which she was reluctant to do. The situation had deteriorated to the point they were unable to discuss issues or make decisions. Using a mediative approach, probing was used to more fully understand the conflict and underlying concerns each had about continuing to work together. What finally emerged were fundamental differences in personality, management style, decision making, and communication that had become exacerbated by the stress of business and financial problems. As this couple came to better understand their needs and differences and attempted to make accommodations, it became apparent that their styles were too dissimilar for them to be able to make business decisions together. They were then able to move to the next stages of negotiation, generating and examining options.

Stage 3: Generation of Options

Ury and Fisher's (1983) negotiation principles can be readily applied to the bargaining stage in couple and family disputes: separate inventing options from judging them; broaden the options rather than looking for a single answer; search for mutual gains; and invent ways of making it easy for others to give you what you want.

Most family members are naive negotiators. The fundamentals of bargaining need to be described, from simple compromise and trade-offs to dovetailing interests, brainstorming, and "sweetening the pie." Each family member is then assisted to develop concrete options to address the specific changes they would like to see in the family system.

Family members can be asked to think of ideas to address the needs of others in the family. Each can be asked what he or she can do differently that might inspire others to give them what they want. They can be asked to think of creative and humorous suggestions that might allow others to achieve their goals. These option-generating strategies are important methods of pattern interruption. Many troubled couples and families are either in avoidant or negative interaction cycles, and most find the bargaining process enjoyable because it replaces long-standing feelings of helplessness and "stuckness" with a sense of hope and empowerment.

In family therapy involving two angry adolescents whose sibling rivalry periodically erupted in violence, the teenagers were asked to come up with ideas that could reduce their fighting. The ideas centered on staying out of each other's rooms, not borrowing anything from the other without permission, respecting each other's possessions, and ceasing name calling. Since there was little trust between them, the discussion turned to assurances that agreements would be followed. They were then asked to brainstorm ideas that would allow each of them to feel more assured; they were encouraged to be as creative as possible in this regard. Soon the notion of assurances was taken to the extreme, with everyone laughing about the kinds of electronic buzzers and silly surveillance devices they could invent. Exploring options in such a hypothetical manner allowed for the safe diffusion of hostility and resulted in a retreat from previous positions.

It is appropriate to take a lighter or even paradoxical approach in the option-generating and bargaining stage of mediation with families. Brainstorming solutions puts all participants on an equal footing since wild and creative ideas are invited and no one is challenged to defend their ideas. By generating options in this manner, changes can be contemplated without parties being threatened. As the mediator lists the most promising options for all to see, the hope that solutions can be found is reinforced and the parties begin to recognize that change is possible.

Stage 4: Bargaining and Decision Making

Marital and family therapy often involves negotiation for change. Powerful resistances to change exist inside each family member's psyche and within the family system. Strategies drawn from mediation theory and brief strategic therapies such as reframing the problem, narrowing differences, emphasizing common interests and goals, reviewing past problem-solving successes, accessing positive memories to realign the accessibility of emotional resources, conjecture or hypothetical questions that lead to an unconscious rehearsal of the future course of events, projecting images of what marital or family life would be like if the dispute were resolved, using "BATNA" (the best alternative to a negotiated agreement—what will happen to the family if matters are not resolved), developing traded assurances, and fractionating (asking for the one thing each wants most from the other) are all important in reducing resistance and helping family members be less fearful of change.

The mediator should make efforts to initially obtain agreement on issues that appear to be the most resolvable, and around which there is likely to be a high degree of compliance. Such simple agreements disrupt long-standing patterns of impasse and attendant feelings of helplessness. The willingness of one family member to make changes for the benefit of other family members conveys caring and can be used to begin to move the family in a positive direction. Decisions made should be put in writing by the mediator as this strengthens family members' commitment to upholding agreements and reduces confusion and the potential for future conflict. At the same time, because of the intensity and frequency of family interactions and the difficulty in changing long-established family patterns, it is important to build in an allowance for imperfect compliance with agreements, and for this to be seen as a normal part of the process of change.

Case Study

An engaged couple was referred to the family therapist-mediator in regard to a dispute between the young woman and her parents over the couple's planned interfaith wedding ceremony. The young couple's relationship with the woman's parents had become increasingly strained in the past year, including a period of eight months when the woman ceased all contact with her parents. Hurt and despairing, the parents felt the fiancée was turning their daughter against them, and had begun to question his character and to make inquiries about him in the community. The growing tension reached a crisis with the parents' refusal to attend or help pay for the wedding because they felt their religious concerns were not being considered. The couple felt that the parents were attempting to dictate the terms of the wedding and violating their right to determine their own marriage vows. All attempts to discuss the wedding turned into power struggles and resulted in further estrangement.

A mediation process was used in this case. The initial meetings were separate caucuses, at the parties' request. It was apparent that each person's major concern was the damaged relationship between the young woman and her parents. Even though the parents had a marked distrust of the fiancée, common goals were identified, including a desire to improve communication, trust, and comfort with each other. Everyone's pain was about not feeling accepted or respected by others in the family, and although they needed to resolve the matter of the wedding, each party's primary concern focused on repairing the relationship.

The family therapist-mediator was forced to grapple with the question of whether this case was better served by family therapy, given that the underlying problems related to longer-standing problems within the family, not the identified dispute. The case may have been approached from the perspective of the daughter's attempts to achieve autonomy from her family of origin. Needing to define herself and her relationship with her parents on her own terms and not continue to routinely accommodate other people's expectations was the overriding psychological issue for the daughter. On another level, however, the breakdown occurred as a result of the dynamics of a competitively oriented approach to conflict, beginning the previous year with the daughter's refusal to participate in an important family event and then escalating to the point of the parties defending their positions and not listening to each other, making assumptions about each other's motives, interpreting events to support their assumptions and positions, and eventually becoming divided by an "us against them" polarization.

In this case the problem definition was reframed in relationship terms: *how the parties can better understand what they expect from each other as family members so that they can create a wedding ceremony in which everyone feels comfortable.* The breakdown in communication was later framed as a difficulty in navigating a normal yet challenging developmental transition; that is, how the relationship between an adult child and her parents changes when the adult child commits herself to a life partner. This reframing helped ease the mother's hurt feelings about the daughter's abrupt cutting off of contact, and normalized the daughter's experience.

The second stage of mediation, identifying needs, interests, and concerns, focused on clarifying past misunderstandings regarding the struggle to redefine the parent-adult child relationship in a way that incorporated the fiancée into the extended family system. Each person spoke about intentions and motivations that had been misinterpreted and described their hopes for the future relationship. Their differences began to narrow. The daughter recognized that her family did not want her to feel obligated or pressured to participate in every family event. The parents better understood the daughter's need to emotionally separate from them and saw that her fiancée was not the cause of her behavior. The young man understood the basis of the parent's mistrust and coolness toward him and had an opportunity to vindicate himself. By the fourth session, with parties feeling acknowledged and understood, it was much easier for them to collaborate in designing a nondenominational wedding ceremony.

Alternatives to Mediation

While there is a place for mediation and mediative strategies in couple and family disputes, there are a number of contraindications. In a clinical setting one invariably faces underlying psychological problems that create obstacles to a negotiation process. There may be a situation involving alcoholism, substance abuse or codependency, with a person unable to identify his or her own needs or feelings; there may be a narcissistic party who is unable to recognize the other's separate needs without feeling a threat to his or her own integrity; there may be a borderline personality disorder or a controlling individual whose self-identity is built on being "right." Mediation and negotiation are rational, economic, decision-making processes in which parties must have at least a minimal ability for rational decision making and perceiving each other as separate, autonomous individuals.

A conflict resolution paradigm on its own is not appropriate where there is significant psychopathology or in cases in which there has been physical violence or spousal abuse. One must also make an assessment in relation to problems of trust. Is there simply a breakdown of trust, which almost always occurs in troubled relationships, or does one of the individuals lack basic trust? The latter will generate a dynamic in which unnecessary conflict erupts because negative motives are habitually assumed and the benefit of doubt is not given. Arguments are not based on actual differences in needs and interests but result from the individual feeling judged, rejected, or slighted.

Mediation is most effective where the dysfunction lies primarily in the parties' inability to effectively handle conflict, whether they are conflict avoidant or highly competitive and argumentative. Clearly identified disputes between and among family members provide a focus for the mediation endeavor. Conflicts between parents and children, disagreements between siblings, and couple and marital disputes about financial management, relationships with extended family members, family work responsibilities, child-rearing and child behavior management, job changes, and relocation are the types of specific issues that lend themselves to a conflict resolution paradigm.

Mediators need to proceed with caution in the realm of couple and family practice. The marital and family practitioner must be clear with clients about his or her method and model of practice, and whether family therapy or mediation will be initiated. Mediation should not be used as a "back door" to family therapy for those resisting it; there must be a clear rationale for one's choice of a conflict resolution process.

During the course of writing this chapter, it became apparent to me just how much my theoretical orientation as a marital and family therapist has been influenced by my work as a mediator. Increasingly, I view marital and family problems as the result of the damage occurring to relationships from the escalation or polarization of differences and family members' inability to negotiate a better "fit" of their needs. For couples and families where there is not serious underlying psychopathology, this has been a useful and benign reframing that allows self-esteem to be maintained and reduces the sense of personal inadequacy.

From the divorce mediation part of my practice, having listened to hundreds of couples tell the story of why their marriage was ending, I have come to see how frequently the root of marital and family disintegration lies in the inability to negotiate difference and resolve conflict. It is not *what* couples fight about but *how* they fight that affects marital and family vitality. A mediation paradigm eloquently addresses this problem, and therein lies its potential in the field of couple and family practice.

References

Amundson, J. & L. Fong. 1986. Systemic/Strategic Aspects and Potentials in the Haynes Model of Divorce Mediation. In J. Lemmon, ed., *Emerging Roles in Divorce Mediation*. San Francisco: Jossey-Bass.

Deutsch, M. 1973. *The Resolution of Conflict: Constructive and Destructive Processes*. New Haven, CT: Yale University Press.

Gadlin, H. & P. Ouelette. 1986. Mediation Milanese: An Application of Systemic Family Therapy to Mediation. *Mediation Quarterly,* No. 14/15: 101–18.

Gold, L. 1993. Influencing Unconscious Influences: The Healing Dimension of Mediation. *Mediation Quarterly,* 11 (1): 55–66.

Gold, L. 1990. Mediation Meets the Unconscious. Presentation at the Academy of Family Mediation Annual Conference.

Haynes, J. M. 1981. *Divorce Mediation: A Practical Guide for Therapists and Counselors*. New York: Springer.

Irving, H. H. & M. Benjamin. 1995. *Family Mediation: Contemporary Issues*. Thousand Oaks, CA: Sage.

Jampolsky, G. 1983. *Teach Only Love*. New York: Bantam.

Kruk, E. 1993. Promoting of Co-operative Parenting after Separation: A Therapeutic/Interventionist Model of Family Mediation. *Journal of Family Therapy* 15 (3): 235–61.

Maida, P. 1986. Components of Bowen's Family Theory and Divorce Mediation. *Mediation Quarterly,* No. 12: 51–63.

Ricci, I. 1980. *Mom's House, Dad's House: Making Shared Custody Work*. New York: Macmillan.

Saposnek, D. 1983. *Mediating Child Custody Disputes: A Systematic Guide for Family Therapists, Court Counselors, Attorneys, and Judges*. San Francisco: Jossey-Bass.

Ury, R. & W. Fisher. 1983. *Getting to Yes*. New York: Penguin.

Wallerstein, J. 1986. Psychodynamic Perspectives on Family Mediation. *Mediation Quarterly,* No. 14/15: 7–21.

Wiseman, J. M. 1990. *Mediation Therapy: Short Term Decision-Making for Couples and Families in Crisis*. New York: Lexington Books.

3

DIVORCE

Comprehensive Divorce Mediation

by Emily M. Brown

Comprehensive divorce mediation is a facilitated decision-making process for couples whose relationship is ending or has ended, and who need to make decisions about financial matters, parenting arrangements, or other "business aspects" of their relationship. Couples in mediation may be married or unmarried, but in ending their couple relationship they need to make decisions for the future about parenting, money, property, and related issues. In this chapter, the terms, *couple* and *spouses* are used interchangeably to refer to these couples and do not reflect a particular marital status. The term *comprehensive* refers to the fact that all issues associated with ending the marriage are addressed within the mediation process, as opposed to dealing only with a single issue, such as parenting arrangements.

All mediation involves a problem or a dispute that needs to be resolved between two or more parties. Most everyday disputes are resolved without the help of a mediator or any other outside assistance. Others are resolved in the most formal of circumstances: adjudication by the courts. Along the continuum between direct negotiation and court determination are mechanisms for resolving disputes ranging from advice-giving relatives, marriage counselors, teachers, elders, diplomats, ministers, and mediators. These mechanisms vary with regard to who makes the decisions, the formality of the process, and the degree to which the decisions are binding.

Mediation is an informal yet structured process in which the parties to the dispute reach their own decisions with the help of a mediator. The mediation process itself is private, as contrasted with a court hearing, which is public. The agreements reached in mediation are not binding unless they are formalized outside the mediation process, such as when both parties sign a legal contract, prepared by an attorney, detailing the decisions and each party's responsibility for carrying them out. However, in many situations, the parties choose to act on their agreements without formalizing them.

In most jurisdictions in the United States and Canada, divorce mediation is offered by mediators in the domestic relations and family courts in the public sector, nonprofit community agencies, and the private sector. Public sector mediation generally focuses only on mediation of parenting arrangements, and sometimes child support provisions. Private sector mediation is usually comprehensive in that it addresses all the practical issues—children, money, and property—that separating couples need to resolve in ending their marriage. The focus of this chapter is on the latter, in which all issues in dispute are seen as interrelated and impacting each other.

The participants in the divorce mediation process are the mediator and both spouses. Mediation usually occurs shortly before or after the couple separates, or may occur at a later time when the spouses are ready to formalize their informal arrangements, or when they encounter a change in circumstances that necessitates changing their existing arrangement. The major issues to be decided are parenting arrangements, financial matters including child support and spousal support, and division of assets and debts. The mediator is responsible for managing the process and the spouses are responsible for making the decisions about their future arrangements. The process is structured, meaning the issues are addressed one by one, with specific steps for considering each issue.

Divorce mediation is unique in the degree of personal investment the parties bring to the process. Most couples come to mediation at the time of greatest emotional upheaval in the process of splitting up—just before or after their separation—at which time the spouses are widely divergent in their thoughts and feelings about the ending of the marriage. The decision to separate is usually one-sided: one spouse has been through a lengthy decision-making process, often without telling the partner until nearing a decision, and has decided to end the marriage; the other spouse, on learning of the decision, is fearful, hurt, and angry, and often tries to forestall the separation (Brown, 1976). When that fails, the partner being "left" typically resorts to blaming, obstructionist tactics, or "falling apart." At this point the two spouses are most out of phase with each other, making mediation extremely timely and potentially beneficial but volatile and highly charged.

Separation is also the time when both spouses embark on numerous far-reaching changes in almost every aspect of their lives (Brown, 1976). Each change is stressful in itself, and each brings with it a sense of loss that must be grieved; in addition, when so many changes occur at once, the physiological toll can be severe (Holmes & Rahe, 1967). Grief at the loss of the marriage is exacerbated by the loss of each spouse's hopes and dreams for their marriage and family. Neither spouse fully understands his or her own contribution to the demise of the marriage. Fear about what the future holds is heightened, and the decisions that will put some fears to rest, those that will be made in mediation, have not yet been made. The high personal investment in the issues to be addressed, the emotional hypersensitivity, and the many difficult practical issues of separation and divorce combine to make divorce mediation a very complex process.

As the marriage is ending, couples embark on several parallel subprocesses that together comprise the transitions of divorce: emotional, social, parental, legal, and financial (Brown, 1976; Bohannan, 1971). Mediation is part of the legal subprocess for making the transition from married to single life. The decisions made in mediation set the base for the parental and financial transitions; aspects of the emotional transition are played out in mediation. The social transition is least evident in mediation.

Divorce mediation grew out of extreme dissatisfaction with the traditional adversarial fault-based process of divorce, which was expensive, polarizing, and highly conflictual. Divorce reform became an important issue in the late 1960s, and the first no-fault divorce law was passed in California in 1969. In the early 1970s, O. J. Coogler, a psychologist and attorney, was the first to design and promote a model of divorce mediation as an alternative to litigation. John Haynes, whose background was in labor mediation, was also instrumental in developing divorce mediation in the late 1970s.

In a relatively short period of time, divorce mediation has proven itself to be a viable alternative to adversarial divorce. Numerous court systems offer mediation and many jurisdictions now require disputing couples to use mediation. Mediation is also readily available in the private sector throughout North America and within nonprofit community agencies as part of a continuum of marriage- and divorce-related services.

Research, Debates, and Trends

Research indicates that couples using divorce mediation have a higher rate of satisfaction with the process, are more likely to honor the decisions they have made, and pay considerably less than those who use the traditional adversarial process. Despite differences in methodology and samples, the studies of Joan Kelly and Jessica Pearson consistently show that mediation has significant benefits for divorcing couples. Kelly (1989, 1990), examining private-sector mediation, reported that litigating couples spent 134 percent more in total fees than couples using mediation to resolve all their issues. She also found that mediating couples had greater satisfaction with their divorce processes and outcomes than litigating couples, and that the mediating husbands and wives perceived that they had had equal influence over the terms of their agreements. Pearson (1991), whose sample included both public- and private-sector mediation, found few actual differences in the decisions made, no matter what forum (mediation, lawyer negotiation, judicial decision, or autonomous negotiation) was used for decision making. However, she found that couples using mediation experienced higher levels of satisfaction and greater cost savings than those who used attorneys to negotiate or litigate a settlement.

A survey of mandatory public-sector custody mediation in California (Slater, Shaw, & Duquesnel, 1992) determined that even with court-ordered mediation, those parents who were able to determine their parenting arrangements in mediation were more satisfied than those who had the arrangement imposed on them by the court. A study by Whiting (1994) indicates that mediation is most successful when there are multiple issues and an ongoing relationship exists between the parties. These factors are present in almost all divorce mediation cases.

Compliance with mediated divorce settlements is high. Meierding (1993) found that 78.3 percent of respondents who had reached agreements in private mediation were in total compliance or had mutually agreed to changes that were necessitated by a change in family circumstances. Whiting's (1992) research on divorce mediation in a community mediation center found that only 3.7 percent of the couples having multiple issues, including both parenting and financial disputes, and reaching agreement failed to comply, while 18.8 percent of single issue couples (those focused on one area of divorce-related conflict) failed to comply.

Controversies

Controversies within the field of divorce mediation relate primarily to concerns about the well-being of mediating parties, particularly women, and the professional issues of standards and credentialing.

Whether mediation is appropriate when physical abuse has occurred between the parties is an important issue. Mediators and women's advocates agree that there are some abuse cases where mediation should not be used; the controversy relates to the "dividing line." Some argue that mediation should never be used if there has ever been physical violence; others believe that with proper safeguards, mediation is a useful tool for some couples who have experienced abuse (Girdner, 1990; Chandler, 1990; Erickson & McKnight, 1990). Factors discussed as having a bearing on whether mediation is appropriate include the woman's level of fear, how recently the abuse has occurred, the nature and severity of the abuse, whether the mediation is voluntary, and whether effective safeguards are in place to prevent further abuse. An issue that has not been sufficiently addressed by mediators is the prevention of divorce-specific violence (Brown, 1995).

Some women's advocates have asserted that divorce mediation is unfair to women, arguing that women are not equal in power to their husbands and thus are not competent to effectively speak to their own needs in mediation. Women are seen to need the help of an advocate (the attorney's role) to protect their needs. This view has been countered by those who assert that there are many different types of power and that shifts in power between spouses occur constantly. Research on comprehensive divorce mediation indicates that women are generally satisfied with the mediation process and with the decisions they have reached (Kelly, 1989; Duryee, 1992).

Professional issues relate to standards and certification of family mediators, and who will make the decisions about standards. Standard setting and certification of mediators has as much to do with who will be allowed into the profession as with competence. The Academy of Family Mediators, founded in 1982, has led the way in setting standards for comprehensive divorce mediators by establishing membership requirements for mediation training, supervision, and experience, as well as professional experience as a mental health professional or lawyer. Standards for court-based mediators vary as they are established by the local court or by the state; the Association of Family and Conciliation Courts has been very active in developing standards for court-mandated mediation, which in some cases is provided by court staff and in other cases by private practitioners.

The Academy of Family Mediators now requires the following for practitioner member status: sixty hours of family mediation training, one hundred hours of family mediation experience, ten completed cases, and the submission of six mediation memoranda of agreement. Core areas that must be addressed in family mediation training include information gathering, relationship, communication, conflict management and problem-solving knowledge and skills; professional mediation values and ethical decision making; conflict resolution, family systems, cycle of violence and negotiation theory; knowledge of pertinent legal aspects of separation and divorce. Practitioner members must also complete twenty hours of continuing family mediation education every two years. The academy assumes, but does not at present require, that practitioner members have a professional degree in mental health, law, or a related discipline.

The question of dual roles is an important one for the mediation field. Mediation standards of practice caution that the use of dual roles (such as therapist and mediator, or attorney and mediator) with the same client may lead to a potential or actual conflict of interest. While a few mediators would like to see this changed (Dworkin, Jacob, & Scott, 1991), most agree that assuming dual roles can be confusing to the consumer and self-serving for the mediator.

One of the most difficult aspects for social work practitioners acting in a mediation capacity is not to confuse other social work roles, such as those of therapist or advocate, with the practice of mediation. For example, how mediators address the emotional issues in divorce is markedly different from how they are addressed in a counseling or therapy situation. The focus in mediation is not on understanding emotions or changing behavior patterns, nor on preventing divorce, but on reaching practical decisions for the future (Kelly,

1983; Brown, 1988). Whereas advocates advise their clients about what to do and negotiate for them, the mediator refrains from taking sides, doing the negotiating for the spouses, and advising them regarding decision making. Mediation is a process of helping clients make the decisions that they will be living with in the future. Divorce mediation differs from custody evaluation: the divorce mediator helps couples develop and assess their options so that they can make their own decisions; the custody evaluator makes a recommendation to the court about custody after studying the situation.

Divorce mediators must have extensive knowledge and excellent process and communication skills. They need to be knowledgeable about the emotional, parent-child, financial, and legal aspects of the divorce process. They need to know how to work with budgets and various financial documents, and to understand the emotions, problems, and logistics of setting up parenting arrangements. They need to have access to a network of family law practitioners and to know how the legal system of separation and divorce works in their community. They need to be able to acknowledge real pain or anger and disallow grandstanding. The mediator must be balanced in working with two spouses who are at odds with each other, and well-organized and directive of the process, while listening, clarifying, and reframing issues in dispute.

It is impossible for the mediator to have absolute knowledge about every issue in a divorce dispute, such as pensions or family businesses, but it is essential that mediators "know what they don't know." The mediator needs to know who does know and make appropriate referrals rather than going beyond his or her area of competence.

Emerging Trends

Courts are increasingly providing adjunct services, particularly parent education programs that help divorcing parents focus on their children's needs. These programs have been effective throughout the country in helping parents enhance their parenting skills and avoid common divorce-related pitfalls. In private-sector mediation, where many mediators are sole practitioners or part of a small group practice, such programs are not as common. This is an area open to development and ideally suited to social workers. Parent education programs for divorcing parents can easily be set up as a precursor or adjunct to a private-sector mediation practice.

Although premediation screening for abuse and for the ability and willingness to mediate has increased in recent years (Chandler, 1990), fewer couples appear to be screened out of mediation (Erickson & McKnight, 1990). This means that those couples engaging in divorce mediation comprise a broader cross-section of the population. Mediators are increasingly called on to deal with a broader range of family dysfunction, as well as to work within culturally specific contexts with their clientele.

The Mediation Process

Purpose and Roles

The participants in divorce mediation are the two spouses and the mediator. The goal is for the spouses to reach agreement on all the issues that must be decided when a marriage ends, when a prior arrangement is not working, or when a significant change in circumstances occurs. As implied, the spouses are the decision makers. The mediator's responsibility is to manage the process.

Managing the process is not a new role for social workers. However the task focus of mediation is quite a different process than that of clinical social work. The emphasis is on the task and not the emotions, despite the fact that emotions run high with separating couples. Effective mediators acknowledge strong emotions, but keep redirecting the focus back to the task. They deal with lesser emotional content, such as a low-level barb, by ignoring it and staying on task. When emotions are so high and persistent that they cannot be dealt with in these ways, the mediator must select another type of intervention that contains the emotional content sufficiently to permit work on the task at hand. Mediation is not about "fighting it out" or, alternatively, reconciliation, but involves a rational, although painful, process of deciding how to allocate responsibilities and resources. Mediators engage the divorcing couple in a cooperative process in which the parties themselves determine what is workable and appropriate.

The spouses' responsibilities in divorce mediation include collecting detailed information about each of the major issues, providing documentation, deciding on the principles and goals that will guide decision making, developing options and assessing them, and reaching agreement on the issues. These tasks are accomplished with the assistance of the mediator. The mediator's role is to decide on the sequence of issues, maintain a step-by-step approach to addressing each issue, direct communication, refer to appropriate sources of information (such as financial planners and educational information about children's needs in divorce), ensure that the information gathered by the spouses provides a complete and accurate picture of the issue in a way that enables each spouse to understand the information, identify problems interfering with the mediation process and intervene appropriately, and draft a memorandum of agreement describing in detail all the decisions that have been made. The mediator does not advocate a particular solution or advise one or both spouses as to what they should do; rather, the mediator sets the stage and manages the process so that the spouses can make informed decisions that meet their own goals.

Stages and Tasks

The essential steps in the mediation process are orientation and contracting, establishing principles and goals, gathering and sharing information, developing options, evaluating and refining options, and decision making. These guide the overall mediation process, and are used in addressing each of the three primary issues in comprehensive divorce mediation: parenting arrangements, financial support, and property division.

The first stage of mediation, the orientation session, is essentially an information exchange. Couples need to learn how mediation works before deciding whether to mediate, and the mediator needs to learn the specifics of the couple's situation to determine whether mediation is appropriate for them. A dialogue ensues about the mediation process, each spouse's concerns, the costs, the most difficult and "easier" issues, and special considerations that need to be taken into account given the family's unique circumstances.

Detailed written ground rules and a written contract to mediate establish the terms of the comprehensive divorce mediation process. The rules describe the general principles of mediation, the roles and responsibilities of the spouses and the mediator, the necessity of full disclosure, and the extent of confidentiality. A typical statement of general principles is the following:

1. Mediation will be conducted in a spirit of cooperation.

2. The major criteria for decision making are

   a. the needs of each family member.
   b. standards of fairness as agreed to by the spouses.
   c. the family's available resources.

3. The marriage will be considered an equal partnership in which each spouse has a substantial right in the contribution of the other, whether as a homemaker or as a financial provider.

In signing the contract to mediate, the spouses agree to the mediation rules and to specific fee arrangements, and acknowledge their understanding that legal advice and legal representation are not given in mediation sessions. During the orientation session both spouses read and discuss the written ground rules and the contract they will sign if they decide to mediate.

The mediator also looks for signs that indicate whether the couple is appropriate for mediation. Considerations include mental illness, alcohol or drug use that interfere with the person's ability to make rational decisions, and domestic violence. When potential violence can be contained or has stopped, mediation may be the preferred process in that it does not pit one spouse against the other or inflame emotions in the manner of the traditional adversarial legal process.

Different couples bring unique issues to mediation. Some have children, some do not. Life stages vary. Parents of young children are most concerned with parenting arrangements and sufficient money. Couples splitting up after many years of marriage are worried about money for retirement. Young couples without children or property may divide the cars and credit cards themselves and not need mediation. Families that have had difficulty making ends meet with one household have different options than those with two professional incomes and comfortable pensions. The mother who will have to return to work after fifteen years out of the job market has different decisions to make than the mother with a professional career and income to match.

The couple's overall goals for mediation are identified in the orientation session. More specific objectives are identified as each of the major issues is tackled. Examples of general goals are "to maintain an amicable relationship," "to protect the children," or "to avoid high legal fees." Typical issue-related goals are "to continue both parents' active involvement with the children," "to ensure that each spouse will have sufficient income in retirement," or "to equally divide the marital property." Couples that decide to mediate are provided with forms on which to organize information about assets and debts, postseparation household budgets, and income. Couples with children are given reading assignments, including Ricci's (1980) *Mom's House, Dad's House*. The mediator decides which issue will be dealt with first, and describes to the couple what information will be needed from them as they begin to examine that issue.

The next stage involves information gathering. The most complicated information needed usually pertains to property, but not all couples have much in the way of property or debts. The spouses are asked to bring in a completed form that includes a brief description of every asset and debt (marital residence at 241 Ames St., 1997 Toyota Camry, debt consolidation loan #12345 from First Federal, Prudential whole life insurance policy, and so on), the current value and how that value was determined, the current equity in the asset, the value at a future date (as in the case of pensions), estimated net proceeds if an asset may be sold, and other details needed to understand the situation. Many couples will be able to prepare this information themselves; some, such as those with extensive assets, debts, or complicated financial situations, will need to collect additional information from external sources. For example, when the debts are greater than the assets, information may be needed about refinancing options. Financial planners, pension experts, and insurance agents are among the resources used by mediating couples to understand their situation and the options available to them. Some couples have their own resources; if not, the mediator makes a referral to the appropriate "experts."

All this information and the related documentation is shared in the session so that both spouses and the mediator fully understand the facts of the situation. The task then becomes one of developing options about the issue under consideration. Couples are encouraged to brainstorm, to expand their thinking beyond the polarized "my proposal" versus "your proposal." Whatever the spouses identify during option development goes on the list, without evaluation. A significant challenge is posed when the only sizable asset is the marital residence; the task of dividing property is easier when there is more than one major asset because a greater number of options and more trade-offs are possible.

Jack and Martha have four major assets: the marital residence, valued at $220,000; Jack's pension, valued at $62,000; joint savings of about $20,000; and a new car purchased for $22,000. They also have an older car, two checking accounts, $4,000 in an IRA for Martha, a household full of furnishings, and a dog. They have a mortgage of $170,000, a car loan of $15,000, and about $1,200 in credit card debt. Their net assets are approximately $141,800. They have agreed to divide their property equally after first putting $2,000 into a college account for each child. The next question is "Who is to get what?" Both Jack and Martha generate several options for dividing their property. As they evaluate their options, they begin to shape what the actual division will be. The most difficult issue is an antique wooden rocking chair that has been in Jack's family for several generations but was lovingly refinished by Martha. They work out a creative decision that is beyond the realm of anything the courts could do: Martha will keep the rocking chair until Jack buys a house, at which point she will give the chair to him. Once they agree on how they will divide all of their property, they move on to the next area of dispute: the post-separation parenting arrangements.

In comprehensive divorce mediation, whatever issue is decided first has implications for the resolution of the other issues. For example, Jack and Martha have decided to keep the marital residence so their children can stay in the same school. Although the major issues in mediation are addressed separately, the decision to keep the house will need to be factored into the arrangements for parenting and financial support.

Even though their marriage is coming apart, Jack and Martha have always cooperated regarding their parenting of Jed, six years old, and Abigail, eight. This suggests that it will not be too difficult to work out their parenting arrangements. (This does not mean that it will be painless or easy, but suggests that Jack and Martha are able to keep their children's needs and interests in the foreground.) The principles they agree to guide them in negotiating their parenting arrangements are that both will be active and involved parents, they will live in the same school district, and they will have equal weekend time with the children.

Information gathering here is simpler than with property. It has to do with the needs and interests of their particular children, their current schedules and activities, which parent has been responsible for what, any special needs, and what changes will be necessitated by the separation.

Jack and Martha brainstormed a number of options regarding the weekday parenting arrangements: Martha stays in the house and the kids are with her during the school week; Jack stays in the house and the kids are with him during the school week; the kids stay in the house and the parents take turns being in the house; the kids spend Monday morning through Wednesday morning with Martha and Wednesday night through Friday night with Jack; the kids spend Monday morning through Wednesday morning with Jack and Wednesday night through Friday night with Martha; the kids are with Martha one week and Jack the next; if either Martha or Jack stays in the house and has the kids during the school week, the other parent will have the kids on Wednesday evening for an overnight; and if either Martha or Jack stays in the house and has the kids during the school week, the other parent will have the kids on Wednesday evening until 9 P.M.

Once they have generated alternatives for weekday parenting arrangements, Jack and Martha are faced with the task of assessing the pros and cons of each option. In the process they further modify their preferred options until they arrive at an agreement that is workable for each member of the family. They do so by suggesting changes, troubleshooting problems, making trade-offs with each other, and deciding where flexibility is possible. The mediator keeps them on task, raising questions about how a particular option would work, walking them through the scenarios, asking Jack to consider what he can offer Martha so that Martha will want to agree to his idea and asking Martha what she can offer Jack so he will want to agree with her idea.

The next step for Jack and Martha is developing and assessing options for the other elements of the parenting arrangement, including the weekend schedule, school breaks, vacations, birthdays and holidays, decision making about major issues (health care, education, religious upbringing, privileges, child discipline strategies, and so on), future changes, and the legal designation: sole, joint, or split custody. Some heated arguments ensue, but step by step they put together the pieces of their parenting arrangement. Then they assess the overall package: Does it meet their goals? Does it take into account their children's needs and interests? Is it workable? Does it cover everything that needs to be covered? When these arrangements are complete (there may be a few loose ends to be finished off before the end of mediation, but Jack and Martha are in overall agreement), the issue of parenting arrangements is put aside, and the focus moves to the remaining issue of financial support.

Financial support refers to child support, and in some cases to spousal support. Because child support orders were honored more by nonpayment than payment, legislation was passed in the United States in 1984 that required each state to establish its own child support guidelines. Both parents are expected to share in the costs of raising their children, but the actual amount each parent pays depends on income and other factors that are addressed in the guidelines. Child support is legally required until children are eighteen years of age, and the guidelines provide mediators with a formula used to determine the amount of support to be paid by one parent to the other. Parents can agree to an amount other than that indicated by the child support guidelines but must document a rationale for doing so.

Spousal support, also called alimony or spousal maintenance, is money paid to a dependent spouse and can be temporary or permanent. In situations involving a permanently dependent or disabled spouse, the alimony will be permanent; that is, paid until the payee dies or remarries, or until the payer dies. The intent of temporary alimony is to enable a spouse to obtain or upgrade career skills that will result in increased earning capacity, or to allow a mother of very young children to stay home with them for a period of time. When the support arrangements are finalized, if no alimony is to be paid this issue cannot be reopened in the future.

Martha and Jack expect financial support to be the most difficult issue for them. Martha has been working two days a week, and full-time jobs in her field are scarce. Jack makes a good income but separation will result in additional costs. Like most couples, the income that has been just enough to support one household will now have to cover two households.

The mediator begins the work on financial support by asking Jack and Martha to establish their principles for deciding on this matter. They agree to maintain a similar standard of living for their children to the extent that is possible, make sure that each household has enough money to cover expenses, and allow Martha to be home part-time with the children for the next year until the stresses of separation subside.

A gap exists between Jack and Martha's budgeted postseparation expenses and their total current income. Martha's income does not meet her budget, and Jack's income is above his budget. Two of the mechanisms available for transferring money from one household to the other are child support and spousal support. The mediator helps Jack and Martha develop options for how the gap in income can be closed, and how much money will be transferred as child support and how much as alimony. Typical options for closing the budget gap are cutting budgets, finding additional sources of income, or using savings. Jack and Martha agree not to touch their savings but work seriously on cutting their budgets and coming up with creative ideas for bringing in more money.

When they are within a few hundred dollars of closing the gap it is time to begin discussing transfers of income from Jack to Martha. The mediator computes the amount of child support that is indicated by existing child support guidelines. Since this amount plus Martha's income still does not meet her budget, they also discuss temporary spousal support. After developing and evaluating several options, they decide on the amount of temporary alimony, and agree that it will stop in one year or when Martha is earning $30,000, whichever comes first. Then comes the fine tuning. The mediator helps them look at the tax implications of what they have decided and explore how to maximize the tax benefits. They decide that Jack will pay Martha an additional amount to cover the taxes that she will have to pay on the alimony she receives. Because Jack and Martha are in different tax brackets, paying alimony, which is a tax deduction for Jack, results in decreasing the total amount paid in taxes by the family, thereby increasing money available to cover expenses.

Other details that Jack and Martha work out are the date the child support and alimony payments are to be made, whether Jack pays the full amount directly to Martha or instead makes the house payment directly to the bank and pays the remaining amount to Martha, which spouse will claim which tax benefits, and how changes in child support or alimony will be determined in the future. They also decide on the amount of life insurance needed to cover the contributions of the other spouse if that spouse should die, and how to handle health insurance for the children now and in the future.

During mediation, the mediator puts the decisions that Martha and Jack have made in writing. By the end of mediation this develops into a memorandum of understanding that details all their decisions and the criteria on which those decisions were based. Martha and Jack then take the memorandum to their respective attorneys. They agree that Martha's attorney will draft the property settlement agreement and Jack will have his attorney review the draft. Neither Jack nor Martha have an attorney, so the mediator gives each a list of names of competent domestic relations attorneys.

Mediation concludes with a review of the memorandum to make sure it is accurate, complete, and all the pieces fit together. As with most couples, Jack and Martha make only minor changes at this point. Then the spouses see their attorneys, whose job it is to translate the memorandum into a legal separation agreement, and to raise questions about any issue that is insufficiently addressed. In practice, few changes are made by lawyers. When Jack and Martha agree that the lawyer's draft represents their decisions, each signs it, and when both have signed, it becomes a binding legal contract. This contract is made part of the final divorce decree at the time the divorce occurs.

The "typical" mediation case addressing parenting arrangements, property, and support takes about eight to twelve hours of mediation time, in addition to time spent putting together the Memorandum of Agreement.

Core Skills of the Divorce Mediation Process

Martha and Jack were a fairly cooperative couple. During mediation they got angry, argued, cried, and got off track, but the mediator was able to get them back on task without great difficulty. Many couples are not cooperative but disorganized, contentious, or "tuned out." Understanding why a spouse is "stuck" is useful in selecting a particular intervention. Mediators have a variety of techniques at their disposal for helping couples move around obstacles or break through impasses:

- *Reframing* takes statements that either or both spouses have made and places them in a more positive context. A reframe may highlight the shared aspect of an issue, defuse a loaded remark, or pinpoint the core of an issue.

- *Operationalizing* loaded and vague words, like *fair,* by asking for specific goals or principles decreases opportunities for argument.
- *Using neutral language,* such as "parenting arrangements" instead of "custody" or "visitation," decreases emotional reactivity.
- *Acknowledgment* of strong emotions tells the person she or he has been heard without inviting discussion of the emotions.
- *Clarification* and *organization* of information using visual materials as well as the spoken word promotes understanding of the issue at hand.
- *Controlling communication* by having the mediator determine who talks and when and decide what issue is on the table cuts off destructive or unproductive comments.
- *Future focus* keeps couples on task and prevents repetitive blaming and recounting of past problems.
- *Mutualizing* focuses on commonalities in interests and keeps the responsibility for making decisions on both spouses.
- *Caucusing* or meeting with each spouse individually can be used to identify why the individual is stuck and to develop strategies to get him or her unstuck.
- *Referrals* to mental health professionals to work on emotional issues and to other professionals to gain specialized information can facilitate the mediation process.
- *Timing* sessions according to the couple's needs allows spouses to ponder an issue, get help, and allay anxiety.
- *Controlling the emotional climate* is important in shifting focus or changing the emotional tone of the mediation session. For example, slowing and quieting can lend calm; listening and attending to both spouses can be reassuring; an empathic but no-nonsense approach discourages diatribes or rambling.
- *Normalizing* reassures the spouses by letting them know that their responses are typical for people in their situation.
- *Refraining* from taking responsibility for the dispute and its outcome keeps the responsibility for problem solving with the spouses.

Some couples remain at an impasse despite the mediator's best interventions. These impasses usually spring from emotional issues such as a desire to "win" above all else (or not to lose), a wish to hurt the spouse, or an unwillingness to face reality. Sometimes impasses cannot be resolved; in these cases couples usually hire attorneys and move into the traditional adversarial process.

Other couples may terminate mediation before reaching agreement. Some reconcile. Others exit mediation to avoid pain. Still others fear being overpowered by a dominant or negative spouse or accede to the questionable advice of friends and relatives.

Alternatives to Mediation

When couples need to make decisions about the practical matter of ending their marriage, mediation is just one of the options available to them. Many couples prefer the traditional adversarial route, with separate attorneys who do the negotiating for the spouses and who advise their own client on how to proceed. In cases where both the spouses and the attorneys are reasonable, this process may be quite satisfactory. When that is not the case, the couple may end up in court. This is an expensive process that pits one spouse against the other, delays decisions, and turns control of the decisions over to the judge. Unlike mediation or attorney-negotiated settlements, where the spouses can do pretty much anything they agree to, the judge is limited to making decisions based on legal statutes and case precedents.

Some couples are unable to use mediation and need to use attorneys to negotiate or litigate the issues for them. This is the case when alcohol or drug addiction is present, mental illness interferes with the individual's capacity to understand or to participate in the mediation process, sufficient safeguards cannot be established to prevent physical or other forms of spousal or child abuse, there is a history of hiding assets or of dishonesty about financial matters, or one spouse deliberately and manipulatively tries to take advantage of the other.

Custody evaluation is another option for couples who do not want to use mediation. A custody evaluator, usually employed by the court, assesses the strengths and weaknesses of the parents and the needs of the children and recommends specific parenting arrangements and a legal custody designation to the court. In some court systems, the court mediator becomes the custody evaluator if the parents do not reach agreement in mediation. Custody evaluation is most useful when parents are so conflicted or contentious that they are unable to reach an agreement about their parenting arrangements through mediation or attorney negotiation, and courts are increasingly ordering custody evaluation before scheduling a hearing on custody. Arbitration is another alternative to mediation but is rarely used; if someone else is going to make the decisions, most people prefer to go to court.

A few couples, usually those without complicated issues or significant assets, choose a "do-it-yourself" process. Seminars provide basic information on issues and options, and some books include samples of separation agreements. Other couples, generally those with no children and no joint assets, just divide their household belongings and go their separate ways, doing nothing formally until one or the other decides to file for divorce.

Comprehensive divorce mediation is not therapy; it does not change the intrapsychic processes of husbands and wives. It can help with the practical matters of separation and divorce through careful and detailed planning for the future. Often this is the first time the spouses have made conscious rational decisions about money matters. Mediation can also make the interactional process between the spouses easier in the future by providing experience in problem solving and by developing a structure for their future coparenting relationship. Most of all, divorce mediation is a respectful process, based on a solid understanding of the facts, that enables parting spouses to arrive at their own decisions for their future and that of their children.

References

Bohannan, P. 1971. The Six Stations of Divorce. In P. Bohannan, ed., *Divorce and After*. Garden City, New York: Doubleday.

Brown, E. M. 1976. A Model of the Divorce Process. *Conciliation Courts Review* 14(2): 1–11.

———. 1988. Mediation in a Mental Health Setting. In Ann L. Milne and Jay Folberg, eds., *Divorce Mediation*. New York: Guilford.

———. 1995. Flashpoints: Identifying and Preventing Violence in Separation and Divorce. Paper presented at the Association of Family and Conciliation Courts Northwest Regional Conference, Skamania, WA, November 3.

Chandler, D. B. 1990. Violence, Fear, and Communication: The Variable Impact of Domestic Violence on Mediation. *Mediation Quarterly* 7(4): 331–46.

Duryee, M. 1992. Mandatory Court Mediation: Demographic Summary and Consumer Evaluation of One Court Service. *Family and Conciliation Courts Review* 30(2): 260–67.

Dworkin, J., L. Jacob, & E. Scott. 1991. The Boundaries between Mediation and Therapy: Ethical Dilemmas. *Mediation Quarterly* 9(2): 107–19.

Erickson, S. K. & M. S. McKnight. 1990. Mediating Spousal Abuse Divorces. *Mediation Quarterly* 7(4): 377–88.

Girdner, L. K. 1990. Mediation Triage: Screening for Spouse Abuse in Divorce Mediation. *Mediation Quarterly* 7(4): 365–76.

Holmes, T. J. & R. H. Rahe. 1967. The Social Readjustment Rating Scale. *Journal of Psychosomatic Research* 11: 213–18.

Kelly, J. B. 1983. Mediation and Psychotherapy: Distinguishing the Differences. *Mediation Quarterly*, No. 1: 33–44.

———. 1989. Mediated and Adversarial Divorce: Respondents' Perceptions of Their Processes and Outcomes. *Mediation Quarterly*, No. 24: 71–88.

———. 1990. Is Mediation Less Expensive? Comparison of Mediated and Adversarial Divorce Costs. *Mediation Quarterly* 8(1): 15–26.

Meierding, N. R. 1993. Does Mediation Work? A Survey of Long-Term Satisfaction and Durability Rates for Privately Mediated Agreements. *Mediation Quarterly* 11(2): 157–70.

Pearson, J. 1991. The Equity of Mediated Divorce Agreements. *Mediation Quarterly* 9(2): 179–97.

Ricci, I. 1980. *Mom's House, Dad's House: Making Shared Custody Work*. New York: Macmillan.

Slater, A., J. A. Shaw, & J. Duquesnel. 1992. Client Satisfaction Survey: A Consumer Evaluation of Mediation and Investigative Services. *Family and Conciliation Courts Review* 30(2): 252–59.

Whiting, R.A. 1992. The Single-Issue, Multiple-Issue Debate and the Effect of Issue Number on Mediated Outcomes. *Mediation Quarterly* 10(1): 57–74.

———. 1994. Family Disputes, Nonfamily Disputes, and Mediation Success. *Mediation Quarterly* 11(3): 247–60.

4

POSTDIVORCE PARENTING

Parenting Disputes in Divorce: Facilitating the Development of Parenting Plans through Parent Education and Therapeutic Family Mediation

by Edward Kruk

The "parenting plan" approach to child custody determination is a relatively new concept, seen by many as the next step in the evolution of child custody law, providing the operational reality to the conceptual progression from fault-based to no-fault divorce, sole custody to shared parenting, and parental rights to parental responsibilities (Tompkins, 1995). It is the antithesis of the concept of "custody," which is seen to reduce the best interests of the child to the idea of individual parental rights, reflecting the premise that children are property to be awarded to the rightful owner. In contrast, parenting plans focus on the best possible postdivorce parenting arrangements that both parents can make for their children (McWhinney, 1995).

A parenting plan is a detailed articulation of postdivorce parenting responsibilities, including specific arrangements regarding time spent by the children in each parent's household, holiday schedules, how decisions are made, and how costs will be allocated. The parenting plan approach to child custody determination involves the negotiation and allocation of parental responsibilities after divorce either directly by the parents themselves, or with the assistance of third parties such as lawyers or mediators, toward a postdivorce parenting arrangement that primarily reflects children's needs and interests, emphasizes parental responsibilities to children over parental rights, and leaves neither parent feeling either overburdened or disenfranchised in relation to these responsibilities.

The idea of parenting plans has essentially grown out of attempts to resolve the sole custody/primary caretaker versus joint custody debate. In Washington, Florida, and Maine in the United States, as well as in Australia, the United Kingdom, and some Scandinavian countries, some form of parenting plan legislation has been enacted and the resolution of this debate has involved the elimination of adversarial and "ownership" language, replaced by new language that emphasizes children's needs and parental responsibilities.

Tompkins (1995) outlines a number of fundamental assumptions underpinning the parenting plan concept. First, it is assumed that parents need a divorce process that helps them to focus on their children's needs at a time when their own multiple transitions and losses render them relatively insensitive to these needs. The parenting plan approach focuses primarily on children's needs, mandating that parents consider the variety of functions that constitute postdivorce parenting and allocate responsibility for these functions. Second, it is assumed that the interests of the majority of children are best served by the substantial and continued participation of both parents in child rearing within some form of cooperative shared parenting arrangement. To this end, parenting plans avoid use of words such as *custody* and *visitation,* which connote images of power, possession, control, and ownership, replacing them with the language of "parental responsibility" and "cooperative shared parenting." Finally, it is assumed that most parents enter the divorce process ill prepared for what lies ahead for them, and need an educational opportunity to obtain the information they lack.

The means by which parenting plans can be formulated include divorce parent education programs and therapeutic family mediation. Courts' involvement in the divorce process changes dramatically, as they are no longer responsible for the determination of custody, except in certain cases. Rather, when an application for divorce or legal separation is made, the requirement that parents in conflict formulate a parenting plan is established by the court. This is followed by an order that clarifies and supports the negotiated parenting arrangement, in which children's needs, parental responsibilities, and the preservation of existing parent-child relationships are emphasized as opposed to parental rights and entitlements.

As the means by which parents are assisted to formulate and determine their own postdivorce parenting plans, mediation is not simply a dispute resolution device, and the goal of mediation is not merely the settlement of disputed issues. Mediation should serve to promote a situation where parents have taken on the responsibility for separating their previous marital conflicts from their ongoing parental responsibilities and are able to develop a parenting plan that is guided primarily by their children's needs and interests. Mediation aims to restructure parent-child relationships in a manner that meets the children's and parents' interests; enhance cooperation between the parents; promote healing by acknowledging deep-seated hurts and helping parents work through emotions associated with the loss of the marital relationship; and transform the parties by empowering them to resolve future disputes via newly developed communication, negotiation, and problem-solving skills, and by allowing them to recognize the core needs of other family members, particularly their children. Mediation thus becomes a therapeutic and educational process that is primarily child focused. Although mediation is not therapy per se, mediators can helpfully draw on the knowledge and skills of family therapy to the extent that the process may well become a therapeutic experience for the parties (Walker, 1993).

Ideally, postdivorce parenting arrangements should attempt to approximate as closely as possible the parent-child relationships in the original two-parent home. In the majority of instances, this would translate into a parenting plan in which both parents have not only equal rights with respect to their children's welfare and upbringing but also active responsibilities within the daily routines of their children's care and development in separate households. North American legislators and policymakers are beginning to recognize that shared parenting after divorce should include not only equal authority in decision making with respect to children's education, medical care, and religious upbringing but also some degree of shared physical caretaking; the granting of parental rights without a concommitant requirement for the assumption of active child care responsibility has the potential for considerable inequity and abuse (Fineman, 1988). While this does not necessarily entail a precise apportioning of a child's time on an equal or "fifty-fifty" basis, it does connote both parents routinely caring for their children in separate households. As the living arrangement most closely resembling the majority of predivorce families and coinciding with emerging models of marriage and parenthood, this type of shared parenting arrangement is regarded by many as the healthiest and most desirable arrangement for the majority of families (Folberg & Graham, 1981; Irving, Benjamin, & Trocme, 1984). The two most salient factors associated with positive outcomes of divorce for children and parents are the maintenance of meaningful, active, and ongoing relationships between children and *both* of their parents, and the parents' ability to minimize conflict and cooperate with each other in regard to parenting and decision making. Cooperative shared parenting may thus be the key to ameliorating the negative impact of divorce on *all* family members.

Parent education and mediation have considerable (and as yet largely untapped) potential in establishing such cooperative arrangements as the norm, rather than the exception, for divorced families. For the most part, parent educators and mediators have avoided directly promoting and facilitating shared parenting arrangements—for diverse reasons. Indiscriminately recommending shared parenting for those who are extremely poor candidates is highly problematic: there are clear contraindications to shared parenting, including cases of child abuse, neglect, or exploitation, the physical or psychological incapacity of a parent, chronic alcoholism or drug addiction, or a stated disinterest in caring for the children; highly conflicted couples may never be able to exclude their marital conflicts from their ongoing negotiations in regard to parenting; abused spouses may continue to fear potential violence within a coparenting structure. While these point to the need for careful screening of potential candidates, the notion of establishing shared parenting plans as an ideal is based on the assumption that in the majority of cases, both parents are capable and loving caregivers and have at least the potential to minimize their conflict and cooperate with respect to their parenting responsibilities. Unless there are compelling reasons to the contrary, children's needs in divorce are assumed to be best met by some form of shared parenting arrangement.

In addition, the promotion of shared parenting in parent education and mediation is antithetical to the neutral stance adopted by many mediators (Roberts, S., 1988; Roberts, M., 1988). Such a therapeutic and interventionist approach, it is argued, reduces client self-determination and may result in a lack of commitment to the mediated agreement and undermines the parties' ability to undertake any necessary renegotiation of parenting arrangements by themselves (Roberts, S., 1988). This chapter will argue that parent education combined with a therapeutic model of family mediation can in fact bolster parents' ability to negotiate and make informed decisions, enhance their communication and problem-solving skills, and ultimately strengthen the durability of negotiated agreements. In addition, the model offers clients the benefit of interventions designed to enhance their negotiations and construct agreements that promote the principles of shared parental responsibility and authority that are associated with the best interests of children in divorce. Mainstream mediation approaches have been particularly lacking in this regard (Bernard et al., 1984; Saposnek, 1983). It will also be argued that mediators have an implicit ethical responsibility to promote postdivorce parenting arrangements that are in children's best interests; they should not make decisions for parents, but they are in a unique position to expand the range of options available to them, point out the costs and benefits of each, and help them weigh the consequences of their choices.

Research, Debates, and Trends

Research

A number of recent North American studies have supported shared parenting plans as a viable and optimal structural arrangement for families after divorce. Ahrons (1981) concluded that shared parenting in fact constitutes a wide variety of parenting arrangements and relationships among families.

Leupnitz (1982) interviewed children as well as parents, and compared sole maternal, sole paternal, and shared parenting arrangements, concluding that children are more satisfied with shared rather than with sole parenting arrangements. Shiller (1984) found that divorce causes less trauma and dislocation to children whose parents opt for shared parenting and that these children appeared to be more comfortable with the status quo, with a more realistic image of what the future will bring. Wolchik, Braver, & Sandler (1985) discovered that children in shared parenting homes report a significantly higher number of positive experiences than children in sole parenting arrangements. In Britain, Lund (1987) compared children and parents in "single-parent/father absent" families with those in "conflicted coparenting" and "harmonious coparenting" families and, using independent teacher ratings in addition to interviews with both parents and their children, concluded that children functioned best in harmonious coparenting families and least well in single-parent families.

Irving, Benjamin, & Trocme's (1984) study of shared parenting used a large data base and a longitudinal design. Contrary to expectations, they found that shared parenting is a realistic consideration for all economic groups, an idea that was obscured by the preponderance of middle- and upper-class families in earlier studies. Also, parents with initial doubts and some reluctance about opting for coparenting were able to negotiate shared parenting plans, and reported positive long-term outcomes. It was not necessary for coparents to be favorably disposed to each other for the arrangement to work, although most respondents reported a change in their feelings toward their former spouses, typically becoming more positive; nor was it necessary for parents to have had a high level of cooperation in sharing parental responsibilities during the marriage. In almost all cases, the initial consideration of the possibility of a shared parenting relationship was first raised by one of the parents rather than by lawyers, mediators, family therapists, or other professionals. Overall, nearly 90 percent of coparents were in favor of the arrangement. The authors concluded that shared parenting is a viable option for a range of divorcing couples, but not for everyone. Good predictors of outcome success included a commitment to parenting, reasonable communication skills, flexibility, the ability to separate previous marital conflicts from matters concerning the children, and good faith with regard to agreements made. Conversely, intense and continuing conflict, weak commitment to active parenting, and irrational hope of reconciliation were all predictors of failure.

An important caveat must be made in interpreting the results of studies of shared parenting, as most involve parents who have independently chosen to make such arrangements. Brotsky, Steinman, & Zemmelman (1988), however, reported on a study of a pilot mediation program in California that promoted shared parenting in cases where at least one of the parties was opposed to the arrangement. When educated about children's needs in divorce and informed of the range of parenting options open to them, 80 percent of participants opted for a shared parenting arrangement. In a one-year follow-up of these mediated arrangements, the authors found that shared parenting provided stability (in 93% of cases), parental satisfaction (68%), valuing of the other spouse (97%), and comfort for the children in relation to both parents (82%). When compared with those in sole parenting arrangements, children in shared parenting homes, like their parents, were reported to be functioning significantly better in all areas.

Debates

Primary Caretaker Presumption. While research studies have provided substantial empirical support for shared parenting as a desirable postdivorce option for families, a number of concerns have been expressed among a number of U.S. legal scholars. Fineman (1988) and Polikoff (1982), arguing in favor of a legal "primary caretaker" presumption, question the degree to which shared parenting actually reflects predivorce family structures, and caution against an uncritical acceptance of the position that women and men make identical contributions to parenting during marriage.

It may be questioned, however, whether sole parenting after divorce is in fact more reflective of predivorce family structures than shared parenting. While mothers generally assume the lion's share of responsibility for child care within two-parent families (although there exists a heterogeneity of parenting roles within families, including greater sharing of care than previously), in the majority of cases both parents form close and salient attachment bonds with their children and remain uniquely influential in their development (Lewis, 1986; Lamb, 1986). This is reflected after divorce, in sole parenting families, in children's pervasive longing for their absent fathers, despite varying amounts of actual parenting involvement by fathers during the marriage (Kruk, 1993a).

Continuing Hostility between Spouses. Another issue of debate regarding shared parenting concerns the ex-spouses' ability to cooperate. It is argued that shared parenting can be calamitous if parents are unwilling or unable to cooperate and their relationship is characterized by high conflict, which typically attends divorce. As Folberg and Graham (1981) point out, however, it is more likely the adversarial nature of the legal system, when extended to the issue of postdivorce parenting, that polarizes parents and exacerbates hostilities. To the extent that the legal system casts divorcing parents in the role of enemies and expects them to be unable to cooperate, a self-fulfilling prophecy is created; legal processes not only exacerbate parental conflict, they often create an atmosphere of hostility in cases where relatively amicable negotiation may have taken place (Kruk, 1991).

Whether the parents are able to isolate their previous marital conflicts from their continuing roles as parents may be the critical issue in the "parental cooperation" debate. There is evidence that shared parenting provides an incentive for cooperation; what often begins as a "front," an appearance of minimal conflict in the children's presence, becomes in time a "normal" pattern of relating, a self-fulfilling prophecy (Irving, Benjamin, & Trocme, 1984). When neither parent feels threatened with the possibility of loss, each is in a healthier position for cooperation (Calvin, 1981). Shared parenting, in providing for a combination of "time off" and enhanced involvement in child care, helps to overcome the problem of mothers feeling overwhelmed by sole responsibility for children and fathers feeling excluded from their children's lives (Folberg & Graham, 1981).

Lack of Continuity in Children's Routine. Another important concern about shared parenting is that it may be disruptive and confusing for children to have two homes, where they encounter two different lifestyles and value systems; shared parenting, it is suggested, inherently creates an unstable, impermanent condition for children. In rebuttal, it has been shown that children have strong attachment bonds and relationships with both parents, and show remarkable tenacity in continuing these under a variety of conditions (Richards, 1982). Shared parenting exposes children to two lifestyles and two points of view, offering a larger array of positive characteristics to model and a greater variety of cognitive and social stimulation; while sole parenting can sever a child's ties with an entire set of relatives, shared parenting permits the child's support group to expand (Folberg & Graham, 1981). In providing for active parenting by two nurturing figures, shared parenting may contribute to a breakdown of gender-differentiated character structures in children (Richards, 1982). Thus, while critics of shared parenting point to the child's vulnerability and need for a consistent and predictable world, proponents emphasize the child's resilience and need for emotional support and stimulation from diverse sources.

Proponents of shared parenting plans have stated their "case" from both the perspective of parents and children. It is argued that most sole parenting mothers feel their children largely overburden and imprison them, and mothers become physically and emotionally exhausted as well as socially isolated (Wallerstein & Kelly, 1980; Sev'er, 1992). It is not surprising, then, that in studies of shared parenting, mothers reported that the greatest advantage of the arrangement is the sharing of care for their children and relief from the sole responsibility of parenting (Nehls & Morgenbesser, 1980). Whereas noncustodial fathers are effectively disqualified as active caretakers of their children (Kruk, 1991), coparenting fathers report that the greatest advantage of sharing care is the opportunity to maintain an active and meaningful role in their children's lives in "normal" day-to-day living situations (Greif, 1979). Finally, shared parenting spares children the disruption and feeling of rejection following the departure of one parent; it ensures the preservation of attachment bonds with both parents in a continuous, secure, and protected relationship (Folberg & Graham, 1981).

Trends

Parent Education as a Precursor and Adjunct to Mediation. It is now generally accepted that it is not divorce per se that results in the difficulties experienced by separated family members; rather, certain critical mediating factors stand between separation and postdivorce outcome for family members (Wallerstein & Kelly, 1980; Hetherington, Cox, & Cox, 1978; Hess & Camara, 1979). These include the extent to which both of the parents and their children are able to maintain meaningful relationships, the level to which the parents are able to support each other in their continuing parental roles, and the extent to which informal social networks and formal judicial, educational, and social welfare institutions are supportive in regard to both.

Given the lack of information available to divorcing families about what to do, what to expect, and the services that might be available to them (Walker, 1993), it may be argued that there is an implicit ethical responsibility for mediators to ensure that such information is made available to parents before instituting any dispute resolution process via some form of parent education program. Parents who are oriented to the divorce process and the impact of divorce on family members are better prepared for mediation and better able to keep the needs of their children at the forefront of their negotiations. Divorce education programs also offer a means to expose divorcing populations to mediation as an alternative mechanism of dispute resolution (Braver et al., 1995).

Further, an educative approach should be an integral part of the mediation process, with a primary focus on children's needs during and after the divorce process. Family mediators with expertise in the expected effects of divorce on children and parents can be instrumental in helping parents to recognize the potential psychological, social, and economic consequences of divorce and, on that foundation, promote arrangements conducive to children maintaining meaningful, positive postdivorce relationships with both parents within a nonconflictual atmosphere.

Mediation and Shared Parenting Plans. One of the most debated issues in the field of family mediation is the extent to which mediators should actively shape the outcome of the agreement: should they assume a neutral or a therapeutic/interventionist role? Neutral mediators seek to avoid influencing the outcome of the negotiations and accept any decision the parents agree on that is not obviously harmful to either. The therapeutic/interventionist mediator, on the other hand, is actively involved in shaping an agreement that includes those factors known to contribute to positive postdivorce outcomes.

The model described in this chapter requires the mediator to assume an affirmative stance in promoting and facilitating the development of cooperative shared parenting plans, where appropriate. It proceeds from the assumption that neutrality in mediation is largely an illusory concept; whether they are made explicit or not, mediators carry with them preconceived notions about what is in the best interests of children and families in divorce, and tailor their interventions accordingly, practicing what Greatbatch and Dingwall (1990) refer to as "selective facilitation" in guiding the mediation process toward arrangements that reflect these notions. It is important for the mediator to declare such biases: that the termination of a marriage necessitates a restructuring of family life that enables children to maintain a meaningful and active relationship with both parents within as cooperative a coparental relationship as possible. If mediation does not exercise its educative and therapeutic function, stressing the desirability of active parenting by both parents, detailing the range of shared parenting possibilities open to families and, where appropriate, actively facilitating and working through the logistics of a shared parenting arrangement, it fails to live up to its true potential.

Mediators also need to pay greater attention to the durability of parenting agreements and the need for parents to continue to improve their ability to cooperate and negotiate with each other after divorce. The challenges facing divorced coparents are numerous; once in place, shared parenting requires an extremely high level of organization, cooperation, and commitment. Mediators can play a key role in helping parents to meet these challenges. To add to its educative and advocacy function, mediation should also include a support and troubleshooting component, a period of follow-up to assist parents not only to share in the parenting of their children but to do so in a cooperative manner.

Facilitating the Development of Postdivorce Parenting Plans via Parent Education and Therapeutic Family Mediation

Parent education regarding children's needs and interests during and after the divorce transition, followed by a therapeutic approach to divorce mediation, offers a highly effective and efficient means of facilitating the development of cooperative shared parenting plans. Within such an approach, parent education is used to introduce the option of shared parenting as a viable structural alternative and to reduce parents' anxiety about a living arrangement that deviates from traditional custody and access arrangements. Mediation then is used to help parents work through the development of the parenting plan and to implement the plan in as cooperative a manner as possible. The process consists of four essential elements of the parent education program and four distinct yet overlapping phases of mediation. The elements of the parent education process are:

1. *Orientation to the divorce process and available services:* stages of divorce/grieving; alternate dispute resolution processes (including mediation); divorce counseling services and other community resources.
2. *Children's needs and interests in divorce.*
3. *Postdivorce parenting alternatives.*
4. *Communication, negotiation, and problem-solving skills.*

The four phases of therapeutic family mediation are:

1. *Assessment* to determine whether the parents are both ready to enter into therapeutic mediation and whether shared parenting is indicated.
2. *Exploration of shared parenting options* and actively promoting a parenting arrangement that meets the children's needs first and the parents' second.
3. *Facilitation of negotiations* toward the development of an individualized, cooperative, shared parenting plan that outlines specific living arrangements, schedules, roles, and responsibilities.
4. *Continuing support/troubleshooting* during the implementation of the shared parenting plan.

Premediation: Parent Education

Families enter the divorce process with a strong need for education and information about the profound changes they are experiencing and how to manage those changes (Tompkins, 1995). Divorce parent education programs, which may be offered in a variety of formats, are designed to inform parents about four major sets of issues: the divorce (and mediation) process, children's needs and interests in divorce, postdivorce parenting alternatives that will serve to meet those needs, and effective communication, negotiation and problem-solving skills. Parent education thus begins the process of helping the parents make an informed choice about the type of postdivorce parenting arrangement that is best for their children and themselves, and as such, may be seen as an essential adjunct and precursor to the family mediation process. The primary goals of parent education are thus to improve the parents' ability to focus on the postdivorce needs of their children by providing them with an improved understanding of the effects of divorce on children and to increase their level of preparedness for mediation. Through a child-focused approach to parent education, it is hoped that parents will be better informed for the decision-making process of mediation (Lehner, 1992).

Parent education programs are most effective early in the divorce process. The format of such programs varies, and includes small group divorce parenting education programs meeting over several sessions, single-session workshops, and individual premediation sessions with parties in dispute. Braver et al. (1995) concluded that short programs (single session, about two hours in length) can sensitize parents to important issues and provide motivation for future learning, but behavioral change and skill development require a more in-depth approach. Bienenfeld (1988) found that the most effective programs are those with multisensory and multileveled presentations of information addressing different learning styles and individual needs. While the content of such programs is educational, the group process typically used in divorce parent education requires a strong knowledge base in family systems theory and child development, and skills in group work and engaging individuals who may be extremely angry or in great personal pain (Salem, Schepard, & Schlissel, 1995).

Parent education begins by focusing on increasing parents' understanding of the divorce process generally, including the process of mediation, and the range of services available to them. It is important to start by normalizing the adult divorce experience, providing an overview of the emotional, legal, parental, spousal, and economic aspects of divorce, phases of the divorce process, and stages of loss and grief. Other specific issues that may be covered, depending on the needs of the parents, include relevant divorce legislation, the mediation process and how it differs from legal resolution of parenting disputes, and alternative models of resolving postdivorce parenting issues. Information is made available about local divorce counseling services and other divorce-related community services.

During divorce, in coming to terms with their own pain, grief, and reduced self-esteem, parents often experience difficulty keeping focused on the needs of their children; they also often lack adequate information about the impact of divorce on children and children's needs at different ages and stages of development (Kelly, 1993; Wallerstein & Kelly, 1980). Focusing on children's needs in divorce encourages parents to begin tuning in to the type of postdivorce parenting plan that will be in their children's best interests, and sets the stage for consideration of alternative arrangements. Parent education programs can be extremely helpful in identifying common problems and offering specific information about what parents can do to ease children's transition to postdivorce family life. These would include: (1) stages of child development and how children of different ages and stages of development respond and adjust to the consequences of divorce; (2) the developmental tasks of children in divorce; (3) how to tell children about the divorce and strategies for helping them through the process of divorce; and (4) the potential negative effects that various manifestations of interparental conflict can have on children.

A third element of premediation parent education examines specific issues to consider in planning for parenting after divorce, and types of post-divorce parenting plans that can be tailor-made to suit the needs of families after divorce, including shared parenting arrangements. Included in this segment would be information relating to the phases of family restructuring after divorce, tasks of coparenting after divorce, and barriers to cooperative parenting.

Finally, parent education incorporates instruction in communication, negotiation, and problem-solving skills, which enable parents to not only make the best use of the mediation process that will follow but to enhance their future negotiation and communication skills regarding parenting concerns. These skills will be essential as soon as parents enter mediation, and a contract for ongoing service is agreed.

Therapeutic Family Mediation

Assessment. Whereas the generic mediation model largely excludes psychological exploration and history taking, focusing almost entirely on the future relationship between the parties (Coogler, 1979; Haynes, 1982), a therapeutic approach involves a detailed assessment process to determine if mediation is appropriate, and an examination of the types of postdivorce parenting structures that are most likely to be in the children's and parents' best interests. It also allows the parties time to tell their story and have their feelings normalized.

Assessment in therapeutic family mediation focuses on four critical dimensions: (1) the degree of acceptance of the termination of the marital relationship by both spouses, which predicts the level to which the parents are able to separate past marital issues from continuing parental responsibilities and the extent to which they will be able to cooperate in the future; (2) the nature of existing spousal relationships, which includes the degree of overt hostility, the presence of spousal abuse, the extent to which one spouse will use mediation to manipulate, threaten, or control the other party, and the degree to which mediation may be used to stall legal proceedings while planning for future litigation; (3) the nature of existing parent-child relationships, which includes the degree of involvement and attachment between each parent and the children, and the presence of child abuse; and (4) the parents' expectations and desires regarding the type of relationship they would like with their children following divorce. At this stage it is important to gather this information in the context of obtaining data about the predivorce family, as opposed to what the parents would like in the way of specific postdivorce parenting arrangements. The mediator's goal is to facilitate the process of building shared parenting agreements step-by-step; the task of the mediator during assessment is to obtain in general terms a statement from each parent about the level of involvement they would like to have with their children after divorce.

The first goal of the assessment stage is to determine whether both parents are ready to enter into mediation, and are suitable candidates for the process. The mediator needs to decide whether to begin the mediation process or delay it, particularly when one partner has a continuing unrealistic hope for reconciliation, or has not come to terms with the reality of the divorce. Setting aside of negative feelings associated with the marital relationship is necessary to make the best use of child-centered negotiations. Referral to divorce counseling may be required before or during mediation, particularly when there is a strong need to allocate blame, point the finger at the other partner, and recite a litany of recriminations, which some have suggested may be an essential step in the process of uncoupling (Walker, 1993).

Contraindications to mediation include cases of physical and sexual child abuse or serious neglect, marked imbalances of power, and situations where abused spouses are unable to contemplate negotiating with their former partners; the option of legal proceedings to settle postdivorce parenting disputes in such cases should be retained. It should be noted that the issue of the appropriateness of mediation in cases involving spouse abuse continues to generate much debate (Kruk, 1994; Corcoran & Melamed, 1990; Hart, 1990). Mediation proponents argue that the process can be highly empowering for abused spouses, enabling them to articulate their needs and interests and have these met within a safe forum of dispute resolution. However, while there are effective strategies to counter imbalances of power between the parties in mediation, continued marked imbalances are unlikely to produce fair outcomes.

The second goal of assessment is to determine whether, given the family's circumstances, a shared parenting plan is indeed appropriate. Contraindications to shared parenting include the inability to care for children mentally, emotionally, or physically, the physical, emotional, or sexual abuse of the children or spouse, significant substance abuse, intractable hostility between the spouses, and an expressed desire of both parents for a sole parenting arrangement. There are a number of valid reasons for one parent to be opposed to shared parenting; however, opposition based on a lack of understanding of children's needs in divorce, a lack of knowledge about shared parenting, or pressure from family, friends, or professionals to reject it as an option should not be seen as sufficient reason not to consider it.

It is particularly critical to assess the nature of predivorce parent-child relationships, including the degree of involvement and sharing of parenting tasks and responsibilities within the marriage, competence in parenting, discipline methods used by each parent, the degree of attachment between each parent and the children, and the degree of influence each parent has in various areas related to children's growth and development. According to Gardner (1984), shared parenting is a viable option when three provisions are satisfied: (1) both parents are capable and loving custodians—their levels of involvement with and attachment to their children are high, and they wish to continue their child care responsibilities; (2) the parents have the potential to cooperate and communicate effectively in regard to parenting concerns; and (3) geographic distance and other logistical constraints are not excessive.

Where parents acknowledge the centrality of their children in their lives and the importance of keeping children's interests at the forefront of their negotiations, the prognosis for shared parenting mediation is good. This is probably the mediator's most powerful lever in facilitating the parents' negotiations.

Exploration of Shared Parenting Options. The second phase of mediation is essentially an extension of the divorce education process, in which the mediator helps the parents to consolidate the knowledge and skills gained during the parent education program. Reinforcement of communication, negotiation, and problem-solving skills is particularly important, as the parties are about to embark on an assisted negotiation process; teaching these skills may include explicit instruction in regard to a particular skill, demonstrating or modeling the skill, enactment, debriefing, and extrasession assignments.

At this point, the mediator clearly declares herself or himself as an advocate for the children in the process, assuming an affirmative stance with respect to establishing the "best interests of the child" as the objective criterion that will guide the parents' negotiations and determination of the postdivorce parenting plan. Where appropriate, the mediator promotes a shared parenting arrangement as best meeting that criterion. The benefits of shared parenting are first examined from the point of view of children and then the parents. Specific information is given about the optimal types of shared parenting arrangements for children at different ages, and for families in different circumstances.

As Walker (1993) cautions, the use of expert knowledge toward influencing outcomes can be problematic in a conflict resolution process that purports to enable the parties to find their own solutions to their disputes. It is important that the mediator not make decisions for parents; however, most parents feel that mediators should help them to generate options and examine the costs and benefits of these in relation to their children's needs (Elwork & Smucker, 1988). Before to the negotiation phase, the mediation process can be used to consolidate the knowledge and skills parents have gained during premediation parent education with respect to children's needs and interests during and after divorce. While the "best interests of the child" are different in each unique family system, mediators who are well-versed in current research on child outcomes in divorce have important and valuable information to impart that can be of enormous benefit to parents in their decision making. After the mediator has examined in some detail both existing parent-child and spousal relationships, she or he is in a unique position to help parents tailor-design parenting plans that are uniquely suited to their situation and reflect existing parent-child relationships.

The mediator's use of language is particularly crucial at this stage: the task is to move parents away from the legal notions of parents' claim to child ownership toward the type of postdivorce relationship that serves the children's (and family's) best interests. Shared parenting should be presented as a "neutral" position, allowing both parents an optimal relationship with their children. In advocating shared parenting, the mediator must be aware of the danger of being perceived by one parent as forming an alignment with the other; caution must be exercised in a situation when one parent wants a sole and the other a coparenting arrangement. This situation may be preempted if parents have been exposed to a divorce education program that has examined the importance of maintaining existing parent-child relationships within some form of shared parenting arrangement, or if this phase of the mediation process remains mediator-directed, in which the mediator educates the parents about children's needs in divorce, stressing the importance of continuing regular involvement of both parents after divorce and then informs them about the range of shared parenting options available. During this time, the parents are not (yet) given the opportunity to indicate their preferred postdivorce parenting arrangement. Rather, the mediator makes clear that the development of the parenting plan will be guided by the principles of maximum parental involvement, parental continuity, and mutual decision making regarding child care.

The mediator should emphasize that shared parenting does not necessarily entail apportioning exactly 50 percent of a child's time to each parent, a misperception that can interfere with the formulation of a flexible and workable plan. At this stage, avoiding the issue of *percentage* of time each parent spends with the children and focusing instead on *types* of schedules and scheduling options may make shared parenting more attractive and likely to be considered. The mediator may thus introduce the parents to a range of shared parenting schedules, while emphasizing that their shared parenting plan will be "tailor-made" for them.

While the actual negotiation and formulation of the parenting plan takes place in phase three, during the option exploration phase the mediator orients the parents toward the development of a plan based primarily on the needs and capacities of the individual child and away from what may be convenient or expedient for the parents. The age and developmental stage of the child are central: preschool children, who have a limited sense of time, in most cases need to have contact with both parents on a relatively frequent basis; with school-aged children, there are more shared parenting options available; adolescents may need the flexibility of not being tied down to rigid schedules so that they have the time available to pursue their own developmental needs and interests. For all children, consistency and (at least initial) predictability of schedule are important; the use of a monthly calendar, which is duplicated so that there is one for each household, gives children a clear sense of where they are going to be and when (and parents a clear picture of their parenting times for the month). The importance of children initially remaining in the same schools and maintaining the same friendship and neighborhood ties should be emphasized.

Before they enter the negotiation phase, it is important for parents to know that, as there is a wide range of family patterns and dynamics, they will be able to select from a range of shared parenting alternatives. Further, whatever parenting plan they formulate will not be irrevocable. They will need to consult each other about their children's changing needs at different ages and stages of development, and are likely to have to modify the arrangement several times during the forthcoming years.

Facilitation of Negotiations. In the negotiation stage, the feasibility of a shared parenting arrangement is examined from the children's and parents' perspectives, and practical needs and constraints in terms of day-to-day concerns and the realities of the entire family are considered. The goal is to help the parents design a parenting plan meeting not only their children's and their own needs and interests, but also their particular schedules and lifestyles. The mediator's tasks at this stage are to reinforce the parents' concern for their children's needs and interests as primarily guiding their negotiations, help each parent to listen to and validate the needs and interests of the other, and identify commonalties in their stated interests—including that of ensuring that the welfare of their children is paramount in whatever outcome they negotiate. Mediation becomes a process of building on areas of agreement, and assisting in the negotiation of issues around which there is disagreement. Each parent will be expected to modify some of his or her own personal desires on the basis of the children's needs, those of the other parent, and the everyday realities of everyone's lives.

In addition, the mediator may wish to meet directly with the children, particularly those who are older, to explore their concerns and preferences regarding postdivorce parenting arrangements. It should be made clear that the parents shall ultimately determine these arrangements, but that it is important for them to have input from the children in arriving at their decisions. The involvement of children in the mediation process may also be helpful toward achieving the goal of parental cooperation in parents' future dealings with each other.

Ricci (1980) outlines three time dimensions and two aspects of decision making as central considerations in the formulation of a shared parenting plan. Time dimensions include overnight stays (how many will there be with each parent?), the actual time the child and parent spend together (time spent in the daily routines of caretaking and parenting), and activity time (time spent together in recreation and special activities). Difficulties are likely to arise if one parent has little activity time but the main responsibility for routine time, or vice-versa, or if all overnights are with only one parent. Parental decision making includes decisions made in the course of daily child rearing, and major decisions (including schooling, religious affiliation and training, and major medical decisions). Again, a plan in which one parent has power to make major decisions without any responsibility for day-to-day decisions can be highly problematic.

The actual negotiations follow a set procedure, established by the mediator. Ware (1982) suggests a process of having each parent develop three lists, in sequence—one from their perspective of their children's needs, one on the basis of their own interests, and one from the point of view of the current realities of their lives—with respect to Ricci's (1980) five dimensions of shared parenting. Kruk (1993b) provides a framework in this regard, including the salient categories to which parents can refer as they draft their three separate lists. After completion, the lists become the foundation for the negotiation and ultimately the final written agreement.

In addition to the three lists, a time survey—having each parent outline what a typical week would look like when the child is living with them—may also help the parents consider realistically what will be involved in parenting as separate entities, think about their strengths and deficiencies as caretakers, and identify the skills they will need to be able to carry through their shared parenting plan.

Through the negotiation stage, proposals and counterproposals regarding various time-sharing formulas are made, and as agreement is reached on particular issues, a parenting plan begins to take shape. Plan formulation proceeds from a skeletal structure to the specifics of the actual shared parenting arrangement; the end product of mediation is a written plan for cooperative shared parenting. In many cases, considerable detail and specificity will be required to avoid initial confusion and conflict, including details of scheduling contact with the children, and a list of which responsibilities are shared and which are held by each parent. The need to keep dates and times absolutely sacred until a degree of trust and cooperation develops should be emphasized.

While shared parenting plans take many forms, it is important to include the following in the written agreement:

1. A general statement to begin the agreement—the parents will cooperatively share the parenting of the children, with cooperative shared parenting being defined as having two central elements: equal responsibility for sharing in important decision making as well as the de facto daily parenting of the children, and parental cooperation in this regard. This includes respect for one another's parenting style and authority; the parents agree to say or do nothing that will harm the relationship of the other parent with their children. A helpful clause to include in this section is, "The parents agree to foster love and affection between their children and the other parent."

2. The sharing of parental rights and responsibilities—the parents agree to confer on all important matters affecting the welfare of the children, including education, health, and religious upbringing. They agree that each will have access to medical and school records. A clause may be added saying that day-to-day decisions are the responsibility of the parent with whom the child is living.
3. The specifics of the actual time-sharing and residential arrangement.
4. Details regarding holidays and special occasions.
5. The agreement time period, and amendments to the agreement—a clause indicating the length of the agreement and that the plan will be reexamined at a later fixed time, or from time to time. If no revisions are deemed necessary after the agreed time period, the agreement is automatically renewable. A clause specifying the manner in which parents will settle disputed issues in the future, with an emphasis on cooperation and a return to mediation if necessary may also be needed.

The aims of cooperative shared parenting mediation are twofold: to help the parents develop their own shared parenting plan, and to help them establish an atmosphere of cooperation with respect to parenting issues. Ricci (1989) emphasizes the importance of moving the parents beyond *parallel* parenting, where there is little or no interaction between the parents, communication is strained or nonexistent, and the child's loyalties are divided, to *shared* parenting within a businesslike working relationship, where parents can talk with each other about parenting issues, and ultimately to *cooperative* parenting, which builds on a spirit of forgiveness and easier give and take, flexibility, and following the "spirit" of the plan rather than the "letter" of the agreement. During the negotiation stage, the minimum expectation is that parents are able to achieve a businesslike relationship; as parents begin the process of implementing the shared parenting plan, cooperative parenting may be established as an objective.

Continuing Support/Troubleshooting. Walker (1993), in a critique of this model, questions whether family members have the capacity and motivation to attain the ideal of cooperative shared parenting after divorce, suggesting that parallel parenting may be the best outcome for the majority of families, given the multiple and complex transitions and losses facing family members.

A follow-up phase at least provides divorced family members with the opportunity to move beyond parallel parenting to cooperative shared parenting. To this end, the mediator monitors the parents' progress and intervenes as needed, helping them work through conflict and reinforcing and consolidating the communication, negotiation, and problem-solving skills taught during the parent education and mediation process.

Explicit guidelines for cooperative shared parenting can be developed at the time the parenting plan is drafted. These may include: (1) respecting the other's parenting rules; (2) avoiding criticizing the other parent, directly or indirectly; (3) avoiding placing a child in the middle of an argument or using a child as a messenger; (4) sticking to the time-sharing schedule and keeping promises, but also being flexible in a way that meets the children's and the other parent's needs (trying to accommodate the other parent's request for changes, but the other parent should remember that even small changes to the schedule that occur with little forewarning can cause major problems); (5) making transitions as comfortable as possible for the child (being positive about the child's stay with the other parent; being courteous with the other parent; once the child settles back in, letting him or her talk freely about the other parent or the other home); and (6) respecting each other's privacy (keeping contacts and communications restricted to set times, and to child-related matters).

Ideally parents should develop a communication system involving routinely scheduled and open forums or "parenting meetings" to which they may bring their stockpiled child-related concerns. Transition times (when children are transferring between their homes) are not appropriate times to discuss important matters, and contacts during stressful times should be avoided.

While the shared parenting plan should generally be highly structured at the beginning, over time flexibility, creativity, and compromise should be encouraged. In addition to teaching parents negotiation and problem-solving skills during mediation, the expectation that changes to the plan are inevitable should be established; it is inevitable that shared parenting arrangements will require reevaluation and change over time, based on children's changing developmental needs and the parents' own changing circumstances. Future changes should not be regarded as indicative of failure of the original parenting plan, but rather of the growth and evolution of a living agreement over time. Mediators should attempt to ensure that parents have developed the tools to negotiate these changes.

Contingency planning sets the stage for future changes. Potential obstacles and areas of conflict regarding parenting can be anticipated and examined; issues such as changing job demands, relocation, and how to deal with children's changing developmental needs need to be discussed. Remarriage or cohabitation and stepfamily formation may affect shared parenting in a significant way as the problem of mistrust often reemerges when new members join the family. Anticipating and preparing for such events can be an important preventative measure.

Once a shared parenting plan has been negotiated and drafted, it should be implemented for a specified trial period, lasting six to twelve months. This is particularly important when shared parenting was not the option of choice of both parents (or had not been considered) at the beginning of mediation. At the end of the trial period, the plan is reviewed and made permanent, modified, or abandoned. Knowing at the outset that the shared parenting arrangement will be reviewed formally after a specified trial period will help parents agree to try the arrangement, despite their anxiety about committing themselves to an unknown way of life. Parents are generally reassured in the knowledge that the plan they negotiate is not irrevocable.

Another important goal during the "troubleshooting" stage is that of assisting the parents in their own and their children's adaptation to living as two households. Establishing a routine and an environment conducive to children's adaptation to the new shared parenting arrangement are critical tasks for both parents. Children are generally anxious to know the specifics of their new routine, and the predictability of a clear schedule facilitates adaptation. They also need to develop a sense of belonging in both homes, and will adapt more easily if they have a place of their own in each house that they have helped to create. Other important considerations include deciding on children's items that need to be duplicated (toothbrushes, nightclothes, school supplies, diapers and baby supplies for infants), those that are divided between the two homes (shoes and clothing apportioned in measure with how much time is spent in each residence, toys, books), and those that will go back and forth between the two homes (cherished toys, bicycles, musical instruments) (Ware, 1982).

The troubleshooting phase will vary in length, depending on the needs of the parents, and their ease of adjustment to the new shared parenting routine and the boundaries of their new coparenting relationship. Where conflict levels are high or when one of the parents is ambivalent about the shared parenting arrangement, continuing mediator support is critical.

In the future, parents may need the services of a mediator to assist in their ongoing parenting negotiations; they should be urged to return for mediation beyond the trial period as future issues develop or past difficulties reemerge.

Use of the Model

Parent education and therapeutic family mediation are adjuncts to the service delivery of social workers and human service professionals working with families during and after the divorce transition period, and represent an alternative to mainstream mediation models emphasizing a neutral orientation to the resolution of postdivorce parenting disputes. The model presented in this chapter is particularly suited to the development of parenting plans; for the majority of families, cooperative shared plans are seen as the best possible parenting arrangements that both parents can make for their children insofar as they reflect parent-child relationships in the original two-parent home.

The model has been highly successful both with couples who have voluntarily involved themselves in the mediation process, and in those cases where one or both of the parents have not entered mediation on a voluntary basis. The model's emphasis on assessment and education in the beginning stages is well suited to work with couples mandated by courts to attempt to develop a parenting plan and provides an effective mechanism for determining the appropriateness of mediation and shared parenting through assessment of the nature of existing spousal and parent-child relationships. Consistent with the findings of Johnston and Campbell (1988), the model has also worked well with high conflict couples who have reached an impasse in their negotiations. The model has been most effective with couples presenting at an early stage in the divorce process, before postdivorce parenting patterns become established and consolidated.

In its exclusive focus on postdivorce parenting issues, the model goes counter to the prevailing (North American) trend in mediation toward assisting divorcing couples in their negotiation of all divorce-related matters, including the financial aspects of divorce (child and spouse support, and property division). Couples benefiting most from the process are those whose primary dispute relates to postdivorce parenting, and either concurrently or subsequently address the financial aspects of divorce within or outside mediation. All parenting plans developed in mediation are made "without prejudice" and are subject to review by the parties' legal representatives, who assist toward legal formalization of the agreement.

In ensuring that children's needs and interests and shared parental responsibility remain at the forefront of the mediation process, the therapeutic mediation/parenting plan model sets the stage toward a high degree of clarity about orders made by the court as negotiations focus on three distinct time dimensions of postdivorce parenting and two aspects of parental decision making: residence and contact are clearly delineated in terms of overnight stays with each parent, actual time spent together, and activity time; parental decision making is broken down to include negotiation of both day-to-day and major decisions.

Conclusion

As Tompkins (1995) notes, no system of conflict resolution in the realm of postdivorce parenting is a panacea; there will always be a percentage of parents that no amount of negotiation assistance or enlightened divorce legislation will help in the construction of a parenting plan. As discussed, the option of traditional legal processes for those who are not good candidates for mediation must be available. In some cases, lawyer negotiation may result in the devlopment of a parenting plan; in others, litigation may be the only means left after such efforts have failed.

Conversely, there will also be a percentage of couples who, no matter what the divorce process entails, will need no assistance in maximizing the positive adjustment of their children to divorce. It is the majority of families who fall between these extremes that will benefit from the advantages of parenting plans developed by means of parent education and therapeutic family mediation.

Cooperative shared parenting plans best meet the needs of most children of divorce and hence are best suited for the majority of divorced families. These plans comprise two essential elements: (1) both parents retain an active parenting role and decision-making authority with respect to their children; and (2) both parents have successfully negotiated the task of separating their previous marital conflicts from their ongoing parental responsibilities. Such an arrangement is regarded as the healthiest and most desirable postdivorce outcome for all family members.

With adequate therapeutic support, the ideal of cooperative shared parenting could become a reality for a significant proportion of separated, divorced, and remarried families. Such an outcome has largely eluded those practicing traditional approaches to dispute resolution in divorce, including mainstream models of mediation. When applied to the divorce arena, the mainstream model, with its highly structured and neutral orientation, is extremely limited in its potential: a pure form of mediation that is strictly rule governed and limited to dispute settlement does not permit the wealth of data related to positive postdivorce outcomes to emerge and guide the mediation process.

A therapeutic/parenting plan approach to family mediation offers an effective alternative to the mainstream mediation model, and may be the key in establishing cooperative shared parenting as the norm, rather than the exception, for divorced families. The model represents a radical alternative to traditional approaches: its goals are therapeutic (facilitating the adjustment to divorce for all family members, restructuring the parents' relationship, restructuring parent-child relationships, enhancing communication and problem-solving skills); the mediator's role is highly interventionist (influencing a settlement that is in the "most adequate" if not in the "best interests" of the child as well as fair to both parents); assessment and detailed history taking with respect to existing coparental and parent-child relationships are emphasized; and interventions are geared toward the promotion and facilitation of cooperative shared parenting after divorce. The mediation process is transformed into a longer-term therapeutic endeavor, focused not only on the production of a shared parenting agreement but on the durability of that agreement.

Mediation focused on the development of postdivorce parenting plans requires a distinct approach; the neutral mainstream model, designed for use in vastly diverse arenas, has shown itself to be an unwieldy instrument in the realm of family transition attendant to divorce. The model presented here is an effective alternative, ideally suited for use by social workers and human service professionals working with families in transition, specifically designed toward the development of postdivorce parenting plans, and operationalizing the principle of shared parental responsibility underlying emerging developments in divorce law.

References

Ahrons, C. R. 1981. The Continuing Coparental Relationship between Divorced Spouses. *American Journal of Orthopsychiatry* 51: 415–28.

Andes, R. H. 1991. A Communication-Instructional Model of Family Mediation: A Compendium of Ideas for Practice. Paper presented at the Annual Conference of the Academy of Family Mediators, Seattle.

Benjamin, M. & H. H. Irving. 1989. Shared Parenting: Critical Review of the Research Literature. *Family and Conciliation Courts Review* 27: 21–35.

Bernard, S. E., J. P. Folger, H. R. Weingarter, & Z. R. Zumeta. 1984. The Neutral Mediator: Value Dilemmas in Divorce Mediation. *Mediation Quarterly* 4: 5–17.

Bienenfeld, F. 1988. Unpublished report: Parent Education Practices in California Family Court Services. San Francisco: Statewide Office of Family Court Services.

Braver, S. L., P. Salem, J. Pearson, & S. R. DeLuse. 1995. The Content of Divorce Education Programs: Results of a Survey. *Family and Conciliation Courts Review* 34: 41–59.

Brotsky, M., S. Steinman, & S. Zemmelman. 1988. Joint Custody Through Mediation Reviewed. *Conciliation Courts Review* 26: 53–58.

Burgoyne, J., R. Ormrod, & M. Richards. 1987. *Divorce Matters*. Harmondsworth, UK: Penguin.

Calvin, D. A. 1981. Joint Custody as Family and Social Policy. In I. R. Stuart and L. E. Abt, eds., *Children of Separation and Divorce*. New York: Van Nostrand Reinhold.

Coogler, O. J. 1979. *Structured Mediation in Divorce Settlements*. Lexington, MA: Lexington Books.

Corcoran, K. O. & J. Melamed. 1990. From Coercion to Empowerment: Spousal Abuse and Mediation. *Mediation Quarterly* 7 (4): 303–16.

Elwork, A. & M. R. Smucker. 1988. Developing Training and Practice Standards for Custody Mediators. *Conciliation Courts Review* 26: 21–31.

Fineman, M. 1988. Dominant Discourse, Professional Language, and Legal Change in Child Custody Decisionmaking. *Harvard Law Review* 101: 727–74.

Folberg, J. & M. Graham. 1981. Joint Custody of Children Following Divorce. In H. H. Irving, ed., *Family Law: An Interdisciplinary Perspective*. Toronto: Carswell.

Gardner, R. A. 1984. Joint Custody Is Not for Everyone. In J. Folberg, ed., *Joint Custody and Shared Parenting*. Washington, DC: Bureau of National Affairs.

Greatbatch, D. & R. Dingwall. 1990. Selective Facilitation: Some Preliminary Observations on a Strategy Used by Divorce Mediators. *Family and Conciliation Courts Review* 28: 53–64.

Greif, J. 1979. Fathers, Children, and Joint Custody. *American Journal of Orthopsychiatry* 49: 311–19.

Hart, B. 1990. Gentle Jeopardy: The Further Endangerment of Battered Women and Children in Custody Mediation. *Mediation Quarterly* 7 (4): 317–30.

Haynes, J. 1982. A Conceptual Model of the Process of Family Mediation: Implications for Training. *American Journal of Family Therapy* 104: 5–16.

Hess, R. D. & K. A. Camara. 1979. Postdivorce Family Relationships as Mediating Factors in the Consequences of Divorce for Children. *Journal of Social Issues* 35: 79–96.

Hetherington, E. M., M. Cox, & R. Cox. 1978. The Aftermath of Divorce. In J. H. Stevens Jr. & M. Mathews, eds., *Mother-Child, Father-Child Relations*. Washington, DC: National Association for the Education of Young Children.

Irving, H. H., M. Benjamin, & N. Trocme. 1984. Shared Parenting: An Empirical Analysis Utilizing a Large Data Base. *Family Process* 23: 561–69.

Johnston, J. R. & L. E. G. Campbell. 1988. *Impasses of Divorce: The Dynamics and Resolution of Family Conflict*. New York: Free Press.

Kelly, J. B. 1993. Current Research on Children's Postdivorce Adjustment: No Simple Answers. *Family and Conciliation Courts Review* 31: 29–49.

Kruk, E. 1991. Discontinuity between Pre- and Postdivorce Father-Child Relationships: New Evidence Regarding Paternal Disengagement. *Journal of Divorce and Remarriage* 16: 195–227.

———. 1993a. *Divorce and Disengagement: Patterns of Fatherhood Within and Beyond Marriage*. Halifax: Fernwood Publishing.

———. 1993b. Promoting Cooperative Parenting after Separation: A Therapeutic/ Interventionist Model of Family Mediation. *Journal of Family Therapy* 15: 235–61.

———. 1994. Divorce Mediation and Woman Abuse: Danger and Potential. B.C. *Institute on Family Violence Newsletter* 3: 20–23.

Lamb, M. E. 1986. *The Father's Role: Applied Perspectives*. New York: Wiley.

Lehner, L. 1992. Mediation Parent Education Programs in the California Family Courts. *Family and Conciliation Courts Review* 30: 207–16.

Leupnitz, D. A. 1982. *Child Custody*. Lexington, MA: Lexington Books.

Lewis, C. 1986. *Becoming a Father*. Milton Keynes: Open University Press.

Lund, M. 1987. The Noncustodial Father: Common Challenges in Parenting after Divorce. In C. Lewis and M. O'Brien, eds., *Reassessing Fatherhood*. London: Sage.

McCarthy, P., B. Simpson, J. Corlyon, & J. Walker. 1991. Family Mediation in Britain: A Comparison of Service Types. *Mediation Quarterly* 8: 305–23.

McWhinney, R. 1995. The "Winner-Loser Syndrome": Changing Fashions in the Determination of Child "custody," *Family and Conciliation Courts Review* 33: 298–307.

Mitchell, A. 1985. *Children in the Middle*. London: Tavistock.

Nehls, N. & M. Morgenbesser. 1980. Joint Custody: An Exploration of the Issues. *Family Process* 19: 117–25.

Polikoff, N. D. 1982. Gender and Child Custody Determinations: Exploding the Myths. In I. Diamond, ed., *Families, Politics, and Public Policies: A Feminist Dialogue on Women and the State*. New York: Longman.

Ricci, I. 1980. *Mom's House, Dad's House*. New York: Macmillan.

———. 1989. Mediation, Joint Custody and Legal Agreements: A Time to Review, Revise and Refine. *Family and Conciliation Courts Review* 27: 47–55.

Richards, M. P. M. 1982. Postdivorce Arrangements for Children: A Psychological Perspective. *Journal of Social Welfare Law* 69: 133–51.

Roberts, M. 1988. *Mediation in Family Disputes*. Aldershot: Wildwood Press.

Roberts, S. 1988. Three Models of Family Mediation. In R. Dingwall & J. Eekelaar, eds., *Divorce Mediation and the Legal Process*. Oxford: Clarendon Press.

Robinson, M. 1991. *Family Transformation Through Divorce and Remarriage: A Systemic Approach*. London: Routledge.

———. 1993. Comment on "Promoting Cooperative Parenting after Separation." *Journal of Family Therapy* 15: 263–71.

Salem , P., A. Schepard, & S. W. Schlissel. 1995. Parent Education as a Distinct Field of Practice: The Agenda for the Future. *Family and Conciliation Courts Review* 34: 9–22.

Saposnek, D. T. 1983. *Mediating Child Custody Disputes: A Systematic Guide for Family Therapists, Court Counsellors, Attorneys and Judges*. San Francisco: Jossey-Bass.

Sev'er, A. 1992. *Women and Divorce in Canada: A Sociological Analysis*. Toronto: Canadian Scholars Press.

Shiller, V. M. 1984. Joint Custody: An Appraisal. Ph.D. diss., Yale University.

Tompkins, R. 1995. Parenting Plans: A Concept Whose Time Has Come. *Family and Conciliation Courts Review* 33: 286–97.

Walker, J. 1993. Co-operative Parenting Postdivorce: Possibility or Pipedream? *Journal of Family Therapy* 15: 273–93.

Wallerstein, J. S. & J. Kelly. 1980. *Surviving the Breakup: How Children and Parents Cope with Divorce*. New York: Basic Books.

Ware, C. 1982. *Sharing Parenthood after Divorce*. New York: Viking Press.

Wolchik, S. A., S. L. Braver, & I. N. Sandler. 1985. Maternal versus Joint Custody: Children's Postseparation Experiences and Adjustment. *Journal of Clinical Child Psychology* 14: 5–10.

5

STEPFAMILIES

Postdivorce Mediation with Stepfamilies: An Overview of Issues and Process

by Lynn Carp Jacob

Demographers tell us that by the year 2000, stepfamilies will outnumber all other family forms (Papernow, 1993). Yet the idealized image of the biological family—mother, father and their children—is still presented as the norm in both the popular media and professional literature, despite the fact that this family form represents only one-quarter of family types in the United States. It is thus not surprising that individuals coming together to form a remarried family compare themselves to the biological family and are not aware that stepfamilies are a unique family form confronted with a unique set of problems and developmental challenges.

In recent years we have begun to think about single parent families and stepfamilies as being new family forms. In fact, even before the increase in the divorce rate in the last half century, single parent families and stepfamilies were common, typically forming after the death of one parent. Historically, divorce and stepfamilies have been tolerated, although regarded as atypical and somehow dysfunctional, a deviation from the nuclear biological family ideal. As stepfamilies become a prevalent family form, however, this is beginning to change, with a recognition of the stepfamily as a legitimate and "normal" family form.

Stepfamilies find themselves in conflict more frequently than biological families for many reasons. First, they are larger and have more complex relationships. Parents do little to prepare themselves and their children for the peculiar stresses of stepfamily life. Given the complexities of remarried families, greater demands are placed on the flexibility of their members, and their problem-solving and communication skills (Ganong & Coleman, 1994).

Disputes develop for many of these families as they struggle with the divorce-remarriage-stepfamily transition.

At the same time that stepfamilies and stepfamily conflict have become more common, mediation has become an accepted procedure for processing family disputes. The increase in the number of disputes being brought before the courts places pressure on the legal system to find another venue for resolution. The types of conflicts that stepfamilies find themselves embroiled in are relational conflicts, and such cases are not readily resolved in the legal arena.

The purpose of this chapter is to provide mediators with knowledge about normal stepfamily development and to outline a model of practice that is specifically designed for resolving disputes with this population. Mediation strategies that are helpful in this unique field of practice will be emphasized.

Theory, Research, and Trends

Stepfamilies

There is no single stepfamily type. Stepfamilies are created by the marriage or cohabitation of two adults, at least one of whom is a biological or adoptive parent of children from a previous relationship. They include households in which children are seldom present, as well as those in which children reside most of the time. Sometimes the biological parent plays an important part in a child's life, at other times not. Stepfamilies encompass households in which the adults have a committed relationship but are not legally married, including same-sex couples who have come together after one or both has given birth to or adopted a child (Visher & Visher, 1993; Robinson & Smith, 1993). Stepfamilies also vary according to the cultural background of the family, and may include grandparents and other extended family members.

There are various ways to categorize stepfamilies. Robinson and Smith (1993) use legal status as their criterion and define four major groupings: the formerly single parent now cohabiting or married; those where the previous spouse of the biological parent has died; those where the biological or adoptive parents have divorced and one or both have remarried; and those who have made a commitment to one another but have not married. Robinson and Smith's classifications, however, obscure some significant characteristics, such as whether just one or both of the partners have children, whether there are any children of the new union, the amount of time the children spend in the household, the amount of contact with the nonresidential parent, and the ages of the children. One might also look at whether couples are in a same-sex or a heterosexual relationship.

Myths. There are numerous myths and misunderstandings about step-families. One of the most common is that stepfamilies are the same as biological families; in fact, life in stepfamilies is radically different from that in nuclear families. The original two-parent family's connectedness gradually emerges through the family life cycle, from courtship to marriage to parenthood. In contrast, a stepfamily must be formed from segments that already possess significant but distinctive links. The road to cohesiveness is rarely smooth. The first stages of stepfamily formation are characterized by a marked ambiguity in rules, roles, patterns of everyday living, norms, and ways of interacting. The stepfamily is made up of either one "minifamily" and an outsider, or two "minifamilies." Some members enjoy a shared history; others are seen as intruding on previously formed routines of living. The first months of stepfamily life are typically an extremely confusing time, as remarried families plunge into instant roles and must adapt. Adults and children in stepfamilies often have quite different expectations; whereas adults may be looking forward to the benefits associated with stepfamily formation, children often do not. Children may feel that they have not been given a choice and act out their angry or hurt feelings by misbehavior or disrespect toward the stepparent, and it is common for a stepparent to feel hurt by a child's angry or hurtful behavior, particularly if she or he is anxious to establish a relationship with the child (Papernow, 1993; Hetherington, Law, & O'Connor, 1993; Robinson & Smith, 1993). Stepparents who try to take on a disciplinary role too quickly impede, rather than enhance, stepfamily integration (Visher & Visher, 1988; Hetherington, Law, & O'Connor, 1985).

Another myth is that after a parent remarries and forms a new stepfamily, withdrawing a child from a nonresidential biological or adoptive parent enhances the relationship with the residential parent and new stepparent. Rarely, however, will alienating a child from one parent strengthen the child's bonds to the other; attempts to withdraw a child from a parent can lead to loyalty conflicts and, in a significant proportion of cases, to parent loss (Kruk, 1993). In stepfamilies, difficult decisions have to be made when two biological parents want to maintain a relationship with a child and participate in activities relating to the child's life. In a biological family, it is acceptable for a child to feel more comfortable with one parent than the other; that child will not be placed in the position of choosing whom to ask to a special event or with whom to spend a weekend (Visher & Visher, 1993).

In stepfamilies, children experience loyalty conflict two ways: when they are caught in the middle of conflict between their biological parents, and when they find themselves in the midst of a struggle between their nonresidential biological parent and stepparent (Martin, Martin, & Jeffers, 1992). The extent and severity of a child's loyalty conflicts depends on the postdivorce relationship between the two parents; the more amicable the contact between the parents, the less severe the loyalty conflicts. Those children caught in the middle of severe parental conflict are most negatively impacted by the divorce of their parents (Johnston & Campbell, 1988, Furstenburg & Cherlin, 1991).

Children do best when their parents can maintain a parenting coalition, a cooperative coparenting relationship that permits children regular contact and a caring relationship with all parental figures (Visher & Visher, 1988). The message children need to hear is that it is acceptable to love both of their parents and have amicable relationships with all family members.

Loyalty conflicts and competition also exist for the adults in stepfamilies. Since the parent-child relationship precedes the new spouse relationship, it is common for adults to feel caught between their children and their new partners; their loyalties are divided between the children they brought into the marriage and the needs of a new spouse. If the remarriage is to succeed, the couple's relationship should be primary; at the same time, the emotional needs of the children are prodigious and require considerable attention.

Tensions between nonresidential parents and stepparents have a profound effect on relationships within the stepfamily. Commonly, the biological parent is threatened by the stepparent's efforts to join the family, which are experienced as a push to replace the noncustodial biological parent; and the stepparent often feels that his or her efforts to join the family are being undermined by the nonresidential parent. Nonresidential parents feel supplanted, while stepparents are jealous of the status of the biological parent. Rivalries between biological parents and stepparents often aggravate dormant hostilities between the former spouses. Thus it is not surprising that postdivorce conflict within families often emerges during the initial stages of stepfamily formation, subsequent to the remarriage of one or both spouses (McGoldrick & Carter, 1989; Furstenburg & Cherlin, 1991).

Loss is a major theme that impacts children and adults in stepfamilies. Children are typically surprised when they learn of their parents' divorce. It is the loss of the "ideal" family that underlies much of the pain of divorce for children and it is common for them to hold onto the fantasy that the family will reunite. When their parents remarry, children face further restructuring of their lives and more changes. Reactions to these changes, transitions, and losses vary with the personality, age, and developmental stage of the child; children in the same family commonly have markedly different reactions to stepfamily formation. An oldest child can suddenly become a second child, with a possible loss of status and responsibility within the household.

Siblings also play a distinctive role in the stepfamily. There are full siblings in which the children have the same parents and half-siblings in which they have only one parent in common. Two children, step-siblings, may live in the same home without being either biologically or legally related. The couple may then decide to have a joint child, further complicating sibling relationships. Reliable empirical data on the prevalence of and dynamics among step- and half-siblings have been difficult to obtain; Ganong and Coleman (1994) report that about three-quarters of the children who reside with a remarried parent have at least one sibling, and one-fifth have a half-sibling.

Finally, the formation of a stepfamily after a death poses special challenges. When a parent has died, children can struggle with grieving the loss of the parent for a protracted period, and they may come to idealize the deceased parent. The loyalty conflicts for a child accepting a stepparent into his or her life while still honoring the memory of the dead parent can be profound (Ganong & Coleman, 1994).

The Stepfamily Life Cycle. Especially in its early stages, the stepfamily is in constant flux as each family member sorts through his or her own interests, needs, and roles. Children may feel betrayed and act out their anger or hurt feelings. Adolescents typically have a particularly difficult time as they may have less investment in stepfamily development when their emotional focus is on separating from the family and developing independent lives. Understanding the life cycle of the stepfamily is important in putting the multiple changes attendant to stepfamily formation in perspective.

How long does it take for stepfamilies families to bond? Papernow (1993) proposes a continuum of cohesiveness in which it takes from two to eight years for families to traverse the basic stages necessary to develop a sense of unity and loyalty in which family attachment becomes primary for all of its members. Stepfamily mediators should be familiar with these stages to be able to help stepfamily members normalize their experiences and restore their often battered self-esteem. Papernow's schema for the life cycle of the stepfamily consists of three main phases with seven distinct stages (see figure 5.1).

In the three stages of phase one, the family remains primarily divided along biological lines, functioning as two "minifamilies." The fantasy stage of anticipation and hope suddenly ends when the new family begins to live together, as the parents hope that the new relationship will heal the pain of the previous marital relationship while children continue to have an investment in the original nuclear family. In the immersion stage, families are often confused as they begin to recognize the differences among their members; unfamiliar situations are common as the family struggles with their differences. Family rituals are affected on three levels: the daily routines of living, family traditions (such as holiday celebrations and religious observances) and rites of passage (such as birthdays, graduations and weddings) (Whiteside, 1988). Parental communication and cooperation is another area in which a great deal of confusion is experienced. There are often different attitudes and beliefs

Figure 5.1   Stages of Development in Stepfamilies

Fantasy	Immersion	Awareness	Mobilization	Action	Contact	Resolution
	Phase One		Phase Two		Phase Three	

about child management and discipline; many parents find themselves unable to judge their efforts against the experience of others in comparable situations. By the awareness stage, family members have begun to see that changes must be made for the new family to remain viable. Conflict and dissatisfaction are likely to peak, and it is in fact during this stage that many stepfamilies decide to separate.

In the middle phase, stepfamilies begin to mobilize themselves and take action toward dealing with dissatisfaction and conflict. As conflicts and disputes surface, family members begin to articulate their needs and move toward making changes. The task of this phase is to negotiate new agreements, roles, and functions within the family. Stepparents speak up about their need for inclusion; a nonresidential parent may express the need for greater involvement; a child may choose to change households. It is at this time that the family is most likely to seek therapy or mediation, either when the conflict is within the stepfamily, as in the case of parent-child, stepparent-child, or sibling conflict, or when there is a dispute between the two biological parents on child-related issues.

By phase three, the new couple bond begins to strengthen and the biological parents begin to cooperate, or at least diminish the level of their previous conflict. By the resolution stage, the family has formed solid and reliable step relationships. Norms have been established, a new family history has begun to develop, and step relationships no longer need constant attention (Papernow, 1993, Visher & Visher, 1988).

Papernow's (1993) research suggests that it is the speed with which families get through the first phase that determines the amount of time it will take them to become a cohesive and functioning unit; those stepfamilies that get through the three stages of the first phase relatively quickly will most rapidly achieve satisfaction and happiness. Some families are able to negotiate the early stages in about a year, others more than four years, with the average taking between two and three years. A family's ease of movement through the early stages is related to the presence of support, validation, and understanding of the intense and painful feelings involved in the early stages of stepfamily life.

McGoldrick and Carter (1989), writing on the basis of their clinical practice, identify four elements that are essential for successful stepfamily functioning. These include the knowledge and recognition of what to expect in this type of family, good couple unity, psychological space for children to continue to relate to all salient parental figures, and cooperative relationships between parental adults. Kelly (1993), in a review of current research on postdivorce outcomes, concluded that for most children, adjustment to the divorce-remarriage-stepfamily transition is furthered by unthreatened and ongoing meaningful relationships with both biological parents within a cooperative co-parental relationship. In a study of successful stepfamily therapy, Elion (reported in Visher & Visher, 1993) found that the most effective therapeutic interventions include validation, education, reduction of helplessness, and the strengthening of the couple relationship. In intervening with stepfamilies, practitioners need to provide this type of support, validation, and education if their efforts are to meet with any measure of success.

When stepfamilies are struggling and seeking mediation, it is likely that they have found themselves unable to negotiate one of Papernow's stages. They may possess little knowledge about how a stepfamily functions. Perhaps the marital couple is beginning to feel comfortable with their relationship and roles in the household but needs help negotiating parent-child roles and relationships, or a child's schedule with an ex-spouse. Knowledge about stepfamily dynamics is essential in stepfamily mediation as this information can be used in a variety of ways to help families transit the complex and often conflictual stages they must master to achieve resolution.

Stepfamily Mediation

Stepfamily mediation is a new and emerging field of practice, with few existing practice models specifically targeted toward this population. It is important to note that stepfamily and divorce mediation are not the same; the stepfamily has reached a different stage of the family life cycle and is at a different point in the divorce transition process than the recently separated family, and the dynamics both within the family and between the biological parents are markedly changed.

There is much debate in the field of family mediation about the place of therapy in the mediation process. Within most mediation approaches, it is accepted that it is the need for the resolution of a specific dispute that brings parties in conflict into mediation, and that while mediation may advance therapeutic outcomes, it should primarily focus on the resolution of the dispute (Haynes, 1994; Moore, 1986). In recent years, therapeutically-oriented mediation models have begun to emerge, including Irving and Benjamin's "Therapeutic Family Mediation," in which family assessment is an important part of the process and the emphasis in mediation is on restructuring family relationships (Irving & Benjamin, 1995).

Stepfamily mediation cases are referred by the courts, lawyers, therapists, school counselors, and the parents themselves. Often conflict is presented as a concern about a child or how family members are relating to one another. A therapeutic approach to stepfamily mediation can be very helpful, including a detailed assessment of family dynamics, and a focus on family restructuring and reorganization, and assisting the family to negotiate the stages of stepfamily development. Underlying many stepfamily disputes are unresolved emotional issues between the biological parents; if these can be dealt with and at least partially resolved, disputes within the stepfamily usually dissipate. A family assessment should focus on the degree to which the stepfamily's difficulties are rooted in unresolved conflicts between the former spouses. Despite stepfamily mediation's therapeutic emphasis, however, it is important for mediators not to lose sight of the primary purpose of the mediation endeavor: the resolution of the conflict or conflicts that have given rise to therapeutic concerns.

The Mediation Process

Most commonly in stepfamily mediation, the primary dispute underlying the difficulties experienced by family members in the stepfamily transition process is between the former spouses, who find themselves enmeshed in conflict over various issues related to postdivorce parenting and the respective roles of parental figures in children's lives, including the stepparents. Ex-spouses may also bring forward unresolved issues from the previous relationship, which impact the new stepfamily in a profound way. While the biological parents should be the "main players" in the dispute resolution process, stepparents have strong feelings about these issues, and have an important role to play in mediation.

Stepfamily mediation usually involves two families, those of the biological father and biological mother. Disputes between the biological parents regarding children are most commonly related specifically to the emerging role of the stepparent, the amount of contact between children and the nonresidential parent, financial matters, and relocation. Disputes also arise when one parent is dissatisfied with the parenting style of the other, particularly if adjustments need to be made subsequent to stepfamily formation. At times, after the remarriage of a former partner, a disengaged parent may wish to reestablish contact after a period of absence. Within the financial arena, either or both parents may request a modification of child support agreements upon the remarriage of one or both. Couples with these types of disputes turn to mediation as an alternative dispute resolution mechanism in an effort to avoid the negative impact of adversarial court proceedings on family members, and to prevent parental disengagement and alienation.

Stepfamily mediation is also found in cases where a parent is divorcing for the second time, and has a child from a previous marriage who has a relationship with the stepparent. In the case of a second divorce for either or both of the parties, it is important for the mediator to inquire about relationships with stepchildren, as well as the stepparent's legal status. It is only through adoption that stepparents can acquire legal parental rights. When conflicts over stepparent visitation are litigated, court rulings tend to favor blood ties over psychological relationships, although more judicial districts are beginning to allow third party requests for visitation (Ganong & Coleman, 1994). Mediation allows couples to voluntarily establish visitation arrangements for the stepparent. In one such case involving a second marriage and divorce for both parents, the couple had an eight-year-old son together. The mother had a twelve-year-old son from her first marriage, who had been living with the couple and with whom the stepfather had a close and caring relationship. The stepfather expressed a strong desire to maintain a relationship with not only his eight-year-old but also his stepson, with whom he had no legal ties as he had not adopted the child. Although the twelve-year-old also had regular contact and a nurturing relationship with his biological father, the biological father had no objections to the stepfather maintaining contact with the child, particularly in light of the close relationship between the two boys. After some discussion, the couple negotiated a schedule in which both boys would be with the stepfather one overnight during the week. Both boys would spend weekends with their respective biological father.

Stepfamilies, by virtue of their complexity, pose special challenges for mediators. As discussed earlier, one of these is the need to be firmly grounded in existing knowledge about stepfamilies, and to be able to use educative and therapeutic interventions in mediation when needed. Stepfamilies place great demands on their members' problem-solving and communications skills. In addition to providing a safe setting for resolving disputes, mediators can discuss with stepfamily members ways of managing the stepfamily transition process and attendant intrafamilial difficulties, and make referrals to therapeutic programs where more specialized intervention is needed. The Stepfamily Association of America is an excellent resource for mediators in this regard.

Stages of Mediation

When stepfamilies seek mediation, they often do not recognize that most of the conflict they are experiencing is related to normal life transitions, involving developmental impasses in the process of stepfamily formation. Instead, the dispute often gets transformed into a legal or quasilegal issue. In light of this, it is important for the mediator to assume the roles of educator, child advocate, and facilitator of problem solving throughout the mediation process.

Initial Joint Meeting with Biological Parents. When stepfamily conflicts involve child related issues, the mediator should begin the mediation process with the biological parents alone, in a joint session. This establishes clear boundaries and defines the conflict as one between the biological parents; it is they who have primary responsibility and decision-making power vis-à-vis the children, regardless of the formal legal custody designation. By starting the process with the parents in a joint meeting, the mediator sets a tone of balance and neutrality in which neither party feels favored; they are together informed about the process and together express their intention to make use of it in a constructive way. This first session is focused on orienting the parties to the process and obtaining their agreement to mediate, and on assessing the nature of existing parent-child relationships, and each parent's perception of stepparent-child relationships. It allows the mediator to assess the nature of the relationship between the former spouses, and to begin to explore the developmental stage of the stepfamily. Rarely does negotiation take place in the initial session.

Specific foci of assessment in the initial joint meeting include: how and why the family in general and the biological parents in particular are "stuck" at this stage of stepfamily formation; what both believe are the core issues to be resolved; how well they can work together in negotiation, and the place of new spouses or partners in the negotiations; the strengths and weaknesses of their pre- and postdivorce coparenting efforts; how they have already attempted to resolve their differences; and their perceptions of their children's needs and present functioning.

Caucus with Each Parent and the New Partner. After the joint session with the biological parents, each is seen in caucus with their new spouse or partner. Stepparents are first included in the mediation process at this time. The purpose of these individual sessions is to more fully assess the stepfamily situation and to build an alliance with each of the parties. The educative function of the mediator, focused on stepfamily formation and stepparenting roles, is emphasized during this stage. The parents and stepparent are given the option of being interviewed alone, although they are seen jointly in most cases.

Whether children become directly involved in the mediation process depends on their ages, the nature of the conflict, and the parents' preferences. Children should be seen when the mediator believes that their input will help the family move toward resolution of the dispute. Children over the age of ten are usually interviewed, and in a few cases grandparents and extended family members are also included.

Negotiation. After the initial joint session and the individual meetings, the actual negotiation may begin. Several negotiation sessions may be required, and these can take place in a variety of configurations: the biological parents together or in alternating individual sessions; the biological parents together with their respective partners or spouses; the biological parents together with their children; and alternating meetings between the biological parents and the children (Jacob, 1991). If the parties are all agreeable and seem able to negotiate flexibly and openly, it is best to include both biological parents and their respective partners, the parenting coalition. Stepparents are often helpful in calming the parent and realistically appraising the situation, as well as assessing different options for resolution of the dispute; in this way, they can function in a comediation capacity. However, the option of only including the biological parents in the negotiation should always be available. If either parent expresses concern about the presence of a stepparent, this must be respected, although the mediator may point out the potential benefits of stepparent involvement. The mediator must also be aware of potential imbalances of power when one parent has a new partner and the other does not, and should structure the negotiation sessions accordingly. The option of "shuttle mediation" between the biological parents should also be available, particularly in cases of power imbalance or extreme conflict. In sum, the decision regarding the negotiation configuration varies with each case, and the mediator should continually seek input from all involved parties regarding their preferences.

A relatively uncomplicated stepfamily mediation process would require an initial joint meeting with the biological parents, one or more individual sessions with each of the parties and their new spouses or partners, and one or more joint negotiation sessions. Postdivorce mediation with stepfamilies involves a total of four to six sessions to resolve specific disputes and provide the educational and support services required for the stepfamily system to move forward developmentally.

Mediator Roles

Stepfamily mediators play a variety of roles. The most important is the role of educator, which encompasses the skills of normalizing, reframing, and helping the stepfamily to develop and evaluate alternative solutions to the difficulties and impasses they are facing. Unrealistic expectations within the family often hinder stepfamily development, and the mediator can act as a reality-tester in this regard, sharing important information about postdivorce parenting and stepparenting. Most importantly, the mediator focuses the stepfamily on cooperative parenting options for the divorced binuclear family system after stepfamily formation (Ahrons, 1994; Blau, 1993; Garrity & Baris, 1994), orienting the family to a variety of parenting schedules that may "fit" the stepfamily's current reality.

Another role for the mediator is that of child advocate. Stepfamily mediators have an important role to play in keeping the mediation process focused primarily on children's needs, as the competing claims of a variety of adults may overshadow children's interests. Parents and stepparents can be guided to evaluate alternative solutions to their conflicts on the basis of children's needs.

Finally, a critical role for the stepfamily mediator is that of facilitator of the problem-solving process. In addition to guiding the stepfamily through the stages of problem solving as they address conflicts and disputes, the mediator teaches family members problem-solving skills, and models problem-solving behavior. The higher the degree of conflict, the more structured the mediator must be in directing the parties through the problem-solving process in mediation; less conflicted families may be guided in a less directive fashion.

Core Strategies in Stepfamily Mediation

Caucusing. A primary feature of postdivorce mediation with stepfamilies is the extensive use of caucusing. The caucus is a private meeting held by the mediator with an individual party or parties in dispute (Moore, 1987). For the caucus to work effectively, it is important that the mediator discuss its utility with the parties in the initial session. The parties are told that whatever is said in caucus may be shared with the other party, unless they ask that specific content be kept confidential.

Caucusing can be used at different stages of the mediation process. In the early stages, it can be an effective strategy for engaging clients and building trust. It is also a good way for the mediator to meet with stepparents and include them in the process. In situations of high conflict in particular, the expression of strong emotions is sometimes best done within caucus, allowing the mediator to keep the parties' anger and other emotions from adversely impacting the mediation. Caucusing can also be used as a recess in the process of negotiation, in two ways. The mediator can help the parties gain insight into how the conflict is being maintained, focusing on their part in the dispute; and can educate the parties regarding stepfamily roles and tasks, effective problem-solving strategies, and available options for resolution.

Caucusing can also be used as a break during stressful negotiations. Either the mediator or the parties can request such a break. When negotiations are at an impasse or strong emotions are being expressed in a way that is not helpful to the process, a caucus may be highly effective in getting the parties back on track. In addition, caucusing can be used to help the parties alter their negotiating positions, or to discuss an emotional issue that seems to be getting in the way of the negotiation (Moore, 1987).

Educating. Rarely are stepfamily members prepared for the multiple tasks and challenges involved in stepfamily formation and family restructuring. Education, with an emphasis on normalizing stepfamily difficulties and reframing these as normal developmental challenges for the family, is thus crucial in a mediator's work with stepfamilies. Mediator monologues and brief stories are particularly useful teaching tools; these may focus on the importance of a stepparent assuming a secondary role when disciplining children, the importance of allowing children to have their own space and not trying to force a relationship, and the difficulties children face when they make transitions between two homes, especially if they are caught in the middle of parental conflict. Some mediators make use of current stepfamily research and refer families to written materials; others relate their personal or clinical experience.

The skill of educating is used throughout the mediation process. The following are fairly typical illustrations at different stages of the process:

- *To a stepparent:* "Your role is a particularly difficult one. Don't expect too much too soon. It usually takes several years for a stepfamily to feel like a functioning family. The best place for you to start is to try building a friendship with the children. It might be easier for you to do activities separately with each of the children."
- *To a parent and stepparent in caucus:* "There shouldn t be a contest between a parent and a stepparent. Such competition will not be helpful. It will, in fact, cause loyalty conflicts for the child. When children are born they get one mother and one father. A stepparent will never be able to be the biological parent. The stepparent role is different from the parental role. The stepparent should, if possible, try to support the biological parent."
- *To a stepparent who is trying to discipline stepchildren:* "Early on, it seldom works for a stepparent to discipline stepchildren. It works best for a child's parent to enforce family rules and do the disciplining. If a parent cannot control a child, we need to talk about this and think about ways to help that person learn to parent more effectively. As the stepparent you should be free simply to be a caring adult or friend to the child. You can help the child feel accepted and welcome in your home."
- *To highly conflicted parents:* "Are you aware of the damage you are inflicting on your children? They love both of you. Putting children in the middle of the conflict tears them apart emotionally and makes it very difficult for them to feel good about themselves. Research shows that the children who do the worst following divorce are those caught in the middle of the conflict."
- *To a biological father who is beginning to disengage from his children's lives:* "It hurts children when they lose a parent. They tend to blame themselves for the loss."
- *To a new stepparent in caucus:* "It sounds like you are working too hard to get the children to like you. I suggest that you give your spouse your input and let him or her enforce the household rules. That will free you to develop a friendship with the children. The reality is that, at the beginning, they will likely not let you parent them. It is best not to try. You can be successful in getting them to treat you courteously and with respect but you cannot mandate love."

Through the skills of educating, normalizing, and reframing, stepfamilies can come to recognize that through the struggles involved in stepfamily formation and development, they can be provided with new possibilities for child rearing and dealing with conflict.

Comediation and Consultation. Stepfamily mediation is a particularly challenging endeavor, even for experienced family mediators. There are two tools that can be most useful in combating mediator stress and burnout. Comediation allows the mediator to work in conjunction with a colleague, to discuss the complexities of each case and debrief emotions that are stirred up by the process. Individual or group consultation provides another forum for discussing cases to combat the isolation and frustration often experienced by stepfamily mediators, particularly those who are in private practice.

Alternatives to Mediation

Mediation should remain a voluntary option for those stepfamilies who are committed to making use of a guided problem-solving process to negotiate the multiple tasks in the divorce-remarriage-stepfamily transition. As stepfamily mediation is one variant of family mediation, referring the disputants to lawyers who will attempt to resolve the dispute through the adversarial or judicial process is warranted in situations where facilitated negotiation assistance breaks down or is contraindicated. Lawyer negotiation or litigation rarely addresses stepfamily relationship dynamics, but decisions are made and disputes are resolved.

Another option for stepfamilies is referral to a family therapist who has the requisite skills and expertise to work with stepfamilies, as well as experience handling postdivorce conflict between former spouses. Joint therapy of ex-spouses can only be effective when couples are willing to commit themselves to the process and work on the issues that have resulted in impasse.

Life in stepfamilies is varied and complex, and vastly different from the nuclear family ideal. At the same time, established roles, expectations, traditions, and patterns are largely nonexistent for these families. Mediation provides a unique opportunity to offer vital educational and support services to stepfamily members, while assisting the former spouses to resolve specific issues in dispute.

References

Ahrons, C. R. 1994. *The Good Divorce*. New York: HarperCollins.

Blau, M. 1993. *Families Apart*. New York: Putnam's.

Furstenberg, F. & A. J. Cherlin. 1991. *The Divided Family*. Cambridge, MA: Harvard University Press.

Garrity, C. B., & M. A. Baris. 1994. *Caught in the Middle*. New York: Lexington Books.

Ganong, L. H., & M. Coleman, 1994. *Remarried Family Relationships*. Thousand Oaks, CA: Sage.

Haynes, J. M. 1994. *The Fundamentals of Family Mediation*. Albany: State University of New York Press.

Hetherington, E. M., T. C. Law, & T. G. O'Connor. 1993. Divorce: Challenges, Changes, and New Chances. In F. Walsh, ed., *Normal Family Processes,* 2d ed. New York: Guilford.

Ihinger-Tallman, M. & K. Pasley. 1987. Divorce and Remarriage in the American Family: A Historical Review. In K. Pasley, & M. Ihinger-Tallman, eds., *Remarriage and Stepparenting.* New York: Guilford.

Irving, H. H. & M. Benjamin. 1995. *Family Mediation: Contemporary Issues.* Thousand Oaks, CA: Sage.

Jacob, L. 1991. Mediating Postdecree Cases. *Mediation Quarterly* 8 (3): 171–83.

Johnston, J., & L. Campbell. 1988. *Impasses of Divorce.* New York: Free Press.

Kelly, J. B. 1983. Mediation and Psychotherapy: Distinguishing the Differences. *Mediation Quarterly* 1: 33–44.

———. 1993. Current Research on Children's Postdivorce Adjustment: No Simple Answers. *Family and Conciliation Courts Review* 31 (1): 29–49.

Kruk, E. 1993. *Divorce and Disengagement: Patterns of Fatherhood Within and Beyond Marriage.* Halifax: Fernwood.

Martin, D., M. Martin & P. Jeffers. 1992. *Stepfamilies in Therapy.* San Francisco: Jossey-Bass.

McGoldrick, M., & E. Carter. 1989. Forming a Remarried Family. In E. Carter & M. McGoldrick, eds., *The Changing Family Life Cycle.* Needham Heights, MA: Allyn and Bacon.

Moore, C. W. 1986. *The Mediation Process.* San Francisco: Jossey-Bass.

———. 1987. The Caucus: Private Meetings That Promote Settlement. *Mediation Quarterly* 16: 87–101.

Papernow, P. 1993. *Becoming a Stepfamily.* San Francisco: Jossey-Bass.

Ricci, I. 1980. *Mom's House, Dad's House.* New York: Macmillan.

Robinson, M., & D. Smith. 1993. *Step by Step: Focus on Stepfamilies.* London: Harvester Wheatsheaf.

Sager, C. J., H. S. Brown, H. Crohn, T. Engel, E. Rodstein, & L. Walker. 1983. *The Remarried Family.* New York: Brunner Mazel.

Taylor, A., & H. Bing. 1994 Settlement by Evaluation and Arbitration: A New Approach for Custody and Visitation Disputes. *Family and Conciliation Courts Review* 32 (4).

U.S. Bureau of the Census. 1995. *Statistical Abstracts of the United States.*

Visher, E., & J. Visher. 1988. *Old Loyalties, New Ties, Therapeutic Strategies with Stepfamilies.* New York: Brunner Mazel.

———. 1993. Remarriage Families and Stepparenting. In F. Walsh, ed., *Normal Family Processes,* 2d ed. New York: Guilford.

Walsh, F., L. Jacob, & V. Simons. 1995. Facilitating Healthy Divorce Processes. In N. Jacobson and A. Gurman, eds., *Clinical Handbook of Family Therapy.* New York: Guilford.

Whiteside, M. F. 1988. Remarried Systems. In L. Combrinck-Graham, ed., *Children in Family Contexts.* New York: Guilford.

6

PARENTS AND CHILDREN

Parent-Child Mediation

by Mark S. Umbreit and Edward Kruk

Parent-child mediation provides a structured yet informal, confidential process in which family members are assisted by an impartial third party to clarify problems and issues in dispute, and to identify steps in their resolution. The primary goal of parent-child mediation is to resolve the conflict and to obtain a balanced and specific agreement that the family believes will meet its needs and to which family members will be able to adhere. The agreement identifies the responsibilities of each family member to make good the behaviors agreed upon, and often includes specific contingencies regarding compliance or non-compliance in this regard. A secondary goal is to achieve a positive change in family system dynamics; this involves learning new skills to negotiate differences and collaboratively developing mutually acceptable solutions when disputes arise in the future.

Parent-child mediation differs from other forms of family mediation in some basic ways. Its aim is to retain the intact family structure, not to restructure or dissolve relationships. Many parent-child mediators would argue that the end result of an agreement is less important than exposing the parties to a process of dispute resolution that will serve to prevent future crisis. Second, the mediator needs to be constantly mindful of the asymmetrical power and knowledge distribution between the parties and to intervene when such disparities threaten to undermine the process.

As is the case with other forms of family mediation, parent-child mediation is not therapy, even though a strong social service or therapeutic component

The authors with to thank Donna and Leonard Lansky and the following members of the Parent/ Teen Mediation Program, Family Services of Greater Vancouver: Jean T. Hannon, Lesley Bennun, Richard A. Singer, Keiron Simons, and Catherine Hobson for their valuable input into the writing of this chapter.

is often present. Child welfare workers, family therapists, and other social workers and human service professionals often refer parents and children locked in conflict to mediation, and following mediation, families sometimes return to counseling. Practitioners of parent-child mediation stress that mediation and therapy should not occur simultaneously.

Many parent-child mediation programs serve adolescent "status offenders" referred to juvenile and family courts for assistance in controlling a variety of behaviors deemed to be illegal or socially undesirable. Attempts to correct these behaviors have met with limited success within the judicial system. The court has limited powers to control children; the most extreme court action is often to remove the child from the parental home. In most of these efforts, the assumption has been that such adolescent behavior is the problem to be "fixed." Family systems theory has provided an alternative perspective, which views such difficulties as residing within the family and more appropriately addressed within that context. It is from the latter perspective that parent-child mediation proceeds.

A variety of parent-child mediation programs has been developed across North America within the past fifteen years. Most programs are conducted under the auspices of nonprofit community agencies, although some are operated by public agencies, such as probation services. Most referrals are made by juvenile courts, with mediation providing a diversion opportunity in these instances; and many referrals are received from child protection agencies, with mediation seen as an alternative to placing the child or adolescent in foster care.

Most programs, private or public, make use of professional human service personnel as well as trained volunteers as mediators. Although there is tremendous variation within the field regarding the use of a face-to-face mediation format versus a "shuttle-diplomacy" approach involving separate sessions between the parties, the "typical" parent-child mediation process uses a multisession approach, follows a number of distinct stages, combines joint and private sessions with the parties, and may use a comediation model.

Rationale

Conflict is inevitable between children and their parents; particularly in the adolescent years, such conflict is reflective of a healthy assertion of the adolescent's individuality and independence. Whereas parents usually regard their children's assertions of autonomy as a challenge to parental authority and control, adolescents perceive their parents' reactions as a threat to their emerging independence. Mediation is particularly well suited to reframing the conflict in neutral terms, moving the parties beyond the power struggles that characterize their conflicts toward an interest- and needs-based type of negotiation.

Adolescence. Adolescence is a transitional stage of development between childhood and adulthood in which significant biological, cognitive, social, and cultural changes occur (Lansky & Lansky, 1996). Erikson (1968) identifies the main conflict of this developmental stage as the need to reconcile the polarities of role diffusion and ego identity in which children gradually shift from a predominantly family to a peer-group identity. Since children in their early teens must continue to depend on their parents for economic and emotional support, they understandably face conflict and ambivalence in their struggle to understand themselves and assert their autonomy. But adolescents do not live in a vacuum; the growing child is part of a family system and parental subsystem responses to an adolescent's assertion of independence often lead to power struggles. Parent-child conflict is thus not merely an issue of "bad behavior" on the part of the child; making family members aware of such complexities is an important part of resolving conflict between and among them. Mediation can play a particularly important role here, as it proceeds from the assumption that parent-child conflict is a reciprocal process and that adolescent behavior needs to be seen from the perspective of the family as a system.

Changing Families. When children are in their teen years, their parents may also be facing significant life changes, including job insecurity, menopause, and the increasing dependence of their own parents. In addition, particularly within the past few decades, the structure of North American families has changed dramatically. Increasingly, children grow and develop within the context of multiple transitions, including divorce, remarriage, and stepfamily formation, and within multiple family forms, including single parent and blended family households. At the same time, the level of poverty and violence within society is placing increased stress and economic hardship on families. In two-parent families, economic need often requires that both parents work out of the home, and the economic consequences of divorce are frequently disastrous for single parent households. Employment demands often result in limited interaction between parents and children, and there are woefully insufficient community-based parent education programs and mutual aid groups to provide much needed support to parents and children.

Even under the best of circumstances, conflict between adolescents and their parents is a normal part of youth development. For some, this shared journey is a temporary inconvenience and irritant that does not threaten the core of the parent-child relationship. For others, adolescence represents a painful, exhausting, grief-ridden, and at times, life-threatening journey that seriously weakens the bond between parents and their children.

What seem to be relatively minor disagreements over a dirty room, coming home too late, not doing chores, or having the wrong type of friends can escalate into major conflicts in which relationships are destroyed or deeply wounded. Parents often perceive adolescent behaviors as violations of family rules and fail to recognize not only their contribution to the dispute but the adolescent's underlying need to establish independence. Often, the more parents attempt to impose and force their will on the rebelling adolescent, the more they push their child in the very direction they detest. A continuously-escalating cycle of conflict, with the child acting out, the parent overreacting, and the child acting out again, can be triggered. Parents may be too authoritarian, which leads to greater adolescent rebellion, or too laissez-faire, which results in not enough structure being provided.

Some adolescents turn inward and become depressed and inactive. Others act out their anger through experimenting with drugs or alcohol, truancy, running away, or breaking the law. Still others respond favorably to parental guidance, no matter how strict or confining it might be. There seems to be no standard technique of parenting that children and adolescents respond to in a favorable manner. Two adolescents within the same family can have very different personalities and needs and therefore respond differently to the same parental approach.

The relationships of families caught in the escalating cycle of conflict can become seriously damaged, a factor contributing to the child or adolescent being referred to child welfare authorities or the juvenile court for behavior such as truancy, running away, or being beyond parental control. Mediation can offer an effective alternative for deescalating the conflict, as referring family conflict to the court system often results in a superficial decision that rarely deals with the core elements of the conflict and often further damages an already tenuous relationship. The adversarial court process pits children and parents against each other, focusing exclusively on the "child as the problem," rather than the family as a system. In contrast, mediation, with its emphasis on joint family responsibility for the problem, empowers both parents and children to assume ownership of the conflict and determine their own solution. Agreements reached in mediation fit the unique circumstances of the people involved, and the process provides the family with a model of collaborative negotiation that they can use in the future, as difficulties, anger, and disputes arise between them. Finally, mediation reframes the situation from behavior that is perceived solely as a violation of family rules or parental authority to a healthy assertion of the child's individuality and independence, and can serve an important educative function for all family members.

In those jurisdictions where parent-child mediation is available, it is usually regarded as a preferred option by both parents and children. As an alternative to the court system, it spares parents and their children the more public exposure of their difficulties and the destructive consequences of what is often perceived as a punitive and arbitrary system of resolving family problems. Also, although it can be used as a way to enable families to enter the therapeutic realm, mediation is often a more palatable option than family counseling or therapy, which connote "deviance" or "dysfunction" in a way that mediation does not. Increasingly, children are being exposed to mediation via school-based peer programs, and have already learned some of the core conflict resolution skills involved in the process. In sum, mediation is regarded as a safer and less intrusive and stigmatizing process than most of the other alternatives available to families in conflict.

Research, Debates, and Trends

Development of Parent-Child Mediation

One of the first formal parent-child mediation programs was developed within the Scottish Children's Hearing system, which replaced the juvenile courts in the early 1960s. This process involved trained volunteers meeting with juvenile offenders, parents, social workers, and school representatives to seek solutions that would benefit the child, family, and community. In North America, neighborhood justice centers developed in the mid to late 1970s, and disputes involving juveniles were addressed by mediation; however, few of these cases were internal family disputes or were considered to involve structured parent-child mediation (Lansky & Lansky, 1996). Parent-child mediation was pioneered in the early 1980s by the Children's Aid Society's Persons in Need of Supervision (PINS) project in New York City and the Children's Hearings Project (CHP) in Cambridge, Massachusetts. These programs focused on diverting juvenile status offenders from the juvenile justice system through participation in mediation with their parents. The stated objectives of these programs were to decriminalize the label "status offender," avoid further involvement with the courts by the use of mediation to resolve disputes between family members, educate both parents and children about the problem-solving and negotiation processes for use with future disputes, and facilitate referral to appropriate community services for needs identified during the mediation process (Lansky & Lansky, 1996).

Over time, the PINS project and CHP expanded their focus and accepted noncourt referrals from social agencies, mental health professionals, schools, and families themselves. Most North American programs today operate from this broader referral base. Phear and Shaw (1989) report that about half of existing programs in the United States operate within statutory social service agencies and courts and half are independent nonaffiliated programs.

Research

Several studies have found that the process of mediating conflict between adolescent children and their parents can generate many important benefits. In both the PINS project and the CHP, evaluation researchers (Morris,

1983; Merry & Rocheleau, 1985) undertook to determine not only whether parent-child mediation was working, but to identify some of the critical components of the process. They found a high degree of compliance to mediated agreements, and most families reported that they had changed the way they handled conflict. Families gained new insights into their intrafamilial disputes, and learned to recognize problematic adolescent behavior as a result of situation and context, not individual volition. They also began to reinterpret conflict as events in which each party shared some responsibility. The mediation process clearly helped to reframe the source of conflict for families.

In the evaluation of the PINS project, Morris (1983) found that the majority of children and parents involved were very satisfied with the mediation process and outcome, with written agreements reached in 73 percent of cases. Seventy-seven percent of the families reported that either moderate or high success had been achieved, citing such factors as the child becoming more manageable, the presenting problem being resolved, or the child not returning to juvenile court within eight months following mediation.

An evaluation of the CHP (Merry & Rocheleau, 1985) found that the most common problems addressed in the parent-child mediation process were truancy, chores, curfews, and the child's social life. Almost 60 percent of the adolescents participating in mediation were girls, with an average age of fourteen, and 66 percent of the families involved in the program were single-parent households from working class neighborhoods. Of the cases referred to mediation, 48 percent were actually mediated; others chose not to participate, despite referral by the court. Eighty-four percent of the families in mediation reached an agreement. Nearly two-thirds of family members in mediation indicated that the mediated agreement helped the overall management of the conflict, and that they were abiding by the terms of their agreement. A high level (83 percent) of satisfaction was reported. Nine of ten respondents indicated that the mediation process was a good or partly good idea. Nearly half of the family members in mediation said it was easier to talk with each other after the session; 41 percent indicated that they learned something new about the other's feelings; and 59 percent stated that they had a better understanding of the other's point of view.

Stern, Van Slyck, and Valvo (1986) used a standardized measure to assess family functioning before and after parent-child mediation as well as an assessment of conflict intensity (the length of the dispute and motivation to resolve it). Their research site was a community-based mediation center in New York in which parent-adolescent mediation was offered as an alternative to court intervention as one of a broad array of mediation services. The study included seventy families, with children ranging in age from eleven to eighteen. Almost half of the children had run away from home at least once; one-third had failed at least one grade in school; one-third had experimented with alcohol, and 20 percent with drugs. Whereas parents identified adolescent behavioral-attitudinal problems as the primary reason for seeking help, the mediators involved identified family dysfunction as a serious underlying issue in each case. Fifty-six percent of the families reached agreement in mediation. More importantly, the perceived intensity of the conflict by parents was related to eventual mediation outcome. Perceived higher intensity of conflict was a motivating factor for parents to successfully complete mediation.

Debates and Trends

Several unresolved issues exist in the field of parent-child mediation, such as targeting of appropriate families, power imbalance, emphasis on separate sessions, presenting versus underlying problem focus, mediation setting, and mediator qualifications. As more parent-child mediation programs are developed in communities throughout North America, these and other emerging issues will require further investigation.

Targeting of Appropriate Families. The process of mediating conflict between parents and their children is not appropriate for all families. For those with multiple problems, including physical abuse, the process may be harmful by masking the need for therapeutic or legal intervention. Participating in parent-child mediation and reaching an agreement may provide an appearance of peace and harmony, but the reality of conflict and violence is likely to continue in abusive families that do not make use of therapeutic processes.

It is unknown to what extent parent-child mediation is appropriate in the context of diverse cultures. Mediation may be seen as a direct threat to the traditional values of some cultures, such as those from Asian or Islamic traditions where filial piety and deference to elders is a core value. On the other hand, mediation may provide a means to resolve escalating conflict arising within the family from the cultural incongruity between the generations when children embrace dominant culture values while their parents endeavor to uphold traditional cultural values.

Power Imbalance. The imbalance of power that is present in the relationship between all parents and children is an important challenge of mediators in this field of practice. Some would argue that effective parenting requires such an imbalance. When conflict emerges between parents and children, parents often rely on the position of power that is intrinsic to their role. As conflicts escalate and give rise to increasingly dysfunctional patterns, however, attempting to resolve them through the exercise of parental power becomes less and less effective.

The issue of power imbalance is closely related to the need to engage the child in the mediation process. It is extremely important that the mediator be continually conscious of ensuring equal participation in the process, creating trust with the child so that he or she will be able to express his or her needs. If the mediator fails to actively address this power imbalance, the conflict is unlikely to be managed well or even resolved and the child is likely to feel further disempowered. At the same time, however, it is important that the mediator not undermine parental authority; the mediator's task is not to rebalance power in the parent-child relationship, but to accord each equal dignity in the mediation process and equal input into the resolution of the conflict (Shaw, 1989).

Emphasis on Caucusing and "Shuttle" Mediation. The process of mediation used by most programs focusing on parent-child conflict typically consists of both joint and separate meetings, or caucuses. In addition, some parent-child mediators rely on "shuttle mediation" throughout the process, with a brief joint session held at the beginning to start the process and orient the parties, and at the end, to formalize and sign the agreement that was negotiated indirectly through separate meetings. The degree to which parent-child mediation relies on the "shuttle" approach varies among existing programs and represents one of the more contentious issues in the field.

Caucuses have several useful functions: to balance power; to allow one party, typically the adolescent, to be heard without the interference of others; and to enable the mediator to use strategies of reality testing and confrontation to enable the parties to reach agreement in a way that does not result in a loss of face in front of the other. There is often such intense hostility between parents and children before to mediation that separate sessions to prepare the parties for direct negotiation are required.

The "shuttle diplomacy" method can be extremely useful in this field of practice. However, the practice of relaying messages back and forth *throughout* the mediation process, in which family members are not encouraged to negotiate directly with each other at any point, raises serious questions about what is being modeled to family members. The opportunity to directly test a valuable conflict resolution process is lost, and it is less likely that such direct communication will take place when the mediator is not present. The shuttle diplomacy model of indirect mediation used by many programs places the mediator in a very active, if not controlling, position. This process leads to family reliance on mediator expertise, rather than empowering the family members to negotiate their disputes directly with each other.

Presenting Problem versus Focus on Underlying Interests. Many practitioners of parent-child mediation have a tendency to focus entirely on the presenting issues in the conflict, such as the child being truant or hanging around with the wrong type of friends. By staying focused on these specific behaviors rather than the underlying interests and needs of all the family members the parties are less able to achieve an improved understanding of each other. For example, the underlying interests of parents in conflict with their children are normally reflective of their love and concern for their children's safety, well-being, and ongoing development; often children have lost sight of this concern. Dealing with only surface issues, such as negotiating an agreement to prevent further truancy, may resolve an immediate problem but does little to ensure that the child will come to understand parental motivation. Similarly, the underlying interests of rebelling adolescents are usually related to their need for independence, rather than continuing to be controlled by their parents, and it is helpful for parents to hear this need expressed. In response, they might be able to adjust their parenting approach even though in the current conflict their focus may be on establishing clear behavioral limits and boundaries. Although mediation must remain a time-limited, task-oriented process focused on specific conflicts, addressing only manifest or presenting problems without some exploration of deeper issues seldom produces an outcome of lasting duration.

Mediation in parent-child conflict often uncovers long-standing family problems that require further intervention. Mediation should be seen as a good first step toward preparing family members to accept and benefit from additional therapeutic and other services.

Mediation Setting. As the practice of parent-child mediation has developed in North America, it has been closely linked to the family and juvenile court system and to statutory social service agencies. Many practitioners believe, however, that parent-child mediation needs to be more closely linked with the school system and community-based agencies. By the time cases have been referred to mediation by the courts, family conflict has escalated considerably. In contrast, if mediation services were school and community based, the mediation process might have a greater impact on preventing escalation of family conflict. The mediation setting must be a safe one for both parties, and a neutral site for the meetings is often preferred. For many, the ideal site is the family home.

Many advocates of parent-child mediation also suggest that services need to be more aligned with diverse communities and neighborhoods. They believe that mediators from diverse communities must be trained to provide culturally specific services and cross-cultural mediation. Mediation should not become a process of imposing white, middle-class values on families from diverse cultures.

Mediator Qualifications. Although existing parent-child mediation programs tend to rely heavily on volunteers, the need for professional personnel with specialized expertise is becoming increasingly emphasized. Prior experience in working with children, adolescents, and families is an important asset, enabling mediators to be sensitive to and to identify some of the factors involved in both healthy family relationships and family dysfunction. An ability to engage and work effectively with children and adolescents is critical, along with a sensitivity to issues related to child and adolescent development, particularly in regard to adolescents' striving for autonomy and individuality. Parent-child mediation training programs should thus address issues that arise during different developmental stages of childhood and adolescence as well as a focus on the family from a systems theory perspective. Other core components to understanding and dealing effectively with parent-child conflicts should include knowledge about effective parenting and child behavior management, child abuse, alcoholism, and substance abuse (Shaw, 1989).

The Parent-Child Mediation Process

Conditions

Two core conditions are essential for nearly all forms of parent-child mediation. First, the participants must have an existing relationship, including some common interests, and they must express a need to preserve the relationship through a resolution of their conflict. Second, they must be in positions of relatively equal power. The process of mediating conflict between parents and their children needs to be examined in the context of these conditions as several important issues are raised by them.

In any family system, parents and children are involved in a complex and reciprocal set of relationships. A good deal of work is required of the mediator to effectively join the family system. It is particularly important that the mediator remain impartial and not allow feelings about his or her own family life to enter the process. Family dynamics are driven by intense emotional power and the mediator must not allow his or her own "emotional baggage" to compromise the process.

When a family enters the parent-child mediation process, its members typically have a strong need to resolve the conflict and preserve the relationship. Other attempts to deal with the tension, frustration, and strain of their conflict have failed. In court-related parent-child mediation, the child's experience of the conflict has been heightened to the point of being brought to the attention of the juvenile justice system.

Whether positive or negative, parents and children usually maintain lifelong relationships. As the Children's Hearings Project states, "This parent-child bond is one fact that makes mediation 'inside the family' special" (Zetzel & Wixted, 1984). However, it is not always successful. When it is, an enhancement of the family's commitment to positive change may be the result. When it is not, the sense of disappointment in a relationship that does not work will increase. It is the job of the mediator to help family members focus on their common interests so that each of them can receive what he or she needs and the overall relationship can be improved (Zetzel & Wixted, 1984).

The condition of participants having relatively equal power is particularly important in the context of parent-child mediation. Childhood is by definition a subordinate status; children do not have the same rights and responsibilities as adults. Therefore, parent-child mediators clearly do not assume that children have equal decision-making power with their parents; parents should and do have more power than their children. Nevertheless, it is important that the mediator ensure that children participate in the mediation process to the fullest extent possible, in equal measure to their parents.

As mentioned earlier, the issues that cause a family to be referred to parent-child mediation almost always involve power struggles. Often it is the child who is increasingly challenging the authority of the parent. The parent may be feeling increasingly powerless and frightened by changing relationships. The purpose of mediation is not to try to restructure the family system by taking authority away from the parent; rather, it aims to clarify expectations, which may lead to a redefinition of some of the household rules and responsibilities. It allows for all views to be expressed by family members and for the negotiation of an agreement to resolve specific issues in dispute. Mediation allows parents to reestablish their power and authority through the establishment of appropriate and realistic limits, which are more likely to be respected if they are mutually negotiated and agreed upon. As the Children's Hearing Project notes:

> Making constructive use of the power struggle defuses it. Moreover, the mediation process, by its nature, helps to offset the seeming inequality between parent and child. The youth is treated as an equal. As mediator, you accord each participant the same kind of respect, listen with the same seriousness to their concerns, pay equal attention to their expressed needs and hopes. The youth is made an active partner in solving the family's conflict. (Zetzel & Wixted, 1984)

There are many types of presenting problems that are suited to parent-child mediation, including school-related concerns (behavior, attendance, suspension), a wide range of concerns related to the child's behavior at home (house rules, curfew, choice of friends), the child running away from home, the child being asked to leave the home, the child living on the streets and looking to reunite with the family, physical aggression against the parent, property damage or stealing, violence against siblings, parental violence toward the child, the child being involved with the juvenile justice system or in criminal activity, the child in the care of the state, the child threatening to harm self, drug and alcohol problems, and intergenerational cultural conflicts.

Phases and Stages of Mediation

Parent-child mediation typically involves a lengthy history of high conflict and thus a multisession model and a comediation team are usually required. Many commentators have emphasized the importance of early intervention; families whose first appointment for mediation is scheduled within a few days of intake are most likely to complete the process.

The mediation process proceeds through a series of distinct phases and stages. Following an intake and orientation session that prepares the family, the actual mediation is scheduled. In mediation, the entire family is first seen together, followed by a series of separate and/or joint meetings between individual family members and the comediators. Finally, the family meets together to finalize the agreement. Often it is necessary to follow-up the mediation by checking on how the agreement is going and making referrals to appropriate community agencies.

The parent-child mediation process involves five main phases: (1) setting the stage, (2) defining the issues, (3) processing the issues, (4) resolving the issues, and (5) making the agreement. These five phases are similar to those in the generic mediation model outlined in chapter 1. Table 6.1 presents the relationship between these phases and the discrete stages or steps in the mediation process.

Cases are usually referred by the court or the social service system. Schools or community agencies may also refer cases to parent-child mediation in an attempt to intervene before these systems become involved. After a referral is received, mediators spend two or more hours preparing the family

Table 6.1   Parent-Child Mediation Phases and Stages

Phases	Stages
A. Setting the Stage	1. Preparation for Mediation 2. Initial Joint Session a. Opening remarks by mediators
B. Defining the Issues	b. Storytelling by family members 3. Mediator Recesses 4. Initial Private or Joint Negotiation Sessions
C. Processing the Issues	5. Interim Private or Joint Negotiation Sessions
D. Resolving the Issues	6. Final Private or Joint Negotiation Sessions
E. Making the Agreement	7. Concluding Joint Session 8. Review and Follow-up

Source: Adapted from Zetzel & Wixted, 1984.

before the initial mediation session. Some programs have only one planned mediation session, usually a lengthy one; other programs may have two to five mediation sessions per case. The length of the mediation itself usually ranges from two to four hours.

There are many differences among existing parent-child mediation programs. The approach presented here is largely based on two models: the Children's Hearings Project model mentioned earlier, which makes frequent use of shuttle mediation, and the Family Services of Greater Vancouver model, which relies on direct face-to-face negotiation as much as possible. Our approach is thus a flexible one in which shuttle mediation can be combined with joint sessions, and makes use of mediator recesses to assess whether joint or private meetings between parent and child are indicated in a particular situation and a particular point in the negotiation process. Within this model, the parent and child are given an equal voice throughout the process to express their concerns and interests while working toward resolution of the conflict. The model is based on the assumption that parents and children have the power and ability to solve their problems and conflicts. The adversarial atmosphere of the court is absent; the parties are encouraged to express their feelings and needs openly in the less formal, more relaxed setting. The process consists of eight distinct stages, as outlined below.

Stage 1: Preparation for Mediation. The primary tasks of the mediators during this phase include tuning in, scheduling, and taking care of preliminaries before meeting with the parties. Early intervention, within a few days after a referral is received, is desirable. It is also necessary to establish who will be the parties to the mediation. In parent-child mediation, it cannot be assumed that the conflict is limited to only one parent and child; most often, all family members have at least some stake in the conflict and need to be included in the mediation process. This form of "multiparty" mediation is a further reason for a comediation approach.

It is particularly important that the comediators carefully decide how to divide responsibilities during the process. One may assume a primary role in working with certain of the parties, the other would do so with other family members. This allows each mediator to lend her or his voice to each of the parties during any subsequent direct negotiations.

Stage 2: Initial Joint Session. The initial joint session with the parties consists of opening remarks by the mediators and the family members' presentation of their perspectives on the conflict. The opening remarks by the mediators set the tone for the mediation sessions to follow. The mediators describe how mediation works by emphasizing its uniqueness in regard to its future focus, and how it differs from juvenile court or public social services. Mediation is presented as a voluntary alternative to the court, one in which family members develop their own solutions to the problems they face. In discussing their role, the mediators emphasize that they are not going to be making any decisions for the family or making judgments about who is right or wrong. Rather, they will assist the family members in constructing an agreement that all parties believe is fair and workable.

It is important to make clear from the outset that mediation is not a panacea, is not intended to instantly resolve a family's long-standing problems, and is not able to resolve every problem. Rather, it can help the family get started in a positive direction and the process can serve as a model for the handling of future conflict.

Ground rules for mediation are discussed and confidentiality is emphasized. The family members then present their perspectives about what is happening. This stage focuses on the tasks of fact-finding, trust building, and observing how the family members communicate with each another. The mediators ask each person to describe the situation from his or her perspective, without interruption. The parties are initially directed to address the mediator, rather than to speak directly to the other family members; this technique of controlling communication, while not embraced by all parent-child mediation programs, is often helpful when working with high conflict and heightened emotionality. During this "sharing of stories," the mediators are trying to create an atmosphere of respect and openness in which the parties begin to identify what they would like to see happen.

This joint session ends when the mediators have obtained a basic understanding of the conflict based on the statements by all parties. It may also be ended if one party is clearly dominating the conversation. Before the end of this stage, the mediators inform the family members that they will be using recesses to review what they have learned and plan for the next stage of work. Prior to proceeding to the next stage of the process, the mediators ask the parties to think about specific things that should change in order to manage the conflict more effectively.

Stage 3: Mediator Recesses. During recesses, which take place between meetings, the mediators review previous sessions to ascertain what they have learned about the family and their perspectives on the dispute. Any factual discrepancies in the parties' accounts are discussed and potential areas of common interest are identified. The mediators' task is to develop a working strategy that includes identifying the issues that seem most likely to be resolved through mediation, and the format of the session to follow: separate or joint meetings. If private sessions are deemed necessary, the mediators decide the order in which to meet individual family members and which mediator should take the lead; each may take the lead on different topics, with different family members, and in different sessions. If family members are making good use of joint sessions, this format should not be interrupted. When joint negotiation sessions are scheduled, the mediator and the parties understand that the option of caucusing is available to them at any time. When caucusing is used, the mediator caucuses with each party for equal periods of time.

Stage 4: Initial Private or Joint Negotiation Sessions. If private sessions are arranged, the mediators meet with the child (or children) first and then the parent (or parents). The mediators repeat that everything that is said is held in confidence. By asking open-ended questions in a nonjudgmental manner, they probe to identify the most important issues and underlying interests of each party, while avoiding counseling or advice giving. The family member is encouraged to continue thinking about the issues, needs, and interests that are important to him or her and to identify potential changes that could help resolve the conflict. The mediators try to show optimism about the potential for change. They clarify what information shared in the private session can be shared with the other party.

If joint sessions are arranged, the mediators' goals and tasks essentially remain the same: identifying and clarifying the issues and underlying interests toward the goal of establishing an agenda for mediation. The parties are given the opportunity to speak without interruption. At some point in the joint session, it is important to caucus with each party to establish that the joint format is working for her or him and to ensure that each party feels that his or her perspective on the conflict has been heard. A common perception of children and adolescents at the beginning of the mediation process is that the adult mediators are likely to side with the parent. It is important to address this perception, at the outset, in caucus with the child. The child should be given ample opportunity to present his or her point of view about the conflict and relationship.

A central precept of mediation practice is to reframe issues in dispute in neutral terms, which is particularly salient during this stage of parent-child mediation. It is important to focus on the needs and interests of the parties, shifting each from rigid positions, and to reframe issues in terms of the goals and future satisfaction of the family (Shaw, 1989).

Before the next stage, the mediators break to further review and discuss the case and make any necessary changes in strategy.

Stage 5: Interim Private or Joint Negotiation Sessions. This stage consists of additional private or joint sessions during which further information can be gathered and expressed concerns and interests clarified. It is also the stage where issues begin to be negotiated, and movement made toward eventual resolution. During private sessions, allowable information is transmitted between the parties; in joint meetings, the mediators are careful to maintain control of the process, and begin to encourage the parties to directly address each other. Issues to be negotiated are further narrowed and reframed in a manner that addresses the interests of all parties. In this regard, attention is focused on the real needs, wants, and fears that underly each party's conflicting initial positions; this ensures that each party begins to understand what is really important to the other.

It is important in parent-child mediation to focus on just a few issues at a time, beginning with a less complex issue around which agreement is more likely to be obtained and a high degree of compliance can be expected (Shaw, 1989). Early experience with success on "smaller" matters predicts future success on the more complex issues in dispute.

Once all of the issues are identified and an agenda is established, each of the parties generates a list of their preferred options for resolution of the first issue in dispute. This is repeated for each of the issues. Reality testing of the various options proposed for resolution of the issues by family members is an important function for mediators at this stage. The mediators use brief recesses to identify any common ground between the parties with regard to proposed solutions. When the parties are far apart, the mediators encourage them to work toward identifying a solution that will meet the interests of both; if this is not possible, a compromise solution is sought. Typically in parent-child mediation, a solution to each issue in dispute will contain two elements: a list of desired behaviors by each party (or changes in behavior expected of the other party); and consequences, positive and negative, of compliance and noncompliance with the desired behaviors.

Stage 6: Final Private or Joint Negotiation Sessions. Working out the details of the agreement is the focus of this stage. Through additional individual or joint sessions, the mediators actively work with the parties to construct the final terms of the agreement. When necessary, the mediators will recess to further review the case.

Balance is extremely important in parent-child mediation agreements, which typically take the form of behavioral contracts. The mediators should ensure that agreements contain a comparable number of both expected behaviors and concessions by each party.

In some cases, this stage might involve only one additional private or joint session; in others, multiple sessions may be required. After a potential agreement is constructed, a final joint session between the parent(s) and child(ren) is arranged.

Stage 7: Concluding Joint Session. To conclude the mediation process, the mediators bring the child(ren) and parent(s) together in a joint session. The agreement developed with the parties during the negotiation sessions is read to all family members. It is then signed and a copy is given to each person. The mediation process can serve as a model for the handling of conflict and crisis in the future, and a discussion about how future conflicts are to be handled is an important component of the ending stage. The session ends with the mediators thanking the parties for the work they have done in resolving their conflict.

While the written agreement outlining expected behavioral changes and consequences is an important goal of parent-child mediation, the objective of exposing parents and children to a negotiation process that they can use in the future, as disagreements, disputes, and conflicts arise, so that crises and ongoing family turmoil can be prevented, is critical. The cumulative benefits of the mediation are a fair and mutually satisfactory resolution of the issues in dispute, a clarified understanding of the perceptions and feelings of each family member, and improved communication and negotiation skills.

Stage 8: Review and Follow-up. After the family members leave, the mediators review the process and its outcome. Particular attention is directed toward what seemed to be the most critical point in the mediation and how it may have contributed to the final outcome. A plan is then developed for follow-up.

It is advisable to follow-up with the family about a month or two after the last contact. It is inevitable that new issues in dispute will have surfaced during this time; the follow-up is an excellent opportunity to assess the degree to which family members are applying their newly-developed negotiation skills to these issues.

Alternatives to Mediation

As far as alternatives to mediation in the field of parent-child conflict are concerned, prevention is the most desirable choice. School systems and community agencies have an important role to play in preventing serious conflicts between parents and their children. Well before their children reach adolescence, parents can be taught effective strategies for managing conflict. Disappointment, frustration, anger, and other strong feelings do not need to escalate to intractable conflict; parenting and child management programs including a dispute resolution component can serve an important preventive function. Further, there are numerous programs in elementary and secondary schools in which children can learn not only about conflict resolution in general but peer mediation in particular. Many children report that they are readily able to transfer their peer mediation skills to their relationships with their parents.

We have discussed a number of "readiness" indicators that suggest the use of mediation in parent-child disputes. A desire to resolve the conflict and preserve the relationship on the part of both parties is central to the success of a facilitated dispute resolution process involving direct or indirect negotiation between the parties and this is particularly salient in the parent-child arena. Second, the relatively equal participation of both parents and children in the process is critical, as the parent-child relationship by definition is one within which an imbalance of knowledge, functioning, and power typically exists. Without these two components, parent-child mediation is likely to fail.

There are a number of other instances when parent-child mediation is contraindicated as a conflict resolution mechanism within the family, including child abuse, violent criminal behavior by the adult or child, or severe mental or physical incapacity on the part of one or both parties. In other instances, there may be a problem of substance abuse by one or both; in such instances, mediation is contraindicated until effective treatment for the problem has been completed or is well in place (Lansky & Lansky, 1996).

Therapeutic and legal intervention remain the primary alternatives to mediation in the field of parent-child conflict. Mediation may also be used as an adjunct to such services. On its own, court-based resolution of disputes remains the least desirable alternative, in most instances, of the three. Wherever possible, parent-child mediation should be offered at least as an adjunct to more punitive measures, particularly in the earlier stages of conflict.

References

Block, J. 1982. *Mediation: An Alternative for PINS*. New York: Children's Aid Society.
Erikson, E. 1968. *Identity: Youth and Crises*. New York: Norton.
Lansky, D. T., & L. M. Lansky. 1996. Parent-Child Mediation. Unpublished paper.
Merry, S. E. 1987. The Culture and Practice of Mediation in Parent-Child Conflicts. *Negotiation Journal* 3(4): 411–22.
———. 1989. Myth and Practice in the Mediation Process. In M. Wright & B. Galaway, eds., *Mediation and Criminal Justice*. London: Sage.
Merry, S. E., & A. M. Rocheleau. 1985. *Mediation in Families: A Study of the Children's Hearings Project*. Cambridge, MA: Cambridge Family and Children's Services.
Morris, M. 1983. *Parent Child Mediation: An Alternative That Works*. New York: Children's Aid Society.
Noland, D. 1983. The Exeter Mediation Program: An Evaluation. Unpublished research report, Exeter, NH.
Phear, W. P. & M. L. Shaw. 1989. *Parent-Child Mediation Manual*. New York: Institute of Judicial Administration.
Shaw, M. L. 1989. Mediating Adolescent/Parent Conflicts. In M. Wright and B. Galaway, eds., *Mediation and Criminal Justice*. London: Sage.
Silbey, S. S., & S. E. Merry. 1986. Mediator Settlement Strategies. *Law and Policy* 8(1):7–32.
Stahler, G. J., J. P. DuCette, & E. Povich. 1990. Using Mediation to Prevent Child Maltreatment: An Exploratory Study. *Family Relations* 39: 317–22.
Stern, M., M. Van Slyck, & S. Valvo. 1986. Enhancing Adolescents' Self-Image: Implications of a Peer Mediation Program. Paper presented at the annual meeting of the American Psychological Association, Washington, DC, August.

Umbreit, M. S. 1991. Mediation of Youth Conflict: A Multi-System Perspective. *Child and Adolescent Social Work*. 8(2): 141–53.

Vorenberg, E. W. 1982. *A State of the Art Survey of Dispute Resolution Programs Involving Juveniles*. Washington, DC: American Bar Association.

Wixted, S. 1982. *Interim Report of the Children's Hearings Project*. Cambridge, MA: Cambridge Family and Children's Service.

Zetzel, G., & S. Wixted. 1984. *A Mediator's Manual for Parent Child Mediation*. Cambridge, MA: Cambridge Family and Children's Service.

7

CHILD PROTECTION
Child Protection Mediation

by Allan Edward Barsky

Child protection mediation (CP mediation) refers to a problem-solving process in which a third party professional assists child protection workers, family members, and others involved in a child protection proceeding to resolve conflicts between them. Although the existence of a child protection proceeding indicates a concern that the child is at risk of maltreatment, the child's immediate safety and welfare must be established before mediation can proceed. Mediatable issues include the types of services the agency will provide, services the family will use, conditions that must be satisfied before a child in placement returns home, alternative child care options, the terms of child-parent visitation, parental expectations for the child, appropriate nonviolent responses to family conflict, termination of parental rights, and open adoption in jurisdictions where permitted by law (Barsky, 1995b).

CP mediation is a peculiar use of mediation, given that one of the clients is a professional who traditionally assumes a mediation role in her own work. When child abuse or neglect are brought to the attention of a child protection agency, the assigned worker is mandated to investigate and intervene to ensure that the child is not at risk. To achieve these ends, the worker can draw on a range of generalist social work roles: enabler, broker, advocate, activist, mediator, negotiator, educator, initiator, coordinator, and group facilitator (Zastrow, 1995). Zastrow defines the mediator role as follows:

> The mediator role involves intervention in disputes between parties to help them find compromises, reconcile differences, or reach mutually satisfactory agreements. . . . A mediator remains neutral, not siding with either party in the dispute. Mediators make sure they understand the positions of the parties. They help clarify positions, recognize miscommunication, and help the parties present their cases clearly. (P. 19)

In the context of child protection, a worker can mediate between disput-ing family members about how they will share responsibility for a child's needs. Similarly, a worker can mediate between parents and foster parents about how and when the parents will spend time with the child. But is a child protection worker able to function as a neutral third party? What if the family members perceive the child protection worker ("CPW") to be biased against them? Can CPWs be neutral if they have a mandate to protect children against abuse and neglect? In this chapter, we explore how a mediator from an inde-pendent service can be used to mediate between CPWs, family members, and other support persons in situations where there are child protection concerns. One of the key questions for advocates of CP mediation is whether the use of an independent mediator contributes anything to the child protection process that could not be accomplished by a CPW skilled in generalist social work practice (including the role of mediator).

Case Study

Paula is a seventeen-year-old, single parent of a six-month-old son named Steve. (For ease of reference, the first initial of each participant's pseu-donym corresponds with the first initial of the participant's role: Paula = Par-ent, Steve = Son, Wendy = Worker, Mel = Mediator.) When Steve was born Paula was abusing drugs and the hospital called the local child protection agency to investigate Paula's ability to care for Steve. The child protection worker, Wendy, met with Paula at the hospital. Paula was scared that Wendy was going to take Steve away from her and decided that it was best for Wendy to know as little about her as possible. Wendy interpreted Paula's minimal re-sponses as indicating resistance and lack of appreciation for the seriousness of the situation. Wendy believed that Paula was not able to provide for Steve's needs due to her age, substance abuse, limited parenting skills, and lack of so-cial support. Wendy placed Steve in temporary foster care and initiated court proceedings to have him made a ward of the state. Once Steve was doing well in foster care, Wendy tried to reconnect with Paula and work out a voluntary plan of care. Wendy told Paula that she had to look out for Steve's welfare, but that she also wanted to help Paula. Paula saw Wendy as a "baby snatcher" and did not trust her. Paula hired a legal aid lawyer to try to win Steve back in court. She believed that if the judge heard her story, he would certainly return Steve to her. After a series of motions and delays, Wendy's supervisor sug-gested that they try mediation.

Neither Paula nor Wendy had any prior experience with mediation. Paula was concerned that the mediator was just another person from the baby-snatching agency, and that they were trying to manipulate her into giving up the court battle. Paula's lawyer was concerned that Paula might say something in mediation that could be used as evidence against her position in court.

Wendy told her supervisor that mediation would not help because she had already tried to mediate and Paula was uncooperative. Wendy feared that going to mediation might be an admission of failure. She was also concerned that if she went to mediation, the mediator might pressure her into making compromises that would put Steve at undue risk of abuse or neglect. She believed that she had already tried whatever was possible without putting Steve at risk. Wendy's supervisor told Paula and Wendy that they did not have to mediate, but they should at least meet individually with the mediator in order to see if the mediator had anything to offer. Feeling a bit pressured, they both agreed to see Mel, a mediator from an independent agency.

Rationale for Child Protection Mediation

Proponents of child protection mediation suggest that mediation is congruent with existing procedures and policies of the child protection system (Palmer, 1989; Wildgoose, 1987). For example, mediation is an extension of voluntary agreements negotiated between front-line workers and family members. The collaborative nature of mediation also fits with the notion that services should be provided, wherever possible, on the basis of mutual agreement. In comparison with court, mediation offers a less intrusive means of family intervention. Further, mediation allows for individualized and future-oriented agreements (Barsky, 1995b).

Although mediation is often seen as a faster and less expensive means of resolving disputes than court (Smith et al., 1992), this is a weak rationale for mediation in the context of child protection. First, the issue at stake—the welfare of the child—should not be sacrificed to save a few dollars in the short term. Second, very few reports of abuse or neglect culminate in a full trial of the issues. Some reports are not substantiated. Others are resolved on a voluntary basis. Even among cases that do make it into the courtroom, most eventually get resolved on consent of the parties. In a study where mediation was viewed as a process to divert cases otherwise headed to court, Smith et al. (1992) found that mediation produced significant savings in legal costs. Still, mediation may be appropriate at earlier stages of the child protection process. If the parties have to wait until they are on the verge of trial, they may be too entrenched in their positions to take full advantage of mediation. Mediation may lead to more timely resolution of issues than litigation, given the formalities of court and the backlog of cases in many jurisdictions. Timely settlement and permanency planning are important in CP cases to minimize the time that children are left in limbo. However, if delays in court are caused by administrative problems, then perhaps these problems should be dealt with rather than simply diverting cases to a cheaper form of dispute resolution (Auerbach, 1983).

The collaborative nature of mediation promotes a more positive working relationship between the parties. Family members and workers essentially have the same goal: to work out an arrangement that serves the best interests of the child. Mediation can help them focus and work together on this goal. The parties could also agree quite readily to work toward ending the relationship between the agency and the family as soon as possible. Paradoxically, the best way to end this relationship is to improve it first. To the extent that the family and agency have a positive working relationship, they will be able to resolve the child protection concerns more readily (Shulman, 1991). The family is also more likely to follow through on arrangements.

The most compelling rationale for CP mediation from a theoretical perspective is that mediation promotes self-determination and empowers family members by creating an environment where they can be more fully involved in decisions directly affecting them (Bush, 1989). Although social workers value the concept of empowerment (Pinderhughes, 1983), a CPW's primary mandate is to safeguard the child against maltreatment. Even the most well-meaning worker may need to use her authority or invoke involuntary measures to ensure that the child is protected (Palmer, 1983). Wendy may have tried to empower Paula by offering choices and by seeking mutually acceptable solutions, but Paula still knows that Wendy has a large say in what happens to Steve if they do not come to an agreement. In contrast, a mediator has no authority or decision-making power.

Research, Debates, and Trends

North American research on CP mediation dates back to the mid-1980s, although there had been some ad hoc attempts at using mediation in CP cases before to this. Early articles reviewed the current literature on child welfare and speculated about how mediation might be used in this context (Mayer, 1984; Oran, Creamer, & Libow, 1984; Palmer, 1989; Wiig, 1984; Wildgoose, 1987). As mediation pilot projects began to develop across North America, researchers started to document the implementation and outcomes of CP mediation (Campbell & Rodenburgh, 1993; Center for Policy Research, 1992; Golten, 1986; Savoury, Beals, & Parks, 1994, 1995; Wildgoose & Maresca, 1994). Most of the research to date has been in the form of program description and evaluation. Interpretation of the data generated by these studies presents a number of problems: the sociolegal context of child protection varies significantly from one jurisdiction to another; the models of mediation employed in various jurisdictions also vary; and the research methods used in many of the studies pose limitations on the generalizibility of the results (with small sample sizes and absence of random sampling, control groups, or matching for comparison).

One of the first empirical studies undertaken, an evaluation of the Denver CP mediation project, examined the reactions of parents, caseworkers, mediators, and lawyers involved in the cases mediated (Golten, 1986; Pearson,

Thoennes, Mayer, & Golten, 1986). Levels of satisfaction with the process were generally favorable across the various groups of participants (70% to 95% were either very satisfied or fairly satisfied with the agreement and the process). In the absence of a control group for comparison, the evaluation made use of expert reviewers (two former child protection workers and a former juvenile court judge). The reviewers were asked to assess the mediation agreements and compare them with their "best estimates" of the outcomes had mediation not been provided in each case. They agreed that mediation had the following positive effects: savings in court time and agency time; reducing the duration of out-of-home placements (in 30% to 40% of all cases); clarifying the plan of action to all parties; producing a plan of action comprehensible to the family; and developing plans early and avoiding delays in treatment. The reviewers also cited the following problems in some of the agreements: when compared to traditional intervention, mediation was less likely to set reasonable time frames for performance; mediated agreements were less likely to include provisions that could be monitored; and mediated agreements did not provide as many safeguards for children. Mediated agreements were seen as more lenient and more complex (Pearson, Thoennes, Mayer, & Golten, 1986).

Mayer (1987, 1989) used an experimental design with a sample from the Denver project to test whether the introduction of mediation affects parental attitudes toward compliance with child protection intervention plans. Mayer assumed that because mediation is a voluntary and collaborative process, parents would have different attitudes towards compliance when offered mediation than under the traditional CP process (which has involuntary and authoritative elements). He found that offering mediation had a substantial impact on parents' attitudes toward compliance: specifically, parents offered mediation "felt less coerced into going along with plans against their will, and that a commitment to the potential value of the intervention for them and their children was more likely to be their predominant attitude" (Mayer, 1989, p. 101). The study did not try to determine whether and how these impacts on attitude might have been associated with actual compliance. Further, the study only examined cases when mediation was *offered* to parents: the research did not determine which attributes of the mediation process had positive or negative impacts on compliance attitudes.

While CP mediation services of varying models and structures have been offered in the Dependency Court in Los Angeles County since 1983, the Family Division of the Connecticut Superior Court since 1984, and the Juvenile Court of Orange County, California, since 1987, completed research of these services is limited (Eddy, 1992). In perhaps the largest-scale study of CP mediation to date, the Center for Policy Research (1992) looked at the experiences of three CP mediation services in Hartford, Los Angeles, and Orange County; the researchers observed thirty mediations, interviewed various professionals involved in or affected by the programs, and reviewed 729 court and/or mediation files. The study confirmed the efficacy of mediation: 60 percent to 80 percent of mediation cases resulted in negotiated settlement. The researchers concluded that participation in the process led to greater commitment to the agreement, parents having a better understanding of the terms of the plan, and mediated agreements being clearer and more specific (Center for Policy Research, 1992).

Factors related to settlement varied greatly across the sites. The only clear pattern that held in all sites was that mediations involving discussion about a child's placement outside of the home were less likely to be settled in mediation. The researchers interpreted this to mean, "In these cases, both sides may view the matter as a non-negotiable issue. Caseworkers perceive it to be a fundamental safety issue; parents believe their ultimate parental rights are being denied" (Center for Policy Research, 1992, p. 83).

In a 1991 article, Thoennes explored two of the main criticisms of child protection mediation: (1) How can parents negotiate as equals with CPWs? and (2) What can be negotiated in CP cases that will not endanger the child? On the former issue, Thoennes notes that there are a number of factors that can contribute to power imbalances: the legal authority of CPWs; the discrepancies in communication skill and systems knowledge between parents and the professionals involved in the case; differences in skill, knowledge, and style of the lawyers representing each of the parties; and intimidation created by having a child removed from one's home. Mediators in the projects reviewed by Thoennes used a number of techniques to try to redress these types of power imbalances: involving legal representatives in the mediation process; directing the process, including the use of individual caucuses and joint meetings; explaining the system, situation, and options to parents to make the process and any agreements understandable to the parties; and helping parties to identify reasonable requests to make of the CP agency. In a follow-up study, Thoennes (1994) concluded that the presence of legal representation in the mediation process was the most important method of balancing power.

Regarding Thoennes' second question, CP mediation practitioners have consistently agreed that a child's safety is not a negotiable issue in mediation; if parents deny that they were abusive or that a protection concern exists, the case is considered not to be appropriate for mediation. If the existence of a protection concern needs to be determined, then traditional child protection investigations and court hearings may be needed. Mediation can only proceed when all of the parties involved agree to work together to negotiate arrangements for the welfare of the child (Mayer, 1984; National Council of Juvenile and Family Court Judges, 1989; Thoennes, 1991). One of the ground rules of CP mediation is that neither abuse nor neglect can continue during or following the mediation; if either continues, then mediation is terminated and traditional mechanisms for child protection are used to ensure the safety of the child.

Eddy (1992) analyzed the theory and practice of CP mediation in Los Angeles by observing two mediations and meeting with CPWs and mediators at a local mediation service agency. His research suggests that the decision makers in CP cases are often afraid of making mistakes. First, information available to the decision maker may be vague and incomplete; second, if a CPW or judge makes a mistake, a child may die and the public outrage may be directed at the people responsible for the decisions. Because of this fear, each decision maker in the system is prone to ratify the prior decision maker's assessment rather than disagree. In mediation, the mediator would support each party's right to disagree with prior assessments. Accordingly, CPWs would be more open to new information and interpretations in mediation than they might be in the alternative processes.

The Children's Aid Society (CAS) of Metropolitan Toronto participated in a demonstration project of nine CP mediation cases from May 1990 to October 1992. In this project, mediation was viewed as a means of diverting cases from court; one of the criteria for referring cases to mediation was that the case was otherwise headed for judicial proceedings. The researchers concluded that the mediation process, as conducted in this project, was a more timely and cost-effective method of resolving disputes than the court system. The majority of clients reported that they were heard fairly, they were able to actively participate in the process, and agreements made were fair and could be followed (Smith et al., 1992). Although most client feedback was positive, some CPWs expressed concern that they were giving up control over the case as a result of turning the management of the mediation process over to a third party. Before mediation, they feared that participation in mediation meant that their bottom-line position and their judgment or professional assessment of the case were being called into question. Most of these concerns dissipated during mediation. Some workers felt that it was much easier to participate when they perceived the court was "ordering" the parties to participate since they did not have to take responsibility for making the referral. Although the mediators advised all parties that participation in mediation was voluntary, referral from the court was seen as a direction to participate (Smith et al., 1992).

The Center for Child and Family Mediation in Toronto (Wildgoose & Maresca, 1994) documented twenty-four cases that came to mediation from 1990 to 1993. This report confirmed the conclusions of Smith et al. (1992) and demonstrated that a broad range of issues can be dealt with in CP mediation: for example, parental access to children in alternative care, state wardship and reviews, terms of supervision orders, placement issues, parent-teen conflict, conflict between foster parents and biological parents, length of alternative care and conditions for return. The report suggested, "[W]hether agreement was reached did not seem to be related to the severity or nature of the child maltreatment" (Wildgoose & Maresca, 1994, p. 32). In fact, mediation helped resolve situations that had been insoluble using other interventions.

Although Wildgoose and Maresca report that 80 percent of the cases were settled in mediation, the question of how to determine "what is a settlement" must be considered. In two of the cases counted as being settled, part of the agreement was that the family would consent to an independent assessment to determine future services and/or living arrangements for the child and family; the question arises about whether or not this is any different from an agreement to have some of the issues resolved in court. Both circumstances could be considered partial agreements. On the other hand, the more significant factor may not be where a case is finally resolved, but how a combination of processes within the CP system can best be integrated. In this sense, mediation would be seen as an option within the CP process rather than simply an alternative to it.

While the above research provides compelling anecdotal support for the use of mediation in actual CP cases, the absence of a control group or matched cases means that the bases for comparison are problematic. As in the evaluative research on the Denver project, the Toronto research by Smith et al. (1992) relied on estimates by CPWs concerning "what would have happened" if not for mediation.

The mediation project in Victoria, British Columbia, used an approach similar to those used in Toronto, except that mediators generally met with both parties together during the first session, and the majority of cases involved parent-teen conflict. In Toronto, the majority of the presenting conflicts were between CPWs, parents, and/or alternative caregivers. Based on a questionnaire distributed to participants in twenty mediations, Campbell and Rodenburgh (1993) concluded that mediation clarified the perspectives of each party, helped participants develop a plan that they could follow, helped parents realize their options for better parenting skills, and provided a supportive environment where parents could express their concerns. Of those parents who did not find mediation useful, some felt that nobody listened to them, problems identified by parents were used against them, or the mediator and CPW had reached an agreement before mediation even started. These concerns reflect potential problems in regard to how mediation was implemented, rather than a condemnation of the mediation process per se.

In summary, a body of research evidence supporting the efficacy of CP mediation has emerged. The preceding studies have identified the following: a significant number of cases that the parties could not settle themselves prior to mediation do settle in mediation; 60 percent to 95 percent of participants in mediation (including family members, child protection workers, and lawyers) report satisfaction with the mediation process; evaluations of initial CP mediation projects recommend that CP mediation services be continued; government agencies in a number of regions are providing financial support to CP mediation services based on the belief that this intervention is a productive process; and CP mediation has been promoted by judges, administrators, children's legal representatives, and other officials in the child protection process.

Mediation is not necessarily better than other CP processes, but it has been demonstrated to be extremely useful in certain cases. In order for CP mediation to be appropriate, participation in mediation must be voluntary and all parties must be competent to negotiate for themselves (taking into account any uncontrolled mental illness, substance abuse, retardation, language impediment, or family violence). CP mediation can be effective even in cases with high levels of conflict and severe child protection concerns. In fact, the emotional and financial costs of protracted legal proceedings in such cases tends to impel parties toward resolution in mediation.

In terms of hard research, more rigorous methods need to be employed if more definitive claims about the effectiveness of CP mediation are to be made; for instance, there is little evidence to support the assertion that CP mediation produces durable solutions and the longer term impacts of mediation on children and families have not been studied. Additional measures for effectiveness also need to be developed.

The literature contains little in the way of critique of CP mediation. However, aspects of the feminist critique of family mediation may be applicable to CP mediation: mediation fails to punish or provide retribution for socially unacceptable behaviour; mediation cannot ensure full disclosure of information; given that mediation is generally a more private forum than the public court system, it is difficult to monitor for mediator bias or for the use of coercive mediation techniques; mediated agreements often depend on voluntary compliance but some situations require mandatory enforcement mechanisms; and mediation can result in outcomes that are based on the relative bargaining power of the parties rather than what is "fair" or "right" in the situation (Fineman, 1988; Girdner, 1990; Ricci, 1985; Saunders, 1994).

Some constituents of the child welfare system are concerned that mediation does not properly safeguard children from neglect and abuse; others argue that mediation does not adequately protect parental rights to procedural justice. In terms of the first concern, critics suggest that mediation encourages compromise and child welfare is not something to be bargained away. They believe that CPWs can negotiate the smaller issues. If the parties cannot come to an agreement on the larger issues, it is argued that the court system is better suited to ensuring the welfare of the child. As for the second concern, critics are concerned that family members will enter mediation with a power disadvantage. Without the procedural checks and balances of the court system, family members may negotiate away their rights or be unduly pressured into agreements (Thoennes, 1994; Mayer, 1987). The feminist-structuralist criticism of mediation suggests that mediation puts most of the responsibility for change on families, and particularly on single mothers, and argues that resources should be used to change broader structures in society (especially to improve the status of women), rather than fund mediation.

Although some of the original CP mediation projects have come and gone, others have become safely ensconced as ongoing programs. Some jurisdictions have incorporated the option for CP mediation into their child protection legislation and regulations. Variations of CP mediation have also been developed to meet the needs of aboriginal communities and other ethnocultural groups. Since most families involved in the CP system fall within the lower end of the economic spectrum, publicly-funded mediation is required. In order to maintain funding, mediation services are impelled to prove that they are cost-effective.

The Mediation Process

The model of CP mediation described here is derived from that used by the Centre for Child and Family Mediation, Toronto (Wildgoose & Maresca, 1994). The term *mediation* is used in different jurisdictions to refer to quite different processes, varying from interventions akin to assessments, pretrial settlement conferences, family group conferences, and single session conciliation. Referrals to mediation are generally initiated by CPWs or lawyers, as they are more likely than family members to be familiar with the process. The Toronto model begins with individual sessions with the CPW first, who can provide an overview of the family's involvement with the child protection agency, and then with family members, usually the parents of the children involved. The mediator explains mediation and assesses the suitability of the situation for mediation. Meetings are held in a neutral setting such as the mediator's office. If the case is appropriate and the parties agree to mediation, front-line workers and family members then meet in joint sessions; lawyers and agency supervisors are generally not involved in these meetings. In addition to trying to work out the legal issues, mediators help the parties build a better working relationship. The goal of mediation is not simply to produce an agreement but rather to create a process in which the parties know they were heard and treated fairly. Tentative resolutions reached in mediation are subject to access to legal advice. They are formalized by a legally drafted agreement or by a court order on consent.

In this model, ten factors are seen to contribute to the efficacy of mediation: (1) establishing alliance between mediators and mediation participants; (2) enhancing understanding; (3) bringing parties together; (4) facilitating communication; (5) focusing the parties; (6) keeping peace; (7) developing options; (8) contracting; (9) neutrality; and (10) fairness.

When family members and CPWs first enter the mediation process, each may be skeptical about it for different reasons. A parent may perceive the mediator as just another person in "the system" and therefore biased in favor of the worker. Paula, for example, may believe that Mel wants to keep Steve away from her or to maintain control over her life. On the other hand, workers may believe that acquiescing to mediation is tantamount to admitting that they could not resolve the issue on their own. Wendy may feel embarrassed if the mediator takes her role and does a better job of it. Accordingly, one of the first tasks of the mediator is to establish a positive working relationship with each of the parties.

Individual sessions with the parties to initiate the mediation process can help the mediator establish an alliance with each of them without posing a threat to mediator neutrality. Paula may need to hear that Mel works independently from the CP agency and the court, has no authority to make decisions for the parties, and will not be formulating any opinions about what type of arrangements will be in Steve's best interests. Wendy may need to hear that Mel is not trying to usurp her job, question her authority, or force her to compromise on what she believes to be in the best interests of the child.

All of the parties need to come away from their intake meetings with a sound understanding of the mediation process, its goals, the role of the mediator, and the voluntary nature of the process. Both Paula and Wendy felt somewhat pressured to try mediation even though they did not really know what the process entailed. Pressure to participate may come from lawyers, the CPW's supervisor, court, or a belief that refusal to cooperate may result in negative consequences. Paula may feel at a disadvantage in negotiating with her CPW. She may be reassured by the knowledge that the process will be fair and that she can terminate mediation without the threat of negative repercussions. If Wendy were concerned that she might be pressured into making a compromise that would put Steve at risk, Mel could reassure her that she can terminate mediation at any point in the process. She can then pursue alternative measures to ensure Steve's safety.

To foster alliance with each party, mediators can use individual sessions to coach the parties on how to negotiate more effectively. Mel can support Paula by coaching her about how to respond if she is feeling put down by Wendy in the mediation session. Mel can help Wendy with partializing her requests for Paula so that Paula does not feel overwhelmed.

One of the key aspects of both individual and joint sessions is that the parties feel heard and understood. Mel does not have to agree with Paula if she says that she wants Steve home right away. He just has to let her know that he understands that she loves Steve and believes that she can be a good parent if Steve were returned home. Similarly, Mel does not have to agree with Wendy's plan to maintain Steve in care. However, he can reflect back her plan to demonstrate that he understands its nature and her reasons for advocating it. Active listening promotes a positive working alliance.

Since CPWs tend to have more education and greater familiarity with the child protection system than family members, the mediator should ensure that both parties use language that is comprehensible to all of the parties. The mediator can reframe legal or social work jargon into plain language and encourage the CPW to do the same. The mediator should also encourage the CPW to indicate the rationale for positions taken by the agency (Tjaden, 1994).

Often, there is no easy solution to a child protection issue. The CPW may be asking parents to agree to leave their children in the care of someone else or to change deeply ingrained ways of caring for their children. Parents may need the authority of the CPW or the court to impose such a solution (Palmer, 1983). Nonetheless, mediation may help the parties' relationship by fostering greater understanding of one another's positions. Whether or not the parties come to an agreement, the CPW and family members will likely need to work together following mediation.

The simple act of bringing parties together can have a profound impact on their ability to resolve CP issues. Parents (sometimes on the advice of their lawyers) may not want to meet with child protection authorities out of a fear that the parents might say something that could come back at them in court. The mediator needs to decide who to invite to the mediation table. In the case study, Paula and Wendy met together but they had not considered meeting together with other interested parties. Mel can explore who the important influences and potential supports were in Paula's life. Paula's parents or Steve's father can be brought into the process as people who can help Paula take care of Steve's needs. Sometimes the presenting problem masks underlying issues. For instance, Paula may be asking for Steve to be returned, but her immediate concern may be a conflict with the foster parents over how access is exercised when Paula comes to meet with Steve at their house. Accordingly, the foster parents can be brought into the process. The mediator can invite CP supervisors, lawyers, or other professionals to mediation sessions, but should consider the impact of their involvement. They can be useful participants because of their knowledge of the legal issues, ability to influence decisions, and bring in objective perspectives. However, these professionals tend to speak *for* the parents or CPWs, reducing the input of the parties most directly affected by the conflict. Although lawyers can negotiate settlement of legal issues, direct communication between the front-line worker and parents is needed to promote a better working relationship between the parties.

Whether or not lawyers and supervisors are involved in the mediation sessions, the mediator needs to keep them apprised of the mediation process and find ways to encourage their support. Agreements in mediation are not finalized until the parties have the opportunity to go back to their lawyers and the CP supervisor. One of the most frustrating situations for parents and CPWs occurs when a mediated agreement is vetoed by the agency or lawyers at the end of the mediation process. Keeping the supervisors and lawyers informed of progress being made in mediation is a vital part of the process.

The question of whether and how to involve a child in CP mediation is complicated. The mediator may want to meet individually with a child to ascertain the child's concerns or to get an idea about what types of arrangements are desirable. Meeting with the child poses a number of potential problems. Since the CPW is responsible for ensuring the welfare of the child, mediators do not need to make their own assessment. If a mediator conducts a meeting with the child, the parties may start to see the mediator in the role of a CPW. Mediators may also lose their neutrality if they are seen as advocating for the child's wishes. Although the wishes of the child may need to be taken into account, their wishes may conflict with their welfare needs (e.g., a child who wants to remain home in a situation with risk of continued sexual abuse). Accordingly, the mediator must be careful not to raise the child's expectations about how the case will be resolved. Many children involved in the child protection system have already suffered traumatic experiences, including abuse, neglect, separation from their parents, and questioning from an array of child welfare professionals. Rather than meet directly with the child, the mediator could consult the child's counsel or other support person to ascertain concerns from the child's perspective that need to be addressed in mediation.

One of the major changes for CPWs when they enter into CP mediation is that they relinquish their role as facilitators to the mediator. The mediator becomes responsible for bringing the parties together, encouraging constructive communication between the parties, structuring the meetings, and guiding the interactions between the parties. Although many CPWs initially find this change in roles disconcerting, they can come to realize that the mediator assumes many of the more tedious functions of child protection work: negotiating people's schedules to agree on a time to meet; setting up the room for the meeting; preparing an agenda for each meeting; dealing with negative comments made by one of the parties; and writing up notes for the parties following each meeting. Because the mediator is responsible for these functions, CPWs are able to concentrate on the substantive issues of the case; what arrangements are needed to satisfy the welfare needs of the child?

In some cases, CPWs and family members can become so invested in the conflict that they lose sight of the best interests of the child. The mediator plays a key role in focusing the parties on the child's interests. The nature of a traditional CP process encourages a CPW to assess and identify past incidents of abuse and neglect to justify intervention. Both family members and CPWs can easily become entrenched in their positions: Paula wants Steve home and thinks Wendy is out to get her; Wendy wants Steve to remain in foster care and believes that Paula is not capable of caring for Steve. Although their positions seem far apart, Mel can probably get them to agree that Steve's welfare is the primary objective and that all parties can benefit from a voluntary solution. Once they agree on these general principles, Mel can focus them on problem solving around the issue of how Steve's needs can best be served, thus taking the parties away from their positions as well as from their personal attacks on one another. Whereas the standard for custody in divorce cases is "the best interests of the child," the CPW's mandate in protection cases is to ensure that the child's basic welfare needs are met. Nevertheless, if the parties can cooperate in mediation, the CP mediators should focus the parties on the best interests of the child. Working toward the standard of "absence of abuse and neglect" establishes an inferior goal and reinforces the reactive nature of the traditional child protection system.

A key role for the CP mediator is to "keep peace" between the family and the CPW, helping them to keep their emotions in check. The mediator acts almost as a referee, setting out certain rules of behavior from the outset and enforcing them if the parties start to stray from the rules. The mediator does not chastise or penalize the parties for breaking the rules but rather identifies counterproductive behaviors and suggests alternate ways of approaching the problem.

Because parties can become entrenched in their positions, the mediator needs to encourage the parties to keep an open mind and consider new options. This may be difficult for Wendy, because she considers herself a competent social worker who has already assessed what is in Steve's best interests. The difficulty for Paula in considering different options may be a lack of trust in Wendy. Mel can use a range of strategies: identify and discuss these underlying concerns; brainstorm; compliment the parties for keeping their minds open; or describe how other clients have found creative solutions to similar types of issues.

Contracting can be a vehicle for change as well as an outcome. As an outcome, contracting is important because it formalizes the agreements, avoids misunderstandings between the parties about their plans and expectations, affirms the parents' role as parents; and fixes the commitment of the parties to follow through on the agreement. As a process, contracting ensures joint participation in decision making and ownership of the agreement, and allows the parties to check out the workability of the agreement before trying to implement it.

Whereas many aspects of mediation are akin to good social work practice, the neutrality of mediators distinguishes them from CPWs. Four aspects of "neutrality" are essential in CP mediation: not siding; absence of preexisting bias; absence of decision-making authority; and no stake in a specific type of outcome. In order to avoid the appearance of siding with one party, mediators need to treat everyone equally, giving everyone the same opportunity to speak and listening to all sides. Mediators need to be particularly careful not to appear to be aligning with the CPW, since family members are often suspicious about the relationship between the mediator and CP agency. If Mel had been a social worker or lawyer for the agency, for example, he would need to declare this relationship. In order to establish that he is free from preexisting bias, he can demonstrate that he has had no prior involvement with Paula's case and has no opinions about how this case should be handled. The fact that Mel has no decision-making authority can also contribute to each party's sense of mediator neutrality. Whereas CPWs must advance their views on how to protect a child's welfare, mediators do not need to formulate an opinion or advocate for a particular position. CPWs are held accountable if a child is put at undue risk, if they intervene too forcefully, or without justification. Because mediators are not mandated to protect children, they have no stake in a particular outcome.

The issue of whether a mediator has a duty to ensure the fairness of the mediation process is a contentious one (McRory, 1981; Stulberg, 1981; Susskind, 1981). Those who argue against such a duty suggest that mediator neutrality is essential, and that attempts to rebalance power violate this principle (Bush & Fogler, 1994). In CP mediation, I would argue that the mediator has a duty to ensure that the process is fair. Balanced negotiations and private ordering cannot be assumed in CP mediation. Child protection agencies and workers tend to benefit from power advantages in negotiating with family members: better resources, familiarity with the system, judicial support, and communications skills training, to name a few. Family members are not without power, and CPWs do not always exploit their power. However, power imbalances are inevitable in CP mediation, and need to be taken into account by mediators. CP mediators are faced with a crucial dilemma: if they act in a purely neutral capacity, ignoring power dynamics, family members are likely to suffer; if mediators take deliberate steps to rectify power imbalances, they risk losing their neutrality and the trust of the CPW (in situations where the power balancing favors family members).

Some writers differentiate between empowerment and balancing power (Bush & Fogler, 1994), suggesting that mediators can empower the parties without losing neutrality. However, they believe that redistributing power in favor of a weaker party is not an appropriate role for mediators. My own research (Barsky, 1995a) suggests that CP mediators, CPWs, and family members do not necessarily distinguish between power balancing and empowerment. Mediators can use of a range of interventions that empower or redistribute power without losing their neutrality: involving another party or support person, helping articulate a position, putting the power issue on the table, spending more time with family members, identifying the family member's concern in front of the CPW, helping the family work out a reasonable plan to present to the CPW, ensuring that all parties are operating from the same base of information, exploring precedents and other options, providing a neutral setting, helping family members to feel heard, and focusing on the best interests of the child.

The question arises, "Why would a CPW submit to the process of mediation, knowing that the mediator will try to empower the other side and/or redistribute power in the family's favor?" The underlying reasons relate to the fact that CPWs are professional parties. CPWs who identify themselves as professional social workers value empowerment and fairness to family members. Unlike private negotiators, CPWs incur the professional obligations that require them to place the interests of others (the child, the family and the child protection system) above their personal interests. Because CPWs are not negotiating out of self-interest, they are more inclined than private parties to trust and support a mediator who is acting to empower or redistribute power in favor of the other mediation participants. A professional CPW is aware of the disadvantages faced by many parents, and understands the reasons that a mediator uses strategies that affect the power relationships between the parties. The CPW should also know that at the end of the process, all parties must give their consent if a settlement is to be reached.

Social work research suggests that empowerment is a clinically important aspect of the helping process (Shulman, 1991). Family members who feel empowered by the mediation process are more likely to follow through and to have a positive working relationship with the CP agency following mediation. CPWs recognize that winning a case in court is only a short-term victory, because what happens following a court decision or agreement is far more important to the child in the long run. If Wendy had prior, positive experiences in CP mediation, she would reenter the process with a better understanding of the mediator's strategies and greater faith in the mediation process. She would not be as concerned about having to make compromises, or having the mediator actively support Paula. Wendy would know that such strategies were necessary to engage Paula and that ultimately the process would be fair.

In my research, CPWs acknowledged that parents must be able to negotiate in a fair manner. In order for mediation to be fair, each party must be able to sufficiently advance its own interests, and the process must be free from coercion or exploitation (Susskind, 1981). In situations where the process becomes patently unfair, the mediator cannot be neutral. The mediator must be able to take steps to either redress the cause of the unfairness or terminate the mediation.

In regard to the extent that a mediator should intervene to balance power, a "least intrusive" standard may be appropriate. In an ideal mediation situation, minimal power related intervention is required: the parents and CPW are able to negotiate in a fair manner; accordingly, the mediator can emphasize the use of facilitative strategies. Since such "ideal" cases are rare, the mediator retains the authority to become more directive in order to deal with power imbalances. For instance, the parties may have been bargaining in a fair manner until a critical issue comes to an impasse, at which point the mediator becomes more directive in order to redress the power issues. Such directive strategies are still less intrusive than imposing a solution on the parties.

In some cases, the mediator may conclude that mediation is not appropriate. If the mediator cannot adequately address power disadvantages between the parties, then the mediator should terminate mediation rather than allow one party to be coerced or exploited. The specific issue of where to draw the line in cases of power imbalance requires further study. However, it can be said that mediation is no longer appropriate when a power imbalance becomes "so severe that no mediator can balance the scale without destroying the mediator's *credibility* and *base of authority*" (Sloan, 1992, p. 7, emphasis added). The mediator must terminate the mediation and refuse to take on the role of advocate (in mediator's clothing). The mediator can discuss alternative processes with the parties and refer them to their lawyers for legal advice.

Alternatives to Mediation

Although there are differences between child protection systems across jurisdictions, most current systems are guided by the same basic scheme. Suspicions of child abuse or neglect first come to the attention of the child protection agency through reports from members of the community, most commonly from teachers, neighbors, family members, or physicians. On receiving a report, the agency is mandated to conduct an investigation into the child protection concerns. If the decision is to have a worker approach the parents, then use of authority may progress along the following lines:

> Initially, the worker's power is limited to approaching families on behalf of the agency. If the clients will not grant them authority [i.e., cooperate voluntarily], workers must negotiate with their supervisors for increased power. This increased power will be limited to a specific function, such as initiating court action to enforce supervision of the family or apprehending a child pending a court hearing. The agency's power is also limited in that its actions are subject to sanction by the court if it apprehends children or wants to enforce supervision on unwilling parents. (Palmer, 1983, p. 122)

The child protection system has a broad range of alternatives to draw from to deal with concerns of child abuse and neglect. The continuum of possible approaches includes no state intervention, voluntary service, solution-focused intervention, case conference, pretrial conference, lawyer-led negotiation, assessment by an independent party, court trial, and imposition of authority by a CPW. Each of these approaches can be legitimate for different situations; however, they can also be used in ways that are inappropriate:

- **No State Involvement:** Under this alternative, child protection authorities assume no role in the investigation or enforcement of welfare standards. This alternative respects the value that families be able to function on an autonomous basis. Families are free to choose whether to make use of support systems in the community. However, the state does not invoke formal mechanisms to address issues of child maltreatment. Current child protection legislation justifies state intervention only in situations where a child is put at a certain degree of risk of harm. CPWs cannot intervene merely for the "best interests" of the child. The child must be "in need of protection." In other words, the state tolerates less than perfect parenting that does not cross into the area deemed to be in need of protection. For example, society may view reading to children as a positive parenting behavior. Still, the state may be reluctant to intervene simply because parents do not read to their children.

- **Voluntary Service:** There are two possibilities for voluntary service. In the first case for voluntary service, the family initiates contact with the child protection system. Here the state assumes a role in child protection if and when the family seeks out help. Families may request that a child be placed in care or may ask for support services that enable them to maintain the child at home. If the family initiates contact with the agency and is agreeable to services, then state intrusion is minimal.

  In the second scenario for voluntary service, the family has initially been brought into the child protection system on a nonvoluntary basis. Some families are brought to the attention of the protection agency by reports of maltreatment. The initial investigation of the CPW is involuntary. However, the family may readily consent to intervention through a voluntary care agreement or voluntary service agreement. Alternatively, the family may agree to make use of supports from outside of the child protection system to redress the child protection concern (e.g., support from extended family or from the voluntary social service sector). The problem that may arise in the context of voluntary service is that it may not be so "voluntary." Because of the power balances that exist between CPWs and family members, what appears to be consent to services may actually be acquiescence to the position of the more powerful agency.

- **Solution-Focused Intervention:** Solution-focused intervention is just one of a number of client-centered approaches to social work that have been tried in child protection contexts. The worker builds on the strengths of the family members rather than focusing on their deficiencies (de Shazer, 1985). Family members are encouraged to develop their own solutions to child protection concerns such that the level of state intrusiveness is reduced and self-determination of the family is advanced (Bernstein, Campbell, & Sookraj, 1993; Boyle et al., 1993). CPWs using solution-focused intervention still maintain their protection mandate. Therefore, they cannot condone or support solutions offered by the family that do not meet the minimum standards of child protection.

- **Case Conference:** Whereas some cases are resolved with relatively informal intervention by the CPW, other cases require more formal intervention. The CPW may decide to arrange to meet with family members to work out a plan of care or other services. The CPW facilitates the meeting and tries to accommodate a mutually acceptable arrangement. Family conferences can take a number of forms (Bernstein, Campbell, & Sookraj, 1993). The common thread is that these meetings are joint problem-solving processes. Both the CPW and the family have input into the decision making. Although the CPW is acting as a facilitator, the CPW also uses the processes of bargaining and persuasion to advance the position of the agency (Palmer, 1983). To the extent that family members have say into how the issues will be resolved, conferences can be relatively nonintrusive. Given the power imbalances between the parties, CPWs may exert their authority or impose unilateral decisions (Tjaden, 1994). Whether or not this is intentional or unintentional, the greater the influence used by the CPW, the more intrusive the case conference becomes. Some jurisdictions have experimented with family group conferences and native circle processes in which CPWs help organize the process, but withdraw from the joint family sessions and encourage family members and community supports to take greater control of the process (Burford & Pennell, 1994).
- **Pretrial Settlement Conference:** A pretrial settlement conference is similar to a case conference in that they are both problem-solving processes that work toward agreements between the protection agency and the family. However, the pretrial conference may take decision making further away from family members for a number of reasons. First, to get to this stage, the case must have already been filed in court by the agency. By filing a case in court, the agency is acknowledging that it needs the authority of the court in order to safeguard the welfare of the child. Pretrial conferences are generally conducted by a judge who may have some power to direct how a settlement will be reached (Bailey, 1994). For instance, the judge may indicate how an issue might be resolved if it proceeded to court. The judge also has the power to make decisions over procedural issues and legal cost awards. This can be used to pressure the parties into compromising their positions and interests.
- **Negotiation by Lawyers:** Negotiation through lawyers is similar to a pretrial settlement conference in that lawyers work toward a solution for the legal issues in a case on behalf of their clients. Unlike a pretrial settlement, lawyer-led negotiations may take place in private, without the benefit of a third party to ensure that the process is fair and that neither party is coerced into an agreement. Ideally, clients involved in lawyer-led negotiations are provided with full information and advice from their lawyers, and the clients direct their lawyers as to what positions to

advocate for on their behalf. Unfortunately, some lawyers do not provide these opportunities to their clients. In some of the worst-case scenarios, lawyers are trying to negotiate a settlement on the doorstep of the court; clients are pressured by the prospects of going into court; they have little time to make a decision; they do not understand the legal issues and ramifications; and the lawyers may be more focused on settling the legal issues than resolving the matter in a way that is best for all of the parties.

- **Assessment by an Independent Agency:** If the CPW and family cannot agree about what is needed for the welfare of a child, one option may be to submit to an assessment from an independent agency. This type of alternative is used, for example, when a CPW claims that a parent had a substance abuse problem and the parent denies this claim. The parent may agree to go for a substance abuse assessment in order to obtain an independent assessment. If the family members are agreeable to an independent assessment, then this option is relatively nonintrusive. However, assessments can be intrusive in a number of ways: the family may only be submitting to the assessment under pressure from the agency; an assessment sometimes requires opening up one's home to the assessor; and an assessment means that the family members will have to disclose personal information to another person outside of their family. The parties can agree for a third-party assessment to be binding in which case the decision-making responsibility has been handed over to a third party. Even if the assessment is to be used as a recommendation, the assessor's recommendation will carry a lot of weight because of the independence of the assessor.

- **Court Trial:** When cases proceed to trial, the decision-making responsibility is vested in the judge. The parties have input into the decision by presenting their evidence and argument. However, since most family members are unfamiliar with legal issues, their lawyers take control over most of this process. When a judge imposes a decision that is contrary to the family's position (e.g., state wardship), this is one of the most intrusive forms of intervention permitted by child protection legislation.

- **Branch Review Meetings:** Child protection agencies engage in periodic reviews of cases in order to assess their current state and to develop strategies for dealing with the case in the future. Various professionals from the agency—including the child and family service workers, their supervisors and agency lawyers—participate in the meeting. Neither family members nor their legal representatives are present at these meetings. Decisions made at these meetings are presented to the family. The decisions may suggest that the workers try to engage the family on a consensual basis. However, the agency may present certain decisions in a unilateral fashion. In this latter situation, the state has not only intervened on an involuntary basis, but the family has had no input into the agency's decisions. Unlike trials, there are no standards for procedural justice and the decision makers are not independent.

- **Imposition of Authority by a CPW:** The most extreme example of uni-lateral decision making by a CPW generally occurs when the CPW makes a decision to remove a child from the care of the family on an emergency basis. Although the agency must bring the case to court in order to give the family an opportunity to respond, even the short-term removal of a child represents a drastic intrusion of state into the affairs of a family. CPWs may also use their authority to motivate family members to change their behaviors. For instance, a CPW may state that in order for a child to be returned home, the parent must successfully complete a drug rehabilitation program. Although the parent may have a legal right to challenge this condition in court, the court option may not seem readily accessible or desirable for the parent. Requiring that family members make fundamental changes in their behaviors or personalities can be extremely intrusive.

The positions of these alternatives along the continuum are not precise. Within each alternative, the process can be implemented in a way that is either more or less intrusive. Mediation falls somewhere in the middle of the continuum. The exact placing of mediation on the continuum would depend on the model of mediation to be used and its implementation. The model of mediation focused on in this chapter is most comparable to solution-focused intervention and case conferencing. Models used in other jurisdictions involve lawyers in the mediation sessions (Center for Policy Research, 1992; Hogan, 1993; Thoennes, 1994), and may be similar to pre-trial settlement conferences.

Child protection agencies are often criticized for their work: if they intervene too quickly or forcefully, they are censured for infringing the privacy, integrity, and autonomy of the family; if a child is injured or dies because they did not intervene immediately or strongly enough, they are blamed for putting the child at risk. Many child protection services also struggle with insufficient resources, high rates of staff turnover, and large caseloads. Despite these challenges, child protection agencies have demonstrated concern for the effectiveness of their services and a willingness to consider new alternatives.

Many agencies have embraced mediation as a positive alternative within the range of services they can utilize. Further study is required to determine factors that indicate which cases are more appropriate for mediation and which for other alternatives. Some workers may be skeptical when mediation services are introduced, having seen many pilot projects and innovative programs come and go. In order to prevent the perception that mediation is just another fad, mediation requires ongoing funding and commitment from the child protection hierarchy. Research and experiences with the first generation of CP mediation services have been promising.

References

Auerbach, J. S. 1983. *Justice Without Law*. Toronto: Oxford University Press.

Bailey, M. 1994. Judicial Encouragement and Discouragement of Settlement in 19th Century England. *Family and Conciliation Courts Review* 32: 445–65.

Bala, N., J. P. Hornick, & R. Vogl. 1991. *Canadian Child Welfare Laws*. Toronto: Thompson Educational Publishing.

Barsky, A. E. 1995a. Essential Aspects of Mediation in Child Protection Cases. Ph.D. diss., University of Toronto Faculty of Social Work, Toronto.

————. 1995b. Mediation in Child Protection Cases. In H. H. Irving & M. Benjamin, eds., *Family Mediation: Contemporary Issues*. Thousand Oaks, CA: Sage.

Bernstein, M., J. Campbell, & N. Sookraj. 1993. Transforming Child Welfare Services in the 90s. Toronto: Catholic Children's Aid Society of Metropolitan.

Boyle, T., R. Tansony, R. Pluznick, & R. Rafael. 1993. "Solution-Focused Assumptions in Child Welfare Practice." Toronto: Catholic Children's Aid Society of Metropolitan Toronto and Oolagen.

Burford, G., & J. Pennell. 1994. Family Group Decision Making: An Innovation in Child and Family Welfare. Paper presented at the National Research and Policy Symposium on Child Welfare, Kananaskis, AB, April.

Bush, R. A. B. 1989. Efficiency and Protection, or Empowerment and Recognition? The Mediator's Role and Ethical Standards in Mediation. *Florida Law Review* 41: 253–86.

Bush, R. A. B., & J. P. Fogler. 1994. *The Promise of Mediation: Responding to Conflict Through Empowerment and Recognition*. San Francisco: Jossey-Bass.

Campbell, J., & M. Rodenburgh. 1994. *Mediation Pilot Project Evaluation*. Victoria, BC: Ministry of Social Services.

Center for Policy Research, Denver. 1992. *Alternatives to Adjudication in Child Abuse and Neglect Cases*. Alexandria, VA: State Justice Institute.

de Shazer, S. 1985. *Keys to Solution in Brief Therapy*. New York: Norton.

Eddy, W. A. 1992. *Mediation in San Diego's Dependency Court: A Balancing Solution for a System under Fire?* San Diego, CA: University of San Diego School of Law.

Fineman, M. 1988. Dominant Discourse, Professional Language and Legal Change in Child Custody Decision Making. *Harvard Law Review* 101: 727–74.

Germain, C. B., & A. Gitterman. 1980. *The Life Model of Social Work Practice*. New York: Columbia University Press.

Girdner, L., ed. 1990. Mediation and Spouse Abuse. Special Issue. *Mediation Quarterly* 7(4).

Golten, M. 1986. *Child Protection Mediation Project*. Final report. Denver, CO: CDR Associates.

Hogan, J. 1993. Mediating Child Welfare Cases. Paper presented at the Academy of Family Mediators Conference, Washington, DC, July.

Mayer, B., ed. 1984. *Child Protection Project Manual*. Denver, CO:: CDR Associates.

————. 1987. *Mediation and Compliance in Child Protection*. Ph.D. diss., University of Denver.

————. 1989. Mediation in Child Protection Cases: The Impact of Third Party Intervention on Compliance Attitudes. *Mediation Quarterly* 24: 89–106.

McRory, J. 1981. The Mediation Puzzle. *Vermont Law School* 6: 85–117.

Murdach, A. D. 1980. Bargaining and Persuasion with Nonvoluntary Clients. *Social Work* 25(6): 458–61.

National Council of Juvenile and Family Court Judges. 1989. *Court Approved Alternative Dispute Resolution: A Better Way to Resolve Minor Delinquency, Status Offense, and Abuse/Neglect Cases: Report to Key Issues Curriculum Enhancement Project.* Reno, NV: NCJFCJ.

Oran, H., J. Creamer, & J. Libow. 1984. *Dependence Mediation Court Project: The First Seven Months.* Evaluation report. Los Angeles, CA: Supreme Court.

Palmer, S. E. 1983. Authority: An Essential Part of Practice. *Social Work* 28(2): 122–26.

———. 1989. Mediation in Child Protection Cases: An Alternative to the Adversarial System. *Child Welfare* 68: 21–31.

Pearson, J., N. Thoennes, B. Mayer, & M. M. Golten. 1986. Mediation of Child Welfare Cases. *Family Law Quarterly* 20: 303–20.

Pinderhughes, E. 1983. Empowerment for our Clients and for Ourselves. *Social Casework* 64(6): 331–38.

Ricci, I. 1985. Mediator's Notebook: Reflections on Promoting Equal Empowerment and Entitlements for Women. *Journal of Divorce* 3: 49–61.

Saunders, D. G. 1994. Child Custody Decisions in Families Experiencing Woman Abuse. *Social Work* 39: 51–59.

Savoury, G. R., H. L. Beals, & J. M. Parks. 1994. Mediation in Child Protection: A Less Confrontational Approach to Resolving Disputes. Halifax: Nova Scotia Department of Social Services.

———. 1995. Mediation in Child Protection: Facilitating the Resolution of Disputes. *Child Welfare* 74(3): 743–62.

Shulman, L. 1991. *Interactional Social Work Practice: Toward an Empirical Theory.* Itasca, IL: Peacock.

Sloan, G. 1992. Power: Its Use and Abuse in Mediation. *Interaction* 4(1): 7–8.

Smith, R., J. Maresca, M. Duffy, N. Banelis, C. Handelman, & N. Dale. 1992. Mediation in Child Protection: Limited or Limitless Possibilities. Demonstration project of the Children's Aid Society of Metropolitan Toronto.

Stulberg, J. B. 1981. The Theory and Practice of Mediation: A Reply to Prof. Susskind. *Vermont Law Review* 6: 49–116.

Susskind, L. 1981. Environmental Mediation and the Accountability Problem. *Vermont Law Review* 6: 1–48.

Thoennes, N. 1991. Mediation and the Dependency Court: The Controversy and Three Courts' Experiences. *Family and Conciliation Courts Review* 29: 246–58.

———. 1994. Child Protection Mediation in the Juvenile Court. *The Judge's Journal* 33: 14–19; 40–43.

Tjaden, P. G. 1994. Dispute Resolution in Child Protection Cases. *Negotiation Journal* 10: 373–90.

Wiig, J. K. 1984. Pretrial Resolution of Child Protection Proceeding. Unpublished manuscript, Los Angeles, CA.

Wildgoose, J. 1987. Alternative Dispute Resolution of Child Protection Cases. *Canadian Journal of Family Law* 6: 61–84.

Wildgoose, J., & J. Maresca. 1994. *Report on the Centre for Child and Family Mediation, Toronto.* Kitchener, ON: Network-Interaction for Conflict Resolution.

Zastrow, C. 1995. *The Practice of Social Work.* Belmont, CA: Wadsworth.

8

ADOPTION

Applying Mediation to the Field of Adoption

by Jeanne Etter

During the past half-century, adoption practices have changed markedly. In the 1930s, the practice of closed adoption with sealed records began, considered a major step forward from previous practices, allowing all of the parties involved in an adoption the perceived opportunity to live free of the stigma of such labels as "bastard," "barren," or "fallen woman." Closed adoption practices based on utmost secrecy and anonymity enabled the adoptive family to maintain the pretense that their family was no different from a biological family. Adoption professionals counseled parents to treat their adoptive children as if they had been born to them, and birth parents to go on with their lives as if the adoption had never happened. It was assumed that adoption required a complete breaking of ties between the biological parents and the child in order to incorporate the child into the new family. In the eyes of the adoption professionals of the day, this approach was viewed as serving the best interests of the child (Nathan, 1984).

By the end of the 1980s, however, lobbying efforts by both birth parents and adoptees began to challenge adoption professionals to allow openness into the adoption process. Closed adoption and its inherent secrecy were no longer seen to be congruent with emerging social norms. In contrast to the recent past, North American adoptive parents today tell their children that they have been adopted, and more than half tell the children before they are three years old (Feigelman & Silverman, 1983).

Research studies have been unequivocal in their finding that within the system of closed adoption, all members of the adoption circle—adoptive parents, adoptees, and birth parents—share a common frustration and disappointment in not receiving adequate information about the adoption and the other parties involved (Sorosky, Baran, & Pannor, 1978). Birth parents report feeling demeaned by closed adoption, perceiving themselves as faceless, voiceless, and considered too dangerous to be a part of the process. Adoptees, after reaching the age of majority, have in large numbers sought out their birth families in attempts to reestablish their connections to their roots.

Theory and Trends in Adoption Mediation

Participants in today's adoptions are no longer willing to submit to rules laid down by practices considered appropriate in earlier decades. Birth and adoptive parents are demanding a voice in a process that will profoundly affect their lives and those of their children and are less willing to turn adoption decisions to professional helpers. They are wanting to fully participate in the adoption decision-making process.

Without a framework for structuring the contact between birth and adoptive parents, both parties and the child are at risk for exploitation, mismanagement, or betrayal. Adoptive placements arise, by and large, out of adversity. The same painful social or personal conditions that make adoption necessary also make the parties to the adoption extremely vulnerable. All participants in an adoption need to have their basic needs protected within a process that allows them to make choices that work for the benefit of all.

Adoption mediation can occur before or after an adoption placement. Preplacement mediation has been used successfully as a tool to plan cooperative or open adoptions. Postplacement mediation is usually the result of a potential or existing legal action, often an attempt to reclaim a child. Mediation can also be used as a tool for resolving differences at the much later stage of adoption reunion, when a participant in a closed adoption searches for another member of the circle and wishes to establish contact with them.

Postplacement mediation between birth and adoptive parents is less frequently used, although once legal action has begun, mediation may be a useful method of engaging the parties in a discovery of points of agreement that could lead to their working together on a plan that is in the child's best interest, and meets the needs of both sets of parents. The issues that typically lead to potential legal action are extreme situations fraught with intense emotions as birth parents who change their minds and use the courts to try to reclaim children are likely to have strong and entrenched positions. A skilled mediator specializing in child welfare mediation and adoption will be able to help both sides step back from their positions and look at their decision making in a different light. In these cases, mediation takes place almost exclusively in caucus with the parties. Joint sessions are scheduled toward the end of the process, after the parties are in alignment on basic issues.

Another type of postplacement mediation addresses conflicts that arise in the course of cooperative or open adoption contact between adoptive and birth parents. The conflict may be as limited as whether a visit happens on a birthday or as broad as whether visits should be discontinued because the adoptive parents are concerned about aspects of the birth parents' lifestyle. Most families can solve these issues for themselves, particularly if their adoption has been planned using a preplacement mediation process. If they cannot solve them alone, mediation offers a reasonably quick option that helps the parties to better handle future problem solving on their own.

Reunion mediation is only beginning to emerge as reunion problems generally have to escalate to the level of legal action before the parties are inclined to seek mediation assistance. As difficulties arise between various parties—adult children, birth parents, and adoptive parents—both before and after reunions, mediation is increasingly becoming regarded as a device for working through feelings and impasses that are likely to arise.

Preplacement mediation is the most common form of adoption mediation and is the primary focus of this chapter. Most frequently, the parties involved are the birth and potential adoptive parents. However, in planning an adoption, disputes also occur between birth mothers and fathers, and between birth mothers and their parents, and members of the extended family. When the birth mother and birth father do not agree on the plan for the child, mediation can be helpful in resolving their differences; however, when one party refuses to work in a mediated setting, the mediator must understand the legal options left to the other party and keep the planning process focused on reality. Birth relatives, other than the parents, do not have legal rights to make decisions about the child's future. They can, however, make the ensuing years very stressful for a birth parent who decides to make an adoption decision in the face of a parent's opposition. Mediators usually make an attempt to encourage support from extended families for plans made by birth parents. Birth grandparents, however, may be opposed to plans that involve placing a grandchild with strangers. When a relative is available to provide a home for the child, placement with that relative may well be in the child's best interest; most often, however, grandparents or other relatives are not in a position to provide a home but are highly apprehensive about adoption, which can be addressed in mediation.

Mediation between birth and prospective adoptive parents is used as a tool for organizing and structuring the adoption process before the adoption is in place and is employed before a dispute has occurred. When parties have differing interests and will be connected for the rest of their lives through an adopted child, mediation focuses on preventing future conflicts. Mediation allows birth and adoptive parents to set the parameters for their contact and, at the same time, begin building a positive relationship that can endure through the child's development into adulthood. Such preventive mediation can help the parties avoid future conflict in situations where they have interests that are distinctly different. Birth parents are most concerned about not having all ties to their children cut off by the legal impact of adoption; they want to know how their child is doing and they want a chance to express their love in a tangible way in the future. Adoptive parents want to have control over how they raise their children, and to ensure that they have a secure family where they feel entitled to be their children's parents. In preplacement adoption mediation, a written agreement keeps birth parents from being shut off from future contact, but also protects and supports the integrity of the adoptive family. Even more important, the process of planning the future with the mediator's help assists the parties in establishing the beginning of a relationship that can grow stronger over the years. Unlike other forms of mediation, if the parties discover they are in conflict over important issues, they need not continue working together. A different decision about adoption or who should adopt the child is then required.

The primary differences between preplacement adoption mediation and other forms of family mediation are based on the realities of adoption law. Unlike other forms of family mediation, adoption mediation works toward an explicit separation of parenting roles. The birth parents are the legal parents until they sign relinquishment or termination of parental rights documents, or have their parental rights terminated by the court. The adoptive parents become the full legal parents after the court decree is issued. Mediation helps both parties face the loss of one role and the transition to another. The birth parent loses the parenting role but can remain connected as an extended family member, perhaps in a role similar to that of aunt or uncle. The adoptive parents will never be biologically related, but they will become the child's parents in every other sense, including legally. The mediated agreement that is designed by both sets of parents provides the framework for ongoing contact and often gives the birth parents the option of an annual visit with the adoptive family.

Preplacement adoption mediation gives parties with different interests the opportunity to structure the future of their relationship in a mutually agreeable and workable manner. In adoption mediation the challenge is great as the agreement needs to cover the years the child is a minor and, ideally, takes the birth and adoptive families into a lifelong cooperative relationship. A well-mediated adoption agreement also needs to provide safeguards for both sides to prevent future differences from disrupting the basic relationship. The agreement also must not overstep the boundaries of either party if it is to be the foundation for lasting cooperation between two sets of parents.

Preplacement adoption mediation also differs from other forms of family mediation in that the parties typically become connected through the adoption process and do not start their mediation with a relationship in place or with a history of conflict. Ideally, the mediation process occurs before a final decision to adopt is made. High levels of conflict during the process or lack of agreement usually mean that the adoption should not take place. Because preplacement adoption mediation involves parties with no relationship history, one of the mediator's roles is to facilitate rapport and trust building between them in the early stages. A key attribute of a good adoption agreement is that it allows parties to continue to build their relationship within a safe structure.

Dealing with misperceptions about openness in adoptions also becomes part of the mediator's task. Adoptive parents are often apprehensive and fearful about the threat of birth parents reclaiming children. In reality, adoption placements being overturned due to birth parents' lawsuits are extremely rare, and an adoption agreement negotiated via mediation can provide safeguards that do not exist in closed adoption.

Preplacement adoption mediation calls for flexibility within a framework. The mediator must have a thorough understanding of the long-term results of choices the parties may make. Options for modifying the agreement are more limited than in other types of mediation because after the legal finalization of the adoption, when full legal rights are gained, the adoptive parents have few incentives to make concessions.

The Mediation Process

Mediation can provide a valuable tool at any point in the adoption process. When preplacement mediation is done well, however, mediation to resolve disputes at later stages becomes largely unnecessary. Difficulties and disputes at the postplacement or reunion stages can be prevented by means of preplacement mediation. Preplacement planning via mediation is particularly important because the legal finality of adoption poses substantial difficulties for postplacement mediation, including marked power imbalances related to the fact that one of the parties has been granted full legal rights of the children involved.

To be successful, preplacement mediation must take into consideration the desires of the parties to have their basic interests and needs safeguarded, both during the mediation process and in the written agreement. An effective mediation process helps birth and adoptive parents discover whether adoption is the right plan for them, agree to minimal obligations for ongoing contact, and develop a cooperative relationship that can grow over the years.

Mediation provides the parties an early opportunity to change their minds about proceeding if they discover that adoption is not the right decision or that the specific match is not the best one for them. It also allows them to come to agreement on basic minimum levels of contact and gives them the framework to develop meaningful relationships in the future.

Unlike other forms of mediation, the parties to adoption-planning mediation cannot simply sit down at the table together and begin working out their agreements. Because they do not have a preexisting relationship, the parties need the mediator's assistance in establishing rapport, trust, and the beginning of a relationship before they can begin to plan the adoption. Effective participation by birth and adoptive parents in the preplacement mediation process requires a high degree of skill on the part of the mediator, particularly in the engagement phase of the process.

Knowledge Base and Skills

Mediators in the field of adoption must be knowledgeable in child welfare issues related to permanency planning and placement decisions, adoption counseling and screening processes for both birth and adoptive families, adoption policies and practices, and family preservation and kinship placement issues. They must also have a good understanding of adoption laws in their state, interstate compact laws and procedures, and national and international perspectives on adoption.

Mediators must be skilled in addressing psychological conflicts as they arise in the course of making adoption decisions, which often continue up to the time of the adoption placement. Referral to a family therapist may be essential for one or more of the parties; impasses may be related to unresolved infertility problems of adoptive parents and "stuckness" in grief and loss for birth parents. Mediators may also need to educate the parties about the needs of adoptees as they grow and develop into adulthood. Finally, information about the process and structure of cooperative adoptions and forms of ongoing contact between birth and adoptive families also needs to be imparted by the mediator.

Core mediation skills include the ability to establish rapport with all parties quickly, the capacity to be comfortable with extensive individual caucuses until the parties are ready to meet, and the ability to build relationships to prevent future conflict. Mediators in adoption need to filter realistic and appropriate options to present to the parties; adoption law and the realities of the birth parent's situation place restrictions on the number of options that are workable in cooperative adoption. Working with birth parents who are low functioning, high risk, and may have done harm to children can be difficult for mediators who are used to working with more articulate parties who have clearly identified issues in dispute and their positions. Most important, mediators need to be able to apply core mediation techniques, such as finding common goals and reframing, in a specialized arena where the focus is on building relationships to prevent future conflicts rather than resolving specific issues in dispute.

Elements of the Preplacement Mediation Process

In addition to the skills and knowledge base outlined above, there are three core elements of effective preplacement adoption mediation between birth and adoptive parents that aim to create positive, long-lasting, cooperative, open adoptions: preparation, generating options and identifying choices, and negotiating written agreements.

Preparation. Careful preparation is the most important tool for mediators working with birth and adoptive parents. When birth and adoptive parents are fully prepared by means of psychoeducational programs, home evaluations, support groups, and individual counseling, the mediated adoption process can work to its best advantage. The time it takes to prepare adoptive parents and counsel birth parents can be extensive. Often adoptions are expected to somehow evolve "naturally" because everyone involved is well meaning. The most common assumption about open adoption is that the birth parent will readily locate prospective adoptive parents and they will all work things out together. These "do it yourself" open adoptions have been likened to giving birth without professional help. Both birth and adoption are natural processes and can certainly be done without help; given a choice, however, having the help of someone who knows the pitfalls and dangers and how to handle them creates better results.

Almost all prospective adoptive parents begin with negative feelings and numerous misperceptions about openness in adoption. They have heard media accounts about birth parents changing their minds, creating future difficulties, and interfering in various ways. Their perceptions of birth parents begin to change after meeting with birth mothers and fathers, asking them questions, and beginning to understand why they are choosing adoption. Further, adoptive parents need to have their desire to protect their family affirmed as a positive parenting instinct, and to be reassured that they will never be put in a position where they will have to agree to a plan for contact that seems risky or dangerous just to make an adoption possible. Prospective parents also need exposure to experienced adoptive parents who are now happily relating to birth parents and raising children in a family that feels entirely "normal." As they hear others' stories and obtain needed information, their fears about openness will dissipate.

Time needs to be planned for premediation preparation for adoptive parents, often in the form of psychoeducational group programs focused on the needs of children for ties to birth relatives, and on how cooperative adoption benefits all of the parties. Adoptees can share their stories about how it feels to have the love of their birth families as a tangible part of their lives. Adoptive families can share ways they talk about adoption with their children at different ages and discuss some of the problems they have encountered with birth parents.

When adoption mediation takes place without prior preparation for adoptive parents, the process is more difficult and less satisfactory. The mediator must do his or her best to focus the adoptive parents on the child's need for connection, and spend time during individual sessions helping the parties understand the benefits to all members of the circle. Describing the safeguards of the mediated adoption process also helps adoptive parents become more flexible as they begin to understand how they will be protected by a written mediated agreement.

Preparation for birth parents usually involves more individual sessions and less group or class time than for adoptive parents. The need for extensive individual caucuses can make adoption mediation look more like counseling than mediation. Preparing both sides to represent their interests is a core aspect of adoption mediation. The extreme power imbalance of a birth parent who cannot keep a child but must negotiate with prospective adoptive parents necessitates extensive preparation with the birth parents in particular. Above all, it needs to be emphasized that it will be their decision whether or not to choose adoption. It is essential that the mediator remain neutral vis-à-vis the adoption itself throughout the process. The birth parents are making a major life decision for themselves and their child. It is only through extensive preparation as they work through their thoughts and feelings in individual sessions that birth parents become ready to represent their interests and take part in building a cooperative relationship with the prospective adoptive parents via mediation.

Generating Options and Identifying Choices. Helping the parties understand the options they have and what to expect as a result of each choice is an integral part of the mediation process. Only when there is choice within a framework that provides safeguards for all parties will adoption mediation achieve its objective.

Due to the legal aspects of adoption, the process will be compromised if birth and adoptive parents choose one another (i.e., are matched) before they have made their choices about the level of openness that works for them. Ideally, adoptive parents should work with an adoptions social worker and discuss and fill out "Comfort Level Worksheets" that focus on their thoughts and feelings regarding postadoption contact and communication with the birth parents before they are matched or chosen by birth parents. Adoptive parents are assured that they will never be asked to work cooperatively with birth parents about whom they have serious concerns. Some adoptive parents may be prepared for a fully identified open adoption; for example, if the birth parent poses no perceived risk to the child. Others may prefer confidential adoption with last names and addresses not revealed, but agreement to meet with the birth parents in a neutral setting such as a playground on prescribed days and at prescribed times. If the child is part of such a meeting, the adoptive parents will always be there with the child. Thus a birth parent who wants the option of visitation would consider only prospective adoptive parents who are open to such visits.

For birth parents, occasional visits (such as one or two annual meetings) are almost always desired as an *option* but not as a *requirement*. The agreement needs to endure until the child reaches legal age, and birth parents, in the midst of making the agonizing decision to find a new family for their child, are not in a position to know what they will be able to manage in regard to the level of contact in the years ahead. Birth parents cannot anticipate how they will feel about and react to having even the first visit. They may find visiting too painful or difficult. The life circumstances that led them to have to place a child for adoption may also make it impossible for them to follow through on visits in a consistent manner. They may not know whether they will *ever* want to have face-to-face contact.

The most workable solution to this dilemma has been to encourage most birth parents to include one or two visits a year as part of the written agreement, but to make visits an option requested by the birth parent, with the time and place of the visits at the convenience of the adoptive parents.

The options explored during the adoption mediation process are tailored to the unique situation and needs of the participants. Mediators walk a fine line between exploring options that are too limited in scope and presenting unlimited and unrealistic options. The former tend to arise from wanting to limit contact between birth and adoptive parents, reflecting the fears and misconceptions of adoptive parents who want to keep birth parents from having a significant role in their children's lives. The latter usually stems from failing to consider the realities of adoption and not understanding the need for simple, achievable goals and agreements. However, when the focus is on relationship building rather than on negotiating strict terms regarding contact, the need for sensible boundaries and simple agreements is clear.

Negotiating Written Agreements. The goal of preplacement mediation is to formulate a written adoption agreement simple enough to be remembered. Some of the core elements of good mediated adoption agreements include visits with the adoptive family as the birth parent's option; visits at the adoptive family's convenience; decisions on paying travel costs; decisions on intermediary services; letter and photo exchange; notification of serious illness, accident, or death of the child; adversarial action by the birth parent invalidating the agreement; future modifications; and mediation or legal action to enforce the agreement. Adoption agreements should address the concerns of both birth and adoptive parents and reflect the best interests of the children involved. A visitation clause is central but the other clauses are also important for setting parameters for other types of communication, making relationships work smoothly and clarifying what will be done if problems arise.

The written mediated adoption agreement is not likely to be legally enforceable unless supported by statute. What then is its purpose? First, and most obvious, if parties to an adoption are going to make a good-faith agreement regarding contact after the adoptive placement, having it in writing can reduce ambiguity and misunderstanding at a later date. Second, emotions are intense while planning an adoption and for the first year or two after the adoptive placement; during this time, even well-meaning people need reminders of what they have agreed to. Finally, if adoptive parents should blatantly disregard their agreement and refuse the contact they have promised a birth parent, the birth parent is more likely to obtain a judicial hearing on the matter if a written mediated agreement can be produced.

Birth parents also have a powerful incentive to keep their agreements. If they break them by showing up unannounced, pressuring the adoptive parents, or otherwise interfering, they may lose their opportunity for future contact. Since any visits are at the birth parent's option and request, *not* visiting will not break the agreement or have a negative effect on future contact. Unpredictable or infrequent contact from birth parents over the years is not necessarily detrimental to children since adoptees with stable adoptive families seem to respond well to even infrequent contact from birth relatives who care about them.

Before face-to-face negotiation of the agreement begins, birth and adoptive parents have chosen, met, and interviewed one another. They have each had a chance to decide independently whether they feel comfortable working with the other party, and if they want to go forward with planning for this adoption. The mediator will have had several individual sessions with each party to clarify their agreement on the basic issues of type and frequency of contact before they meet to work out the details. They know that they will not be asked to compromise their most basic desires.

The parties meet to negotiate their written adoption agreement about four to six weeks before the adoption placement and after premediation counseling and individual preparation. The mediator has thoroughly assessed the parties' needs and preferences in regard to ongoing contact and knows they are reasonably well matched on the central issues. Only then are the adoptive and birth parents ready for their initial match meeting. If, after that first meeting, they both decide to proceed, the mediator talks with each set of parents separately in preparation for future meetings to plan their agreement. When the parties have indicated that they are ready to go forward, the mediator establishes a time for the first session to negotiate the agreement.

When the parties sit down to plan their agreement, they already have a fairly good picture of the kind of relationship they wish to structure. If major disagreements between them were evident in the preparation phase, the mediator would not proceed to the negotiation; conflict at that point would be an indication either that adoption was not the right choice for the birth parent or that the birth-adoptive parent match was not the right one. Since their relationship usually exists only because the birth parent has chosen the prospective adoptive parents, there is no reason to continue a relationship that is not cooperative.

Elements of the Mediated Agreement

Once the negotiation session is underway, parties are encouraged to remember that they may decide to modify the written agreement in the future, as long as they all agree, but they will be obligated to do no less than the agreement specifies. The core issues that are addressed and written into the agreement in simple, nonlegal terms are as follows.

Visitation. Starting with a generic mediation agreement form, the mediator helps the parties draft their agreement as they decide each issue regarding visitation. Agreements usually provide the birth parent with the right to visit the minor child with the adoptive family in a neutral setting a certain number of times per year. The visits are at the option and request of the birth parent, and at the convenience of the adoptive family. Sometimes supervision by an intermediary agency and/or an assessment before to the visit are part of the plan but only when safety concerns exist based on past visitation experiences. Provision is also made for the payment of transportation costs.

With careful preparation as a core part of the process, adoption mediation clients rarely have problems agreeing on the terms of visitation. Even birth parents who do not think they will want direct contact will usually want to include an optional annual visit in the agreement in case of future changes in their circumstances.

The frequency of the visits stipulated in agreements varies, although twice a year access is common. Both parties realize that they can increase the frequency of meetings if the visitation is successful and if they agree that more contact will serve to meet the child's needs as well as those of the parties.

Sometimes it helps clients to think of the written agreement as an "insurance policy" in case the relationship between the birth and adoptive parents becomes strained. If the relationship becomes tenuous, they can "fall back" on the safety of the minimum level of contact in the agreement.

The follow-through required by both parties to honor the mediated visitation agreement is usually fairly minimal and rarely requires a large investment of effort on the part of either birth or adoptive parents. Having one or two guaranteed annual visits at their convenience, including time and place, is not an onerous requirement for adoptive parents. The pressure is off and they feel reassured that they have the legal right to decide what is best for their child. Since visits between the child and birth parents take place with the adoptive family present, the dynamic becomes similar to that of a visiting relative.

Communication. Parties agree to communicate either directly or through an intermediary agency. Most mediated agreements have a clause providing for the adoptive parents to send letters and pictures on a regular basis and allowing the child to send and receive letters from the birth parents. The adoptive parents usually agree to inform the birth parents of serious illness, accidents, or the child's death.

Financial Responsibility. Both parties determine who pays which costs, including paying back any assistance given birth parents if they decide not to go through with the adoption, depending on state or local legislation in this regard.

Incorporation into Decree. The parties decide whether the agreement "may" or "shall" be incorporated into the decree of adoption. The adoption agreement is then, if appropriate, attached to the petition to the court.

Invalidation. A clause stating that the adoptive parents will no longer have to comply with the visitation and communication clauses if the birth parent assumes an adversarial rather than cooperative relationship with the adoptive parents is always included in the written agreement. The purpose of such a clause is to make birth parents fully aware that if they take legal steps to regain the child or pressure the adoptive family in any way, the relationship with the family is changed. If they want to have ongoing contact and communication, cooperation and goodwill are essential.

Other issues that the written agreement might address are enforcement, modification, severability, and liaison fees for those who communicate through an agency.

Written mediated agreements are the foundation for successful cooperative adoptions in which the adoptive family stays in contact with the biological relatives. These agreements are designed to be both achievable and durable through the years as the child grows and develops.

Alternatives to Mediation

The principal alternatives to mediated cooperative adoptions are traditional closed adoptions, open adoptions where clients work out all arrangements for future contact themselves, and arranged contact after the adoption that is limited to one-way correspondence, such as adoptive parents sending birth parents an annual update on the child's progress. Other options include approaching prospective adoptive parents after adoption planning is underway and asking them or their attorney how much openness they are willing to offer to the birth parents. Despite their reservations, prospective adoptive parents usually agree to open adoption with the recognition that they likely will not be able to adopt the child in any other manner.

Mediation should not be used in adoption when either party is manipulating or exploiting the situation for their personal benefit. Birth parents have been known to use a pregnancy and potential adoption to see how much they can get from one or more sets of potential adoptive parents. Adoptive parents are in a position in some states to be able to exploit a birth parent's misfortunes and make promises that they never intend to keep. A mediator who senses that either party is trying to take advantage of the other should make efforts to examine this perception and withdraw from the case if he or she is not completely satisfied that both parties are negotiating in good faith. Mediation is also not useful when the court is needed to make a determination about a crucial issue such as whether someone who claims to be the father has legal rights in the case.

Adoption mediation involves a considered, carefully thought through process based on the realities of adoption and the needs of both parties and focused on the best interests of the child. Well-mediated adoptions give children who cannot remain with their biological parents a chance for new homes with loving parents while not losing touch with the best from their birth parents and their heritage.

Adoption Mediation as a Tool for Permanency Planning

Adoption mediation can also occur within the context of permanency planning for children who are in the care of child welfare authorities. Although permanency planning mediation is a variant of the adoption mediation process described above, there are a number of considerations and specialized procedures unique to this field of practice. Allegations of child neglect and abuse have been made and substantiated, a child welfare agency has become involved, and the termination of parental rights has been deemed necessary. The tasks involved in permanency planning are particularly complex, and the mediation process must be tailored accordingly.

Trials to terminate parental rights are costly and time consuming. Children suffer, often waiting several years in foster care for the court process to free them for adoption. Specialized mediation for permanency planning offers an alternative to traditional, lengthy, adversarial termination proceedings. Unlike court determination, the mediation process is voluntary, cooperative, noncoercive, and relationship building.

In the permanency planning process, birth parents whose children are in foster care due to abuse and neglect are given the option of working voluntarily with an independent child welfare mediator. Through mediation they are able to participate in planning for a permanent home for their child and remaining in contact with their child in the future. The mediator, who is not connected with the child welfare agency or the court, engages the parent and the child welfare agency in a thoughtful decision-making process focused on the needs of the child. Most of the mediation, particularly in the early stages, is done in individual sessions or caucuses with the parties. The parties to the permanency planning mediation are initially the birth parent(s) and the child welfare agency; the goal of the process is to agree on a plan for the child in care. Thereafter, if adoption is the plan for the child, the parties to mediation become the birth parent(s) and the prospective adoptive parents.

Mediation is uniquely suited to making permanent plans for children who cannot return home. A court trial to terminate a parent's rights is highly adversarial and charged with negative emotions. An excessive amount of time and expense are typically invested by child welfare authorities to develop a case and to establish that a mother or father has been and will be unfit to parent their child. Those who have information about the parent's problems, misdeeds, faults, and inadequacies become witnesses against the parent. Building a case strong enough for the court to decide to permanently terminate parental rights and responsibilities is extremely difficult, and increasingly so as appeal courts overturn decisions that might have stood in the past.

In contrast, referring a case to a specialized independent mediator is relatively low cost and low risk. Parents referred to mediation can decide if they want to participate and, by participating, have a voice in what happens to their child. The mediation process helps parents to gain an understanding of their child's needs and realistically assess their own abilities. Even after months of failed attempts to reunite with their children, some parents will be able to negotiate and follow through with realistic permanency plans. Cooperative adoption, kinship adoption, guardianship, and permanent foster care are options that mediation can explore when the child cannot be returned to the biological parent.

Mediation serves children in care and their families in a multitude of ways. First, mediation speeds up the process of child placement. In a few months the child can be in a permanent home rather than waiting years for a court release. Second, children benefit when their foster, adoptive, and birth parents, as well as child welfare workers, focus their energies on a cooperative process rather than a combative court battle. Most important, however, permanency mediation lays the groundwork for a future positive connection between the birth parents and the family who will raise the child.

Cooperative adoption is desirable when children have ties to their birth families. The mediation process involves screening the birth parents' capacity to participate in a long-term connection with the adoptive family. As a structured process, mediation safeguards everyone's needs, and the mediated agreement provides protection to all the parties. Mediation makes it possible to build solid and lasting relationships within a limited framework for both birth and adoptive parents. The enhanced cooperation between their birth and their permanent families helps children know their roots, and they can know that they continue to be loved by their birth family in spite of past problems and abuse. The benefits of this connection endure into adulthood.

The adversarial nature of protective services, foster care, and permanency planning puts requirements and restrictions on child welfare agencies while making parent participation difficult. Mediation can ease many of the restrictions within the court process to terminate parent's rights that are detrimental to voluntary participation in planning for a child's future.

As neutral facilitators who are not representatives of the child welfare agency or the court, mediators are in a unique position to be able to establish trust with birth parents. Birth parents are often willing to discuss plans for their children with mediators when communication has broken down with the child welfare agency, particularly after reunification efforts have failed. Because the mediator is protected from being required to testify in court, parents can talk openly and freely knowing the mediator cannot be called as a witness. When foster parents are beginning the process of adoption, mediators can help them to address and resolve their ambivalences as well as their fears of birth parents.

Nationally, the foster care population has grown phenomenally. An estimated six out of every thousand children under age eighteen are in foster care (Kroll, 1992). Children who have already suffered emotional and physical harm suffer further as they wait in temporary foster families for the system to release them and make them available for adoption. Bottlenecks in freeing and placing children for adoption are endemic. In spite of U.S. federal policy, outlined in Public Law 96-272 requiring permanence for children, the ratio of one finalized adoption for every 2.4 adoptions in planning demonstrates the pressing need to move children more expediently from foster care into adoptive families.

The adversarial court process of terminating parental rights is the most frequently used method to free children for adoption when family reunification efforts have failed. However, involuntary termination of parental rights damages both children and parents in critical ways. First, while it permanently and irrevocably severs legal connections between the child and the birth family, it does not cut the emotional connections as cleanly. Most foster children who are adopted have memories and attachments to their birth parents and kin. Their ability to form healthy attachments in an adoptive family is related to their ability to grieve the loss of their birth family. Knowledge of and contact with birth family members can mitigate the effects of loss by focusing on actual changing relationships rather than on fantasy relationships and can help children adjust to adoption (Fahlberg, 1991). The adversarial nature of termination of parental rights trials, however, makes it very difficult for birth parents to cooperate and establish positive ongoing communication with adoptive parents.

Adversarial termination of parental rights trials are also expensive. Thousands of dollars are required to prepare for trial, litigate, and appeal cases. In addition, the time it takes to try a case takes a significant emotional toll on children who live for months or years in the uncertainty of foster care, waiting to be placed for adoption. At the same time, termination trials cost birth parents their self-esteem and put at risk any future contact with their children.

Mediation as an Alternative Process of Permanency Planning

Permanency mediation begins with the referral of a case, usually from the child welfare agency or department responsible for ensuring that children acquire permanent homes if they cannot return to their parents from foster care. The child welfare agency will be proceeding toward freeing the child for adoption, usually through filing a petition to begin proceedings toward termination of parental rights through the courts.

Often a child welfare worker will attempt to engage the parent in adoption counseling, discussing the option of a voluntary relinquishment or surrender. If the birth parent makes no significant progress that could lead to reunification and refuses to consider adoption, the case enters the adversarial track. The length of time between staffing and a trial depends on court dockets and the backlog of cases needing legal processing. A trial within six months gives the birth parents and their attorneys, as well as the child welfare agency, sufficient time to prepare their cases; in some jurisdictions, however, cases linger months or years waiting to be staffed, and then even longer to move to trial and through the appeals process.

With mediation as an option, parents and child welfare agencies are able to work toward resolving their impasse before the adversarial process is initiated. Ideally, all biological parents involved in permanency planning initiatives should be given the option of using mediation; in reality, child welfare agencies currently select those cases they have determined to be most appropriate for mediation. Restricting parental access to mediation, with one party to the mediation deciding which parties will be offered the opportunity to use mediation, may compromise the neutrality of mediation programs; however, decisions need to be made regarding the appropriateness of mediation in permanency planning cases. Permanency planning mediation can be effective for a broad range of clientele, including parents who have tried and failed drug or alcohol treatment programs, those who are incarcerated, those who are involved in criminal proceedings, those who have made some mention of adoption or having someone else raise the child, and parents who visit the child regularly but understand that they cannot adequately manage the job of parenting. Cases that are inappropriate for mediation are ones in which a parent is not considered competent to make legal decisions and cases where parents decline the option of mediating the impasse; permanency planning mediation must always remain an entirely voluntary endeavor.

Permanency planning mediators must be knowledgeable and skilled in abuse and neglect, child protection, foster care, permanency and adoption, termination of parental rights, cooperative special needs adoptions, court process, and culturally-specific practice. When a case is referred to a mediator or mediation agency that has contracted with the child welfare agency to provide permanency planning services, information regarding the parent(s) and child(ren) who will be involved, the potential adoptive family, safety concerns about the birth parent having future meetings with the child and the adoptive parents, and other relevant factors must be obtained before the mediation process can proceed. The permanency planning mediation process involves two distinct phases: mediating the permanency plan, and then mediating a cooperative adoption, guardianship, or long-term foster care.

Phase One: Mediating the Permanency Plan: Premediation Preparation and Consideration of Options. The permanency planning mediation process begins with the mediator's initial contact with the child welfare worker (who represents the child welfare agency) followed by contact with the birth parents. The mediator makes contact with the child welfare worker to be briefed on the case, and then contacts the birth parents' attorney to gain permission to contact the parents. Either the child welfare worker or the attorney may ask the parents if they are interested in the possibility of mediation, a voluntary and cooperative process that will allow them a say in what happens to their child. It is explained that the purpose of mediation is to help the parties work together on a mutually agreeable plan that is in the child's best interests.

The attorney for the birth parents may wish to be present at their first meeting with the mediator, held without the child welfare worker, to help explain the nature of confidentiality and the fact that the mediator is not an employee of the child welfare agency or the court. Parents may discuss their past experiences with the child welfare agency, and are encouraged to share their reservations about the mediation process. If they agree to mediation, they are asked to sign an agreement to mediate form before the next meeting. The parent knows that the mediator will share only specific information that he or she has been given permission to pass on to the child welfare worker, with the exception of any new information regarding harm or potential harm to a child.

Many professionals new to this specialized type of mediation express concerns about how an extremely resistant parent can possibly be engaged in the process. A birth parent who does not trust the mediator enough to agree to mediate or who is too angry to talk with anyone will simply not continue after the first session, and it can be expected that a proportion of cases referred for permanency planning mediation will not complete the process; the parents may decide not to participate, a key party is not locatable, or some other impediment to mediation is discovered in the initial meetings.

Several individual sessions with the parents focusing on psychoeducational issues may be required before the child welfare worker is directly introduced into the process; these are designed to prepare parents for thinking through their child(ren)'s need for permanency. Workbooks illustrating core issues regarding children's needs for permanency planning are used, in addition to questions that lead parents to examine their present life situation, their own experiences as children, and their child(ren)'s current experiences and needs.

Parent advocates have expressed concerns about permanency planning mediation related to the fact that parents may be coerced into adoption by the mediator. The permanency planning mediation process, however, is specifically designed to empower parents to think clearly about their children's needs and to take responsibility for planning their future. Discussion of options insufficient psychoeducational preparatory work has occurred to enable the parent to focus on the child's needs.

Once the parents begin to express what they want for their child, the child welfare worker and parents are brought together to begin to explore realistic options. It may be that parents are able to overcome their barriers to parenting and will be able to reunite with their children; however, since permanency planning mediation referrals are typically cases where long-standing efforts toward family preservation have failed, mediated permanency plans to reunite the child with the parent are relatively rare. When this occurs, however, mediation is terminated upon the drafting of an agreement that includes a service plan between the parent and the child welfare agency and an agreement to return to mediation in the future if the parent does not succeed. When family reunification is not possible, the mediator focuses the parties on selecting among the remaining options: adoption, guardianship, or long-term foster care. When the parents and the child welfare worker reach agreement in this regard, phase two of the process can begin.

Phase Two: Mediating Cooperative Adoption, Guardianship, or Long-term Foster Care. The parties in phase two are the birth parents and the prospective new parent(s), with the child welfare worker playing a less active role in the mediation process.

Guardianship and long-term foster care are much less stable than cooperative adoption and are thus less favored by child welfare agencies as an option in permanency planning. Even when relatives will be raising the child(ren), adoption allows for many more possibilities, including an ongoing adoption subsidy in some cases. Once their fears and concerns are addressed, relatives usually find that they are eager for the protection offered by making the placement legally permanent. Their concerns about taking the child away from the birth parents disappear when they realize that everyone wants a successful placement and that the parents have made these plans willingly and voluntarily.

In the child welfare context, the majority of families adopting children are relatives or foster parents: new adoptive parents become involved in only a minority of cases. Adoption mediation is significantly different when relatives or foster parents are adopting rather than new adoptive parents recruited in cases where abused and neglected children are wards of the court.

Parents have considerably less choice when adoptions are planned for children who have been in foster care for a lengthy period of time. Birth parents may have no voice in deciding who adopts, particularly in the case of foster parent adoption, and adoptive parents may have little choice about the birth parent with whom they will continue to have a connection. Options are often quite limited in the adoption phase of the permanency planning mediation process.

Separate caucuses with the prospective adoptive parents follow a similar psychoeducational process to that in preplacement adoption mediation.

Before adoptive parents begin to consider options, they need to understand how their interests will be safeguarded through a mediated agreement, and the importance to the child of maintaining a continuing positive connection with his or her birth family. The mediator explains the importance of a simple, easy-to-keep agreement that establishes the foundation for a continuing cooperative relationship with the birth parent, including a baseline for visits and the exchange of information.

Bringing foster parents into mediation is more difficult than working with new prospective adoptive parents. They will have knowledge about or have met the birth parents, and often know firsthand of the harm they have caused the children. Foster parents may see themselves as the "rescuers" of innocent children and view the birth parents as undeserving of consideration because of their "unforgivable acts." The mediator must be creative in showing the positive and human side of the parents, as well as the children's need to have access to their heritage and continued connection with their birth family.

After such a psychoeducational process with the prospective adoptive parents, and once a common desire to form a positive link for the sake of the child has been expressed by both sides, the birth and adoptive parents need an opportunity to meet and get further acquainted. If they already know one another, they need to meet with a focus on learning more about one another's values and views about parenting, the child's needs, and their common interests and concerns. The initial joint meeting with the mediator provides a forum for the parties to begin exploring their ability to relate and cooperate for the child's sake. The mediator establishes mediation guidelines that ensure safety and promote mutual respect. The parties are instructed to refrain from negotiating the terms of contact until the next session, giving them time to think over their desired contact after the "get acquainted" session.

Once both sides have agreed to proceed with the adoption plan and feel that they can relate positively to one another, mediating the terms of the adoption agreement can begin. If they are uncomfortable with each other or about the adoption plan, the mediator must help the parties back away gracefully by suggesting that everyone needs time to think over whether or not they are ready for this next step.

A "shuttle mediation" process is then used to negotiate the terms of future contact until agreement on the major issues of concern has been established. Following this process, the parties are brought back together. When the parties have agreed in caucus sessions that two annual meetings a year, for example, are desirable, they can come back for a joint meeting to discuss transportation arrangements, whether the adoptive parents can supervise the visits or will need professional assistance, whether the child can correspond with the birth parents, how often the adoptive parents will send a photo and update letter, and so on.

The mediated agreement must be as general as possible, in contrast to most other mediated agreements, which can be highly specific. As up to eighteen years could be involved in carrying out the agreement, if specific dates and times are included or conditions made, there is a strong likelihood that one or the other party will not be able to keep their side of the agreement, even with the best of intentions.

Both sets of parents need to know from the beginning that they will have to adapt to major life changes, such as one or the other moving, new marriages, and major illness. Parties are encouraged to talk about their hopes related to future relationships, such as being able to visit on the child's birthday; they may want to talk about what to do if either party relocates. A distinction should be made between their wishes for how they hope to handle future possibilities and the written agreement. Cooperative adoption requires that future disputes will have to be worked out as they arise; the mediator works toward developing a positive relationship between the parties that will make it possible for them to handle future issues as children's and families' needs change. The written agreement, however, should be general enough to cover a variety of future possibilities.

As in other forms of adoption mediation, the birth parents must be given the option but not the obligation of visiting. No one can predict how they will be able to manage visits in the years ahead, particularly in the context of an already damaged relationship. Past problems may keep them from being available to the child and the adoptive family in the future. Children are better able to handle inconsistencies when they have the security of stable parenting from their adoptive parents; the adoptee may miss the birth parents and wish to see them, but usually responds well when reminded of tangible evidence of the birth relatives' caring. Mediators can support maintaining contact by encouraging birth parents to allow the adoptive family to contact other family members who might know how to find the birth mother or father in the future should direct contact be lost.

Parties are encouraged to plan the timing and content of the events surrounding the legal voluntary relinquishment or surrender, the signing of the adoption agreement, and the transition to the new home. The child will need preparation and time to adjust and assimilate the changes that adoption will create. Psychoeducational materials help prepare birth parents for all phases of the process, and can also be used to help adoptive parents to understand what to expect. As they are building the foundation of a lifelong relationship through their mutual connection to the child, the more both sets of parents can feel involved and in control of the process, the more satisfactory the results will be.

Permanency planning mediation resulting in cooperative adoption provides for less secrecy without sacrificing needed privacy. Families often share first names only and plan to exchange letters through a third-party intermediary. The adopted child gains access to information about the birth family without endangering his or her feeling of belonging to the adoptive family.

Conclusion

Permanency planning mediation is provided by specialized child welfare mediators who first engage parents in a psychoeducational process focusing on the needs of the child and then explore choices and responsibilities. Mediators employ a two-phase mediation process leading to an agreement between the birth parent and the child welfare department regarding the best permanency plan for the child in the first phase. In cases where the plan is adoption, mediation then leads to a written cooperative adoption plan jointly negotiated between birth parents and prospective adoptive parents in the second phase.

Traditional permanency planning is the major alternative to permanency mediation. When adoption is determined by the child welfare agency to be in the child's best interest, adversarial processes to terminate the parent's rights begin. Attorneys for both sides begin building their respective cases, and caseworkers carefully document all evidence indicating the parent's inability to ever provide a safe home for the child. Birth parents are counseled to refrain from talking to caseworkers about adoption, other options, their feelings or any plans they may be making because what they say will be part of the record and can be used against them in court.

In some cases, where family reunification efforts have failed, there will always be the need for an adversarial court process to free children for adoption. Some parents will refuse to participate in mediation, be impossible to locate, be considered legally incompetent to make their own decisions, or have criminal proceedings against them that prohibit mediation. A sound, timely, and effective court process to resolve such cases will always be a necessary part of permanency planning for children.

However, there are many difficulties with adversarial resolution. First, the process takes a great deal of time, often years; appeals, which are common, may add years to the child's wait in foster care, and trials to terminate parent's rights are among the most costly to litigate. Battles over children's futures jeopardize their ability to move quietly and humanely into a home where they can begin to heal from the effects of their early trauma. Finally, when the court terminates parental rights, the child is deprived of an ongoing connection with his or her birth parents and heritage.

Adoption and permanency planning mediation serve the needs of children, birth parents, adoptive parents, and child welfare workers, and are a melding of the best social work practices and mediation techniques. These processes help birth and adoptive families establish lasting relationships and develop postplacement communication agreements that safeguard all of the parties. Children are the main winners in this more humane process that forges positive links with their birth heritage and encourages the adults in their lives to cooperate and work for a positive future.

References

Fahlberg, V. 1991. *A Child's Journey Through Placement*. Indianapolis, IN: Perspectives Press.

Feigelman, W., & A. Silverman. 1983. *Chosen Children*. New York: Praeger.

Kroll, J. 1992. Still No Data on Foster Care and Adoption. *Adoptalk,* 1: 1–4.

Nathan, J. 1984. Visitation after Adoption: In the Best Interests of the Child. *New York University Law Review* 59: 633–75.

Sorosky, A., A. Baran, & R. Pannor. 1978. *The Adoption Triangle*. New York: Doubleday.

9

AGING

Mediation in the Aging Field

by Ruth J. Parsons and Enid Opal Cox

The North American population is getting older. In 1995, persons sixty-five and over numbered 12.7 percent of the U.S. population (about one in eight Americans), and it is projected that by 2030, 20 percent of the population will be in this age group, twice as many as in 1990 (U.S. Bureau of the Census, 1995). However, as the life span continues to increase, and the percentage of older persons in society grows, incapacity is not predicted to change. An increased life span with functional impairments requires an adjustment and change in status on the part of the older person from independence to some degree of dependence.

The two most rapidly expanding dependent groups of elderly persons are women and the "old-old" population (Brody, 1983a, 1983b), with the eighty-five-plus population twenty-eight times larger than it was in 1900 (AARP, 1995). While only 5 percent of persons sixty-five to seventy-four years old need the care of another person with the basic activities of daily living, 33 percent of the population eighty-five and older need such care (Ory, 1985). The majority of elders who need care will remain in the community, not in institutions, and the family will remain as the prime caretaker (Ory, 1985). These population shifts will require more and more families to become involved in difficult decisions around elder care, such as hospital discharge planning, hospice placement, nursing home placement, assisted living care arrangements, home health care, and family caregiving.

The decisions facing families with elder members include the type and level of elder care, who will be involved in their care and in what way, who will pay, and how much. Participants in these decisions may include elder family members, children of elder family members, siblings of elder members, family members of designated caregivers, and friends and neighbors. The core issues facing elders, their families, and their significant service providers relate primarily to elders' loss of autonomy and increased dependence, and discrimination against the elderly in society. The younger elder population (sixty-five to seventy-five) face decisions regarding employment and retirement wherein their rights are often disregarded in deference to profit interests and other corporate motives. Employment institutions may offer negotiated retirement packages that may require third party mediators, or elders may find themselves the victims of direct discrimination in regard to employment and retirement. As older elders (seventy-five years and older) are faced with increasing frailty, resulting in loss of autonomy and need for quality of care, increasing numbers of human service agencies, including residential facilities, will find themselves in the position of having to make important decisions regarding elders and their families. And as resources decrease and the service delivery system for elders and their families adapts to increased privatization, decision making around elder care will likely become more complex and conflicted.

Theory, Debates, and Trends

Sources of Conflict in Caregiving Decision Making

While elder caregiving by families is a common occurrence in our society, decision making with respect to care arrangements is typically not a harmonious process. This is reflected by the fact that family conflict resolution is one of the five most frequent interventions by social workers in home health care agencies serving dependent elders (Levande, Bowden, & Mollema, 1987). Sources of family conflict around elder care decisions involve feelings of guilt, grief connected with the decline of the elder family member's health, decreased family resources, disparate investments and interests in the caregiving arrangements of elders, scarce resources for elder caregiving (which demand commitment and substantial sacrifice from family members), limited experience with joint decision making, and the rejuvenation of previous conflictual family dynamics through the decision-making process.

The unequal burden of caregiving is a major source of conflict in families. The bulk of care falls principally on a single caregiver, usually a female adult child (Brody, 1983a). While women do the major portion of caregiving, they are frequently considered less critical to decision making regarding elder care. Many family members who are removed from actual caregiving nonetheless tend to become active in the decision-making process. Feelings of resentment in this regard are bound to occur and with the escalation of conflict within families, caregiving decisions are often sabotaged.

There is substantial evidence that unresolved conflicts among family members regarding caregiving arrangements are associated with decreased decision-making ability. The greater the conflict, the less family members consult with one another regarding future decisions, resulting in a compartmentalization of effort and reduction in the effectiveness of the family's total capacity. Family support plays a critical and intervening role in an elder's coping with illness and even its outcome (Berkman, 1983). Moreover, evidence exists that breakdown in the elder's network increases the possibility of institutionalization (Berkman, 1983) and elder abuse in the caregiving situation (Knight, 1985). Family members often become more isolated from one another and feel less empowered to handle caregiving decision-making responsibilities. In this situation, everyone loses, particularly the elder family member.

In addition to family disputes in regard to elder care, many disputes arise in the context of human service agencies and residential facilities. In a study by Hall (1990), adult children were asked what kind of help they most commonly provided for their elderly parents. Bureaucratic mediation was among the top three services identified, along with psychological support and personal care. Care conflicts in nursing homes between staff and the elder, staff and family members, and family members and the elder in nursing care are commonly identified (Wood and Karp, 1994). The role of the ombudsperson in nursing care is increasingly one of mediating between conflicting interests rather than only advocating for clients' rights (Kahana, 1994). Many nursing home conflicts are not merely elder rights issues requiring advocacy, but conflicting "rights" that lend themselves to a mediation framework. Mediation is also being used in medical ethics committee disputes in health care in regard to elder care issues (Gibson, 1994).

Cox and Parsons (1992) report on a demonstration project where seniors were trained as volunteer mediators and offered mediation services to elders through a centralized commission on aging. The most common disputes were within senior residential facilities and included violations of tenants' rights to privacy and the use of common facilities, safety, and evictions. Other disputes involved landlord/tenant conflict in single family units, board and care home disputes, and public utility, consumer/business, neighbor/acquaintance, and social service agency disagreements.

The American Bar Association's Standing Committee on Dispute Resolution and Legal Problems of the Elderly has identified disputes that affect the elderly and lend themselves to alternative dispute resolution processes. These include consumer, neighborhood, housing, age discrimination, public benefit, estate and long-term care planning disputes; conflicts with organizations such as nursing homes and home care programs in regard to quality of life issues; and multiparty public policy disputes, such as legislative and policy initiatives directed toward long-term care benefits, housing, and public utilities (Kester & Wood, 1988).

The destructive potential of the problems and conflicts that impact elder populations highlights the need for early intervention to resolve disputes, promote cooperation, and improve communication between and among elders, family members, and community agencies and service providers. While current policy and practice promotes a philosophical stance toward family oriented and community-based approaches to service provision, Circirelli (1986) points out that with the emphasis on diseases and conditions that affect individual elders, the strong influence of the family system on the care, condition and outcomes of intervention with the elderly is frequently ignored. The medical orientation held by many service providers prevents agencies from considering more community-based interventions such as mediation and arbitration.

Many disputes in the aging field involve complex problems and multiple parties. Families are usually involved in aging disputes, increasing the emotional stake in problem solving, and the potential for destruction of relationships. In disputes where future relationships are important to the care of elders, mediation may be essential given its potential of preserving relationships.

The authors propose that mediation is an appropriate intervention strategy for moving toward a more family- and community-based approach to elder issues, and that social workers and human service professionals have a direct role to play in this regard. At the same time, it should be recognized that in many cases, elders themselves have ample capacities to become trained as volunteer mediators in the community and social workers also have an indirect role to play in the training and supervision of these volunteers.

The Social Worker as Mediator

The role of mediator is central in social work theory and practice. The social work function, in fact, is often viewed as essentially one of mediation between clients and environmental systems, wherein social work problems are the result of a dysfunction or breakdown in systems linkage (Hearn, 1970; Schwartz, 1961). What distinguishes the mediation role from clinical or advocacy functions is related to the fact that the social work mediator intervenes in a process of interaction between systems as a neutral facilitator for the purpose of assisting those systems to reach agreement about disputed issues (Parsons, Jorgensen, & Hernandez, 1994). No attempt is made either to advocate for a system or to change the way that system functions (Connaway & Gentry, 1988). In addition to its focus on individual parties in dispute, mediation is a recognized method of organizational conflict resolution (Blake & Mouton, 1984) and community building (Walton, 1969).

Principles of Mediation. Mediation is an intervention between conflicting parties to promote reconciliation, settlement, compromise, or understanding. It is a behaviorally oriented problem-solving intervention, seeking mutually agreed-upon behavioral contracts. Mediation focuses on the facilitation of the problem-solving process, and the ability of the parties in dispute to isolate issues, interests, positions, alternatives, and resources in order to find mutually agreed-upon solutions. While Connaway and Gentry (1988) point out that few theoretical conceptualizations exist for the interaction process observed in mediating conflicts, recent studies undertaken from the perspective of exchange theory, system linkage, field theory, and negotiation theory have begun to systematically examine these interactions.

The focus of mediation is on the process of problem solving, not the behavioral or personality dynamics of the participants. Personal changes are a secondary outcome of agreement-seeking, based upon the assumption that changes in interaction create choices in that interaction which can improve significantly the quality of life for the parties (Connaway & Gentry, 1988). While the potential exists in mediation for elders, family members, organizational staff, and neighbors to improve their understanding of one another and their communication processes, the primary goal of mediation is task accomplishment.

Mediation has empowering qualities not present in other forms of conflict resolution. One such quality is found in its educational focus. The mediator educates each participant to negotiate to get his or her needs met, and empowers all participants to negotiate on their own behalf. Meyers-Chandler (1985) describes this aspect of mediation as "joint advocacy," in which the social worker actively promotes the interests of each participant. Other empowering aspects include the emphasis placed on each participant's own responsibility for decision making and outcome in mediation. Mediation assumes that the participants have the capacity to examine facts and make rational choices with the assistance of a third-party neutral (Connaway & Gentry, 1988). The responsibility for the outcome always rests with the participants.

It is theoretically optimal for the mediator to be viewed as neutral, committed to helping all of the parties in dispute, with no interest in the outcome other than participant satisfaction, fairness, and the workability of the plan. However, it may be argued that complete neutrality is not feasible or desirable within the framework of professional social work values, particularly in the case where the elder is unable to negotiate for him or herself. There is little doubt that the concept of complete neutrality on the part of the mediator is a controversial issue in mediation. Specifically, the social work mediator may have to assume an interventionist stance where marked power differentials exist or the elder is otherwise unable to make optimal use of the negotiation process.

One distinction between nonprofessional mediators and a professional social worker assuming a mediation role in practice relates to the use of multiple roles. In agency-based social work practice with client systems, the social worker typically assumes various roles: conferee, broker, mediator, advocate, and sometimes guardian (Parsons, Jorgensen, & Hernandez, 1994). An important task of the social worker taking on a mediation function as one of many roles with an elder client is to assume a stance of neutrality for the purposes of conflict resolution. According to the National Association of Social Work Standards of Practice for Social Work Mediators, social work mediators should enter into a dispute as mediators only when they can maintain a stance of impartiality and neutrality, and are responsible to the system of parties involved in the dispute or decision-making process rather than to any single party or client. This must be discussed in view of the agency context, the role of the worker in the agency, and with all parties involved. When the social worker is no longer in the position of being a mediator, however, she or he is able to work with the elder client in a very different manner, as advocate, counselor, or even guardian; this too needs to be made known at the outset to all parties in mediation. The social work mediator must remain vigilant in trying to avoid any potential conflicts that may result from multiple roles.

Mediators in the field of family disputes regarding elder caregiving need to have expertise in the substantive area of the conflict being addressed. They should be knowledgeable about the physical, mental, and emotional conditions of aging, as well as issues related to power of attorney, durable power of medical attorney, and protection of rights. Cognitive functioning in the elderly is a major consideration in the determination of an elder's capacity to use the mediation process. Likewise, mediators need to have knowledge regarding entitlements, service policies, and consumer rights, and be familiar with the policies and laws regarding custody and guardianship issues and protective service law. In addition, the mediator should be fully cognizant of the long-term care options for elder persons so that alternative solutions may be understood and/or suggested; when a mediator is familiar with the array and availability of services, she or he is better able to facilitate agreements about caregiving plans.

Conflict. While often viewed as negative, conflict is a normative part of human life. It is highly visible at the family, group, organizational, community, and societal levels, and is a necessary part of social change (Coser, 1956). Much of the negative connotation attached to the word *conflict* comes from the association with the "win-lose" outcome assiociated with competitive conflict resolution. Mediation, on the other hand, seeks solutions that are "win-win" in nature, in which each party to the conflict experiences some satisfaction of his or her interests.

Conflict often surfaces around substantive issues, whether or not substance is actually the key element in the conflict. Substantive conflict comes from participants having different data, disparate interpretation of the same data, or disagreement on procedures. Unsuccessful attempts to resolve conflict often create hard feelings around the issues in dispute. The emotional arena of conflict grows out of mistrust created from a history of conflict resolution attempts, or negative relationship components existing before to the conflict, and includes stereotypes, repetitive negative behavior, and poor communication. Out of these emotions, entrenched positions develop. At times conflict grows out of differences in values, which results in disputants' inability to define ways to agree or to disagree. The mediator's role is to move the conflict from the emotional and value arenas to the substantive arena, where negotiation is possible. Once the emotional barriers are broken down, negotiation can occur around data and its meaning.

Controversial Issues in Mediation in the Aging Field

The Elder Participant. An important question both from the perspective of the effectiveness and ethics of mediation is the role of the elder in the mediation process, particularly in family matters. Elders in need of family caregiving may not be equal participants in regard to their ability to negotiate in the decision-making processes regarding their care; rather, they should be viewed as on a continuum of capacity to incapacity to participate in a mediation process. Incapacity in elders may be due to mental, physical, or emotional conditions. Moreover, elders may be reluctant or unwilling to participate in an open discussion of family problems around which there is conflict. The strong socialization in our society against open discussion of conflict, particularly among the aging, mitigates against the acceptance of family mediation on the part of elder members. Elders are likely to feel guilty about being perceived as the cause of family conflict and, as a result, downplay, disregard, or deny its existence. On the other hand, younger elders may view a more open and direct approach to conflict as normative and acceptable. The willingness and capacity of elders to negotiate for themselves must be carefully assessed before the mediation process can begin.

Adhering to the principle of empowerment of elders toward self-determination (Cox & Parsons, 1994), and in the interest of due process, elder family members should be involved in the mediation process to the extent that they are able and willing to participate. A decision must be made about exactly how to involve the elder member in the process. Three approaches are possible. The first and most desirable way is direct involvement whereby the confrontational aspects of the conflict may have to be negotiated informally (Gibson, 1994) so that elders feel more comfortable with the process. If the elder member cannot or will not participate in the mediation, his or her interest may be represented by a support person or advocate, who takes responsibility to ensure that any agreements made meet the needs and interests of the elder as defined by the elder and/or professional assessments of the elder. A third alternative is that the elder member is represented by a formal guardian *ad litem,* who is appointed to serve in the best interests of the elder. Elders often prefer an informal or indirect approach in negotiating differences with family or with service providers with whom they have an ongoing relationship, but the latter may be a preferred option if the conflict is intense and multi-layered.

Not All Conflicts Are Mediatable. All conflicts are not appropriate for mediation. In order to be mediatable, the issues in dispute must be negotiable; that is, there must be more than one way to approach or settle the issues. Second, disputants must be competent to negotiate. Persons with serious and longstanding alcohol or drug addiction are not considered reliable risks for keeping mediated agreements, and persons who are mentally incompetent cannot be expected to negotiate agreements and keep them. Life-threatening situations are not amenable to mediation intervention and must be handled in a more direct and arbitrary manner. Meyers-Chandler (1985), in her comparison of mediation and other social work interventive strategies, proposes that mediation is most successful when there is ongoing personal interaction between disputants, all parties are willing and able to express personal wants and needs, and there is a relatively egalitarian relationship between the disputants. When the latter condition is not present, the mediator can assume a "joint advocacy" approach, working to equalize status differentials between the parties.

The presence of elder abuse may preclude the use of mediation in family conflict. As is the case with domestic violence in general, conflict resolution strategies that deny or minimize an individual's civil rights must be used with extreme caution. In most cases of domestic violence, mediation is not indicated unless the violence has been reported to legal authorities and some form of legal sanction and/or therapeutic involvement has resulted. Elder abuse may be physical, emotional, or financial (Pillemer & Wolf, 1986). When symptoms of physical abuse are present, removal of the elder from the abusive situation must be given primary consideration to prevent harm. Legal sanctions must be used when appropriate, and no mediation or negotiation of abusive situations should substitute for civil or human rights. Emotional abuse is harder to detect and establish, and depending upon its severity and nature, a mediation intervention may be useful to help the two parties establish some ground rules for interacting with one another. In cases of severe emotional abuse where significant power imbalances exist, mediation is not indicated.

The area of elder abuse that may lend itself to mediation is the financial arena. Specific financial agreements may be reached between an elder and his or her family members via mediation, including the primary caregiver, which can halt continued financial abuse. In such cases, power differentials between the parties should be carefully assessed and monitored. If the power imbalance between two parties is too great, or if the fear is expressed that financial abuse will continue, the use of mediation may not be appropriate unless an outside authority is available to monitor and enforce the agreement.

An important factor in whether mediation is an effective strategic choice is the presence of a "shadow of the future." To what extent are the disputants likely to interact with one another in the future? If the shadow of the future is such that family members will continue their relationship, the motivation for negotiating workable agreements is increased. If, on the other hand, there will not necessarily be substantial interaction, the motivation for families to enter into negotiation is reduced.

An important and related concept is Fisher and Ury's (1991) "BATNA," or "Best Alternative to a Negotiated Agreement." If a disputant's BATNA is quite positive, and there are some desirable alternatives to negotiating, the disputant may be less motivated to negotiate, and therefore a poorer candidate for mediation intervention, and vice versa. In most cases of elder mediation, family members' alternatives to some form of negotiation are limited, and they are all likely to experience negative consequences if their conflicts are not resolved. The key question is whether the alternatives to a negotiated solution are as good, better, or worse than a negotiated agreement. While some family members may believe that litigation is a better alternative than a negotiated solution, with most families, the shadow of the future is such that litigation or other more coercive forms of resolution are not desirable in the long run. These two concepts should be considered in case selection and used as leverage to help families stay in mediation when their negotiations reach an impasse.

The Mediation Process

The processes of negotiation and mediation are quite similar. Negotiation is a bargaining relationship between parties who have a perceived or actual conflict of interest, and mediation is an elaboration and extension of that process. Mediation involves the intervention of an acceptable and impartial third party who has no authoritative decision-making power and who helps the parties to negotiate their own mutually acceptable settlement of issues in dispute (Moore, 1986). An assumption in mediation is that if disputants are able to negotiate solutions to problems without the assistance of an outside person, there is no need for a mediator to act as a facilitator of negotiation.

Stages of Mediation

The mediation process in the field of aging begins with an agreement to mediate among the significant parties, and a decision regarding the formality or informality of the process. This is followed by strategic behaviors on the part of the mediator to facilitate that process, which include getting the salient issues in dispute on the table and clarifying the parties' various definitions and perspectives, identifying the interests underlying the parties' stated positions, creating options that will satisfy the interests of the parties, making selections from these options, and reaching agreement.

Agreement to Mediate. All participants in a conflict situation must be contacted and invited to participate in the mediation process. In elder mediation, this would normally involve all family members that are salient individuals in the elder's life. An assumption of mediation is that it is a voluntary process for all participants. The process must be explained to each party, and the role of the mediator clearly outlined. The mediator should contact each person individually and get an agreement from him or her to participate. At the time of the individual contact, the mediator may ask the family member about his or her interests and concerns in order to guage the level of commonality among the parties regarding issues in dispute and interests. Even though a disputant may tell his or her side of the story to the mediator before the first mediation session, each disputant is asked to repeat that information during the first session. At the first session, the mediator again explains his or her role as an impartial third party and lays the ground rules for the negotiation to follow.

A critical issue during the initial phase of the mediation process is the need to assess the capacity of the elder to participate in the negotiation. There may not be agreement among family members or institutional staff in this regard; although an elder may have the mental and emotional capacity to negotiate for him- or herself, there may be a denial of this capacity by other parties in the dispute and therefore a tendency to discount the elder's stated needs and interests. If an elder is going to participate in the negotiation, the other parties must accept and validate that participation even though some participants may disagree with the positions taken by the elder. The mediator needs to clearly establish that the elder has the capacity to negotiate and make good decisions for him or herself. A decision must then be reached regarding the formality or informality of the negotiation to follow. As mentioned, some elders may be uncomfortable with the traditional approach to mediation, with all parties to the dispute in the same room, taking turns speaking, and openly disagreeing. It may be necessary for the mediator to meet with the parties individually in order to get the negotiation started and the air cleared before a more formal and open approach is used. Another possibility is that elders may need to be prepared for negotiation through discussion, role play, or by viewing videotapes on the mediation process.

Separate the People from the Problem. The next step in the mediation process is to get problems clearly defined and stated. Conflict around any significant issue usually carries with it a great deal of emotion. Often the other party is identified as the "problem," not the issue around which there is conflict. The perception of the "person as the problem" mitigates against effective negotiation.

Ted, ninety years old, was very independent, living alone in his own home. His son, John, was concerned because he saw his father leaving the stove on, forgetting what he was doing, and unable to keep his living conditions sanitary. John decided that Ted needed a live-in housekeeper. Ted did not like this and found fault with each successive housekeeper, making life so difficult for each that they finally quit. The first step in mediation between John and Ted was to separate the people from the problem. Ted needed to understand that his reactions to the housekeepers, or the people, were actually his form of resistance to the problem, decreasing independence. His son, John, needed to recognize that his father's behavior was reflecting a fear about losing his autonomy and not simply the result of ill-temper and obstinance. The mediator facilitated this mutual recognition by asking each participant to describe the problem and his or her feelings about it separately. Time was allowed for each participant to let off steam and express his emotions around the issue. The mediator used active listening skills to reflect and validate each person's perceptions and feelings. Each was encouraged to use "I-statements," and listen to the other's concerns and recognize them as legitimate. The mediator validated each participant's experience, while listening for common interests between them. An agenda for work was established from the concerns and issues presented. Finally, the mediator maintained control of the process so that the two parties were able to perceive the situation as safe for their participation.

A unique aspect of this stage of elder mediation is the strong emotions most people have about aging and the elderly. For children of the elderly, the recognition that their parent is losing strength, health, and autonomy may be very difficult, and can result in feelings of anger, guilt, loss, and grief. Elders experience a loss of autonomy, which may elicit feelings of resentment and fear. Emotions run very high in family disputes regarding elders, and separating the emotions from the problems to be resolved is a very delicate process.

Focus on Interests Instead of Positions. Positions are predetermined solutions to a problem from the participant's own perspective; interests are common human needs underlying positions. A position of, "My mother will not, under any circumstances, go to a nursing home," may reflect an underlying interest of, "I need to feel that my mother is getting the best treatment or care available," or, "I need not to feel guilty about placing my mother in a nursing home." The key to effective negotiation is to find common interests among the parties, which are basically common human needs such as security, economic well-being, belonging, recognition, and control over one's life. Interests are the "silent movers" behind conflicts. The mediator identifies the interests behind the positions as each participant presents his or her views on the issues in dispute. Optimally, some of the interests behind disparate positions will be held in common and will serve as the basis of future agreements. Some techniques for identifying participants' interests when not apparent include asking why participants hold the positions they do, why their position is important to them, what the impact of their position is on the other party, and what they are going to need from the mediation in order to be satisfied with it. If the adult children of an elder family member can agree that, behind their various individual positions, their common interest is the best care for the elder member that the family can afford, the mediation process is well on its way to finding mutually agreed-upon solutions. Often, commonality in interests is hidden behind emotional barriers, and the mediator's task is to break down those constraints. In elder mediation, family members usually share the interest of the well-being of the elder, regardless of divergent views regarding how to provide for that well-being, and this common interest can be used as the foundation for the negotiation to follow.

Create Options That Satisfy the Interests of the Participants. Once common interests are identified, many options that provide mutual satisfaction can be generated and explored as participants come to see that there is more than one way of resolving their impasse. The technique of brainstorming may be used to generate options. If the social worker has expertise in the substantive area of aging, he or she may think of alternatives and resources not considered by family members.

A seniors housing facility had a mandatory food program that violated the nutritional requirements of a resident. The facility would not waive the contract to permit the resident to remove herself from the food program, even with a doctor's note explaining her dietary needs. The core interests of the two parties were financial requisites for the seniors' facility and proper diet for the elder. This dispute became resolvable when the following options were generated: the facility could decide to meet the dietary requirements of the elder, contract the meals of the elder out to a third party, waive the policy in this case, find special resources to cover the costs of the special diet, or secure help from a nutritional expert to create different options for meeting the elder's dietary needs.

The generation of as many options as possible creates many possibilities for problem resolution. Knowledge of resources for the elderly is critical to the process of option production; a mediator who is fully aware of available resources is a better facilitator of option generation for mutual gain.

Select Criteria for Choosing Alternatives. Finally, each of the alternatives must be evaluated and one or more options selected. The mediator focuses the disputants on the objective standards that will guide them in option selection. In elder care mediation, those standards are likely to be based on the principles of economic feasibility or shared economic responsibility, autonomy of the elder, and quality of care. Once objective standards or criteria for judging alternative solutions has been agreed upon, the mediator can help the disputants choose from the range of alternatives they have generated. When solutions are chosen, they are written down and copies distributed to all participants for further clarity and agreement. Fisher and Ury (1991) suggest that effective negotiation produces an agreement that satisfies the interests of all the participants. Choosing options based on objective criteria is critical to such an outcome. Objective criteria on which to evaluate potential solutions in an elder care dispute might include affordability of the solution, compatibility with medical opinion regarding the elder's condition, and agreement from the elder. These criteria are decided upon before option selection, and they guide the process of decision making.

In a community conflict, Mrs. L., over ninety years old, with severe locomotion disability, had a bus stop a few feet from her house. People waiting for the bus were often noisy and caused considerable damage to her property. She was fearful and unable to clean up the damage. She had complained to the bus company and called the police on a number of occasions, with no positive results. The mediator was able to talk to the bus company consumer representative and to provide Mrs. L. the opportunity to talk directly with the representative in her home. In selecting criteria for choosing alternatives, it was determined that Mrs. L.'s ultimate need was that she feel comfortable and safe in her own home. The two criteria for assessing options for resolving the dispute between Mrs. L. and the bus company were that Mrs. L. felt comfortable and safe in her home and that the bus company would not have to interrupt its projected routes and connections. The bus company agreed to move the bus stop to the other end of the block to correct the problem.

Through these stages, the mediator guides the participants toward decision making in regard to the issues in dispute. Getting an agreement to "come to the table," in whatever form that may take, is the first step. After the parties to and the format of the mediation have been established, the next stage involves separating the people from the problem, and the emotional aspects from the resolvable problems. This is particularly challenging in disputes involving elders, given the strong emotions associated with aging and attendant difficulties. Finding mutual interests is the next task, followed by generation of options for mutual gain. Expertise in the field of aging can greatly facilitate this process. Choosing criteria for selecting options is a difficult but necessary step toward selecting options for mutual agreement.

Alternatives to Mediation in the Field of Aging

As noted above, late life is associated with loss of independence and autonomy. Elders increasingly find themselves in conflicts regarding their rights, which are often overlooked by family, social service organizations, and the legal system. The need for elder care and the necessity of preserving elder rights are often in conflict. Mediation provides an opportunity for these two aspects of aging to achieve some measure of reconciliation.

Not all elder disputes, however, are appropriate for mediation and other options must be considered in these cases. One such alternative is a less formal application of the skills and knowledge needed for conflict resolution by service providers who interact with elders and their families. As suggested by Cox and Parsons (1992), elderly individuals, particularly women, often have been socialized to avoid conflict. Service providers can use conflict resolution strategies such as clarity of communication, separating the people from the problem, and brainstorming outside the structure of a formal mediation process to assist elderly clients to maintain their autonomy and assert their personal rights. Experience with such strategies may help elders to participate in more formal mediation efforts when they become necessary.

An option to mediation of elder conflicts is to educate and train elders to negotiate for themselves. By learning specific negotiation strategies, elders may be able to communicate, negotiate and clarify their own options and rights within a family or institutional dispute. One such effort, initiated by Cox and Parsons (1992), trained elders in residential facilities in personal communication skills, resulting in elders' becoming more assertive and able to identify their needs to family members and service providers.

The absence of mediation may result in an "efficient" solution that generally leaves the elder's rights in jeopardy. Elders may use legal means to obtain their rights, thereby turning the decision making over to a third party who imposes a formal settlement. Families may go to court for what they see as a "quick" solution, which often exacerbates conflict, splits the family apart, and renders it ineffective as a support system for the elder. The costs of such a process are high, both for the elders and their families. A less adversarial option than litigation is arbitration, but this method also has the potential of damaging future relationships. In nursing homes and residential facilities, an elder advocate may stand in the place of an elder in pursuit of elder rights.

Mediation can provide an intermediary mechanism to leverage elders' rights without the formal engagement of the court system. Social workers and allied professionals are in a unique position to offer this service while not necessarily compromising the other services they can provide elder popultions, within the context of multiple roles.

References

American Association of Retired Persons. 1995. *A Profile of Older Americans.* Washington, DC: AARP.
Berkman, L. F. 1983. The Assessment of Social Networks and Social Support in the Elderly. *Journal of the American Geriatrics Society* 31: 743–49.

Blake, R., & J. Mouton. 1984. *Solving Costly Organizational Conflicts*. San Francisco: Jossey-Bass.

Brody, E. M. 1983a. Women in the Middle and Family Help to Older People. *Gerontologist* 21: 471–80.

———. 1983b. Women's Changing Roles and Help to Elderly Parents: Attitudes of Three Generations of Women. *Journal of Gerontology* 38: 597–607.

Circirelli, V. G. 1986. The Helping Relationship and family neglect in later life. In K. Pillemer & R. Wolf, eds., *Elder Abuse: Conflict in the Family*. Dover, MA: Auburn House.

Connaway, R. S., & M. E. Gentry. 1988. *Social Work Practice*. Englewood Cliffs, NJ: Prentice-Hall.

Coser, L. 1956. *The Function of Social Conflict*. New York: Free Press.

Cox, E. O., & R. J. Parsons. 1992. Senior-to-Senior Mediation Service Project. *The Gerontologist* 32(3): 420–22.

———. 1994. *Empowerment-Oriented Social Work Practice with the Elderly*. Pacific Grove, CA: Brooks/Cole.

Fisher, R., & W. Ury. 1991. *Getting to Yes: Negotiating Agreement without Giving in*. New York: Penguin.

Gibson, J. M. 1994. Mediation for Ethics Committees: A Promising Process. *Generations* 18(4): 58–60.

Hall, B. 1990. Families of the Hospitalized Elderly: Untapped Resource. *Canadian Journal of Community Mental Health* 9(1): 179–89.

Hearn, G. 1970. Social Work as Boundary Work. Paper presented at the Third Annual Institute on Services to Families and Children, School of Social Work, University of Iowa, April.

Kahana, J. S. 1994. Reevaluating the Nursing Home Ombudsman's Role with a view toward Expanding the Concept of Dispute Resolution. *Journal of Dispute Resolution* (2): 217–33.

Kestner, P., & E. F. Wood. 1988. *Mediation: The Coming of Age: A Mediator's Guide in Servicing the Elderly*. Washington, DC: American Bar Association Standing Committee on Dispute Resolution and Commission on Legal Problems of the Elderly for the National Institute for Dispute Resolution.

Knight, B.G. 1985. The Decision to Institutionalize. *Generations* 10: 42–44.

Levande, D. I., S. W. Bowden, & J. Mollema. 1987. Home Health Services for Dependent Elders: The Social Work Dimension. *Journal of Gerontological Social Work* 11 (3/4): 15–17.

Meyers-Chandler, S. 1985. Mediation: Conjoint Problem Solving. *Social Work* 30: 347–49.

Moore, C. 1986. *The Mediation Process*. San Francisco: Jossey-Bass.

Ory, M. G. 1985. The Burden of Care: A Familial Perspective. *Generations* 10: 14–18.

Parsons, R. J., J. D. Jorgensen, & S. H. Hernandez. 1994. *The Integration of Social Work Practice*. Pacific Grove, CA: Brooks/Cole.

Pillemer, K. A. & R. S. Wolf. 1986. *Elder Abuse: Conflict in the Family*. Dover, MA: Auburn House.

Schwartz, W. 1961. Between Client and System: The Mediating function. In W. Roberts & H. Northern, eds., *Theories of Social Work with Groups*. New York: Columbia University Press.

U.S. Bureau of the Census. 1995. *Demographic and Socioeconomic Aspects of Aging in the United States.* Current Population Reports, Series P-23, #138, pp. 1–16. Washington, DC: U.S. Government Printing Office.

Walton, R. E. 1969. Two Strategies of Social Change and Their Dilemmas. In R. Kramer & H. Specht, eds., *Readings in Community Organization Practice.* Englewood Cliffs, NJ: Prentice-Hall.

Wood, E. & N. Karp. 1994. Mediation: Reframing Care Conflicts in Nursing Homes. *Generations* 18 (4): 54–57.

10

HEALTH CARE

Caregiving Mediation in Health Care Settings

by Edward Kruk, Freda Betz Martin, and Jennifer O'Callaghan

Health care institutions and providers have a great deal of implicit power in North American society, and it is often difficult for patients and their families to make themselves heard (Dubler & Marcus, 1994). Hospitals in particular can be intimidating institutions where the tendency is toward the depersonalization of patients and erosion of their confidence in decision making.

The principal role of hospital social workers is to address the psychosocial aspects of health care, the impact of illness and disease on patients and their families, and the implications for their living arrangements and need for community resources. Medical social workers also deal with a wide range of disputes as the arena of health care is replete with conflict. These include disputes between hospital staff members, hospital staff and patients, patients and family members, hospital staff and family members, and others. Organizational complexity as defined by the number of people potentially involved in disputes in health care settings is only one of the characteristics of health care conflict that distinguish it from conflict in other settings; Dubler and Marcus (1994) also cite factors of ambiguity, forced choice, high stakes, competition and hierarchy, stress and pressures, and the context of change as dispute characteristics unique to this field of practice.

Most often the disputes in health care settings relate to patient caregiving decisions that need to be made, including discharge planning and bioethical disagreements. The former have been traditionally regarded as a central component of medical social work practice; the latter are rapidly expanding as medical technology is increasingly able to sustain human organ function in the absence of an integrated and aware personality, and as medical care becomes more fragmented and complex (Dubler & Marcus, 1994). Mediation in health care settings thus focuses not on conflict resolution per se but on assisting the parties in their care planning, decision making, and searching for the best possible outcome.

Mediation is a process of dispute resolution ideally suited to the arena of caregiving decision making in health care settings. Mediation provides patients, their families, and hospital staff with a process to help them sort through medical facts and care choices available in searching for solutions. Mediation thus promotes good patient care by providing a decision-making structure that assists the parties to understand relevant medical, social, psychological, legal, and ethical issues in searching for creative solutions that meet the interests of all concerned.

The medical social worker has a unique understanding of the people, professions, roles, and relationships of those who work in the health care setting; is the primary liaison with the patient's support network, including family and community support systems; and in a period of swift policy and social changes, the medical social worker has access to pertinent health care policy and legislation, as well as the ethical dimensions of a case, crucial to providing the parties with required knowledge for decision making. The social worker is thus in a unique position to formally or informally assume the role of mediator in caregiving decision making in health care settings.

Mediation as a method of caregiving decision making has been most frequently applied to the task of discharge planning, traditionally regarded as a core element of the role of the medical social worker. Caregiving decisions in health care settings have most often involved elder patients, their families, and staff, and the model described in this chapter has been mainly used in that context. It can, however, be applied to all patients who require caregiving, including younger persons with chronic conditions or debilitating illness.

Theory, Debates, and Trends

Each day more families face the dilemma of what to do with a relative who is unable to cope with independent living and will require ongoing care, or when critical medical decisions have to be made. Most often this dilemma is played out in the hospital after the family member has suffered some medical emergency, is in failing health, or is otherwise unable to continue to manage independent living. For the medical social worker, this often means becoming involved in a difficult and emotionally laden care-planning process. Often this scenario includes a patient who fears eventual placement in a long-term care facility and who wishes to continue living at home; a family that is overburdened with the tasks required to keep the relative safe and healthy at home, and feeling guilty that they are increasingly unable to manage to meet their relative's need to be safe and to remain in their own home; and a caregiving planner, usually a social worker charged with the task of discharge planning. The social worker is responsible for assessing the patient's abilities, disabilities, home situation, financial situation, current living situation, and wishes and plans for receiving ongoing care; the caregiver's abilities, coping mechanisms, current emotional and physical condition, financial situation, support network, and wishes and plans for providing, or not providing, ongoing care; and the community resources available to assist the patient and the caregiver to achieve their individual and combined requirements and goals. In most cases the patient and family do not agree on the type of care that will be required or the manner in which it will be delivered.

The current model of practice for social workers involved in discharge planning in hospitals is problem solving and advocacy for the patient's rights and wishes. This model is often inadequate in addressing the need for both patient and family to be fully heard by the other, the desire for a harmonious ongoing relationship after discharge, and the need for a combined effort to overcome challenges. It also fails to address the highly emotional nature of the dilemma facing both patient and family.

Though not always labeled as such, medical social workers have also acted informally as mediators in disputes arising from health crises. Although mediation is well suited to this specific area of medical social work practice, there is little recognition in the health care literature of the need for formal mediation practice in this field. Family disputes between patients and their caregivers must meet a number of essential criteria for the use of mediation: there is not a marked imbalance of power between them, there are clear issues in dispute, the parties will have an ongoing relationship, there is commonality of interests, and nonadversarial resolution is desired by the parties (Moore, 1986). The use of a formal caregiving mediation model, where discharge planning includes a dispute between a patient who is not coping with independent living and his or her family, which is currently providing partial or complete ongoing care, would thus serve to enhance the overall provision of social work services in health care settings.

The Parties

Most often, the parties to caregiving mediation in health care settings are elderly patients and various family members. The people most likely to provide care to the frail elderly are close family members such as spouses and adult daughters. In the absence of those close family members, the responsibility devolves to, in order of frequency, daughters-in-law, sons, sons-in-law, other relatives, neighbors, and friends (Toseland & Rossiter, 1994). Stone, Cafferata, and Sangl (1987) discovered the following about the elderly who receive assistance from family members: their average age is seventy-eight years; 28 percent are over eighty-five years of age; 60 percent are female; 51.3 percent are married; 41.3 percent are widowed; 11 percent live alone; and 89 percent live with caregivers providing either primary or secondary care. Caregivers are primarily female; one-third are over sixty-five years of age; 29 percent are wives; 23 percent are adult daughters; they often suffer from their own chronic health problems; and they are often also responsible for young or teenaged children.

The projected increase in the number of elderly people over the next several decades necessitates an increased role for social work in meeting the demands of this population. The increasing numbers of frail elderly will also place a heightened demand on caregivers. A long-term commitment to elder caregiving can be extremely taxing. In addition, the relationship between the caregiver and the frail elderly person does not remain static; changes and uncertainty in regard to the health status of the elderly person continually place additional demands on the caregiver. The social worker must thus be sensitive to the shifting dynamics of the elder-caregiver relationship (Toseland & Rossiter, 1994).

Families seeking help from health care professionals are unlikely to specifically request mediation. In the hospital, most people approach or are referred to the social worker at a time of crisis. An acute illness or injury has put the elderly family member in the hospital and suddenly the caregiving arrangement that had been in place is no longer feasible. This change in care needs is rarely anticipated. While families are sometimes successful in negotiating new discharge plans on their own, or in consultation with medical staff, often these negotiations break down, or the stress of the health crisis renders their normal patterns of communication ineffective. For the sake of "keeping the peace," anger and frustration have often been suppressed and may surface during a health care crisis, resulting in marked family friction, which seriously impedes successful negotiation. Mediation can provide a forum that allows family members to say honestly what they want regarding caregiving rather than leaving such a painful subject to default and risking hard feelings (Lemmon, 1985).

The Mediator

Given the fact that the medical social worker is an employee of the health care institution, he or she may be initially seen by patients and their families as representing the interests of the institution, thereby compromising the neutrality deemed essential to the mediation endeavor. Yet caregiving mediation in health care settings demands a knowledge of the administrative and political workings of the particular institution, as well as relevant medical and legal knowledge, and ready access to health care staff within the institution. The mediator should have sufficient knowledge and background in health care to effectively mediate: to clarify the core issues in the dispute, identify options that the parties may have overlooked, and help the parties evaluate those options. In the process of resolving disputes within health care settings, formal neutrality must thus be balanced against education, knowledge, and access (Dubler & Marcus, 1994).

In the process of resolving caregiving disputes, social workers must be seen as sufficiently independent to qualify as neutrals in dispute resolution. This is a challenging yet fundamental task and involves careful interpretation and negotiation of the social worker's mediation role, as distinct from other roles that may be assumed within the health care setting. Social workers who mediate caregiving disputes must be particularly cautious in regard to the potential dilemmas resulting from the taking on of dual roles with their clients; the mediation role must be seen by all parties as compatible with their other roles within the institution.

Core Issues in Caregiving Mediation

Power Imbalances. It is essential in caregiving mediation to explore the potential for power imbalances in the patient-caregiver relationship. This is particularly salient with elder patients, as elder abuse is an increasingly recognized phenomenon and a testimony to heightened levels of caregiver burden. Though imbalances of power may not be obvious during mediation, the potential for abuse may restrict options for living arrangements after discharge. Premediation meetings with both parties are important for screening in regard to abuse concerns, as well as potential power imbalances related to money and property. In the case where abuse or power imbalance exists, the social worker must assist the patient to make arrangements according to his or her wishes and in his or her best interests.

In addition, the mediator has obligations that arise from the intimidating nature of the health care setting and the imbalance of power and knowledge between patients, their families, and medical staff. Without compromising neutrality, the mediator must use caucusing and other means to empower those patients and their families in conflict with the health care setting to adequately represent their interests in the mediation if a principled resolution is going to emerge from the negotiation.

Mediator Neutrality. It is essential in caregiving mediation that the mediator be recognized by the parties as neutral, both in regard to the patient-family relationship and the patient/family/health care staff relationship. In regard to the patient-family relationship, if the social worker has acted in an advocacy capacity on the patient's behalf in regard to caregiving issues, he or she is unlikely to be regarded as possessing sufficient neutrality to impartially resolve caregiving disputes. The same dilemma arises when he or she is seen by the patient or family to represent the institution's interests in the dispute. The hospital or health care institution's position is often regarded by the patient and family as requiring an expedient discharge of the patient with little regard for the patient's or family's interests.

In the process of generating options in caregiving mediation, it is often necessary for the mediator to take on an educative role as families are usually unaware of the resources available to them. In doing so, it is important to remain as neutral as possible in regard to desirable outcomes and to refrain from emphasizing one option over another. Families know their own needs best; it is important to trust that providing a forum to discuss their conflict will enable the family to find their own resolution.

Therapeutic Mediation Approach. A therapeutic, family systems orientation is an intrinsic part of social work practice in health care settings. As such, careful attention should paid to the emotional issues underlying family conflicts and caregiving decision making. The goal of mediation is thus not restricted to settling the issues in dispute, but also to enhancing understanding and restoring harmony between the parties, and establishing a healthy framework for their continued relationship. The therapeutic model of mediation is best suited to the work involved with health care patients and their caregivers. The primary focuses of therapeutic mediation are on positive family relationships and the underlying emotional issues that may be causing the parties to cling to their positions and remain unable or unwilling to understand the other's needs and interests. The role of the mediator following this model is to facilitate negotiation, educate the parties regarding each other's circumstances and interests, teach the process of negotiation as a portable skill for future use, and restructure relationships so that they may develop beyond the agreement reached in mediation. Within this model, the mediator can help parties to develop or enhance communication and problem-solving skills that will result in a durable agreement and a functional and ongoing relationship.

For the patient who requires ongoing care, and for his or her family who is providing care, this model respects and assists relationships that may be stressed as a result of changing circumstances, expectations, and roles. The therapeutic model also emphasizes premediation assessment toward understanding the complexities and the subtleties of family relationships in flux, which may be a contributing factor to ongoing disputes.

The Mediation Process

Moore (1986, p. 14) defines mediation as, "the intervention into a dispute or negotiation by an acceptable, impartial, and neutral third party who has no authoritative decision-making power to assist disputing parties in voluntarily reaching their own mutually acceptable settlement of issues in dispute." Medical social workers, by the nature of their learned skills, are able to intervene or enter into an ongoing system of relationships, to come between or among persons for the purpose of helping them, and to assist them to express their needs and goals. At the same time, they do not have the authority to impose a particular type of resolution where caregiving or discharge planning is concerned; this would be seen to contravene the principle of client self-determination. There is a high degree of compatibility between medical social work practice and health care mediation in relation to values, goals, roles, and tasks; the process of mediation closely parallels the stages of generalist social work practice.

Criteria for Mediation: The Parties

A number of criteria must be met for the parties to be considered to be good candidates for mediation. Specifically, the parties must be:

1. *Interdependent and able to rely on the cooperation of one another in order to meet their goals or satisfy their interests.* Health care patients and their caregivers are usually highly interdependent and the emotional and physical well-being of each party relies on the cooperative actions and decision-making abilities of the other.
2. *Able to influence one another and to undertake or prevent actions that can either harm or reward.* For patients and their family members, the other's actions have a direct and significant effect on their own health and well-being. This reciprocal influence has been developed over the course of their life together. Pronounced power imbalances, however, may warrant against the use of mediation.
3. *Pressured by deadlines and time constraints and share an impetus for early settlement.* A resolution in the hospital is critical, as the care plan needs to be completed by the time the physician determines that the patient is medically stable and fit for discharge. The caregiver often sees discharge as an opportunity to introduce significant changes or modifications to the care plan for the patient. For these reasons, both parties are anxious to reach a resolution before discharge.
4. *Aware that alternative procedures and outcomes to a negotiated settlement are not as viable or desirable as a plan that they negotiate themselves.* Although caregiving decisions rarely end up being decided in a court of law, each party has the ultimate power to make independent and binding decisions. The patient has the power (if deemed mentally competent) to refuse any and all care provided by the community, including nursing care at home or institutional care. The family member has the power to refuse to provide any type of care.
5. *Able to identify other concerned parties and involve them in the problem-solving process.* The primary parties to caregiving mediation are

normally the patient and the patient's caregiver(s). Health care staff, however, may also be one of the parties in the mediation, as can other family members not directly involved in caregiving.

6. *Able to identify and agree on the issues in dispute.* In most cases, both the patient and caregiver are able to identify and agree on the issues in dispute, which usually have to do with where, when, and what type of care will be provided, and by whom.

7. *In a situation in which the interests of the parties are not entirely incompatible.* Often, some combination of home and facility care is agreeable to both parties, or in the event of a patient requiring permanent institutional care, some arrangement of home visits or visits by the family to the facility will satisfy both parties.

Using the criteria above, mediation to resolve the conflicts that arise in hospital and other health care settings involving caregivers and their relatives may be the option of choice in most situations. It is also a useful alternative in disputes that arise between patients and health care staff, or between family members and staff. In regard to the latter, the social worker in the mediation role needs to be able to clearly establish him or herself as a neutral facilitator and not aligned, as an employee of the health care facility, with health care staff.

Roles and Functions of the Mediator

As mentioned, the roles and the functions of the mediator are highly compatible with those of the hospital social worker. Specifically, the health care-based social work mediator is:

1. *The opener of communications channels.* This is a primary function of the medical social worker, who must often uncover the underlying interests and issues that contribute to an individual's social and medical circumstances.

2. *The legitimizer who helps all parties recognize the right of others to be involved in negotiations.* Often, in caregiver-patient disagreements, the goal of the social worker is to attempt to have the patient understand the caregiver's right to participate in the decision making regarding the patient's ongoing care, and to have the caregiver understand the rights of the patient to participate in the determination of the type of care he or she will receive.

3. *The process facilitator who provides procedure and chairs negotiations.* Medical social workers are often called upon to chair family conferences and multidisciplinary meetings and facilitate internal process changes.

4. *The trainer who educates in the negotiation process.* When working with families, medical social workers must often provide a structure and

process for communication when members are in disagreement or are inappropriately confronting one another.

5. *The resource expander who links the parties to outside experts and resources.* This is a primary function of the medical social worker who must coordinate community resources for patients and their families.

6. *The problem explorer.* A critical function of the medical social worker is to define the factors impeding the patient's return home and help the patient to overcome these obstacles.

7. *The agent of reason.* Medical social workers often have to work closely with patients to assist them to come to terms with their limitations or decreased functioning. While in the protective hospital environment, patients are not always realistic about their ability to cope with their acute or chronic illness at home. In the hospital, their nutritional intake significantly improves, they may receive regular physiotherapy, and they have the benefit and assurance of twenty-four-hour nursing care. Generally, they feel stronger and healthier than they did before admission and often develop false confidence that they will be able to function without formal care arrangements after discharge.

8. *The scapegoat who may take some of the blame for an unpopular decision.* Medical social workers must often suggest a manageable compromise between what a patient requires and what a caregiver is or is not willing to provide, or between what a patient requires and what resources a patient is willing to accept. In many cases, the social worker is able to absorb some of the responsibility for helping to make difficult decisions as it is his or her mandate to develop and implement a discharge plan.

9. *The leader who takes the initiative to move the negotiation forward.* One of the primary functions of the hospital social worker is to initiate discussions that will result in an appropriate discharge plan for patients so that they may return to the community.

The goals of the social worker in a health care setting are to combine family and community services and resources in a way that meets both the patient's and family's needs, and to enhance the safety, security, health, and social aspects of the patient's life. The objective of mediation in caregiving decision making is to have the patient and family agree on the type, amount, and delivery of services and resources required to meet each of their needs.

Stages of Caregiving Mediation

The current model of practice used in health care settings in care or discharge planning has not been entirely effective in dealing with the fluctuating roles and functions of the patient and caregiver, or with the tensions this produces. Moreover, the medical setting provides limited opportunity for long-term or ongoing therapy; often, the hospital social worker has only a few days in which to make significant changes toward resolving complex and important issues.

The following model of caregiving mediation addresses these limitations in a manner that enhances the role of the social worker without compromising the goals of mediation.

Premediation Phase.

1. *Collecting background information:*
   a. The patient is screened at admission for potential problems and caregiving issues around which there may be conflict, and a referral is made to the care planner for caregiving mediation.
   b. Before meeting with the parties, the care planner reviews the medical chart and consults with the health care interdisciplinary team. The care planner may convene a meeting with all involved medical staff to establish the medical facts, including the patient's medical history, present condition and prognosis, and implications for care planning.

2. *Initial assessment:*
   a. The initial assessment of the patient's and the caregiver's current medical, social, family, and home circumstances assists the care planner in beginning to develop strategies for linking the family to outside resources and services, and develop options that the parties may later consider. The initial assessment is best done with the parties separately in order to better understand their positions and interests.
   b. The care planner ascertains who the parties to the mediation will be.

Beginning Phase.

1. *Clarifying the role of the mediator:*
   a. The care planner's position in the hospital should be openly discussed. It is explained that the care planner's mandate in working with the parties as a mediator is to provide the parties and the health care setting with a care plan that addresses the needs of the patient and caregiver in a timely fashion.
   b. It is important to assure the parties that the decision they reach will be independent of hospital influence and that the care planner-mediator's role is to aid the parties in developing and implementing the plan.

2. *Assessing the negotiation abilities of the parties:*
   a. The mediator determines whether or not the patient is capable of making decisions.

b. The mediator assesses whether the parties are emotionally ready, psychologically able, and agreeable to participation in the mediation process.

c. Power imbalances are also assessed and addressed at this time.

3. *Building trust with both parties:*
   a. Before negotiation each party needs to be provided the opportunity to tell his or her story and express her or his feelings. Often, it is the caregiver who has been allowed a voice and the patient may feel silenced. In order to continue to build trust and establish rapport, each party must feel understood and legitimated.
   b. At this point it may be determined that one or both parties may require ongoing support or grief counseling following mediation.
   c. Patients may believe that family members have the power to unilaterally decide that they will be "put away" into a long-term care facility. The patient must be assured that he or she will not, and cannot, be accepted into any care facility without verbal and written consent.
   d. It is important to acknowledge the family member's caregiving struggles and recognize burnout symptoms. In addition, it is vital for the caregiver to understand that decisions cannot unilaterally be made on the patient's behalf, and that he or she is not required or expected by the acute or long-term care system to continue to provide ongoing care for the patient.
   e. A statement regarding the neutrality of the mediator should be made to assure both parties that all caregiving options will be examined and all positions heard.

4. *Selecting a strategy to guide mediation:*
   a. In order to best structure the mediation process, it is important for the mediator to be aware of the communication style of each party and the issues that may impede effective communication. Affected by stress or guilt, the caregiver may not adequately hear the concerns of the patient. Frustrated by lack of acknowledgment, the patient may repress anger, become uncommunicative, or express frustration in ways such as aggressive behavior. Communication patterns will vary widely. Being familiar with the temperament of the parties is important in guiding the mediation process.

5. *Designing a plan for mediation:*
   a. The social worker provides a complete explanation of the mediation process.
   b. The framework for mediation is set, including establishing a time to meet, who will attend, and the issues to be discussed.

Middle Phase.

1. *Defining the issues:*
   a. At this time, issues for negotiation must be agreed upon as well as the order in which they will be handled.
   b. In care planning, these issues will essentially be where the patient will live and who will provide care.

2. *Identifying interests:*
   a. Often a patient's complete refusal to consider facility placement has to do with a feeling of lost autonomy in all areas of life or a fear that the family will abandon the patient once they are not directly responsible for his or her ongoing care. Also, the patient may equate institutional life with substandard living, restraints, and overmedication. These fears are often manifested as rejection of facility care.
   b. For the caregiver, the unmet demands of the patient's care often result in guilt and a feeling of failure that can manifest itself as anger toward the patient. An honest discussion of what is and is not possible for one person to accomplish with respect to caregiving relieves the caregiver of guilt and accompanying anger. It may also serve to reduce the patient's demands that all care be provided by the primary caregiver.
   c. It is important to respect the emotional content of the issues raised in mediation and to assist each party to deal with his or her discomfort. Emphasizing shared commitment and ongoing relationships rather than conflict sets the tone for emotional expression that is productive to the process.
   d. Introducing the parties to or reminding them of the various home support services available often reduces tension and directs the attention of the parties to a middle ground.

3. *Generating options for care:*
   a. Once positions are softened, the exploration of community services and resources can begin in earnest. Various caregiving possibilities, including facility care, home care, homemakers, meal preparation services, nursing assistance at home, home visits, emergency notification systems, shopping services, volunteer visitor/driver/ shopper services, physiotherapy compliance, financial constraints, respite care, day care, medication compliance, and bathing assists, are generated.
   b. This is also a critical time for the mediator to intervene with issues of safety, health, and social aspects of the patient's and the caregiver's

lives. These will then become components of the resource/service allocation on which they are deciding.

4. *Exploring resources independently:*
   a. "Homework" for each party may include tours of long-term care facilities, an assessment of home support needed, a review of resources available for support and calls to independent home support agencies.

Ending Phase.

1. *Cost/benefit analysis of proposed options:*
   a. The mediator helps the parties identify options that are safe, viable, and desirable for both the patient and the caregiver.

2. *Final bargaining:*
   a. The agreement is struck by way of mutual agreement or compromise and a final review and summary of the agreement is presented so that each party fully understands the content and the arrangements involved.

3. *Achieving formal settlement:*
   a. Formalizing the agreement consists of processing various long-term care forms required by the health care setting and coordinating any type of ongoing care provided by the community.
   b. As an option, for visiting schedules and temporary care provided by the community or family on a private basis, a document may be prepared by the mediator that outlines this part of the agreement, which will accompany the long-term care agreement forms.
   c. The mediator should review the process taken to reach agreement and commend the parties for their commitment to the process and their success. They have demonstrated that they have the skills to renegotiate an agreement should circumstances change. It is important to advise the parties that changes, particularly to the patient's health, should be anticipated.
   d. In closing, reminding the parties of their common interests and goals and their ability to negotiate effectively with each other can set the tone for compliance with the mediated agreement, and provide an incentive to renegotiate the agreement should their circumstances change.

Postmediation Phase.

1. *Short-term follow-up:*
   a. The patient may remain in hospital pending discharge to a long-term care facility, or awaiting the arrangement of home support service.

2. *Long-term follow-up: Offering support to the patient and caregiver:*
   a. Decision making regarding care arrangements can have quite a profound impact on both parties. A unique feature of the mediator's role in this setting is that he or she will remain in contact with the patient and family through the duration of the patient's hospital stay.
   b. Much of the support the parties receive at this time is in anticipation of significant changes in living arrangements and the effect these changes will have on their relationship.
   c. In the postmediation phase, the care planner-mediator maintains the integrity of the professional-client relationship, demonstrates a commitment to the process, and shows respect for the family's choice.

This model has been described as it is employed in hospital settings. In fact, it is the crisis invoked by acute illness, injury, or deteriorating chronic condition causing hospitalization that most frequently provides the impetus for mediation. However, its application is not restricted to use in hospital discharge planning. It is equally effective if not more advantageous in mediating care agreements between individuals and their caregivers while the person requiring care is still at home. Mediation of such a relationship before a health crisis would prevent the escalation of conflict in the event of hospitalization. In the community, the role of the mediator could be filled by a community case manager or by a private practitioner familiar with supportive resources and sensitive to the issues involved in a caregiving relationship.

This model of caregiving mediation is applicable to many areas of health care. It is particularly well suited to medical social work in regard to discharge planning disputes between patients and the people—usually family members—who provide their care. Precipitous discharges often result in rapid readmissions to hospitals and escalating frustration of patients, families, and health care providers. The use of this model of mediation in hospitals for this population of clients benefits the hospital by reducing the recidivism rate and benefits the medical social worker and other health care staff by providing the means to expedite discharge and care plans, and the patient and family by assisting them to come to mutual agreement, and improving the quality of their relationship.

References

Dubler, N. N., & L. J. Marcus. 1994. *Mediating Bioethical Disputes.* New York: United Hospital Fund.

Lemmon, J. 1985. The Mediation Method Throughout the Family Life Cycle. *Mediation Quarterly* 7: 5–21.

Moore, C. 1986. *The Mediation Process: Practical Strategies for Resolving Conflict.* San Francisco: Jossey-Bass.

Stone, R., G. L. Cafferata, & J. Sangl. 1987. Caregivers of the Frail Elderly: A National Profile. *The Gerontologist* 27 (5): 616–26.

Toseland, R. & C. Rossiter. 1994. Social Work Practice with Family Caregivers of Frail Older Persons. In M. J. Holosko & P. A. Taylor, eds., *Social Work Practice in Health Care Settings*. Toronto: Canadian Scholars Press.

11

MENTAL HEALTH

Mediation: An Intervention to Facilitate the Empowerment of Mental Health Consumers

by Jeanne A. Clement and Andrew I. Schwebel

Although mediation has been in use as a dispute resolution process in the health care field for some time, the idea of using this alternative with persons who have a mental illness is relatively new (Mazade, Blanch, & Petrila, 1994). Events in the last decade have prompted some groups and individuals to rethink the conventional wisdom that suggests that persons with serious mental illness would not be able to participate in such a cognitively oriented problem-solving process.

In this chapter, the authors describe two of the major forces currently influencing reform in the mental health field: the advent and growth of managed care, and the increasingly visible mental health consumer and family member movements that advocate for the vision of "recovery." The convergence of these forces has created an environment in which mediation programs could serve many useful functions.

Conflict is inevitable among mental health consumers, family members, and caregivers. Following an overview of the mediation process and a case study depicting how mediation can empower mental health consumers and their families to resolve their own disputes, the authors discuss conflict resolution alternatives for mental health consumers. The chapter concludes with a discussion of future possibilities for mediation in the mental health field.

Reform Movements: Managed Care

The mental health system is currently in a cycle of reform and change (Goldman, et al., 1992; Inglehart, 1996), largely driven by forces interested in lowering the cost of care. These same forces also challenge the system to demonstrate that the care given produces high-quality outcomes. The current reform cycle is rooted historically in the Community Mental Health Centers Act (U.S.), enacted in 1964, that resulted in the "deinstitutionalization" of persons with serious mental disabilities (Goldman et al., 1992). Contrary to the planners' expectations, the downsizing of state psychiatric hospitals fostered both the "transinstituionalization" of persons with serious mental illnesses (SMI) into nursing homes and other long-term care facilities, and an influx of others with SMI into communities. The comprehensive community mental health centers that had been developed through direct federal funding failed to provide the services needed by this latter group as well as those needed by young persons with serious mental disabilities who had never been hospitalized (Mechanic, 1989).

In response, the movement that developed in the 1970s was concerned with the rehabilitation of individuals living in the community already disabled by severe mental illness (Goldman et al., 1992). Using the Community Support Services (CSS) model developed by the National Institute of Mental Health (NIMH) and implemented in demonstration projects, this movement aimed to build a network of services that would support and maintain individuals with SMI within the community.

Full implementation of the CSS plan did not occur. The 1980 repeal of the Mental Health Act (U.S), the use of block grant funding to states (as opposed to direct federal funding to CSS programs), and other factors resulted in decreased funds for community support services for persons with SMI. By the mid-1980s services for persons with severe and persistent mental illness were described as disastrous, and the problems associated with their care had increased (Goldman et al., 1992).

Exceptions to the general downward trend in providing adequate services for persons with severe mental illness are found in several states (Goldman et al., 1992). For example, the Ohio State Legislature, at the urging of a diverse coalition that included mental health consumers, family members, professionals, labor, and other stakeholders, passed a comprehensive mental health bill in 1988 that provided for the development of an integrated system of care in the public sector. This bill placed both funds and responsibility for service provision in the hands of local mental health authorities (Hogan, 1992). Mental health boards at the county (and in some cases multicounty) level were charged with the development and implementation of comprehensive CSS programs (Hogan, 1992).

CSS programs necessitate a multiservice systems approach, with the client or consumer clearly at the center (First, Greenlee, & Schmitz, 1990).

Case managers are the service providers charged with the responsibility of aiding mental health consumers in dealing with the system. Case manager responsibilities include aiding mental health consumers to access the most appropriate services, increase their ability to function on a day-to-day basis, and maintain themselves in the community (First, Greenlee, & Schmitz, 1990).

Although CSS services, where available, have been successful in reducing the number of days mental health consumers spend in hospitals, and increasing consumer access to community services, many are left feeling disenfranchised (ODMH, 1993; Hogan, 1992; Goldman et al., 1992). Specifically, consumers feel that their lives are under the control of others, and that the quality of their lives is far from optimal (Campbell & Schraiber, 1989). Family member groups also argue that current CSS approaches encourage dependency on the service system (ODMH, 1995).

The issues of control of service and dependency on the service system will grow in importance as managed care expands, limiting the use of services (Inglehart, 1996). New visions and services that promote the health of the consumer are necessary if the mental health system and mental health consumers are to thrive in a managed care environment.

Reform Movements: Recovery

In a recent paper, Hogan (1994) discusses the concept of "recovery" and the role it can play in guiding the development of programs for persons with SMI. Programs that support recovery incorporate new beliefs concerning rehabilitation that encourage hope and "rational optimism" on the part of consumers and professionals alike (Hogan, 1994). These goals require that professionals, family members, and consumers collaborate in a search for new methods and processes that will provide consumers with the skills needed to have their voices heard and their choices exercised within the mental health system as well as in other areas of their lives.

The current definition of recovery, growing out of the consumer self-help movement, has a complex and future oriented focus that involves risk taking. When mental health consumers experience recovery, they move from receiving prescriptive interventions to taking personal action, from faith to hope, from following routines to promoting change, from being protected to personal freedom, and from dependency to self-reliance (Plum, 1987). As it is currently used, recovery implies a dynamic process in which an individual who has an illness moves beyond chronicity, a condition that becomes irrelevant when life has meaning. The concept of recovery challenges beliefs that disability must limit an individual's ability to achieve his or her optimal potential if social supports and personal resources are fully developed (Moxley, 1994). To cope, and to develop meaning in their lives, mental health consumers must experience increased satisfaction, self-care, and self-efficacy, which demands action on their part. Moxley (1994) notes that

> recovery is not compatible with passive consumers who accept what professionals want for them. (A need exists for) rehabilitative and clinical approaches that support people in articulating their desires, making choices about treatment, and evaluating the quality and relevance of the services they receive . . . the achievement of an active voice on [the] part of consumers is perhaps the most vital ingredient of the recovery process. The achievement of voice is linked to self-determination, empowerment, and self-efficacy. (P.13)

Recovery suggests that consumers should be partners with professionals in all aspects of programming, from inception through evaluation.

Research, Debates, and Trends

The needs of managed care companies and those of consumers in recovery appear to be contradictory. However, the needs of both are served by processes like mediation, which promote skill development, self-efficacy, and self-responsibility in persons with SMI. The issues raised in the development and implementation of such programs include involving mental health consumers and family members in the design and implementation of the programs; addressing existing power imbalances related to the disenfranchisement of mental health consumers; conducting research to identify at what point in the system, and for whom, new programs such as mediation would be most useful; and adapting the mediation process to ensure that persons with serious mental illness can participate as fully as possible in the process.

Involvement of Mental Health Consumers and Family Members

Critical to the recovery movement is the need for consumers to take more personal responsibility by assuming an active role in managing their lives and making their own choices in regard to issues and decisions that they confront. Being involved in program development and management is a new experience for many consumers, and antithetical to past practices. Many consumers report that they experience other people (family members, providers, and so forth) as having more control and power over their lives then they do themselves (Coursey, Farrell, & Zahniser, 1991; Schwebel & Clement, in press). Moreover, during the course of their care, persons with SMI often feel that their thoughts, feelings, and experiences are not taken into account or heeded. For example, many consumers reported personally diminishing experiences while being admitted to a psychiatric hospital (Coursey, Farrell, & Zahniser, 1991). Rubin et al. (1993) noted that the consumers they interviewed, although valuing the emergency services they received, nonetheless felt that they were not treated in beneficial ways during points in their treatment.

Addressing Existing Power Imbalances

In a series of forums on recovery in Ohio, mental health administrators, chief clinical officers, mental health consumers, and family members noted that current practices in the mental health system tend to foster dependency. To correct the imbalance that results in a milieu of dependency, programs that support recovery empower and encourage consumers to rely more heavily, and in healthy ways, on themselves, and less on caregivers and mental health professionals. This increased responsibility allows consumers to see themselves as deserving of the rights and responsibilities of full membership in their communities. To help consumers achieve this goal, these programs support the development of skills for both consumers and professionals that promote partnerships and collaborative relationships (ODMH, 1995). Such clinical interventions "need to focus more upon decreasing stigma and enabling patients to be more active, self-reliant and future oriented. Therefore, not only are expressive and cognitive interventions required, but also those that are psychobehavioral and focus more extensively upon skill-training: for developing and sustaining social relationships (e.g., social competency); for coping with information regarding health and illness (e.g., self-management and anticipatory guidance); and for reducing stress (e.g., setting reasonable goals, maintaining physical exercise and leisure activities)" (Plum, 1987, p. 291).

Participating in mediation, a process rooted in the concepts of fairness and the assumption of responsibility for solving one's own problems, has the potential to foster skill development and to facilitate self-determination and empowerment. Parties in mediation are guided through a problem-solving process in which they have an equal opportunity to have their opinions and explanations heard and respected. Thus, the process itself provides the parties with an opportunity to simultaneously increase control over their own lives and to learn useful life skills.

Research in Mental Health Mediation

Although the growth of the recovery movement (Hogan, 1994), national trends toward managed health care (Freeman & Trabin, 1994), and initiatives such as the Americans with Disabilities Act (Daar, Nelson, & Pone, 1993) suggest the value of providing self-empowering programs such as mediation to mental health consumers, little has been done to investigate their potential impact, or to implement pilot mediation programs in mental health settings. The assumption that mental health consumers may not be able to benefit from me-

200 Jeanne A. Clement and Andrew I. Schwebel

diation continues to prevail (Schwebel & Clement, in press). Mental health practitioners, as well as family members, have indicated that interventions such as mediation might not be effective for a number of reasons. Mazade, Blanch, & Petrila (1994) cite the following assumptions underlying the belief that persons diagnosed with serious mental illness lack the capacity to engage in the mediation process: "When consumers' symptoms exacerbate, they may be unable to adhere to mediated agreements; having been systematically disenfranchised, consumers would enter mediation sessions relatively powerless compared to other parties; many mental health consumers, especially those taking medication, may be unable to engage in a process that involves sophisticated cognitive processing" (Pp. 436–37).

However, in a series of focus groups with consumers and family members examining mediation as a possible addition to current services, most participants expressed the belief that consumers could participate in mediation and abide by the agreements made when their symptoms were in remission, or in the early stages of exacerbation (Schwebel & Clement, in press). Further, many consumers and family members indicated they would use mediation, if available.

Given the paucity of mediation programs in the mental health field, it is not surprising that few empirical studies exist that evaluate the effectiveness of its use with consumers. Krajewski and Bell (1992) describe the successful use of mental health-related mediation to resolve disputes related to a number of issues, including treatment, seclusion and restraints, quality of the hospital environment, alleged abuse, and admission, discharge, and transfer of hospital patients. In the project they studied, mediation was one part of an advocacy/grievance program instituted in a state hospital in which consumer advocates mediated between physicians, other health providers, and consumers.

Schwebel and Clement (in press) conducted focus groups with mental health consumers and family members to ascertain their perceptions of the potential use of mediation in the community. Consumers and family members generally expressed interest in using mediation programs, and they identified multiple areas in which mediation could be of use. These fell into four categories:

1. *Treatment issues:* Disputes identified as appropriate for mediation in this category included the development of treatment plans that fit the consumer's lifestyle (when to use hospitalization and medication, timetables for accomplishing treatment goals, and housing options), disputes between consumers, family members, and other caregivers regarding the timeliness and quality of services, and the development of advanced directives for treatment choices.
2. *Issues in daily living:* Disputes identified as appropriate for mediation in this category included household responsibilities and rights in cases

where consumers and family members share quarters, similar disputes in group homes, and disputes related to the Americans with Disabilities Act (ADA).

3. *Interpersonal conflicts:* Disputes that could be mediated in this category included conflicts between consumers and between consumers and family members, friends, and those with whom consumers conduct business, and disputes that might arise at times of transition, such as when consumers return to or leave their parents' home.

4. *Personal responsibilities:* Disputes that could be mediated in this category included behavior appropriate for different settings, managing anger and violent behavior, and disputes related to consumers' romantic relationships, including those about marriage and cohabitation, the use of birth control, and the care of children.

While mental health consumers would be one of the parties in mediation in the above disputes, the other parties could be family members, friends, fellow employees, employers, people with whom consumers do business, police officers, neighbors, managed care staff, caregivers, and other mental health consumers. Psychiatrists are another category of individuals who might constitute the other party. However, both consumers and family members expressed the belief that many psychiatrists might not have the time or desire to participate, and that the amount of power they saw physicians as holding within the medical system might present an irreconcilable power imbalance (Schwebel & Clement, in press).

Some consumers in our focus groups indicated that they had invested a great deal of time and effort in past attempts to resolve conflict situations. Mental health professionals also spend a significant amount of time dealing with conflict and its consequences. We surveyed mental health professionals in Ohio, as well as mental health service planners on mental health boards, eliciting their perceptions concerning the utility of including mediation as an adjunct to mental health services currently provided. A range of human service professionals—psychiatrists, nurses, social workers, psychologists, counselors, lawyers, and educators—responded. We found that mental health professionals spend about 15 percent of their time dealing with conflicts between themselves and their consumers or family members, and between consumers and family members.

In sum, the mental health professionals we surveyed favored developing mediation programs, and expressed the belief that, under certain circumstances, mental health consumers could be active participants in the resolution of disputes. Some differences existed along disciplinary lines; psychiatrists were less likely than others to believe that mental health consumers would adhere to mediated agreements (Schwebel, Clement, & Sullivan, in preparation).

The precise impact of mediation on the recovery of mental health consumers has yet to be determined by research, and the true potential of mediation in reducing the number of preventable difficulties within mental health systems is unknown.

The Mediation Process in Mental Health

The generic mediation process, as outlined in chapter 1, stresses how important it is that clients have a clear picture of the overall goals of mediation, the role of the mediator, and the nature of the interventions used. The mediator who is working with mental health consumers has to be particularly vigilant in this regard. Fully orienting mental health consumers to the mediation process may require a unique blend of approaches, an expanded time frame, and frequent repetition of the material covered.

Schwebel et al. (1994) describe four approaches to divorce mediation: the legal, labor management, therapeutic, and communication models. Although there are many commonalities in these models, particularly in the beginning stages where mediators establish an atmosphere of hope and respect, each has its distinct characteristics. Among the major distinctions identified by the authors germane to the application to the mental health field include the roles played by the mediator and the assumptions made concerning how change is facilitated. In the legal model, mediators maintain a neutral, nondirective stance, functioning as rule setters and evaluators of fairness. Change is believed to take place in a structured environment in which rules encourage cooperation and discourage the expression of emotions. In the labor management and therapeutic models, mediators assume a more active and directive role. Mediators who employ a labor management approach may act as coaches, teaching mediation skills if one of the parties is less knowledgeable or skillful; this approach is designed to equalize the power between the parties so they may more equitably engage in bargaining and negotiation. Therapeutic mediators intervene by encouraging controlled expression of emotions when feelings block progress toward a settlement. Finally, the communication model employs an interdisciplinary approach with an attorney-therapist mediation team; here the underlying assumption is that the parties can solve their dispute when communication skills are improved and they have appropriate information and guidance from two distinct sources.

Concepts from all four models have utility in the mental health mediation arena. The high structure and low emotionality of the legal model fits the needs of people with schizophrenia, who manifest fewer symptoms in an environment low in expressed emotions, particularly negative emotions (Kuipers & Bebbington, 1988; Parker & Hadzi-Pavlovic, 1990).

Persons with serious mental illness may have cognitive processing difficulties related to neurological impairment due to their illness and/or the medication they are taking. Additionally, some people with a SMI may not possess the degree of communication, problem-solving or negotiation skills to make optimal use of the mediation process, particularly if the age of onset of their illness was in their early or late teens, as emotional growth and development tends to slow with the onset of the illness (Burns, Clement, & Wagner, 1993). Thus, in designing the mediation process, mediators may decide to employ strategies from the labor negotiation model, coaching one or both parties before the session, and strategies from the communication model, preparing consumers to participate in mediation, and to "level the playing field."

Strategies used by mediators who employ the therapeutic model have particular relevance in work with mental health consumers. Persons mediating in the mental health field need to be expert in the use of therapeutic communication techniques designed to enhance the self-esteem of parties who may have had previous experiences that were self-diminishing and who do not trust new people or situations. Another strategy from the therapeutic model to expedite effective problem solving with mental health consumers is to work on an individual basis with the consumer, encouraging the identification and controlled expression of the emotions connected with the issues in dispute.

A Mediation Process Adapted for Mental Health Consumers

Building an effective mediation program to serve persons with serious mental disabilities requires certain fundamental adaptations to traditional mediation procedures, including who conducts the mediation sessions. In the focus groups described above, consumers and family members expressed the belief that the success of mediation programs in the mental health arena is predicated on the presence of mediators with working knowledge of mental illness and the mental health system. The focus group participants strongly supported the idea of training mental health consumers and family members as co-mediators.

Our experiences in conducting such training sessions produced further considerations regarding how the mediation process could be better adapted for persons with serious mental illness. Mediator neutrality, essential to the mediation process, is not a concept familiar to most mental health consumers. Consumers have, however, had considerable exposure to the advocacy role as the recipients of advocacy services. Consumers who are used to having others speak on their behalf are not used to allowing their own voice to be heard. As parties to the mediation process, mental health consumers need a detailed description of the concept of mediator neutrality, and the implications of this for their participation in the process. The issue of confidentiality must also be fully discussed as consumers, rightly or wrongly, often fear retaliation by individuals in the medical treatment system if they express their opinions. Role reversal is one technique that can be adapted by mediators for use in orienting participants to mediation and as an interventive technique during sessions. Other considerations in mediating with mental health consumers include the need to repeat detailed explanations of what to expect; the use of chalk board or flip charts to write out established rules and the stages of mediation; and for consumers manifesting high anxiety levels or low attention spans, more frequent breaks and shorter sessions.

The mediation process adapted for use with mental health consumers involves a sequenced series of phases and associated strategies, together with phase-related activities for the mediator (figure 11.1).

Although the mental health mediation process does not differ significantly from the generic mediation model discussed in chapter 1, a number of adaptations are necessary in working with mental health consumers. These relate to the overall length of the process, and greater emphasis on the premediation assessment phase. The introduction phase may need to be extended, as might some of the other phases. Caucusing during sessions can greatly aid in the expanded coaching functions assumed by mediators in the mental health field; however, the advantages of caucusing may be outweighed by its disadvantages if the mental health consumer comes to believe that there is collusion between the mediator and other party, or the consumer is not able to tolerate being alone while the other party is caucusing.

Case Study

The following case study illustrates a typical dispute faced by many mental health consumers and family members, and how mediation can be adapted to this special needs population. Joe, a twenty-six-year-old single man diagnosed with schizophrenia, moved back with his parents after being released from the state psychiatric hospital. A few days after his return, two health-threatening concerns became apparent to his parents. First, Joe had returned to drinking both in and out of the house; and second, he was not taking his medication as prescribed. For the parents, this was a familiar pattern of behavior that, in the past, had resulted in Joe becoming uncommunicative and withdrawn, the first steps on a downward spiral, resulting in either trips to emergency services or hospitalization. At the same time, Joe was unhappy and resentful of his parents' concern about what time he returned home in the evening. Although he sometimes forgot to take his medication, he believed that this was his responsibility, not theirs, and he felt that his parents were treating him like a child. Both Joe and his mother complained about the situation to Joe's case manager, who referred them to mediation.

During the assessment process, the mediator decided to involve only Joe and his mother in the mediation sessions. Joe's father had not shown the same level of interest as had his mother, and it was felt that having both parents in mediation might adversely affect the power balance in the sessions.

Figure 11.1   Phases of the Mediation Process for Mental Health Consumers

---

Phase 1: Premediation assessment
Strategies:
  Educate about the process.
  Assess for emotionality.
  Explain neutrality and confidentiality.
  Determine need for involvement of a support person.
Phase-related mediator activities:
  Use of therapeutic communication and empathic responding.
  Individual coaching.
  Directive approaches.
  Use of role reversal.

Phase 2: Introduction: Beginning the session
Strategies:
  Reinforce neutrality.
  Establish ground rules for sessions, including signals for when breaks are needed.
    Write ground rules on flip chart.
    List phases of mediation and what is done in each on flip chart.
    Establish what mediator will do to make sure ground rules are followed.
  Acknowledge the level of anxiety present.
  Repeat instructions until understanding is demonstrated.
Phase-related mediator activities:
  Frequent repetition of concepts and processes.
  Use of simple, clear language.
  Caucusing or terminating session if anxiety level becomes too high.

Phase 3: Story telling and issue identification
Strategies:
  Be alert for increased anxiety level.
  Watch for nonverbal cues of anxiety.
  Use caucusing judiciously.
  Consistently reiterate directions.
Phase-related mediator activities:
  Assessment of level of emotionality and ability to listen to the other party.
  Frequent use of summarization.

Phase 4: Solution generation
Strategies:
  Help parties to develop more than one solution.
  Explore workability of solutions.
Phase-related mediator activities:
  Use of role reversal and caucusing.

Phase 5: Selection of mutually agreed-upon solution(s)
Strategies:
  Careful exploration of mutuality may be necessary.
  Detail specific actions the parties will take.
Phase-related mediator activities:
  Use of summarization, and caucusing if necessary.

Phase 6: Detailed review, writing, and signing of agreement, and anticipatory planning
Strategies:
  Review how the dispute was settled and other accomplishments in mediation.
  Determine specific course of action if either party is unable to keep the written agreement.
Phase-related mediator activities:
  Generalization: connect problem-solving process to other areas of the parties' lives.

The mediator learned during the assessment that the family had a history of domestic disputes, and that neither Joe nor his mother had ever participated in a structured problem-solving process. In order to enable them to fully participate in mediation and to lower their anxiety about taking part in a new experience, a trained mental health mediator met with Joe and his mother separately before the first joint session. The mediator outlined the mediation process in detail, and educated each party about what to expect from the mediation, and what might be anticipated in the session, given the dispute and past relationship history. The mediator explained that both would have ample opportunity to express their concerns and fears about the current situation. Both would also have the experience of listening to the other without the pressure to "help the other do something." The mediator reassured them that the process of mediation is highly structured, which helps the participants to keep their emotions from getting out of control and helps them to solve their problems in a way that is satisfactory to both.

The mediation session was scheduled in a meeting room at the local library. This neutral site was chosen over the family home, which might have had many negative cues, and the mediation office, which was in the local court building, a site that had unpleasant associations for Joe.

During the mediation session, Joe expressed his wish to keep the part-time job he had just started, and to be able to hang out with his friends at the neighborhood bar. Mother shared her concern that if she left Joe to his own devices she would feel responsible for his getting ill again. When each was satisfied that they had expressed all they wished regarding their conflict, Joe and his mother were able to isolate the various issues contributing to the conflict, and agree on mutually beneficial solutions to those issues. Joe agreed he would drink only on weekends with his friends, at the house, and that during the week, he would refrain from drinking alcoholic beverages. Joe's mother agreed that during the week the refrigerator would be stocked with nonalcoholic malt drinks and the cupboard with Joe's favorite snack cakes. Further, mother agreed that she and Joe's father would let Joe's friends come into the house on weekends and that they would provide a private place for them.

As the discussion progressed, Joe expressed his frustration with having to take pills several times a day, and talked about how infantalized he felt when his mother would check to make sure he had taken them, or would bring them to him. After discussion of some of the side effects Joe had experienced and an expression of empathy on the part of his mother, Joe agreed that he would try taking long-acting injections instead of the daily pills his psychiatrist had originally prescribed. In return, mother agreed that she would not ask him to be home at any particular hour, as she would no longer need to worry about his drinking at the tavern. Joe agreed that his parents would be permit-

check him for alcohol without any forewarning on any night he was out. At the end of the mediation, the mediator drafted a written agreement for both to sign.

A second mediation session was held about a month later following an episode in which Joe drank on a week night and arrived home loud and disruptive. Both parents came to this session, with Joe's agreement. Both parents reported feeling frustrated and betrayed. Joe thought they were overreacting, but was also able to acknowledge that he had reneged on the mediated agreement. The new agreement negotiated during this second session stipulated that any future episodes would be avoided by Joe going to a designated consumer-run "safe house" or crisis center rather than coming home drunk.

In this case, the mediator coached Joe and his mother in the mediation process, and reduced their anxiety by letting them know what to expect in this novel situation. The mediation took place in a location considered neutral by both parties. In addition, frequent breaks were called during the sessions, as Joe's anxiety rose, or if he seemed to need more time to process the information he was receiving. At one point, the mediator asked Joe and his mother to reverse roles, which helped them understand each other's position.

This case study illustrates several ways in which mediation can be adapted for use by mental health consumers. In general, the main adaptations for mediating with mental health consumers fall into the realm of structure and technique. Structural adaptations may include the use of a trained mental health consumer with a professional mediator, a more detailed and longer orientation to the process in the premediation assessment phase, more frequent breaks, careful attention to choice of site for the session, and shorter sessions if necessary. Technique adaptations include the use of role reversal, judicious use of caucusing, increased sensitivity to power imbalances and emotionality, and helping the mental health consumer connect mediation to past and future experiences.

Alternatives to Mediation

Conflict is inevitable in human relationships. Whereas conflict has the potential to destroy relationships and create distance between people, when properly handled it can help to heal or restore relationships. Often problems that arise as a result of a dispute between people are the result not of the conflict itself, but of how it is handled and the type of outcome it produces. When the outcome of conflict is perceived as a loss by one or all of the participants, the potential for heightened conflict dramatically increases.

There are several ways for mental health consumers to deal with conflict regarding their treatment and care. One way consumers can attempt to resolve their disputes is to contact a client rights officer (CRO), a position mandated by state law for mental health agencies. The role of the CRO is to serve as a client advocate: "Advocates operate in the expressed interest of clients rather than necessarily the imputed best interest of the client. The advocate does not make clinical judgments but gives voice to the expressed wishes of the mental health client" (Campbell & Schraiber, 1989, p. 131). The CRO assists the mental health consumer in finding a resolution to a grievance. The CRO is mandated by law to be an advocate for the consumer and is therefore not neutral; it is assumed within this approach to dispute resolution that consumers need such assistance as they are not able to advocate for themselves (Schauer, 1995). The CRO also provides advice to consumers, and recommends actions that they might take on their own behalf. If consumers are unable or unwilling to act for themselves, the CRO will act on their behalf.

Another way mental health consumers can resolve disputes, and voice their opinions and concerns about the mental health system, is through the use of a grievance procedure. What constitutes a grievance, and the grievance process itself, are mandated by state legislation. The definitions of what is a grievable issue and the procedure to follow are posted in all state hospitals, mental health boards, and agencies. In these institutions, structured procedures provide consumers with specific steps to follow to file a grievance.

The use of client advocates and grievance procedures are preferred processes when there has been an alleged, or clear, violation of the law such as in cases of physical or sexual abuse, theft, or other criminal act, or where the consumer is incapacitated and unable to fully participate in the process. Mediation should be considered as an alternative dispute resolution process when the consumer has the ability to speak on his or her own behalf (with support from others if needed), and when the dispute falls into the categories identified earlier: treatment issues, disputes in daily living, interpersonal conflicts, and personal responsibilities.

Although the potential of mental health mediation remains largely untapped, two major trends in the mental health field—managed care and the recovery movement—have created an environment in which mediation programs could be useful. Mediation has the potential to positively affect mental health consumers by empowering them to resolve their disputes, increasing their sense of self-efficacy, and providing them with skills that can be used in a variety of settings. Further, the mental health system can benefit from the adoption of mediation as a dispute resolution mechanism in the form of lower costs and higher levels of consumer satisfaction. If the goal of mental health services is directed toward consumer independence and self-responsibility, mediation provides a "win-win" alternative in many cases.

References

Banyan, C. D. & J. R. Antes. 1992. Therapeutic Benefits of Interest-Based Mediation. *Hospital and Community Psychiatry* 43(7): 738–39.

Burns, E. M., J. A. Clement, & J. D. Wagner. 1993. Brain-Mind-Behavior and the Effects of Psychoactive Drugs: A Review with Special Sections on the Family and the Homeless. In E. M. Burns, A. Thompson, & J. Ciccone, eds., *An Addictions Curriculum for Nurses and Other Helping Professionals*. New York: Springer.

Campbell, J., & R. Schraiber. 1989. *The Well-Being Project: Mental Health Clients Speak for Themselves*. Sacramento, CA: California Department of Mental Health.

Coursey, R., E. Farrell, & J. Zahniser. 1991. Consumers' Attitudes toward Psychotherapy, Hospitalization, and Aftercare. *Health and Social Work* 16(3): 155–61.

Daar, M., T. Nelson, & D. Pone. 1993. *Durable Powers of Attorney for Health Care Manual: An Advocacy Tool for Mental Health Consumer Empowerment and Patient Choice*. Sacramento, CA: Protection and Advocacy, Inc.

First, R. J., R. W. Greenlee, & C. L. Schmitz. 1990. *A Qualitative Study of Two Community Treatment Teams*. Columbus: Ohio Department of Mental Health.

Freeman, M. A., & T. Trabin. 1994. *Managed Behavioral Healthcare: History, Models, Key Issues, and Future Course*. Washington, DC: U.S. Center for Mental Health Services, SAMHSA, Department of Health and Human Services.

Goldman, H. H., J. P. Morrissey, S. M. Ridgely, R. G. Frank, S. J. Newman, & C. Kennedy. 1992. Lessons from the Program on Chronic Mental Illness. *Health Affairs* 11(3): 51–68.

Hogan, M. 1994. Recovery: The New Force in Mental Health. Paper presented at the National Forum on Recovery, Columbus, OH, October.

Hogan, M. F. 1992. New Futures for Mental Health Care: The Case of Ohio. *Health Affairs* 11(3): 69–83.

Inglehart, J. K. 1996. Health Policy Report: Managed Care and Mental Health. *New England Journal of Medicine* 334(2): 131–35.

Krajewski, T. F., & C. Bell. 1992. A System for Patients' Rights Advocacy in State Psychiatric Inpatient Facilities in Maryland. *Hospital and Community Psychiatry* 43(2): 127–31.

Kuipers, L., & P. Bebbington. 1988. Expressed Emotion Research in Schizophrenia: Theoretical and Clinical Implications. *Psychological Medicine* 18: 893–909.

Mazade, N., A. Blanch, & J. Petrila. 1994. Mediation as a New Technique for Resolving Disputes in the Mental Health System. *Administration and Policy in Mental Health* 21(5): 431–445.

Mechanic, D. 1989. *Mental Health and Social Policy*. Englewood Cliffs, NJ: Prentice-Hall.

Moxley, D. P. 1994. *Serious Mental Illness and the Concept of Recovery: Observations from a National Forum*. Unpublished manuscript.

Ohio Department of Mental Health. 1993. *The Results of Reform: Assessing Implementation of the Mental Health Act of 1988*.

———. 1994. *Summary of the Statewide Regional Recovery Forums*.

———. 1995. *The Recovery Concept: Implementation in the Mental Health System*.

Parker, G., & D. Hadzi-Pavlovic. 1990. Expressed Emotion as a Predictor of Schizophrenic Relapse: and Analysis of Aggregated Data. *Psychological Medicine* 20: 961–65.

Plum, K. C. 1987. How Patients View Recovery: What Helps, What Hinders. *Archives of Psychiatric Nursing* 1(4): 285–93.

Rubin, W., J. Traynor, M. B. Snapp, L. Ossa, J. Ossa, & S. Stone. 1993. *Understanding the Experience of People Brought for Potential Commitment.* Paper presented at the NASMHPD Research Institute Annual Meeting, Annapolis, MD, October.

Schauer, C. 1995. Special Report: Protection and Advocacy: What Nurses Need to Know. *Archives of Psychiatric Nursing* 11(5): 233–39.

Schwebel, A. I., & J. A. Clement. In press. Consumer and Family Member Perceptions of Mediation. *Psychiatric Rehabilitation.*

Schwebel, A. I., J. A. Clement, & B. Sullivan. In preparation. Mental Health Professionals Perceptions of Mediation as an Intervention for Persons with Serious Mental Illness.

Schwebel, A. I., D. W. Gately, M. A. Renner, & T. W. Milburn. 1994. Divorce Mediation: Four Models and Their Assumptions about Change in Parties' Positions. *Mediation Quarterly* 11(3): 211–27.

12

DISABILITIES

Mediating Disputes Involving People with Disabilities

by Peter R. Maida

As mediation matures as a profession, it is increasingly regarded as the preferred dispute resolution technique when people, groups, and organizations have conflicts and disagreements. The reasons for its growing popularity include efficiency, preservation of civility between disputants, and cost-effectiveness. For many years people with disabilities have been parties in disagreements and mediators have attempted to accommodate their needs. Many mediators, however, have found themselves ill-equipped to work in situations when one or both parties are disabled. This results from not being able to accommodate the needs of the disabled party, reservations about the capacity of the disabled individual to participate in the process, stereotypical thinking about disabilities, and discomfort about working with disabled populations.

In 1990 in the United States, the passage of the Americans with Disabilities Act (ADA), fueled the interest in the relationship between disability and dispute resolution, particularly mediation. In Title V, Section 513, the ADA encourages the use of dispute resolution in resolving complaints involving discrimination against people with physical and mental disabilities. Some disability advocacy groups were alarmed at this development, fearing that hard-won battles for legal rights could be negotiated away if dispute resolution did not acknowledge the voice of the disabled in crafting resolutions to disagreements (Maida, 1994).

Consequently, after passage of the ADA, interest in how mediation is practiced when a person with a disability is involved increased. A new stridency and critical look at mediation when a person with a disability is involved characterized the thinking about whether mediation was helpful or harmful. This was partly the result of the work of disability advocates, and partly the self-consciousness, discipline, and critical thinking characteristics of the coming of age of mediation as a profession.

This chapter will present the mediation perspective in providing service delivery to people with disabilities. Does the convergence of the mediation process with the presence of a disability in one or both clients create special responsibilities, reflecting the particular needs of people with disabilities as well as the ethical standards of mediation? In answering this, we will discuss what we know and what we need to learn about mediation and conflict resolution when one or more clients has a disability.

Theory, Debates, and Trends

Using mediation to resolve disputes in which one of the parties is a person with a disability has until recently met with opposition, particularly by disability advocates. Concern about erosion of legal rights, combined with anecdotal reports of how poorly people with disabilities have fared in mediation has resulted in resistance. Unfortunately, what is included under the rubric of "disability mediation" are a number of practices that strip the parties of their right to self-determination. Although client control of outcome is a cornerstone of mediation, mediators working with disabled populations are often at risk of imposing their opinions about how a dispute can be resolved. Often this is the result of paternalistic and stereotypical attitudes about the competence of a person with a disability. In other instances, bureaucrats as well as direct service practitioners maintain an institutional imperative to fit people into categories that make running the system easier. People with disabilities are not unfamiliar with others' attempts to control their lives. The thought of voluntarily participating in a procedure that is just an extension of this coercion would quite naturally be repugnant to them.

Another source of resistance to the use of mediation in dispute resolution involving people with disabilities is the belief among mediators that both parties must be able to fully communicate and negotiate. Two problems arise here, one related to communication, the other with balancing power. Effective communication in mediation requires not only competence but techniques allowing everyone to understand what is being communicated (Donohue & Rogan, 1989). Particularly in the area of mental and emotional disability, many question the use of mediation with someone who does not have full mental capacity. The determination of whether a person is competent enough to make optimal use of the mediation process should be done on a case-by-case basis, and this requires mediators themselves to be competent to make such determinations. Complicating the situation is the fact that some disputants' mental capacity is intermittent. Would it be appropriate, for example, to conduct a mediation with a person diagnosed with a mental disability during periods of lucidity?

Mediators have an obligation to ensure that parties participate fully in the mediation process, and that their interests are adequately represented. Any situation, condition, or factor that interferes in their full participation must be addressed by the mediator. Accommodations must be made to facilitate communication for all parties in mediation. The ADA requires mediators, doctors, lawyers, and other professionals who offer their services to the public to make such accommodations to people with disabilities to ensure effective communication.

In regard to potential power imbalances in mediation with a disabled and nondisabled party, there are a number of strategies at mediators' disposal that should be used in the disability field. An uneven playing field has not kept mediators from mediating disagreements involving parties of unequal power in other mediation contexts and fields of practice, including parent-child, landlord-tenant, employer-employee, and citizen-government disputes. Mediators have an ethical obligation to intervene to reduce power imbalances where such inequities have the potential to harm one of the parties, and if they are unable to create a level playing field for negotiation, mediators are ethically bound to terminate the process. In the disability field in particular, when imbalances of power or functioning are such that the disabled party is unable to represent his or her interests to the fullest extent possible, mediators must intervene; if marked power imbalances continue subsequent to intervention, the parties should be referred to more traditional dispute resolution alternatives.

Mediation and Conflict Resolution

Regardless of one's field of practice or the substantive area of a dispute, mediation involves the use of an impartial third party who helps those having a disagreement communicate productively to reach a mutually acceptable resolution of that disagreement. The mediator directs the communication between the parties, keeping them focused on the future and not mired in the past. The mediator ensures that each person is fully informed about possible ways to resolve the disagreement so as to make a thoughtful decision. This in turn, ensures a fair agreement. Thus mediation is about providing for accessible communication between the parties and a safe, accessible physical environment for the negotiation process.

Mediation is not therapy (Kelly, 1983). The mediator is interested primarily in how people having a disagreement will communicate with one another in the future. Consequently, if psychological or emotional issues emerge, a mediator will keep the parties on track discussing the presenting issue. Acknowledging emotions is important but mediation must not dwell on emotions or examine in depth why a client is expressing certain feelings. If emotions or psychological factors interfere in the mediation, referral to or consultation with a therapist may be in order.

Probably the most important feature of mediation is collaborative negotiation, which stands in contrast to competitive negotiation, in which one party wins at the other's expense. In assisted collaborative negotiation, mediators make every effort to help each party understand the other's interests, avoid positioning, look for mutual solutions to problems, share information rather than withhold it, and communicate with their adversaries in a constructive manner. Three core principles guide mediation practice: neutrality and impartiality, doing no harm, and client self-determination.

Commonly, we speak of mediation as a series of stages, beginning with an introduction or orientation to the mediation process. Sometimes, participants are asked to sign an agreement indicating they have had mediation guidelines explained to them and they agree to abide by them. Everyone is asked to describe what has brought them to mediation in the subsequent fact-finding stage. In mediation, the goal of fact-finding is not to determine who is right and who is wrong. In a disagreement, parties position themselves by stating that their version of what has happened is correct and that a single resolution to the disagreement, theirs, exists. The mediator helps the parties to identify their interests, that is, their underlying concerns or what they really hope to accomplish by staking their position. The parties often discover that their interests are either mutual or interlocking in some manner and this leads them to a consideration of solutions that will meet the core needs of both.

A mediator must be careful not to focus on past behavior and fact validity; a future focus is another cornerstone of mediation. Where positioning is based on unsubstantiated claims, parties have to be encouraged to focus on what they would like to have happen in the future. The mediator discerns what the issues are and validates them with the parties. Next, each person is asked to think of ways to resolve the disagreement. Mediators facilitate communication between the parties to help them collaborate, being careful not to rule out any suggestions before the brainstorming is finished.

The negotiation stage has the parties evaluating possible resolutions, keeping in mind that any resolution has to meet the needs of both. Parties to the dispute bargain with one another to reach a resolution of their agreement, with the mediator responsible for balancing power differences and controlling the process. Finally, the mediator may record the decisions in a memorandum of understanding or agreement.

Disability

Disability can be defined as any physical or mental condition that significantly affects an individual's ability to perform major life activities such as physical movement, breathing, thinking, eating, working, and self-care. These activities are necessary to sustain an independent and self-sufficient lifestyle. Nondisabled persons are not reliant on changes in the physical environment as it exists; disabled persons require these changes to be able to perform necessary life activities.

In recent years, professional dispute resolution organizations, community mediation centers, and individual mediators have focused on human diversity in mediation theory and practice, including the role of gender, race, sexual preference, ethnicity, and social class. Yet sustained and serious interest in disability as it relates to the mediation process is of more recent origin (Johnston & Campbell, 1988; Retzinger, 1990; Saposnek, 1983; Schwebel, Gately, Milburn, & Renner, 1993). Six developments have prompted this increased attention. First, the Americans with Disabilities Act (ADA), enacted in 1990, encourages the use of dispute resolution including mediation in the resolution of complaints made against employers, local and state governments, and the business sector. Second, two federal administrative agencies, the U.S. Department of Justice and the U.S. Equal Employment Opportunity Commission, funded several projects to test the efficacy of using mediation in resolving complaints filed with their agencies by people with disabilities. A flurry of interest in the use of mediation to resolve disputes involving civil rights infractions of people with disabilities grew out of these government initiatives. Third, with the passage of the ADA, disability rights groups have been instrumental in initiating dialogue with mediators about what they need to know if they are going to provide services to the disabled. Interest among disability advocates in learning more about mediation and conflict resolution has been motivated on the one hand by the fear that mediation might erode the civil rights of the disabled guaranteed them under the ADA, and on the other by the promise that mediation may be the way for an underemployed and unemployed population to achieve their rights quickly and inexpensively. Fourth, the use of mediation in health care delivery systems such as hospitals and nursing homes is increasing every day (Dubler & Marcus, 1994), raising important issues with respect to patient competence and the use of mediation. Fifth, financially strapped educational systems are searching for ways to avoid costly litigation, and are examining mediation as an alternative dispute mechanism in areas such as special education placements and procedures for students with learning disabilities. Sixth, mental health consumer groups have a need not only to be employed but also a need to remain employed. Interest in mediation among these consumer groups has pushed the envelope with respect to identifying the conditions of mediation when mental disability is a component. The desire for a "voice" in negotiating employment issues makes mediation seem ideal (Chamberlain, 1990; Maida, 1995; Mancuso, 1993).

Types of Disability. One of the difficulties with identifying the conditions necessary to mediate disputes when one or both parties has a disability is that communication and physical setting needs will differ. To be an effective service provider, mediators must understand these differences. The variation within disabilities is great; adaptations in mediation practice and setting for people with disabilities will largely depend upon the particular type of disability of clientele.

A broad distinction may be made between physical and mental disabilities. Physical disabilities include any physical condition, regardless of its origin, that affects one's ability to move, hear, and speak. Possible origins for physical disability can include injury, physical disease, obesity, or congenital conditions. Mental disabilities can be cognitive, emotional, or learning in nature.

From a mediation perspective, intervention is necessary to ascertain whether any factor or condition in the mediation session plays a major role in determining if the process is fair in order to level the playing field. A disability could affect the mediation process to the extent that it would be unethical to continue. Some of the key considerations in the mediator's assessment include whether it is possible to provide an auxiliary aid to facilitate communication, whether stereotypical attitudes about disabilities are able to be overcome, whether the mediator has enough understanding of the particular disability to be able to facilitate communication between the parties, or whether the physical demands of mediation, such as too much noise and distraction, make the process unfeasible.

After assessing how physical and mental disabilities might affect their service delivery, mediators must make a judgment on a case-by-case basis about whether and how they must adapt their practices. In the disability community one hears, "If you want to find out how to make something accessible for a particular person with a disability, ask that person. People with disabilities are experts on their disability."

Disability and Mediation

Disability impacts the process and practice of mediation in a number of ways. The most prevalent is when one or more of the disputants, regardless of the particular problem or substantive content, has a disability. Second, an increasing number of mediations involve disputes covered by civil rights acts; these disputes arise because of alleged discrimination. Third, a disability can be present, but the mediator may be unaware of it. The nonapparent or hidden disability manifests itself but the mediator does not respond in an appropriate manner, thus preventing the disabled person from being a full participant in the process. This raises ethical concerns regarding the mediator's responsibility to ensure full participation of all disputants in the process; mediators are expected to conduct the mediation in a manner that is not discriminatory or demeaning to either party.

Disputes involving family members and those involving a discrimination complaint merit special mention. In family disputes, whether separation or divorce, parent-child, sibling, family business, or probate, the interrelation between family relations and the disability presents many challenges to the mediator. Family mediation rarely can avoid addressing emotional dynamics that grow out of close personal relationships. Sometimes the emotion is connected to the fact that the family has had to adjust to the disability of one of its members. For example, what effect does caring for a learning disabled child or an elderly parent have on the marital relationship? How do these effects figure into the mediation? What must the mediator do to keep the parties focused on the issues if past history interferes with decision making? In disagreements involving discrimination the mediator is less likely to be faced with managing the dynamics of close personal relationships. These disagreements characteristically occur within in the workplace or other public sphere and are the result of discriminatory attitudes. The person with the disability has generally been marginalized by an institution that would prefer not to integrate people with disabilities; added to this is an able-bodied person thinking about and behaving toward the person with a disability in a stereotypical fashion. In this instance, social distance rather than intimate relations must be addressed in mediation. The mediator must thus be aware of the social context within which discrimination occurs, the consequences of the lack of productive communication between the parties, and the legal implications of discrimination.

Several new developments are emerging in the field of disability mediation. First is the recognition that mediators in this substantive area must be prepared to address emotional issues. The extent of emotionality attendant to disability has surprised many mediators, who have been trained to contain the parties' expression of strong feelings. Second, the inclusion of legal processes as an adjunct to mediation, particularly in ADA complaints, is essential if a dispute involving people with disabilities is to be managed efficiently; the interface between mediation and advocacy is just beginning to be examined in the disability arena. Third, discussion about lifestyle differences and how they relate to types of disabilities has begun as a way to determine how mediation is to be an appropriate dispute resolution technique in disputes involving people with different disabilities. Finally, the key to self-determination is providing opportunities for people with disabilities to empower themselves without being paternalistic. Mediators are beginning to explore less directive and more client-led approaches to the mediation endeavor.

The Mediation Process

When mediating disputes involving people with disabilities, a number of considerations must be kept in mind. First, mediators should conduct a thorough and informed assessment of the needs of the parties. The initial contact with each party should establish whether any special accommodations will be necessary. Particularly in the instance of nonapparent disabilities, the mediator should pay careful attention to determine whether any emotional, cognitive, or learning disability is present, validate this in an appropriate fashion, and determine what accommodation is necessary to facilitate the mediation. If a person's disability, apparent or not, has the potential to harm that person in mediation, the mediator has an ethical obligation to examine alternatives to mediation. Termination of the mediation must be done in a manner that does not put either party at risk or is embarrassing to the parties.

Second, mediators have an ethical obligation not to facilitate a process in which the rights of the disabled are left unprotected. Thus, a mediator must understand the array of civil rights laws enacted to protect people with disabilities against discrimination. Mediators have standards of practice that mandate bringing the highest level of expertise to the resolution of any dispute. Those who do not understand civil rights laws should not be resolving complaints involving people with disabilities, as mediation may jeopardize their legal rights. Agreements should be avoided that deny a person with a disability full participation in the life of the community.

Third, the advantages and disadvantages in using mediation to resolve a disagreement should be considered. It should not be assumed that the common advantages of mediation, including quickness, efficiency, maintenance of the relationships between parties, and ensuring equal participation of the parties, will apply to working with people with disabilities. For example, if the presence of a disability will substantially increase the amount of time for the mediation, the parties should be informed; if the parties are paying for the mediation, the mediator must adjust the fee so that the parties are not paying a surcharge because of the disability. A surcharge to account for added expenses because one or both parties have a disability is discriminatory in the United States under the ADA.

Fourth, as mentioned, disabilities vary in their impact on the mediation process. Differences within categories of disability make every mediation involving a person with a disability a unique challenge. An understanding of these differences and how they impact not only on the mediation process but also the outcome of the process is crucial. Involving people with disabilities directly in the dispute resolution process by asking questions about necessary accommodations is essential to ascertain their unique needs.

Fifth, under the ADA, mediators are considered public servants, and as such, must ensure that the mediation process is accessible to any party with a disability. A mediator should determine what is necessary to make the mediation process accessible, whether this would involve providing auxiliary aids such as interpreters to facilitate effective communication, alternate format materials such as Braille or audio types, or removing structural barriers by providing ramps, allowing people using wheelchairs to gain access to the mediator's office. Regardless of civil rights statutes, a mediator has an ethical obligation to ensure full and equal participation of the parties in the process.

Sixth, a standard protocol for mediators is checking on whether the participants have the same understanding of what is communicated between them. In the case of individual disabilities, however, a mediator may have to learn how accessibility to the dispute resolution process affects meaning. For example, will an interpreter convey the specific nuance associated with a proposal to settle? Dispute resolvers ordinarily have ways to determine the accuracy of communication sent and received by parties in the mediation; working with interpreters poses particular challenges in this regard.

Seventh, institutionalized power differences may exist between parties in dispute vis-à-vis a disability. Stereotypes and misinformation about people with disabilities create an unequal bargaining field and attendant emotions on the part of both parties may run high. Mediators must educate, counteract stereotypes, be prepared to handle emotions, and attempt to equalize the power differential between the parties before any negotiation between them takes place. Any agreement that results from misunderstanding and power imbalances will not be equitable. When obstacles to fair negotiation cannot be overcome, the mediator must decide whether mediation of the disagreement is still appropriate.

Eighth, mediators are impartial third parties. It is mandatory for them to understand how societal expectations about people with disabilities affect them, people with disabilities, and other parties involved in the disagreement. Overprotectiveness, hostility, fear, stereotypes, and paternalism can affect both the process and outcome of mediation. The mediator's use of language should be carefully considered; certain ways of referring to people with disabilities demonstrate a lack of sensitivity. For example, using the word *handicapped,* or saying someone is "bound to a wheelchair," is offensive to many people who use a wheelchair. Referring to the person first and the disability second is essential.

Ninth, accommodating the needs of the person with a disability is achieved by means of a variety of changes in the workplace and marketplace. Whether the mediator is accommodating the person with a disability or the disagreement is over an accommodation, technology is involved. Mediators whose clients have disabilities have an obligation to understand the technology involved in reasonable accommodations, auxiliary aids, and structural barrier removal. A number of organizations can provide assistance and information about available technologies. Mediators should have a resource list to help with technological issues that arise in mediations involving people with disabilities.

Tenth, resolving disagreements in which one or both parties is disabled may require relying on input from other professionals. Impartial experts who are disabled and individuals who understand technology may be helpful. For example, an impartial expert could be called upon to inform the parties in the mediation about the available technologies for a reasonable accommodation in the workplace. Mediators should have a methodology for triaging with others if an issue related to the disability emerges in the mediation.

Eleventh, the Society for Professionals in Dispute Resolution, the Academy of Family Mediators, and a number of other professional groups and organizations have developed mediation practice guidelines. Mediators should have sufficient experience in dispute resolution and knowledge of the impact of disability on mediation service provision. Mediators are obligated to inform their clients about the role of confidentiality in the process, disclose any conflict of interest, explain fees, and educate clients about mediation, and should ensure that these are clearly communicated to disabled participants.

Specific Considerations

Disability impacts on mediation in different ways during different stages of the process. Mediator interventions can be tailored accordingly. At the initial contact, usually by phone, mediators can determine if either or both of the parties need any accommodation to avail themselves of the mediator's services. The first session provides another opportunity for the mediator: Are the restrooms wheelchair accessible? Can the person using the wheelchair even get into the building and the office? Are written materials accessible? Does a learning disabled client require more time to read through written information? A client with an emotional disability may require a particular seating arrangement, muted lighting, time-outs, and other accommodations. Is a sign language interpreter needed for a hearing impaired client?

After the orientation phase, mediation clients are asked to communicate their perspectives about what has happened to bring them to mediation. Knowing what the other person is communicating is an important part of the mediation process. Does each fully understand what the other has said? Sometimes people having a disagreement have not directly communicated with each other and are unaware of the other's position on the issue(s) in dispute. Are auxiliary aids for effective communication necessary? Would an interpreter or computer facilitate the exchange of information? More often than not, frustration is caused not only by the disagreement but by communication difficulties related to the disability. What remedies will effectively reduce these frustrations?

Later in the process, mediation clients are asked to think about ways their disagreement can be resolved. Does the person's disability interfere in brainstorming? The mediator may have to modify the option-building phase to account for the disability. For example, option-building may be broken down into parts that make the task more manageable by a person with an emotional, cognitive, or learning disability. Some mediators like to write options on newsprint for the parties to see. Periodically reading aloud and referring to these options would be helpful to a person with a sight disability.

Negotiating over options also may be influenced by disability. Taking time, ensuring that what is communicated is understood in the same way by each party, allowing each party whatever is needed to communicate about the option or options that party would be willing to settle for, and checking to see if the option or options decided on to resolve the disagreement are clearly meeting the needs of the person with the disability are important strategies.

How the agreement at the end of the mediation is written and its contents may also require consideration. Do agreements requiring mobility reflect the fact that persons with a disability affecting mobility may need certain contingencies if they are to honor the agreement? Is the level of detail in the agreement sufficient to be workable for a person with a stress-induced disability? What about future changes in the condition of the person with the disability and the ability to live up to the agreement? Multiple disabilities in one or both parties increase the complexity of the mediation case.

The Mediation Process: Case Study

When mediators are asked to resolve a disagreement, they bring both a set of skills and strategies, and a particular theoretical framework to the process. These inform decisions they make about appropriate courses of action in mediation. The following case analysis will demonstrate how a mediator might think before and during the mediation.

Ginger, who uses a wheelchair, wants to buy a toaster at Center Appliance. Three steps prevent her from getting to the door of the store. A clerk at Center opens the door and asks Ginger what she wants and, according to Ginger, insists that Ginger would have to enter the store to be waited on. Ginger asks to speak to the proprietor but the clerk indicates that she is busy and cannot come to the door. Ginger, discouraged, goes home and calls the proprietor to complain. Indicating that Center is a small store, and might not be able to afford any architectural changes, the proprietor apologizes to Ginger and says she can buy a toaster elsewhere, and why make such a big deal of this? Ginger indicates that she knows that Center has the best selection of toasters in town and that she does not want to buy any ordinary toaster. When the conversation takes a turn for the worse, Ginger says "goodbye," and hangs up. The proprietor at Center is annoyed, and Ginger is furious about how she has been treated. Ginger calls the local consumer complaint bureau and registers a complaint. The consumer complaint bureau recommends that Ginger take her complaint to a local mediation center for help.

Preliminary Assessment. Mediating disputes involving people with disabilities begins with an assessment before the parties begin negotiation. This is necessary for a number of reasons. First, it helps the mediator decide if mediation is the appropriate dispute resolution alternative. Second, an assessment will determine whether any accommodation is needed for the person with a disability. In this case, the mediator has implemented a number of changes in the physical environment: the office and restroom are wheelchair accessible, and mediation materials are available in alternate formats.

Once mediation is determined to be the appropriate procedure for resolving a particular disagreement, the mediator must also determine whether he or she has the qualifications to mediate the case. In our example, we will assume mediation is appropriate as the parties are able to communicate with one another and litigation might be an economic disaster for Ginger and Center's proprietor.

Caucusing with the parties would be useful, particularly if their level of emotional functioning interferes with the mediation process. Factors that signal the need for separate meetings with the parties include the need for emotional venting, an inability to discuss the disagreement because of intense emotions, expressed marked distrust of the other party, and an unwillingness to shift from one's stated position on the issue(s) in dispute. Resistance encountered during the initial stages can be dealt with by discussing the consequences of continuing the disagreement, helping the parties find common interests in resolving the disagreement, and encouraging the parties to trade assurances about how their future behavior toward one another will be fair and thoughtful.

Reviewing the "Rules." Mediation guidelines should be reviewed once the mediator and the parties have decided to proceed in the assisted negotiation. In the case involving Ginger and Center, the rules consist of the following:

- Each party agrees to abide by the rules of confidentiality established for mediation.
- Both agree that their presence at the mediation is voluntary. They may terminate the process any time they wish.
- Each party has the opportunity to fully explain, without interruption by the other, what happened to bring them to mediation.
- They agree that all information relevant to resolving the disagreement must be shared with the other.
- Excessive hostility and threats will not be tolerated and each agrees to treat the other with respect.
- The focus of the mediation will be the future and not the past. They will refrain from assigning blame onto the other.
- Each will be expected to propose solutions to resolve the disagreement, taking into consideration not only their own interests but also those of the other.
- The final responsibility for making decisions about how this disagreement will be resolved rests with the parties.

An agreement may be signed affirming that the parties have had an opportunity to consider the rules, understand the guidelines, and agree to abide by them.

Collecting Facts—"Story Telling." Since Ginger filed the complaint, she is asked to present her impression of the situation. She is allowed to speak uninterrupted as she relates her story. If the proprietor of Center interrupts, she is assured that she will have her turn to speak. During this phase, the mediator begins to identify the salient issues around which there is dispute or disagreement. The mediator checks for details that may need to be documented, assesses the level of emotionality, tests for Ginger's willingness to actively participate in discussions with the Center proprietor, thinks about whether this is a case where litigation or some other dispute resolution would be more appropriate, asks clarifying questions if Ginger's description is vague, and assesses Ginger's potential power if she must negotiate with Center's proprietor.

Center's proprietor is given her chance to describe what has happened. She also has the opportunity to speak uninterrupted. The mediator critically evaluates the proprietor's story in the same way Ginger's story is evaluated and then decides if gaps in information necessitate additional questions of the parties. If not, the mediator frames the issue(s) for discussion and negotiation in neutral and mutual terms.

In the present case scenario, let us suppose that the facts in dispute are what the clerk said to Ginger (the clerk, when questioned by the proprietor, had no recollection of his conversation with Ginger), and what transpired in the conversation between Ginger and the proprietor. Ginger and the proprietor of Center cannot agree on what actually happened. The proprietor states that she would have sold Ginger a toaster had she known she was at the door. Ginger doesn't believe this but is willing to discuss the matter further. In complaints such as this one, the matter of discrimination based on disability is considered by the mediator. Does local, state, or federal legislation prohibiting discrimination against people with disabilities apply in this case? The fact that Ginger has not raised the issue of discrimination does not absolve the mediator from being aware of the legal overlay and ramifications of the disagreement. The mediator cannot give legal advice, but must be aware that the issue of whether Center Appliance will or will not comply with the law is not negotiable; negotiation may only be over the conditions of compliance with the law. Otherwise, ethical issues for the mediator with respect to doing harm are raised.

Isolating the Issue(s). During the fact-finding process with Ginger and the proprietor of Center, the mediator begins isolating the main issues of the disagreement. They may argue about what the clerk actually said but that is not the main issue. Ginger clearly wanted to buy a toaster and could not. How can

Ginger buy the toaster if she cannot access the store? The crux of the disagreement is about Ginger's ability to enter the store. The proprietor claims that it is not necessary for Ginger to enter her particular store since Ginger can shop in other stores that are wheelchair accessible. Ginger claims that she has a right to enter the store just like anyone else.

Generating Options. The parties are encouraged to come up with ways to resolve their disagreement. Option building is a challenging phase since each party has usually selected their preferred alternative, which is in opposition to the solution of the other party. Mediators use a number of strategies to get the parties to generate new options that meet both parties' needs and interests for resolving the disagreement. A mediator exercises caution not to suggest how the parties may want to solve their disagreement; rather, he or she empowers the parties to determine their own solution.

In the Ginger-Center case, the following resolutions to the disagreement were identified by the parties: (1) Ginger could enter the store through a back door over an accessible threshold until it can be decided when Center can afford to install a ramp at the front entrance. After a study of the cost is completed, Center will provide a ramp to the front door if the cost is less than $6,000; (2) Center will proceed next week with construction to install a ramp to the front door. The ramp will be completed in five days. To compensate for the delay Ginger has to endure before she can buy a toaster, Center will give her a discount on the toaster; (3) Ginger will look at toasters brought to the front door of Center. She will purchase a toaster but will not pay for it until Center installs a ramp at the front door; (4) Ginger will buy a toaster shown to her at the front door and Center will give her a generous discount on the toaster; (5) Center will not install a ramp at the front door but will find Ginger the name of another appliance store that is accessible. Each of the parties took part in suggesting the options. The mediator, for the sake of protecting the brainstorming exercise, refrained from making any comments about the validity of the options.

Negotiating the Options. The next step for Ginger and Center's proprietor is to negotiate by means of evaluating each of the options, eliminating those they do not agree on and keeping those that represent both their interests. The mediator facilitates the negotiation. The parties may want to generate some other options or refine the existing options. When the Center's proprietor argues that they cannot afford to install a ramp, the negotiations come to a halt. The cost of a ramp and how long it would take to install it are still unknown. The mediator might suggest that an independent contractor be asked to help determine the cost. Center could also make some inquiries before the next mediation session to investigate the cost of a ramp and how long it would take to install it.

Agreement. After obtaining necessary information about the cost of installing a ramp, Ginger and the proprietor negotiate further and arrive at the following resolution of their disagreement. Center will hire a company to install a ramp. They have an estimate of $5,500 for the installation. The contractor will allow Center to pay for the ramp in monthly installments. The ramp will be installed in five days. If it takes longer, Ginger agrees to wait. After the ramp is installed, Ginger will go to Center to purchase the toaster. Ginger agrees to tell the members of her disability network about the cooperation of Center in an effort to create more business for Center. Ginger also agrees not to go further with her complaint. The mediator thanks the parties for their cooperation and places their agreement in writing.

Postscript. In this case study, disability played a key role; it was central to the reason for the disagreement. Resolving the agreement hinged on providing access to goods and services. The mediator's services also had to be accessible. If they had not been, Ginger might also have had a grievance with the mediator, which could have risen to the level of a civil rights complaint.

The effect of the disability on communication centered on the reaction of Center's proprietor to making structural changes to her business based on another's disability. The initial responses of the proprietor and clerk on one side, and Ginger on the other, were such that anger and intense emotions prevented further discussion and negotiation without a third party to facilitate the process. One can only hypothesize about whether the business' failure to adequately serve Ginger was an outcome of a socially supported reaction to disability. In this scenario, the parties' anger did not interfere with the eventual resolution of the dispute. Resolving the conflict required acknowledging the presence of the disability, as well as recognizing and giving legitimacy to the interests of a person with a disability.

Alternatives to Mediation

Mediation is a model of conflict or dispute resolution. It is not the only possible way to help people who are having a disagreement (Folberg & Taylor, 1984; Moore, 1986; Singer, 1990). Mediators occasionally decide against mediating a disagreement. What alternatives do they suggest and why? The first possibility is that of the parties negotiating themselves to resolve their disagreement. A mediator may suggest that the parties negotiate the solution themselves without the help of anyone else to see if they can be successful. When power imbalances cannot be remedied, litigation is a way of resolving a disagreement. Assuming that the parties are able to afford litigation, each party is (ideally) equal before the court. The current increase in the use of mediation in the disability arena is a reflection of the degree to which equality before the court is achieved in reality. However, in a case involving a person with a disability, if legal rights are at stake and if a precedent will result from litigation, this alternative may be preferred.

In some disputes, a social, mental, or legal impediment may interfere with the ability of the parties to negotiate. In these cases, mediators should make referrals to therapists, social service agencies, or attorneys before considering mediation. In cases involving people with disabilities in the United States, a useful component of mediation is to ensure that all parties are informed about the ADA at the outset, particularly if discrimination is a factor in the dispute. This may necessitate a referral to an outside legal professional or paraprofessional for information before mediation can begin.

Another useful adjunct to mediation in the disability field is the provision of written information to help the disputants become informed so they are better able to negotiate. Suggesting reading material informs the parties of their options and sometimes frees them from the emotionality of their dispute, thus setting the stage for future negotiation.

Interest in mediation in the field of disability is increasing among social workers and other human service professionals who are looking for alternative dispute resolution processes when conflicts arise in the lives of their disabled clients. Their interest is fueled by a desire to give voice to people with disabilities by means of a dispute resolution model that is known for providing a voice to all of its participants.

We need to share the knowledge about how disability impacts the mediation process; contributors to this knowledge include people with disabilities, mediation practitioners, and researchers. Only then will mediation in the field of disability begin to realize its full potential, with the development of the specialized skills and models of practice necessary with this population. The potential benefits of mediation for people with disabilities are clear: mediation promises equal participation and fair outcomes. When the disability of an individual potentially compromises his or her equal participation in the process and the achievement of a fair outcome, mediators have a professional obligation to make the necessary accommodations to ensure that mediation is indeed a preferred alternative of dispute resolution for all of the parties involved in the dispute.

References

Chamberlain, J. 1990. The Ex-Patients' Movement: Where We've Been and Where We're Going. *Journal of Mind and Behavior* 11: 323–36.

Donohue, W. A., J. Lyles, & R. Rogan. 1989. Issue Development in Divorce Mediation. *Mediation Quarterly* 24: 19–28.

Dubler, N. & L. Marcus. 1994. *Mediating Bioethical Disputes*. New York: United Hospital Fund of New York.

Folberg, J & A. Taylor. 1984. *Mediation: A Comprehensive Guide to Resolving Conflicts Without Litigation*. San Francisco: Jossey-Bass.

Grillo, T. 1991. The Mediation Alternative: Process Dangers for Women. *Yale Law Journal* 100(6): 1545–1610.

Grose, P. 1995. An Indigenous Imperative: The Rationale for the Recognition of Aboriginal Dispute Resolution Mechanisms. *Mediation Quarterly* 12(4).

Irving, H. & M. Benjamin. 1992. *Family Mediation in Canada and Israel: A Comparative Analysis*. Occasional Paper 1. Jerusalem: Hebrew University of Jerusalem.

Johnston, J. & L. Campbell. 1988. *Impasses of Divorce: The Dynamics and Resolution of Family Conflict*. New York: Free Press.

Kelly, J. B. 1983. Mediation and Psychotherapy: Distinguishing the Differences. *Mediation Quarterly* 1: 33–44.

Kelly, J. B. & M. A. Duryee. 1992. Women's and Men's Views of Mediation in Voluntary and Mandatory Settings. *Family and Conciliation Courts Review* 30(1): 43–49.

LeResche, D. 1993. Special Issue: Native American Perspectives on Peacemaking. *Mediation Quarterly* 10.

Maida, P. 1992. Diversity: Some Implications for Mediation. Special Issue. *Mediation Quarterly* 9(4).

———. 1994. Using Mediation to Resolve ADA Complaints. *Michigan Municipal Review* 67(7): 266–67.

———. 1995. Mediation, Mental Health, and the ADA. *Journal of the California Alliance for the Mentally Ill* 6(4): 38–39.

Mancuso, L. 1993. *Case Studies on Reasonable Accommodations for Workers with Psychiatric Disabilities*. Sacramento: California Department of Mental Health.

Moore, C. 1986. *The Mediation Process: Practical Strategies for Resolving Conflict*. San Francisco: Jossey-Bass.

National Institute for Dispute Resolution. 1994. *Mediation and Disability: Targeting Disability Needs: A Guide to the Americans with Disabilities Act for Dispute Resolution Programs*. Washington, DC: NIDR.

Retzinger, S. 1990. Mental Illness and Labeling in Mediation. *Mediation Quarterly* 8(2): 151–60.

Saposnek, D. 1983. *Mediating Child Custody Disputes: A Systematic Guide for Family Therapists, Court Counselors, Attorneys, and Judges*. San Francisco: Jossey-Bass.

Schwebel, A., D. Gately, T. Milburn, & M. Renner. 1993. PMI-DM: A Divorce Mediation Approach That First Addresses Interpersonal Issues. *Journal of Family Psychotherapy* 4(2): 69–90.

Singer, L. 1990. *Settling Disputes: Conflict Resolution in Business, Families, and the Legal System*. Boulder, CO: Westview.

The Americans with Disabilities Act. 1990. 42 U.S.C. Sec. 12101, Title V, Section 513.

13

COMMUNITY

Community Mediation: The Grassroots of Alternative Dispute Resolution

by Harry Kaminsky and Ann Yellott

Two neighbors find themselves engaged in a heated argument. In a fit of anger, one kicks the car door of the other, causing $500 in damages. Legal charges are pending.

An entire neighborhood finds itself in conflict over the noise disturbance caused by a barking dog. What began as a minor dispute between two neighbors has escalated into a full blown conflict over personal rights and individual freedoms.

A dispute receives headline attention in the local newspaper when a group of homeless individuals camping in an open field are confronted by neighboring residents determined to pressure local politicians into forcing the homeless to move elsewhere. Advocates for the homeless also gather to protest the continued harassment of these men, women, and children struggling to create homes for themselves.

These examples are typical of disputes being successfully resolved every day in community mediation programs. Each case involves parties that to some degree have an ongoing relationship and are engaged in a dispute that has underlying interests that must be addressed to resolve the dispute in such a way as to prevent escalating future conflict (Kaminsky, 1988). The resolution of community-based conflict allows for and promotes the development of positive values among citizens within a more cohesive community.

Historical Overview

The history of community mediation programs is rich. Community mediation is built on the conviction that when disputing parties are empowered to resolve their own conflict in a noncoercive environment and with the assistance of an impartial facilitator familiar with the dynamics of the community, a mutually beneficial resolution can be found. This is not a new concept as it has been informally practiced in diverse cultures for centuries. Whereas in some traditional cultural contexts the formal role of community mediator is well established, in most instances this facilitator was likely to be a friend, family member, spiritual advisor, or community elder. These individuals were selected because they were respected within their community and demonstrated commitment to and understanding of those in conflict. The modern equivalent of these historical pioneers share similar values and attributes.

It has often been said that the modern roots of community mediation originate with the social action movements of the 1960s. In 1965 a Presidential Commission on Law Enforcement and the Administration of Justice called attention to problems associated with judicial resolution of community disputes, including overloaded court dockets. The U.S. Community Relations Service was established by the Civil Rights Act of 1964 in part to prevent violence and create dialogue between conflicting parties. It began to use the process of mediation, previously used primarily in labor disputes, to resolve conflicts in schools, prisons, and government institutions (NIDR, 1991).

In 1969, the U.S. federal government, the American Arbitration Association, the Philadelphia District Attorney, and the Philadelphia Municipal Court jointly created the Philadelphia Municipal Court Arbitration Tribunal, which was funded through the Law Enforcement Assistance Administration (LEAA). Although it provided arbitration as an option for resolving disputes, it paved the way for mediation as a creative dispute resolution alternative (NIDR, 1991).

The Columbus Night Prosecutor's Program, also created with LEAA funds, evolved from the Philadelphia model and established what is still considered to be a model community mediation program. Its goal was to help resolve an array of minor disputes that were overwhelming the courts; mediation was seen as an effective method of diverting cases from the court system. The City of Phoenix Community Mediation Program, established in 1986, is one of the many examples of such a diversion model, and is now administered by the diversion program administrator for the city. As LEAA funding continued, neighborhood justice centers were established in Atlanta, Kansas City, Los Angeles, Honolulu, Houston, and Washington, D.C. (NIDR, 1991).

In San Francisco in 1976, under the banner of the Community Boards Program, one of the best known and frequently duplicated programs was established. The Community Boards Program strives to develop a neighborhood justice system in which volunteers are trained to mediate community disputes as well as to provide other services. The result is that the individual volunteer experiences personal growth through civic involvement, which in turn serves to combat alienation within urban communities. Many community disputes are resolved amicably via the use of volunteer mediators, and the entire community benefits through the greater cohesion and enhanced self-esteem of its residents (Shonholz, 1984). An enhanced community spirit is one of the many benefits of the community board model.

There are many issues that confront community mediation programs today, including the demise of federal and state funding. Yet programs continue to flourish and expand. The essential concept underlying all community mediation programs is firmly grounded in the assumption that those directly engaged in conflict have the potential to find their own solutions to resolve their disputes. If we empower individuals and groups in the community by providing a safe forum for dispute resolution with an impartial facilitator, we will continue to see creative workable solutions that provide numerous benefits to all citizens.

Theory, Debates, and Trends in Community Mediation

Community mediation programs (CMPs) or neighborhood justice centers (NJCs) have thrived since their initiation during the 1960s and 1970s, despite predictions that the demise of federal funding would lead to their disappearance. Their numbers have steadily increased from a handful of projects in the early 1970s, to approximately 180 in 1988 and at least four hundred programs in 1992 (Drake & Lewis, 1988; Bell, 1992). Thousands of communities have been impacted by these predominantly grass-roots organizations. Citizens and groups have been provided with a forum for no- or low-cost dispute resolution processes, and community institutions such as schools, government agencies, and businesses have used an increasingly varied range of conflict resolution services offered by these programs.

Over the course of the more than quarter century that community justice programs have existed in North America, a variety of issues and debates have surfaced in this field of practice. Research is beginning to contribute some answers or at least a better foundation for addressing these challenges. Considerably more study is needed on all of these issues, and practitioners and researchers need to collaborate more effectively in the future in this regard (Birkhoff, 1995).

The Illusive Goal of Social Change

As Drake and Lewis (1988) point out, much of the idealism and personal commitment that nourishes the dispute resolution field is rooted in the com-

munity justice center movement. The establishment in 1994 of the National
Association for Community Mediation (NAFCM) reflects a continuing commitment to the transformative power of collaborative problem solving and social change as a long range goal for CMPs. However, as Herman (1994) notes,
transforming communities is not a job for the faint hearted or the thin skinned.
Several studies reviewed by Herman suggest that many CMPs may actually
support the status quo by failing to provide an environment that consistently
upsets socially sanctioned power relationships. For example, Herman's review
of 603 Albuquerque small claims cases settled either through adjudication or
mediation demonstrated that white claimants received significantly higher
monetary settlements than visible minority claimants. Minority disputants
paid out more and received less than their white counterparts, with differences
being even more significant in mediated cases than in adjudicated ones. It is
interesting to note that the involvement of two minority comediators eliminated the disadvantage for minority disputants in mediated settlements of the
claims, while mixed race comediation teams did not significantly improve the
situation for minorities (Herman, 1994). Such research, limited in scope as it
may be, raises significant questions about the social justice claims of CMPs
and has important consequences as the field seeks to address questions about
standards of practice and training of mediators.

Administrative Structures of Community Mediation Programs

The issue of the relationship of CMPs to courts and legal systems, and
the relative advantages and disadvantages of close ties to the courts has been
vigorously debated. Some have argued that the survival of CMPs is furthered
by their being directly sponsored by courts. While CMPs need a steady stream
of cases to mediate, and contracts with court systems are one of the most effective ways to assure the availability of an adequate caseload, others would
argue that it is important to keep the programs located in the community, independent of court systems. The NAFCM in particular has emphasized the importance of autonomy from the judicial system. According to the NAFCM,
community mediation "provides direct access to the public through self-
referral and strives to reduce barriers to service including physical, linguistic,
cultural, programmatic, and economic barriers" and "provides an alternative to
the judicial system at any stage of a conflict" (NAFCM, 1994).

Currently, North American programs that call themselves community
justice or mediation centers have a wide variety of administrative structures, including being part of the judicial/legal system, such as multidoor courthouse
programs or projects sponsored directly by a court or prosecutor's office (e.g.,
the Cochise County Superior Court Alternative Dispute Resolution Program in
Arizona and the Phoenix Mediation Program in the City of Phoenix's Prosecutor's Office); being sponsored by a government (nonjudicial) jurisdiction, such

as a city or county (e.g., the Dispute Settlement Program of the Charlotte-Mecklenberg Community Relations Committee in North Carolina); being an independent agency with its own board of directors (e.g., the New Mexico Center for Dispute Resolution, the Community Boards Program in San Francisco, and Neighbor-to-Neighbor in Salem, Oregon); and being part of a larger social service agency (e.g., the CMP of Our Town Family Center in Tucson). Programs that are independent of the courts typically have contracts with their local or state judicial systems and provide dispute resolution services for cases referred by the courts, police, and prosecutors. Often these referrals form the majority of cases handled by the program. Herein lies a potential danger for the survival of community programs; as more judicial systems increase their commitment to using alternative dispute resolution processes such as mediation, arbitration, and settlement conferences, the courts are more likely to take over the administration of comminity programs. CMPs having long-standing and positive relationships with courts and prosecutors may experience the loss of substantial sources of funding and cases, as those judicial systems claim the alternative dispute resolution services for their own multidoor courthouse programs.

Another challenge that relates to the issue of CMP governance is found in those programs that are part of a larger social service agency. Staff and volunteers in these programs can find themselves facing a series of ethical dilemmas. The goals of the larger umbrella organization may have little to do with mediation and conflict resolution, as agency policies and procedures are set by boards of directors that contain few people knowledgeable about the field of dispute resolution. Grant monies, donations, and fees that come directly into the CMP may be incorporated into the larger agency budget to cover the administrative overhead for non-CMP services. Given the substantial numbers of CMPs in North America, research into the question of benefits and disadvantages of different types of program governance is needed. Such research could assist CMPs in taking action to create the most beneficial system of administration for their programs, and the field as a whole would stand to benefit.

Funding and Fiscal Realities

The need to develop a diversity of funding sources is repeatedly cited as a key to the survival and growth of community mediation. Funding for CMPs comes from federal, state, and local government and judicial systems, bar associations, the United Way, foundations such as Hewlett, Ford, and Surdna, corporations and businesses, sales of training manuals and other materials, fundraisers, and increasing administrative, service, training and/or membership fees. The search for sufficient monies to run quality programs is a never-ending process. The growing competition for sources of public and private funding continues to be a challenge for community mediation as for all social services.

One approach to dealing with financial constraints is for CMPs to charge fees for their mediation, facilitation, and training services. Many CMPs still use their grant monies to provide free mediation and training services; increasing numbers of programs, however, recognize the need to collect monies for complex cases or projects that are not covered by existing grant funds, particularly as CMPs expand into areas such as school-based peer mediation, environmental or public policy conflict resolution, and family disputes. Many CMPs are now charging for their training services. These practices pose the challenge of how to administer a mix of free and fee-based services, and how to move no-fee services to a sliding fee or set rate.

Quality Control and Certification

In many ways CMPs have led the mediation field in dealing with issues of quality control. Since CMPs get much of their funding from public sources, they have been held accountable in regard to numbers of cases handled, agreements reached, durability of agreements, and disputant satisfaction. This information provides feedback to the program mediators that can be used to make needed changes. Unfortunately, often due to limited staff, this statistical information is used in reports and grant proposals for funding purposes, and often not applied to actual programmatic changes.

CMPs generally require their beginning mediators to complete twenty- to forty-hour training programs, attend continuing education and case-management sessions, and comediate with more experienced mediators. Many CMPs have set up procedures for evaluating mediator competence. Many have successfully involved volunteers as trainers while others predominantly use staff, or contract out for their training. The quality of CMP training programs vary, thus impacting the qualifications and competence of their mediators.

Complexity and Range of Cases Handled by Community Mediation Programs

Most CMPs started by dealing with cases involving barking dogs, noisy stereos, or minor property damage. Over the years, however, they have expanded their services to include the handling of complex community disputes, environmental and public policy cases, victim-offender reconciliation work, training of peer mediators in elementary and secondary schools, and family mediation services. Numerous challenges have arisen in regard to the expansion of services from "micro-level" neighborhood disputes to more "macro-level" issues. The first challenge relates to the provision of adequate additional training of community mediators to enable them to comfortably and effectively deal with such cases. The second is the necessity of obtaining additional funds or developing a system for charging fees to cover the costs of providing these new services. Public policy mediations are particularly time consuming and protracted. If a CMP begins to take on multiparty community, environmental, or public disputes without adequate preparation and finances, the volume of work substantially rises and can rapidly overburden program staff. Some CMPs have charged for these more complicated community disputes and paid volunteer mediators minimal stipends in an attempt to deal with the fiscal challenge.

Collaboration, Not Competition

An important issue within the community mediation field is the need to encourage collaboration at the national, state, and local levels. Limited funds, as well as principles of cooperation and communication, contribute to the focus on creating collaborative structures among alternative dispute resolution organizations. Both NAME (National Association for Mediation in Education) and NAFCM now share space with the National Institute for Dispute Resolution, thus cutting administrative overhead and encouraging direct communication between these national organizations. The emergence of NAFCM as a viable membership organization for CMPs speaks to the need of neighborhood justice centers for networking and collective advocacy for common goals.

Many CMPs are active members of statewide, regional, or local dispute resolution organizations. Such networking is critical for the continued survival and growth of community mediation. Community mediation needs to become more outspoken and prominent locally and nationally to ensure that the field of conflict resolution is able to contribute to the goal of transforming communities and creating a more just and equitable society.

The Community Mediation Process

Models of Mediation

There are two primary models for mediating community-based disputes—the caucus and systems models of community dispute resolution. Both can be practiced in a pure form, although a hybrid approach is most often used.

The caucus model replicates a mediation model frequently used in labor and employment disputes as well as commercial disputes. As the name implies, the mediator frequently caucuses (involving private privileged communication) with each party in dispute. The parties generally meet in a joint session to discuss common concerns such as rules and ongoing procedures, and then arrange for ongoing individual sessions with the mediator.

In the private session, the mediator helps to identify the discrete issues in dispute and the interests underlying stated positions, and assists each party in identifying their "Best Alternative to a Negotiated Agreement" (Fisher & Ury, 1983), the standard each disputant will use in evaluating any proposed solutions made in negotiation that may resolve the dispute. The private caucus allows for a confidential exchange that permits each party the opportunity to explore creative options without appearing weak to the other side, which may result in posturing and a loss of face.

The systems theory-based approach is rooted in the assumption that when two or more parties are in conflict, the system within which they interact is also "conflicted." Therefore, to adequately resolve the conflict all parties that contribute to it must be present and interacting. A positive impact on one party (one part of the system) will also impact another. A transformation may occur between the parties, as well as within the system, that can bring positive change far beyond the scope of the dispute. This is sometimes referred to as the transformative approach to mediation.

The systems model incorporates these concepts and requires that all parties to the dispute be present and in the same room with the mediator. Caucusing takes place only as an impasse strategy and only when absolutely necessary. In most instances, the parties remain together throughout the process and interact, modeling the mediator's positive communication and problem resolution style.

In most community practice settings, a hybrid model combining the two approaches is used. A private caucus session is frequently used to diffuse anger or other strong emotions, but problem exploration and alternatives for resolution are conducted within the systems context.

Number of Mediators

The number of mediators used to facilitate a mediation process also varies within existing programs. The use of a single mediator is common for several reasons; it is easier to schedule sessions and many mediators prefer to work within their own creative style, feeling constrained by the input of another mediator. Frequently, in a case mediated by a single mediator, it will take less time to reach a mutually acceptable outcome. Single mediators are less expensive, an important consideration in light of the fact that many community mediators are volunteers who receive little financial remuneration.

A comediation model is used by many programs for the perceived advantages inherent in working within teams. The old expression, "two heads are better than one," clearly applies to dispute resolution. A comediation model provides an extra set of ears and eyes to better listen to and observe the communication between parties. The interplay between the mediators can also spark a range of creative alternatives generated by the parties. Positive modeling of behaviors between the mediators can serve to demonstrate the possibilities available to the parties through cooperative efforts.

Another benefit of the comediation model relates to working in the context of human diversity. For example, imagine that two neighbors are having a conflict regarding the volume of noise generated by a stereo system playing rock music. The complaining neighbor is an elderly African-American female; the neighbor playing the music is a young caucasian male. After agreeing to mediate in response to receiving a telephone call from a case coordinator at the local community mediation program, they walk into the mediation room and meet their mediator for the first time. The mediator is a college age caucasian male. The possible perception of the complaining party may be that the mediator will be inherently biased against her, as he is similar to her neighbor in appearance. If perception impacts conflict resolution then it may be important to find ways to balance these perceptions. One way is to create mediation teams that address possible concerns related to gender, race, culture, age, socioeconomic status, and disability.

Comediation also provides for the combining of experienced and novice mediators. It provides an opportunity for the new mediator to gain experience without carrying the full responsibility as the facilitator of the process; for the experienced mediator, each mediation session provides both teaching and learning opportunities as it is debriefed.

A variant of the comediation approach is the panel/board model in which members of a community may sit on a panel or board and assist in conciliating disputes. The benefits are similar to the comediation approach as issues of human diversity that may assist in the settlement of the dispute are addressed.

A possible negative aspect of comediating relates to stylistic differences. Sometimes these differences provide the necessary creative diversity to enhance options. However, when stylistic variances cannot be reconciled, these differences negate the positive modeling that disputants need to observe. If disputants sense a conflict between mediators, even if a conflict of style rather than substance, this perception could impair the positive resolution of the dispute.

Process of Mediation

Both the systems and caucus models use a similar structure for mediation, and the basic steps of the process, with some variation for larger community disputes, are the same: introduction; problem description; identification of interests; options for solution; agreement; and conclusion.

Introduction. The introduction to the process of community mediation is extremely important to the eventual outcome. The mediator welcomes the parties and establishes that the outcome of the process belongs to them. The dispute is theirs and the opportunity for a creative and beneficial resolution lies with them as well.

The mediator establishes her or his own role as a skilled facilitator of communication between the disputing parties. No outcome will be imposed by the mediator, and if mediation is not successful the parties may leave without a solution once they have attempted to earnestly work out their differences. The mediator will also help the parties build positive expectations and garner confidence in both the process and the mediator.

The mediator will strive to establish credibility by assuring the parties that she or he is neutral and has no direct interest in the outcome of the dispute. The mediator may discuss the extent of the training he or she has received in conflict resolution, the number of cases she or he has previously mediated, and her or his commitment to the betterment of the community. It is important to develop the expectation of success as a positive, self-fulfilling prophecy.

Rules of conduct for the mediation session will also be discussed. Although the process is informal it is important to establish rules and gain the commitment of the parties to these rules in order to build trust and confidence. Most parties feel that it is the other that will violate a rule, at the expense of the first party. By gaining a commitment from each, a safer and more comfortable environment is created. Once a rule is agreed upon it is essential for the mediator to enforce that rule.

Rules of conduct vary according to the type of program and nature of the case. However, some rules seem to be universally appropriate, including no interruptions while the other party is speaking, no name-calling or put-downs, and no screaming or shouting. Other rules, such as no physical violence, may be appropriate for cases involving harassment, minor assaults, and property damage, but may seem out of place in a community dispute over the installation of speed bumps on a road.

The final task in the first stage is an overview of the mediation process itself. Most parties in community mediation have never participated in the process and are nervous about the unknown. A brief description of what will occur, step by step, can decrease anxiety.

Problem Description. Stage two of the process gives each party the opportunity to describe the problem situation that has led to the need for mediation. Usually the complaining party will begin to describe his or her perception of the problem. When they have fully described the situation from their point of view, the other party will have the chance to ask any clarifying questions. This process is intended to better understand the perspective of the other and is not an opportunity for rebuttal. The mediator must delicately facilitate this stage. She or he may also need to ask clarifying questions for her or his own understanding of the situation.

After the first party has had the chance to express his or her understanding of the problem, the other party will give their perspective. Once again clarifying questions may be asked and the step repeats itself.

Identification of Interests. At this point in the process each side should be clear on how the other views their situation, and together they proceed to define their interests. This is done by answering a simple question posed by the mediator, "What do you want to see happen in order to remedy the problem as you see it?"

The response is frequently stated in the form of a position rather than an interest. They may say, "I want my neighbor to get rid of their barking dog." This is clearly a position, and one that is unlikely to be acceptable to the other side. The choice is to meet the position, sacrificing one's own interests, or to say no, leaving the parties at an impasse. However, through exploration of the position, it may be determined that the underlying interest of the complaining party is to be able to sleep through the night undisturbed by the barking dog. This is an interest that may be able to be met through the creative exploration of options.

Once the interest of one side is better understood by the other, this step is repeated with the other side identifying their own wants and interests. We may discover that the dog owner keeps the barking dog as a watchdog in order to meet their personal interest of greater security in their home. With the understanding of the desire for security, solutions that were not apparent previously may be able to be found.

Options for Solution. The understanding of each other's interests can now lead to an exploration of possible solutions. Rather than trying to meet the conditions of a position, which usually leave two options—"Yes, I'll do it" or "No, I won't"—the parties now can explore a rich mix of creative alternatives to their mutual problem. In the example above, the dog owner may agree to bring the dog into the house during certain night hours to give their neighbor a chance to sleep undisturbed; in return the complaining party may offer to involve the dog owner in the Neighborhood Block Watch to meet the interest of greater home security.

Agreement. When the parties feel as if the problem will be rectified by means of a course of action that will satisify both their sets of interests, they have in fact reached an agreement that is mutually acceptable. Many programs finalize the agreement by means of a written memorandum, which serves as a reminder of what each side has willingly stated they would do. A good agreement will have each side responsible for making the agreement work. It should also be specific in answering the questions: Who will do what? When? Where? How? and How much?

Conclusion. The mediation session ends after each side acknowledges their understanding of the agreement and commitment to making it work. However, there is usually an extra benefit provided by the mediator as the parties debrief the mediation. New discoveries are often made by the parties and a better understanding on how to define interests and communicate them more effectively in the future are realized and discussed. In this way the mediation session becomes a learning experience and a possible precedent setter for the future.

Case Study: Neighborhood Dispute

Fred Cranmer and Charles Smith have been neighbors for three years. They are not close friends but they are cordial and generally neighborly. Both live active lives and between their commitment to work and family do not frequently interact. Their driveways are separated by some hedges that Mr. Cranmer planted and has maintained for several years, even before Mr. Smith moved in.

One night Mr. Smith pulled into the driveway and accidentally drove into the hedges, damaging them. The next morning Mr. Cranmer knocked on Mr. Smith's door and screamed insults, accusing him of having no regard for property and driving while intoxicated. Mr. Smith began to apologize for driving into the hedges but felt so abused by Mr. Cranmer's language and the false accusation that he was driving while drinking, that he screamed back telling Mr. Cranmer to get off his property and then slammed the door.

For several days the two did not see each other. Then on a Saturday morning, while Mr. Cranmer was working on replanting the hedges, Mr. Smith pulled into the driveway. Mr. Cranmer demanded that Mr. Smith pay him for the cost of the new hedges and for his time. Mr. Smith, not liking the tone of Mr. Cranmer's voice replied, "I don't care about the hedges and your time is not worth anything."

Fred Cranmer was not a violent man, but he was so outraged by Mr. Smith's reply that he picked up a garden shovel and smashed the tail lights and back fender of Charles Smith's car. Mr. Smith's wife, observing from the window of her house, called the police. Mr. Cranmer was sited for the misdemeanor offense of criminal property damage.

The prosecutor's office reviewed the case and decided that before charging Mr. Cranmer, both he and Mr. Smith might benefit from the opportunity of mediating their differences. Although prosecuting may help Mr. Smith in obtaining restitution for his damaged vehicle, it is unlikely to resolve ongoing differences between him and Mr. Cranmer. Since it is likely that they will remain neighbors for some period of time, it is important for both to put past differences behind them. They were each told about the option of mediating this case rather than going to a hearing before a judge. Mediation might spare Mr. Cranmer the stigma of being prosecuted while helping Mr. Smith to collect restitution for his damaged vehicle and reduce the tensions and potential for future violence.

Both Mr. Smith and Mr. Cranmer received a phone call from a case co-ordinator with the local community mediation program. She obtained their consent to schedule a mediation session at a time convenient to each of them and obtained enough information regarding the two different perspectives about the dispute to select two mediators from the community where Mr. Cranmer and Mr. Smith reside.

The mediation took place approximately two weeks after the initial incident. It lasted a little over one hour and was resolved to the satisfaction of both parties using the mediation process previously described. The city prosecutor did not go forward in charging Mr. Cranmer, as the dispute was settled to the mutual satisfaction of the parties.

The agreement reached contained details of the restitution Mr. Cranmer would make and Mr. Smith's acknowledgment that the dispute was resolved so that the complaint could be dropped in the precharging stage. The key to the resolution however, was the discussion that took place, facilitated by the mediators. This discussion included Mr. Cranmer's building hostility toward Mr. Smith for never offering to contribute toward the maintenance of the hedges, and Mr. Smith's feelings about never being welcomed to the neighborhood by Mr. Cranmer. This level of discussion and intimacy could never have unfolded in a court of law but is common in mediation sessions. Both the parties and the mediators concluded that this type of discussion was not only crucial for resolving the dispute at hand but also for the prevention of future disputes.

Case Study: Multiparty Community Dispute

The Desert Ashram found a suitable site to set up their substance abuse residential treatment program, and approached the city government for the necessary zoning change to allow the project to operate in what was a low-income, predominantly Hispanic inner-city residential neighborhood. During the process of public notification and hearings about the requested zoning change, it became clear that many neighbors were extremely concerned about placing yet another controversial social service residential center in their community. Speaking for the local community was the Ortega Neighborhood Association (ONA), which pointed out that too many residential shelters for homeless people or drug addicts get "dumped" in low-income and predominantly minority neighborhoods such as theirs, reducing property values and residents' safety. The Ashram program would be only one block away from the neighborhood's elementary and middle schools. The Association felt that community residents had made many efforts to "clean up" their neighborhood, discouraging drug dealing and gang member activity, and to restore a positive image of their community. Residents indicated that they had worked too hard to now cave in to the city on this zoning change. Thus adults and children appeared with signs and loud voices at the meeting of the zoning commission and the subsequent public hearing, demanding that the city deny the request for a zoning change. In addition to harsh words about the drug addicts who would be coming into their community, ONA members expressed considerable suspicion and distrust of the white-turbaned Ashram staff.

The zoning commission, along with several city council members, were finding themselves growing weary of the trend of various neighborhood associations protesting placement of shelters and social service programs in their local communities, with diminishing sympathy for this kind of "not in my backyard" phenomenon. They decided to refer this controversial situation to the local community mediation program to see if an acceptable resolution could be reached. The CMP agreed to mediate despite the knowledge that this would be a very time-consuming process that would likely take several months of meetings before any hope of a resolution was forthcoming, and the fact that funding from the city for the CMP was in short supply. However, it was hoped that this case would provide an opportunity to demonstrate the worth of alternative dispute resolution processes to local politicians who had been reluctant to use mediation or facilitated problem solving to address public policy disputes.

A small mediation team of two staff and three volunteers were selected to work on this case, including two Hispanics and a staff member who had previously worked in a drug treatment agency. Initial arrangements were made to meet with both the Desert Ashram project staff and the Ortega Neighborhood Association. The purpose of these initial caucuses was to explain the mediation process and obtain a commitment from both sides to participate in the process, determine an equal number of representatives for each side for the mediation itself, and establish a mechanism for reporting back to the larger groups and getting approval for any agreements that began to develop. It was necessary to identify a neutral location in the community for conducting the mediation meetings, get an agreement regarding interacting with the various media who had been reporting on the initial clashes between the two groups at City Hall, and decide whether the mediation sessions would be open for community members who were not part of the mediation team to attend. Particularly within the Ortega Neighborhood Association, which was made up of sixty-three families, there was a strong distrust of the mediation process, and a concern that the city was just using this procedure to pressure association members into concessions and again forcing them to accept something that they did not want in their neighborhood. They felt that if they were wealthier and whiter, city council members would have been quick to uphold their objections and refuse this zoning change, thus forcing the Ashram group to move elsewhere.

In meeting with the Ashram staff, it became evident that they believed the association was opposed to the residential center because Ashram represents a "different" religious belief system and because Ashram staff "look different" with their white turbans and robes. The Desert Ashram had been offered a particularly good deal on the house they wanted to buy and use for the residential treatment program. They also felt that they could offer some valuable substance abuse education and treatment services for the local schools and community. One of the reasons they were particularly attracted to this neighborhood was the proactive stance of the ONA to "take back the parks and streets" from the drug dealers and gang members.

The CMP's first task was to obtain the trust of both groups, especially the ONA. After initial separate meetings to establish rapport and engage each party, five joint mediation sessions followed, spread out over four months. Interspersed between the joint sessions were several individual meetings with the two groups, as well as many discussions by phone and in person with various city officials and others involved in this dispute. A critical development to the process was the inclusion of several groups who had not been involved originally as parties to the mediation, including a small merchants association in the neighborhood, the local schools, and representatives from the youth gang located in that part of the city.

The eventual resolution included the following items: the Ashram pledged 5 percent of its resources to the ONA for use in its educational and community building efforts; the Ashram staff and clients, several gang members, three local merchants, and four neighborhood families formed a speakers' bureau to offer ongoing presentations to local schools, community groups, and the media; the Ashram agreed to hire one of the local gang members who had been involved in the mediation process as a peer advocate, contingent on his staying clean, and to provide a small summer job training program for local youth, using grant money provided by the city; the merchants' association agreed to provide several minimal wage part-time positions for youth in the community; and all groups agreed to participate in a monthly neighborhood "clean-up" campaign to be organized by the ONA and the elementary and middle schools. Further, there would be monthly meetings in the first year to determine whether the parties were living up to their obligations, and whether there were any problems occurring in the neighborhood involving Ashram clients; after the first year, these gatherings were to become part of the regular meetings of the ONA. The city agreed to pay for notices of the meetings to be mailed out, along with any minutes and educational materials created for use in the neighborhood. Finally, three members of the ONA would be added to the Ashram's Residential Program Advisory Committee. The parties thus collaboratively decided that the plans for the Desert Ashram residential treatment center could proceed.

Conclusion

Community mediation can be delivered from a variety of practice venues. One alternative is to house mediation services within the court and use community volunteers as the mediators. This approach preserves some of the enthusiasm and idealism of the community mediation field, through the involvement of trained volunteers. However, what is lost is the goal of directly impacting the community's ability to resolve disputes nonviolently and without resorting to overcrowded and typically adversarial judicial systems.

Another option is using private dispute resolution providers to resolve these conflicts. This approach helps to strengthen those mediation programs that are seeking to expand their services. However, many of the cases that are handled by CMPs come from people and groups with limited incomes and/or minimal awareness about mediation as a means for resolving disputes. CMPs have acted as a vehicle for extending mediation and other collaborative problem solving processes to individuals and groups who would otherwise not use them. Given that the general public is still largely uninformed about mediation and arbitration, we cannot overlook the important educative role played by community mediation programs in regard to the benefits of mediation as an alternative dispute resolution process.

An important alternative to community mediation is community development and organization, which can assume many forms (Rothman, 1974). In the multiparty case study described above, the ONA might have used a locality development approach to empower the neighborhood in its efforts to resist the placement of a residential drug treatment program within its boundaries, and to make a statement for the rights of low-income and minority neighborhoods to exercise more control over their own communities. The Desert Ashram might have used a process of social action to challenge the city and community regarding the rights of substance abusers involved in treatment programs and society's obligations to this population. The city might have used a social planning model to assess the treatment needs of substance abusers in the city as well as the impact of locating a program such as the Ashram residential center in the Ortega neighborhood.

Community mediation can empower neighborhoods to assess and meet their needs or, conversely, discourage them from pressuring political or corporate entities to meet their demands. Advocates and practitioners of community mediation need to remain vigilant about the potential misuse of mediation in the service of dominant power groups. There are times when a class action suit, for example, may be needed to address inequality and discrimination in a particular community.

The ever-increasing level of violence in our society speaks to the need for maintaining and enhancing new avenues for peacemaking. Rather than asking what alternatives exist to community mediation, a more fruitful question may be to ask how can we ensure that increasing numbers of our citizens gain an appreciation for and ability to use more effective communication and nonviolent conflict resolution skills. Community institutions such as schools, churches, businesses, and governments could offer educational opportunities and in-house mediation programs, which would draw upon the talents and skills of both community justice centers and private dispute resolution providers. The substantial paradigm shift needed to move from aggression, violence, and competition to collaboration and cooperation will require a range of alternative dispute resolution options.

References

Bell, G. 1992. Improving the Administration of Justice. *NIDR Forum* 24: 5–9.

Birkhoff, J. 1995. Marketing Isn't Everything: The Importance of Research in Dispute Resolution. *SPIDR News,* 19 (3): 1–12.

Drake, W. R., & M. K. Lewis. 1988. Community Justice: A Lasting Innovation. *NIDR Forum,* 20: 3–4.

Fisher, R. & W. Ury. 1983. *Getting to Yes*. New York: Penguin.

Herman, H. S. 1994. Reflections on Transformation. *NIDR Forum* 26: 17–22.

Kaminsky, H. 1988. Community Mediation. *Arizona Attorney* 25 (3): 24–25.

National Association for Community Mediation. 1994. Competition for Limited Mediation Funds: Sound Familiar? *NAFCM News,* Winter.

National Institute for Dispute Resolution. 1988. *How Community Justice Centers Are Fairing*. Washington, DC: NIDR.

———. 1991. *Community Dispute Resolution Manual: Insights and Guidance from Two Decades of Practice*. Washington, DC: NIDR.

Rothman, J. 1974. Three Models of Community Organization Practice. In F. Cox et al., eds., *Strategies of Community Organization,* 2d ed. Itasca, IL: Peacock.

Shonholz, R. 1984. Neighborhood Justice Systems: Work, Structure, and Guiding Principles. *Mediation Quarterly* 5: 3–30.

┌─────────┐
│   │
│   │
│   │
└─────────┘

14

EDUCATION

Mediation in the School System: Facilitating the Development of Peer Mediation Programs

by Nancy M. Kaplan

Violence among young people is a significant problem. Over 3 million assorted crimes—about 11 percent of all crimes—occur each year in U.S. public schools (Sautter, 1995). Children are being shot in school hallways, classroom doors are locked so that unwanted students cannot disrupt classes, teachers are being attacked by students. The atmosphere of fear prevalent in the school system is clearly not conducive to learning, and educators know that change needs to occur.

Mediation in the field of education has become increasingly important because violence in schools has significantly increased, and because the ability to problem solve is recognized as a necessary life skill. The most prevalent form of school-based mediation is peer mediation, which aims to provide a more effective and appropriate method for resolving conflict than suspension, expulsion, or court intervention by allowing young people to resolve their own disputes. By increasing students' knowledge of nonadversarial conflict resolution, and enhancing their communication, negotiation, and problem-solving skills, mediation can lead to a perception of conflict as a positive force that allows for personal growth and institutional change (Davis & Porter, 1985). Peer mediation in elementary and secondary schools is relatively new, with the first U.S. programs beginning in the early 1980s. Today, peer mediation can be found in over five thousand U.S. schools, and there are over a hundred variants of peer mediation programs from which to choose.

Although this chapter focuses on peer mediation and how it is used in school settings, it is important to recognize that peer mediation is only one type of mediation found within the school system. Mediation programs are in fact used by educational institutions in a variety of ways. Preschool teachers use mediation to settle conflicts between young children. In elementary and secondary schools, faculty are trained in mediation techniques and mediation is taught and modeled in the classroom. Some elementary and secondary schools are conducting parent training classes, educating parents of young children to use mediation to settle sibling disputes. Conflicts between parents of special needs students and school districts regarding special education placements and services are being mediated by dispute resolution professionals both from within and outside the school system, including school social workers. Intergroup racial conflicts in schools are being responded to by means of intergroup mediation programs.

At the college and university level, a variety of disputes are settled through the peer mediation process, and student-faculty disputes are often referred to mediation. In addition, many colleges and universities are incorporating mediation training programs as part of elementary and secondary education programs. The National Institute for Dispute Resolution (NIDR) and the National Association for Mediation in Education (NAME) have developed a training curriculum for in-service and pre-service educators *(Conflict Resolution in Teacher Education: A Manual for Educators),* which presents the concepts, skills, and techniques of conflict resolution in a series of adaptable modules.

There are also other types of student-based conflict resolution approaches that have been initiated by school systems, many of which contain elements of the mediation model. Peer Helpers is one such program in which students are trained to provide one-to-one counseling for other students who come to them with emotional and personal concerns, and to make referrals for counseling or other assistance when needed. Other widely used methods of conflict resolution are anger management programs, such as Second Step, developed by the Committee for Children. This curriculum is presented by classroom teachers to students in elementary and middle schools, and instructs students to defuse and resolve conflict in an effective, conciliatory manner. Another program is Cooperative Learning (Johnson & Johnson, 1994), where students are encouraged to work together in groups to accomplish various tasks, a process that often leads to conflict, which is regarded as an opportunity to engage in conflict resolution in a protected environment. Yet another interesting approach is the Peace Table, where young students are given time to settle their differences directly with one another. Group meetings are also used where an entire class of elementary students sits in a circle to discuss and work out a problem presented by one of their fellow classmates.

One principal difference between peer mediation and other conflict resolution programs is that peer mediation programs offer a structured system where student mediators are given the opportunity to practice the skills they

have been taught. Most anger management training programs and conflict resolution programs teach skills and concepts to students and then assume that
the students will transfer them to their daily lives. Peer mediation involves assigning mediations to students trained in the process, and having them directly
facilitate the process of dispute resolution, with the "arms-length" support of
school personnel.

There is little doubt that peer mediation programs pose many challenges
for school systems. These programs do not "run themselves," and preliminary
mediation training is not enough to create and maintain a successful program.
There is an administrative requirement not only to train students but also to as-
sign mediators and to keep records. The effectiveness of the program varies with
the commitment of school faculty and the comprehensive nature of the program
itself. Further, the fact that peer mediation programs are associated with significant changes in the roles of teachers and school staff and a fundamental shift in
power relations within the school system results in considerable wariness on the
part of some school administrators about instituting such initiatives.

Do peer mediation programs reduce violence in schools? Violence in
our society is produced by a myriad of causes, and teaching mediation skills
and approaches in school may not counteract these influences. Socioeconomic conditions, racism and other forms of oppression, the media, and child
abuse are all contributing factors. Because peer mediation programs are relatively new, and there is little quantitative research on them, it is premature
to categorically conclude that these programs alone reduce violence in the
school system.

Peer mediation programs may not be a panacea, but they are an important step toward helping develop effective, positive ways to deal with conflict.
Giving young people the responsibility for guiding their peers toward settling
their disputes is an empowering experience for the mediators and beneficial
for disputants. The process defuses disagreements, disputes, and conflicts that
could erupt into violent situations, and is an enlightening experience for all
involved. Peer mediation clearly has the potential for positively improving
school climates both immediately and in the long term.

Research, Debates, and Trends

History

Peer mediation is a form of conflict resolution in which students are
taught to act as neutral third parties, using a structured process to help other
students resolve conflicts. Existing research reveals mixed results regarding
the effectiveness of conflict resolution and peer mediation programs in school
settings, and relatively few studies have directly examined the efficacy of current programs.

One of the first U.S. peer mediation programs was initiated in 1981 by the Neighborhood Justice Center in Honolulu. Reports from the project indicate that the majority of cases referred to peer mediation were resolved, and that the high schools involved experienced marked decreases in fights where mediation programs had been instituted. In 1982 the Community Board School Initiatives (CBSI) program in San Francisco initiated its peer mediation program for elementary, middle, and high school students. The CBSI curriculum is widely used today throughout North America. The School Mediators' Alternative Resolution Team (SMART) program began in 1983 in New York City, initiated by the Victim Services Agency and funded by the New York City Youth Bureau. Positive effects on school climate and disciplinary practices, on the self-image and confidence of student mediators, and on the longer-term behavior of student disputants were noted as a result of the program.

In 1984, the National Association for Mediation in Education (NAME) was formed subsequent to a meeting of fifty interested educators from fifteen states to discuss peer mediation in the schools. The original goal of NAME was to be a clearinghouse for mediation in educational institutions. The organization was to produce a directory of school-based programs, a quarterly newsletter (*The Fourth R*), and sponsor annual conferences. Future goals included conducting research, experimenting with new models, and giving technical assistance to start-up programs. NAME has now merged with the National Institute for Dispute Resolution (NIDR), and continues to be the leading national organization in the field of school-based mediation.

Current Research

A modest number of studies have begun to identify some of the positive outcomes of school-based mediation programs, including peer mediation, and are beginning to identify some of the salient factors associated with successful programs. Research on the SMART project (Moore & Whipple, 1988) reveals that at one site, Bryant High School, of the 134 cases referred to peer mediation, 116 were accepted, and 93 agreements were reached. Mediation agreements were adhered to in more than 90 percent of cases, and the school administration reported that suspensions fell by 50 percent, which was viewed as a positive outcome of the project. Araki (1990) reported the results of the Honolulu initiative, and found that the success of school-based mediation, particularly peer mediation, is largely dependent on the effectiveness of the start-up phases. Effective training and orientation, involving students, teachers, and school administrators, sets the stage for a successful program. The Honolulu project included a full-time district coordinator of mediation, who played a key role in organizing the orientation and training, and establishing and monitoring referral of disputes to the programs. Again, a high rate of agreement (92 percent of cases referred) was found in regard to a wide range of disputes, including gossip or rumors (27 percent of all referrals), verbal arguments (20 percent), and aggressive behavior and harassment (27 percent). Particularly successful student mediators were confident, had the ability to write clear agreements, possessed leadership qualities that gained the respect of their peers, demonstrated empathy and positive regard, made good use of questions, and listened well.

More recently, Yau (1994) and Brown (1994) reported on two Toronto-based research endeavors examining teacher and student attitudes toward conflict and conflict resolution. Yau analyzed questionnaires given to 847 elementary grade students and 134 teachers in ten schools, seven of which conducted peer mediation programs for at least two years. There were some interesting discrepancies in perception: teachers did not think that conflict was as prevalent as did students, especially boys; and trained student mediators were more positive regarding the efficacy of conflict resolution than were untrained students. Brown's research involved students and faculty at the secondary school level, and used questionnaires, focus groups, and individual interviews to explore attitudes and perceptions. In his research, not only did perceptions of teachers and students differ in regard to conflict but there were also differences between boys and girls. Whereas teachers defined "conflict" as a physical confrontation, students also used rumors or gossip in their definition. Most teachers felt conflicts were resolved when teachers acted as mediators, while only one-fourth of the students agreed. These findings may have implications for future research on perceptions of conflict. As Brown points out, whereas most U.S. research studies on school-based mediation have focused on the reduction of violent crimes in the schools, the Toronto board program focuses on raising awareness and skills in order to recognize, manage, and resolve conflicts effectively and peaceably. He concludes that further research on the noncriminal effects of conflict resolution programs is critical, as violent crime is only a small proportion of the total conflict in a school.

Two studies by Johnson and Johnson (1992, 1994) present the effectiveness of mediation programs for elementary school children. Their first study discusses the effects of conflict resolution and mediation training with two groups of middle-class, suburban elementary school children, one that had training and one that had not. After mediation training, referrals to teachers to resolve disputes dropped by 80 percent, and referrals to the principal dropped completely. Students used their skills outside of school, and videotaped simulation posttests given six months after the training indicated that trained students knew and were generally able to apply the negotiation sequence; untrained students did not use conflict resolution skills to resolve disputes and took longer than the trained students to come to resolution. The untrained students were twice as likely to go to the teacher to resolve a dispute as were the trained students. Johnson and Johnson's later (1994) research included ninety-two elementary-level children and involved a pretest, a posttest two weeks after training, and a second posttest four months after training. Conflict resolution and mediation skills were taught to the students for thirty minutes per day over a six-week period; once training was complete, two students were chosen to be peer mediators each day. Results showed that children referred fewer conflicts to the teacher, integrated core mediation skills, and increased their use of these skills (Johnson & Johnson, 1994).

Gentry and Benenson (1992) studied whether school mediation training transfers to the home setting. Twenty-seven elementary students were trained to be conflict managers, and pretest and posttest questionnaires were given to the children and their parents. Parents reported that student conflict managers showed a marked decline in conflicts with their siblings, and that when in conflict, they significantly improved in their ability to communicate effectively. Parents also reported a decline in their own interventions in sibling conflicts; and students reported a significant decline in the intensity of their conflicts.

The Ohio Commission on Dispute Resolution and Conflict Management (1993) initiated a three-year project to establish school peer mediation programs. Two types of conflict resolution programs were taught: one was a classroom curriculum teaching negotiation concepts to all students in the school; the second consisted of negotiation skills taught to all students and peer mediation skills taught to a select group of students who would then act as mediators for students in conflict. After the second year, surveys were administered to 10,000 students from the twenty schools involved in the project. Children in grades kindergarten to three showed a greater acceptance of other children seen as "different"; children in grades four to six reported increased willingness to stop fights and choose nonviolent options, and expressed increased confidence in their communication skills; students in grades seven to eight expressed an increased willingness to stop fights and to talk rather than fight; and high school students made use of their newly developed mediation skills in a variety of settings, both within and outside the school.

Eisler (1994) reports on a mediation project initiated in fifteen middle schools in New York City in 1991–92, called Schools Teaching Options for Peace (STOP), which expanded to thirty schools in 1992–93, with the second group named the Teen Mediation Project (TMP). Training for schools in the STOP group included peer mediation in-class training for select students and parent mediation training. Training for the second group of schools (TMP) involved only peer mediation training. The evaluation of the two projects noted fewer fights, reduction in suspensions, growth of personal relationships at school and home, and a more positive school climate. The curriculum component appeared important, but the time needed to present the material in every class was noted as a problem. Parent training was important to reinforce the skills learned at school but was difficult to administer due to problems recruiting parents and reaching non-English speaking populations. All respondents agreed that peer mediation was essential, primarily because it provided real-life opportunities for students to put conflict resolution concepts into practice (Eisler, 1994).

Jones and Carlin (1994) found in their study that females are generally more satisfied with peer mediation training than males, adults more than students, and Caucasian students more than African-American, Hispanic, or Asian-American students. There is no mention in their research of the race, gender, or age of the trainers involved, potentially key factors influencing their findings.

Faris (1996) reports on a study conducted in the Memphis school system that involved eleven secondary schools, and compared students trained in mediation who had the opportunity to mediate peer disputes with those who had been trained but had not mediated. Seventy-six percent of students who had mediated (versus 55 percent for students who had not) felt that their ability to resolve conflicts had improved significantly, 66 percent (versus 55 percent) felt that their ability to communicate had increased, and 81 percent (versus 70 percent) reported improvement in self-esteem. Over 50 percent of both groups reported using mediation outside of school either in sports, with friends, or with family. These results suggest that mediation training is more effective after trained students actually use their skills in peer mediation cases.

Horowitz and Boardman (1994) summarize the status of conflict resolution programs in schools and suggest directions for research, which include the need to test and expand conflict theory while stressing the importance of conflict prevention and deescalation, the need to develop cross-cultural and culturally specific mediation models, the need to study a range of third-party interventions (comparing different mediation models, and mediation with other types of intervention), the need to develop methods of dealing with disputants who do not want to participate in mediation, the need to consider different ages in theory and practice, the need to conduct interdisciplinary research, and the need to assess the effects of parent training and early intervention.

Because peer mediation programs are relatively new, special consideration must be given to the validity or lack of validity of research conducted on recently created programs that include small samples of participants. None of the research to date is definitive in establishing the absolute value of peer mediation. There is general agreement that although peer mediation seems like a good idea, we have not been able to prove that it is always effective in changing behavior or reducing violence. Most professionals agree that more quantitative research needs to be conducted over an extended time period. It will be some time before the effectiveness of these programs is clearly demonstrated, and it may take several generations to determine the degree to which mediation impacts social skills development, as young people trained in mediation mature into adulthood.

Debates and Trends

Debate continues in the field as to whether peer mediation programs actually reduce violence. But beyond this debate lies the question of whether violence reduction should be the ultimate goal of peer mediation. Many educators believe that teaching students the life skills of conflict resolution and "being your own mediator" are of paramount importance. Others argue that schools should teach only academics and question whether schools should be assuming responsibility for tasks that, they believe, belong to parents.

As mentioned earlier, one source of resistance to the implementation of peer mediation programs is those educators who tend to rely on strict disciplinary codes and practices that punish student misbehavior. Mediation is a direct threat to such systems as it necessitates a fundamental shift in power dynamics within the school. Students become empowered to settle their own disputes, and gain skill and confidence in doing so. Mediation requires significant changes in the school culture as students learn to respond more favorably to a respectful, collaborative mode of communication than to an autocratic style of behavior management.

One of the central debates in the field relates to whether peer mediation should be limited to the resolution of student disputes only. Some argue that it is inappropriate for student-teacher conflicts as it can weaken teacher authority; others believe that a double standard is present when mediation of disputes is not available in the student-teacher arena. Increasingly, schools are training not only students but teachers and all school staff in the mediation approach so that conflict resolution skills can be modeled by teachers, and teachers too can participate as both mediators and parties in the process.

Peer Mediation at the Elementary and Secondary School Levels

School social workers and human service professionals working within school systems are uniquely situated to aid in the establishment of the full range of school-based mediation programs, including peer mediation. With respect to the latter, they can serve as program initiators, consultants, planning committee members, trainers, and organizers. School social workers in particular have not only assumed the mediation role as an integral part of their mandate but have been instrumental in the development of peer mediation programs throughout North America.

Research has demonstrated that the most effective peer mediation programs are those that target as many students and teachers as possible within a school. Ideally, all faculty and students are exposed to mediation concepts, and the school becomes a community focus for the dissemination of mediation techniques and courses so that parents and others can use mediation skills in their daily lives.

Despite the broad range of programs in North America, most peer mediation programs follow common guidelines. There are, however, fundamental differences between peer mediation approaches at the elementary and secondary school levels. Mediation at the elementary level is a microcosm of the structured mediation model outlined in chapter 1 of this book, although it is simplified to meet the developmental abilities of young children. Generally speaking, the negotiation phase of the mediation process is quite brief, usually lasting only a few minutes. At the secondary level, students are able to explore and negotiate issues in dispute in much more detail, and use more sophisticated techniques, which significantly expands the negotiation phase of the process.

Elementary school mediations are generally conducted on the playground. Although some elementary school mediators actually conduct mediation by means of a "sit-down" approach similar to secondary schools, the playground model is most common, involving a structured approach to problem solving that takes only a few minutes. Teams of two "conflict managers" (also called conflict mediators, problem solvers or peacemakers) wear brightly colored hats, armbands, or T-shirts to identify themselves. Equipped with clipboards and several contracts, they are assigned to walk around the playground at recess looking for students in conflict. When a conflict is spotted, the managers approach the students in dispute and ask if the students would like them to help solve the problem. When permission is granted, the students move away from the scene of the conflict to a quieter place. The conflict managers then proceed to follow a set process: each disputant agrees to the rules of conflict management; the conflict managers help the disputants to define the problem; the conflict managers probe for information by asking open-ended questions; and the conflict managers help the disputants to brainstorm solutions to the problem and come to agreement.

Most of the conflicts at elementary school involve disputes over property such as balls or jump ropes. There are also name-calling incidents and concerns over lack of fair play in games. No violent conflicts are mediated by conflict managers unless playground teachers, who intervene in violent situations, believe that the disputants have calmed down sufficiently to make effective use of the process.

Secondary school peer mediation programs are more sophisticated. Two student mediators and two or more disputants sit around a table in a private room, usually adjacent to the school counseling office. In most schools, adults are not present during the mediation process. Mediations include issues such as dealing with rumors, name calling, boyfriend-girlfriend disputes, racism, sexual harassment, and teacher-student disputes. Some schools use mediation as a prerequisite to students' returning to school after having been suspended for fighting. Most administrators realize that suspensions may "cool down" students, but do not address underlying causes of conflicts. Peer mediation is seen as a way to deal with the latter. Certain issues are clearly not appropriate for peer mediation, including incidents involving weapons, drugs, or any situation where the possibility of violence exists.

Peer mediations are assigned by school faculty coordinators. School social workers, counselors, or teachers may act as peer mediation coordinators, but not administrators (such as the principal or assistant principal), as they are generally regarded by students as arbitrators and disciplinarians. Administrators, faculty, and students may make referrals to peer mediation. When an appropriate referral has been received by the coordinator, two student mediators are chosen and briefed about the situation, the disputants are called out of class, and the process begins. At the secondary school level, mediations are generally concluded in a time span of five to sixty minutes. There are exceptional cases where peer mediations last several hours or where several sessions are scheduled.

There are variations of the mediation process at the secondary school level. Some programs require peer mediators to meet with each disputant separately before beginning the joint mediation; others believe that such caucusing may cause further polarization and distrust. Thus they meet with both disputants throughout the process unless exceptional circumstances dictate otherwise. Some schools believe the disputants should be interviewed by the faculty coordinator before each mediation; others require that the coordinator be present at each mediation. The most successful programs, however, empower students as much as possible, which means allowing the student mediators to conduct sessions without adults present (although program coordinators are available to help students prepare for and debrief each mediation session).

Stages of the Peer Mediation Process

The three stages of the peer mediation process at the secondary school level are the introduction, exploration of the problem, and finding solutions/reaching agreement. The primary task of the introduction phase is to set the stage for the process to follow, including the ground rules to which each party must adhere, and to determine the mediation agenda, including a listing of the issues in dispute. Confidentiality is extremely important. If confidentiality is violated, students can quickly lose their confidence in the mediation endeavor and the process may be jeopardized. Limitations to confidentiality must also be discussed; any disclosure of any information that indicates illegal behavior or suggests that disputants may harm themselves or others needs to be reported, and participants must be made aware of this fact.

Setting the structure for mediation is a challenging task, as many students are reluctant participants. Often students are faced with a choice of disciplinary action or participating in peer mediation. Mediation is thus seen as the "lesser evil," and participants may be present at the mediation in body but not in spirit. This attitude may be manifest in disruptive, oppositional, or withdrawn behavior, creating special challenges for the mediators. Student mediators learn to cope with these behaviors by setting and firmly enforcing ground rules, structuring the process so communication guidelines are clear, and asking open-ended questions to elicit information.

The mediation process begins with the mediators introducing themselves to the disputants, orienting them to the mediation process, and explaining their roles as peer mediators. The ground rules of mediation are presented one at a time, including confidentiality and a range of other guidelines, such as telling the truth, making an honest and good faith effort to solve the problem, and not interrupting, gossiping, name calling, or fighting. After agreement to these ground rules is reached, the disputants sign the mediation contract. The first disputant is then asked to describe the problem, to outline his or her perception of the situation, to tell his or her story. After the problem is presented, it is restated by one of the mediators. The process is repeated with the second disputant, and the second mediator restates. Notes are taken by the mediators listing the issues to be negotiated. The mediators summarize the issues presented and with an agenda of issues to be resolved, they continue to the second phase of the process.

The focus of the second phase of mediation is to help the disputants "explore the problem," to teach them how to communicate with one another more effectively and, through a mutual examination of feelings, encourage them to begin to empathize with one another and understand each other's point of view. Some of the strategies used at this point include teaching the disputants to use "I-messages," paraphrasing what the other disputant has said, and reflecting feelings. The mediator, through the skillful use of open-ended questions, collects salient information to understand the dimensions of the dispute and moves the disputants from position-based to interest-based negotiation. This shift requires a fundamental change from the disputants clinging to their positions in the conflict to their recognition of their own and the other's core concerns and needs underlying the dispute.

When the disputants have fully discussed one issue, the mediators guide them to the third and final phase of the process: "finding solutions and reaching agreement." The task here is to help the disputants reach an agreement that is fair and with which they can feel comfortable. To begin this phase, the mediators ask the disputants, "What can you do to solve this problem?" If no solution is found, the mediators ask, "What do you think will happen if you don't solve this problem?" If there is still no solution, brainstorming is the next technique, and only when the disputants have exhausted their options may the mediators suggest options for settlement. Student mediators are careful to suggest at least two options at a time to give the disputants a choice, so that mediators will not appear invested in a particular outcome. When the disputants have reached agreement, they sign the contract prepared by the mediators, and the mediation is concluded. After the disputants have left the room, the faculty co-ordinator assists the student mediators in debriefing. The signed contract is kept in the private files of the faculty coordinator and is used to monitor compliance and to maintain records for evaluation purposes.

Establishing Peer Mediation Programs

An important role for social workers and allied professionals working within the school system is to advocate and obtain support for peer mediation from both school and school board administrations. These might include the director/superintendent of education, principal and assistant principal, counselor, activities coordinator, nurse, and security staff. After obtaining the support of key administrators, a faculty presentation is made, in which teachers learn about how the program works, how and when student training will be conducted, and how student mediators will be chosen. It is also important to point out issues that are not appropriate for peer mediation. Teachers are assured that all student mediators must receive their teacher's permission to be released from class, and that although counselors who are running the program are expected to be available to the mediators, teachers are required to do little more than allow students out of their class.

It is important to choose a cross section of students to be peer mediators. There must be a racial, cultural, and socioeconomic balance as well as a selection of students representing the unique social groups within the school. Students with anger management problems, shy students, students with learning disbilities, and bright and "bossy" students as well as those who are good listeners and natural problem solvers need to be included in the selection. The program holds special therapeutic value for each of these groups: for angry, oppositional students, mediation offers a way to redirect energy in a positive manner; for shy students and those with a learning disability, mediation programs can help raise self-esteem; for bright and "bossy" students, being a mediator means waiting for the disputants to arrive at a solution, which can be a challenge. Umbreit (1995) notes the following as desirable attributes of student mediators: leadership ability, whether it has led to positive or negative behavior; respect and trust of peers; good verbal skills; and commitment to serve for the entire school year.

At elementary schools, "conflict managers" are usually nominated by teachers. At the secondary level, choosing students is best accomplished by making brief presentations to students at each grade level. A discussion of existing school disciplinary practices is a good way to introduce peer mediation as an alternative. Often, far more students than can be accommodated volunteer, and the challenge becomes how to choose the students to be trained.

After key school faculty attend an initial mediation workshop, training for student mediators begins. This training is best conducted over several sessions during a two-week period. At elementary schools, the training sessions are usually two hours; at the secondary level, they last up to three hours. Although sessions may be conducted back-to-back over a two-day period, the wealth of information presented is best assimilated when the sessions are a few days apart. The training focuses on ways to deal with conflict, the mediation process as a method of conflict resolution, communication and listening skills (particularly reflecting feelings and using "I-messages"), problem-solving skills, negotiation skills, diversity and conflict, and dealing with difficult situations.

Once the student training is complete, a more intensive training is conducted for the entire faculty. This three-hour introduction to mediation concepts and skills gives faculty the opportunity to learn about mediation and to observe what their students have learned, as the newly trained student mediators are used to help supervise faculty role plays. Most faculty are surprised and impressed by what their students now know about mediation. Other goals of the faculty training are to ensure appropriate referrals for the mediation program and to create an awareness that mediation concepts and techniques can be taught as part of the curriculum and used in the classroom to resolve disagreements and conflicts.

Many schools use teams of trained student mediators to teach mediation skills to all students in the school. As they teach mediation to others, student mediators reinforce the concepts and skills they have learned in their initial training. In addition, faculty and trained student mediators can offer mini training sessions for parents; mediation thus becomes a mode of conflict resolution and problem solving not only within the school but also in the local community (Kaplan, 1996).

Finally, once student mediators are trained and peer mediation is established within a school, it is imperative to provide ongoing support and training opportunities for the student volunteers. The initial training process provides a foundation for the learning of more advanced skills and competencies during ongoing training, as student mediators continually find themselves faced with new challenges and opportunities in their conflict resolution work.

Case Studies

Developing peer mediation programs and maintaining them as effective school-based conflict resolution mechanisms requires a high degree of skill commitment on the part of many. Creativity is important, as the types of disputes that are presented to peer mediators are varied and call for a certain amount of artistry on the part of the student mediators. The following vignettes illustrate some of the issues that may surface within such programs.

The Best Mediators Are Far from Perfect. One of the most exciting elements of peer mediation training is its therapeutic effect upon young people. Darrel was a sensitive, insightful eighth grader with multiple behavior problems. In fact, he was suspended from school during the course of the mediation training. Darrel was so intrigued by mediation that he secretly came back into the school building to participate in the after-school training. He eventually became one of the school's most effective mediators. He significantly changed his behavior, went on to high school, and graduated.

"Eight Is Enough." A multiparty mediation occurred at a suburban junior high school. Eight students were in dispute over the use of the school gym: four were football players known around school as "jocks," and four had long green hair and black fingernails, and were referred to as "alternative lifestyle." All eight students sat in mediation for a total of three hours. It was an argumentative and exhausting experience for the disputants and the three student mediators. After this marathon session, it was reported by one of the "jock" disputants that the participants were surprised to find out that under their various "costumes" the two groups had many common fears, concerns, and life goals.

Teacher-Student Disputes. An interesting outcome of mediation training is the personal growth experienced by many young mediators. One young man described his experience "balancing power" between a teacher disputant and student disputant. He reported that, when the teacher refused to listen to the mediators and insisted on taking over the mediation, he (the student mediator) simply moved his chair to the head of the table, leaving the teacher rather isolated. This student assumed a "power" position, and the teacher gradually became more cooperative. After reporting this technique, the young man admitted rather sheepishly, "I really took mediation training only to get out of class, but now I actually can see that mediation works!"

Being a Mediator Is Empowering. Some students who benefit from mediation training are initially shy and withdrawn. Diane was a high school student who hardly said a word during the mediation training. About two weeks after training, she was chosen to help at a faculty training by supervising role plays. After observing Diane calmly and confidently instructing faculty on the process and techniques of mediation, the school counselor said in amazement, "What happened to Diane? What a change! It's a miracle!"

Conclusion

School-based peer mediation is not a panacea. There are situations in which it is contraindicated, and alternative means need to be considered. When illegal behavior or student abuse is involved, adult-led interventions are clearly required; when student mediators find themselves unable to effectively deal with certain situations, even with ongoing support, other means are likely necessary.

Despite its limitations, mediation has an important place in the school system and has yet to reach its potential in that field of practice. The opportunity to resolve one's own conflict with the assistance of an impartial third party is foreign to most young people. At home, parents arbitrate; at school, the principal, assistant principal, teachers, and even counselors impose decisions on students. Young people are surrounded by adults telling them what to do and how to resolve disputes. Within such an atmosphere, young people will continue to be frustrated and possibly infuriated by their inability to resolve and deal with conflict. While arbitration is sometimes an effective way to obtain closure to a conflict, it often creates more tension between the disputing parties and does not teach them the skills to communicate, negotiate, and problem solve more effectively in the future.

Some believe that increasing security by hiring police to patrol school halls, using metal detectors, or locking classrooms will ameliorate the situation. These measures appear to be a reaction to the underlying problem; they are certainly not a cure. They leave young people feeling disenfranchised. Creating more restrictions and taking punitive action cannot help but make the situation worse.

Peer mediation is an empowering experience for both the mediators who are helping others and the disputants who are assisted to resolve their own conflicts. Although research on peer mediation in schools is limited and inconclusive, most school-based practitioners believe that mediation has considerable and far-reaching benefits. Violence prevention is only one of the potential positive impacts of peer mediation. If the majority of young people develop the conflict resolution skills to effectively deal with their own conflicts and the ability to help others resolve disputes, they will possess a facility that could lead to significant societal change.

References

Araki, C.T. 1990. Dispute Management in the Schools. *Mediation Quarterly* 8(1). 51–62.

Brown, R. S. 1994. *Evaluation of Conflict Resolution Programs at the Secondary Level*. Toronto: Toronto Board of Education.

Conflict Resolution Unlimited. 1995a. *Conflict Manager Training for Elementary School Students*. Bellevue, WA: CRU, Inc.

———. 1995b. *Mediation Training for High School Students*. Bellevue, WA: CRU, Inc.

———. 1995c. *Mediation Training for Middle School Students*. Bellevue, WA: CRU, Inc.

Davis, A. & K. Porter. 1985. *Tales of Schoolyard Mediation*. Chicago: American Bar Association Special Committee on Youth Education for Citizenship.

Eisler, J. 1994. *Schools Teaching Options for Peace (STOP) Teen Mediation Project, 1993–94*. Brooklyn, NY: New York City Board of Education.

Faris, J. 1996. *Peer Mediation Program*. Memphis, TN: Memphis City Schools.

Gentry, D. B. & W. A. Benenson. 1992. School-Age Peer Mediators Transfer Knowledge and Skills to Home Setting. *Mediation Quarterly* 10(1): 101–9.

Horowitz, S. V. & S. K. Boardman. 1994. Managing Conflict: Policy and Research Implications. *Journal of Social Issues* 50(1): 197–211.

Johnson, D. W. & R. T. Johnson. 1994. Constructive Conflict in the Schools. *Journal of Social Issues* 50.

Johnson, D. W., R. T. Johnson, & B. Dudley. 1992. Effects of Peer Mediation Training on Elementary School Students. *Mediation Quarterly* 10(1): 89–99.

Jones, T. S., & D. Carlin. 1994. *Philadelphia Peer Mediation Program: Report for 1992–1994*. Philadelphia, PA: Temple University.

Kaplan, N. M. 1996. *Student Mediation: Opportunity and Challenge*. Westlake Village, CA: National School Safety Center.

Moore, P. & C. Whipple. 1988. *Project START: A School-Based Mediation Program*. New York: Victim Services Agency.

Ohio Commission on Dispute Resolution and Conflict Management. 1993. *Dealing with Conflict in Ohio's Schools: Teaching Students New Skills to Resolve Conflicts Without Violence*. Columbus, OH: Ohio Commission on Dispute Resolution and Conflict Management.

Sautter, R. C. 1995. Standing Up to Violence. *Phi Delta Kappan 76(5): K1–K12*.

Umbreit, M. S. 1995. *Mediating Interpersonal Conflicts: A Pathway to Peace*. West Concord, MN: CPI Publishing.

Yau, M. 1995. *School Climate and Conflict Resolution: A Survey of the Toronto Board of Education Elementary Schools (1994)*. Toronto: Toronto Board of Education.

15

WORKPLACE HARASSMENT

Mediating Workplace Harassment Complaints

by Judy Mares-Dixon

Allegations of workplace harassment are on the rise, confusion about how best to respond to these charges is mounting, and managers and supervisors, human resource personnel, and union representatives are looking to social workers and other human service professionals for services in this area. Sexual harassment, one form of workplace harassment, has been recognized as an offense in the United States under Title VII since 1977. During the five-year period from 1987 to 1992, the number of sexual harassment complaints filed with the Equal Employment Opportunity Commission nearly doubled. Fifty to 85 percent of working women will experience some form of sexual harassment in their place of work, but research indicates that up to 90 percent will not report the incident, for reasons such as fear of retaliation and loss of privacy (Stamato, 1992). The typical "Fortune 500" firm spends $6.7 million per year (or $280 per employee) on legal fees related to disputes involving sexual harassment. In the United States, 64 percent of cases that lead to a jury verdict are decided in favor of the complainant; judgments can reach $300,000, and defense costs $80,000 on the average (ibid.).

In the realm of physical harassment, over 2 million people employed in the U.S. private and public sector experience workplace violence each year, and over 4 million employees report that they have felt threatened in some way by a fellow employee. Hostility, violence, and other intimidating behaviors in the workplace are a growing problem resulting from a multiplicity of factors, according to social services agencies and other professionals who provide training and support services for local, state, or federal agencies and a wide range of private businesses. Mounting pressures in the workplace due to downsizing associated with longer working hours and increased workload are cited, as is the fear of job loss. Increased stress levels may cause one's unresolved conflicts to escalate while depleting one's ability to cope with work and remain loyal to the organization.

According to recent human rights legislation, an employer is responsible for harassment that is endured by employees and can be held liable. The employer is also liable for the discriminatory conduct of employees, including managers, supervisors, coworkers, and even clients or customers. Employers have an obligation to provide a healthy and respectful work environment, including preventative measures in the form of a clear and easily understood workplace harassment policy. Specifically, it is the employer's responsibility to make clear that harassment will not be tolerated, establish a formal harassment policy, ensure that employees understand the policy and how to use it, inform managers and supervisors of their responsibility to provide a harassment-free workplace, promptly investigate and resolve problems as they arise, and take appropriate corrective action when required (Burdine, 1996).

Theory, Debates, and Trends

The mediation of workplace disputes involves a third party who helps employees in conflict to negotiate an acceptable settlement of contested issues and who is frequently used to avoid or overcome an impasse when employees have been unable to negotiate an agreement on their own. Workplace harassment mediation is a more specialized form of workplace mediation that seeks to find remedies to complaints or allegations of various forms of harassment. In workplace harassment cases, the parties to the mediation are referred to as the "complainant" and the "respondent"; the complainant is the person(s) who believes that she or he is being harassed, and the respondent is the person(s) who is being identified as the harasser. Workplace harassment mediation is a complainant-driven process and seeks remedies for a situation rather than resolving a dispute per se.

Workplace harassment includes a range of behaviors that undermine the dignity, morale, safety and respect of individuals or groups in the workplace. It can be defined as verbal, visual, or physical conduct that has the effect of unreasonably interfering with an individual's or group's work performance or that creates an intimidating, hostile, or offensive work environment (Burdine, 1996). Harassment complaints may involve charges of discrimination or sexual harassment, or claims of personal harassment or intimidation. Forms of workplace harassment include humiliation, threats, intimidation, abuse of power, rumors, back-stabbing, blackmail, exploitation, ostracizing, isolating, actual or threatened physical assault, bullying or taunting, malicious teasing, offensive gesturing or abusive language, and defacement or destruction of property (Burdine, 1996).

Sexual harassment is a particularly invasive form of workplace harassment and requires even more specialized procedures. According to the U.S. Department of Regulatory Agencies, sexual harassment behavior includes unwelcome sexual advances, requests for sexual favors, and other verbal or physical conduct of a sexual nature. Conduct may be labelled sexual harassment when submission to such conduct is made either explicitly or implicitly a requirement of employment, the individual's response to such conduct is used as the basis for decisions that deny that individual's rights protected by law, work performance is affected, or such conduct creates an intimidating, hostile, or offensive work environment. Forms of sexual harassment include obscene gestures, staring or leering, sexually suggestive comments about an employee's appearance, unwelcome touching, displaying sexually oriented pictures, and requesting sexual favors in return for a job or other employment benefit (Burdine, 1996).

Workplace harassment complaints are usually mediated by experienced conflict resolution professionals who have a background in the human services with expertise in employment law, civil rights, and personnel management. Workplace harassment mediators need to have a thorough understanding of pertinent legislation regarding various forms of harassment and discrimination in the workplace. They also need to be familiar with the employing organization's policies regarding the prohibition of harassment and the remedies available to the complainant if the respondent is guilty of harassing behavior. Finally, while workplace harassment mediators are neutral third parties, they should not be "neutral" in the sense of being void of opinions or values regarding discriminatory behavior, sexual harassment, or other forms of unacceptable conduct in the workplace. Mediator neutrality does require workplace harassment mediators to carefully assess whether their personal experiences, opinions, and values will permit them to treat both the complainant and respondent with respect and allow each of them to make full use of the mediation process to remedy the situation. Mediators who have themselves been victims of discrimination, physical violence, or sexual harassment should not automatically rule out the possibility of mediating workplace harassment cases. An honest assessment of one's ability to view these cases with an open mind, however, is fundamental.

Why Is Mediation an Appropriate Procedure for Resolving Workplace Harassment Disputes?

The forces impelling private corporations and public organizations toward the use of mediation to resolve workplace harassment situations include the escalating costs of litigation, the strain on human resources during a period of downsizing, the pressure to increase productivity in the face of increasing competition, and the need to provide a safe and respectful workplace for all employees by eliminating violence and other forms of harassment. Mediation can build workplace morale and enhance communication. If the parties in harassment mediation can be assisted to find a suitable remedy and work through their impasse together, the need to appeal to outside sources and rely on cumbersome external procedures will be minimized. Litigation and arbitration of harassment disputes are on the rise primarily because employees believe that these procedures will protect their interests. Mediation is successful only when both management and nonmanagement employees believe that the process is accessible, fair, and impartial, the mediator is respected and supported within the organization, and employees' concerns and interests are fully addressed.

Mediation is less formal and more expedient than the more formal processes of hearings and legal procedures, and it prevents unnecessary time delays and paperwork, and the stress and frustration that may result. In mediation, decision-making authority is retained by the employees. As a result, mutual ownership of the settlement is enhanced, and the likelihood that any remedies negotiated and agreements reached will be honored is increased. Mediation places the decisions in the hands of the people who are usually in the best position to know which solution will work and which will not. They can usually best evaluate the impact of each proposed solution on their future working relationships and careers.

Workplace harassment mediation programs, when administered correctly, protect confidentiality, allowing the parties to identify what most concerns them, prioritize and focus on that which is most important to resolve, and reach agreements on how to deal with future problems. Mediation also offers greater flexibility in regard to the possibilities for agreement. Often, solutions that are imposed by a third party are viewed as unjust, unhelpful, ambiguous, or simply unacceptable. Mediation enables employees to avoid the trap of deciding who is "right" and who is "wrong." Instead, employees can focus on clarifying what actually occurred, how each felt (including both the intent and impact of the behavior), what could have been done differently, and how the situation can be rectified. They can "expand the pie" and develop solutions that address their underlying concerns in a way that is satisfactory to each party and effectively deals with the problematic behavior. These typically include offering and accepting apologies, and outlining specific behaviors and expectations that are designed to ensure that problems will not recur.

The fact that mediation does not focus primarily on attributing fault does not mean that a harasser cannot and will not be disciplined. Rather, the respondent will discover how his or her behavior affected the complainant and how the complainant would like to see the situation rectified. Mediation offers the harasser the opportunity to apologize for his or her behavior, clarify intentions, and accept, if not agree to, appropriate disciplinary action that is dictated by organizational policy or management prerogative.

Mediation is usually considerably less expensive than arbitration or litigation. The costs involved in using internal or external mediators is usually less than that of lawyers. Furthermore, the cost of discovery is eliminated, as are the costs involved in the delays that accompany most formal and legal processes. Employers spend an average of $200,000 on each complaint that is investigated in-house and found to be valid, whether or not it ever gets to court (Fisher, 1993). Using mediation to resolve harassment cases that might otherwise lead to expensive and humiliating lawsuits can also help save valuable public resources.

Mediation protects relationships and individual careers. Mediation that results in genuine agreements addressing each person's needs helps, where appropriate, to preserve and enhance a future working relationship. When one or both employees agree to discontinue their relationship, the mediator can help them negotiate the procedure that outlines how the relationship will end while seeking to protect reputations, confidences, and career opportunities.

When Is Mediation an Appropriate Procedure for Resolving Workplace Harassment Disputes?

The question of whether mediation should be used to resolve workplace harassment complaints, especially sexual harassment cases, continues to be debated. Mediation is not appropriate in every situation. When an employee feels physically threatened, coerced, or otherwise unable to express his or her concerns and negotiate for solutions to remedy the situation, engaging in mediation is clearly contraindicated for safety and other reasons. On the other hand, when a complainant wishes to resolve the issue quickly and confidentially, while limiting the number of personnel who might otherwise be involved in the case, mediation may be the ideal forum to meet his or her needs (Stamato, 1992). When the complainant and the respondent wish to "clear the air" and maintain a professional working relationship with one another, the mediation process offers the opportunity to share perspectives, clarify outstanding questions and rebuild strained or damaged relationships. One of the difficult dynamics in harassment cases involves doubt: doubt on the complainant's part about the respondent's motives at the time of the incident and doubt on the respondent's part as to whether the complainant understood his or her intent. The respondent may have second thoughts, or even regrets, about the incident. A clear sign of respondent readiness to proceed in mediation is an openness to listen to the complainant's perspective, to learn about the impact his or her behavior had on the complainant. The impact, not the intent, is the salient factor in workplace harassment mediation.

When a complainant reaches the point of being able to negotiate with a respondent without fear of retaliation or loss of face, the mediation process can offer a powerful opportunity to describe what happened, how the complainant was impacted at the time and after, and what is needed to begin to move beyond the situation. One of the most difficult aspects of sexual and other forms of harassment is that employees do not have secure opportunities to express their feelings of embarrassment, anger, humiliation, or fear.

In order to determine whether a case is appropriate for mediation, the mediator needs to: review existing workplace policies regarding harassment; be aware of the full range of existing dispute resolution processes and procedures, including the availability of employee support services; determine whether the respondent has been involved in a single incident or has a history of harassment; assess the complainant's ability to negotiate without fear; assess whether the respondent is willing and able to negotiate and is ready to listen to the impact of his or her behavior; determine if there have been any counterallegations on the part of the respondent; and clarify the reporting requirements to the organization. Prior to accepting a case for mediation, the mediator should know the answers to the following questions: When and how has mediation been presented as an option to the complainant and the respondent? How has the respondent been notified of the complaint? How does the organization define the role of the mediator—as a neutral, an advisor, or both? With whom does the mediator liaise before, during, and after the mediation? How much time is allowed for premediation preparation and postmediation follow-up? Does the organization's policy require a written agreement from the mediation? If so, who will review it, and who has access to it? What, if any, documentation or other communication does the organization require if the conflict is resolved (or unresolved)? What is the role and responsibility of the mediator if the immediate conflict is found to be symptomatic of a larger, more systemic problem (Burdine, 1996)?

Mediation is most effective when it is an integral part of a larger dispute resolution system within the workplace that offers support services and is governed by policies stating that the organization will not tolerate any form of harassment. These policies should specify that a supervisor who harasses or solicits favors from an unwilling subordinate in return for promotions, increased wages, job security, or any similar promise will be disciplined or terminated. They should also indicate that unwelcome sexual propositions and hostile or threatening behavior between and among workmates constitute harassment and will not be tolerated.

Verifying that a clearly understood policy that prohibits physical violence, sexual harassment, and other forms of hostile or intimidating behavior is in place is the first step in determining whether the organizational culture truly prohibits such behavior. The mediator also needs to know whether this policy is consistently enforced throughout all levels of the organization. If the policy is adamantly enforced in some departments and not in others, or if it is enforced at staff levels but not at the senior management level, it will be difficult, if not impossible, for the aggrieved party to reach an agreement that will be supported by responsible officials within the organization. In fact, if the organization is not committed to the consistent enforcement of its harassment policy, it is likely that mediation could serve not as a process for resolving painful and difficult issues but as a method of "pushing the issues under the rug," where the aggrieved employee is placated to the point where she or he is no longer willing to pursue the matter internally through the organization's formal grievance procedures or externally through litigation.

Workplace harassment mediation requires a period of premediation assessment and preparation, which involves separate meetings with the complainant and respondent. First, the mediator needs to understand the history of the relationship between the employees involved in a workplace harassment allegation. A history of violence between the parties or a record of repeated harassment charges is a sign that a case may be better suited to more formal procedures for resolution. A critical point is that violence, sexual harassment, and other forms of intimidating or hostile behavior are not, themselves, mediatable. The focus of workplace harassment mediation is the relationship problem that is caused by the harassment and the development of a plan to remedy the situation.

Mediation can be successful only if the complainant is willing and able to negotiate with the respondent. The mediator's initial critical task in any harassment case is to determine the extent to which an employee is feeling physically safe and the degree to which he or she is emotionally vulnerable. The key question to be addressed is, Under what conditions, if any, is the complainant willing and able to negotiate with the respondent? During the initial private interview with the complainant, the mediator should pose open-ended questions to uncover the nature and degree of the harassment and the level of threat for speaking out. A nonthreatening, confidential environment in which the complainant may talk about the situation should be ensured. It is usually necessary for the complainant in mediation to not only talk about what occurred but also express feelings of shame, anger, and fear. He or she may have never talked about the harassment beyond indicating that there might be a problem. He or she may believe that harassment, including sexual harassment, is simply part of the "package" he or she must accept in order to keep his or her job or be successful in the workplace. In many cases, there is considerable fear of retaliation.

The mediator needs to ask open-ended questions to thoroughly explore the situation with the complainant. These include: How would you describe what happened? How would you like to see the situation resolved? Have you attempted to discuss this situation with the respondent? If so, what happened? How has your relationship with the respondent changed since the incident or since the harassment began? How closely do the two of you have to work together? Do you feel afraid of the respondent? How has the organization responded to your situation thus far?

The complainant who readily assumes blame for the harassment or who is reluctant to engage in a discussion of the situation may not be a good candidate for mediation. In cases involving sexual harassment in particular, verifying whether the complainant is in need of and has access to support services is important prior to initiating mediation.

A thorough assessment of the respondent's willingness and ability to engage in mediation is also necessary. It is possible that this employee also feels victimized, either because he or she was harassed by the complainant or by the way the organization is responding to the situation. Whether he or she is a suitable candidate for mediation is largely dependent on his or her willingness to accept the fact that there is a problem and that the situation may be viewed very differently by the complainant. He or she must be open to recognizing the impact of his or her behavior on the complainant. The employee who is unwilling to make concessions or take responsibility for hostile behavior or unwelcome advances may not be a good candidate for mediation. Mediation is not appropriate when the respondent trivializes his or her actions or believes that there should be no consequences for his or her harassing behavior, or if there is any hint that he or she may use the process to humiliate the other party in any way.

Workplace harassment mediation is more likely to meet with success if there is at least some consistency between the parties regarding the facts of the situation. Commonality of interests, the necessity of an ongoing relationship between the parties, and a stated desire by all involved to remedy the situation are signals that mediation may be the option of choice for dealing with a harassment complaint.

When should mediation occur? Resolving workplace harassment situations by means of mediation is usually most effective and expedient, and less stressful, when initiated early in the process of a harassment complaint, before formal grievance procedures are used (DeLeon, 1994; Skratek, 1990). Often workplace harassment situations involve tensions that have been allowed to escalate over several months or even years, causing relationships and communications to deteriorate and hostility and frustration to escalate; such a situation does not bode well for negotiation focused on remedying the problem.

Issues and Challenges

The use of mediation to resolve workplace harassment issues is clearly on the rise and is likely to become an increasingly important option in dispute resolution systems throughout the private and public sectors. In the future, social workers and allied human service professionals will be more likely to occupy positions in which they function as workplace mediators or are called upon to establish workplace mediation programs, policies, and procedures.

There are many questions and concerns that need to be addressed if their interventions are to be optimally effective.

One of the key issues facing workplace mediators is how to assess an organization's readiness to accept mediation as a viable procedure for resolving harassment complaints. Although mediation is no longer an unfamiliar practice in the corporate world, it continues to be confused with arbitration and other forms of mediation, particularly labor mediation. One reason for this is that human resource personnel and union representatives are thoroughly accustomed to arbitration, often a final step in most grievance processes, and to labor negotiation.

There are a number of reasons why an organization might decide to incorporate mediation into its grievance procedure. It may have been confronted with a high conflict, high-cost harassment situation and is looking to reducing its risk in the future. The organization may be in the throes of a protracted litigation that, according to its legal counsel, may cost a substantial amount of money and time. It may be suffering from continued chronic conflict that is not being addressed by its current systems. Finally, many organizations adopt mediation as a result of the influence of an internal champion. This person usually has credibility, established rapport, and access to the decision-makers in the organization; has had a positive personal experience with mediation, has previously practiced as a mediator, or has had training in mediation; and has a vision for how the union, management, and specific employees can benefit from an interest-based, nonadversarial process of conflict resolution.

Another issue facing mediators in the workplace is balancing the need for privacy versus the "right to know." Mediating workplace harassment cases requires confidentiality procedures that protect employees' rights to participate in a process that is private and confidential. This allows employees to express feelings, own responsibility, apologize, and explore possible options for agreement without exposure or formal internal or external pressures. Such a confidential process, however, may have the unintended consequence of protecting those who reoffend; if no record is kept of charges of harassment, a pattern of such behavior may be difficult to establish. Specific limits that protect employees against future harmful acts by another may thus need to be imposed. It is imperative that confidentiality requirements not allow repeat offenders to use mediation as a way of sidestepping disciplinary action, including termination, for such behavior.

How do we deal with fears of retaliation? An employee who has been harassed by his or her supervisor or another upper-level manager is usually fearful of retaliation. A harassment allegation may surface during a complainant's performance review and can affect the opportunity for promotion, transfer, and access to positive references. Perhaps the most subtle and damaging form of retaliation can occur in the day-to-day activities of the team or department. For example, the employee who files a grievance because he or she has been harassed may experience a "chilly climate" in the workplace, may not be invited to socialize with the rest of the group, may be passed over for all the "exciting" projects, or simply may be ignored. The mediator's challenge is to enable employees to talk about their fear of retaliation and then assist the parties to reach agreements on how fears of retaliation can be addressed and productively resolved. The mediator cannot absolutely ensure that retaliation will not occur; however, it must be made clear in mediation that any form of retaliation will be treated as a form of harassment and will be dealt with according to the organization's harassment policy.

The management of power imbalances is a particularly important task for the mediator of workplace harassment complaints. Although many harassment cases involve a supervisor who is accused of harassing a subordinate, the power differential between them does not have to prohibit the parties from engaging in mediation. Each party to a dispute has both actual and potential power that can be mobilized to remedy the situation. Power comes in many forms: credibility, technical expertise, control over resources (such as money, labor, and materials), charisma, leadership (formal and informal), access to the media, access to and support from advocacy or consumer groups, relationships with upper management, access to a board of directors or to funding sources, and access to legal counsel. The mediator's challenge is to assess each employee's sources of power and enable each to utilize his or her power in creative and productive ways, as opposed to using it to inflict harm, to humiliate, or to blame the other party.

One method of addressing a real or perceived power imbalance is to legitimize each party's participation in the mediation process by validating everyone's need to be heard and understood and discussing the benefits of reaching agreement or some resolution of the issue. By understanding the history of the relationship, the mediator can structure a process that acknowledges the differing points of view of the complainant and respondent, incorporates different styles of communication, and sets forth the expectation that the parties will take responsibility for adhering to the ground rules of mediation.

How can we assure that employees who have experienced harassment and who are unwilling or unable to report the incident due to cultural, class, language, or other barriers have access to the mediation process? Part of the answer to this dilemma lies in the importance of preserving legal and institutional safeguards. Mediation is not meant to replace these safeguards; rather, it should be seen as a way to augment existing systems by offering a less formal and adversarial, interest-based process for dealing with harassment complaints. Mediation should be seen as one component in an organization's harassment policy, a voluntary option backed up by a range of institutional safeguards.

These questions are indicative of the challenges facing conflict resolution practitioners, corporate executives, labor unions, and the entire work force as workplace harassment mediation continues to grow and develop as an alternative method of resolving harassment complaints. They are also signs of its importance and relevance in the workplace and corporate sphere. They reflect the fact that whether or not to utilize mediation to deal with workplace harassment problems is no longer the issue; rather, current debates regarding workplace harassment mediation focus on the most effective and safe means of implementing the process, in a manner that preserves and strengthens existing workplace harassment policies and legislation.

The Mediation Process in Workplace Harassment Situations

Currently, there are many types of workplace mediation programs that deal with harassment and numerous variations on the process. The types of disputes considered by different organizations to be appropriate for mediation vary, as do definitions of what constitutes "harassment." The reporting requirements placed on the mediator vary from one setting to another. Organizations also differ in regard to whether mediation is instituted as part of the organization's overall process of dealing with harassment complaints or offered on an ad hoc basis. A number of governmental organizations, for example, have established formal mediation services, whereas many colleges and universities utilize the expertise of existing staff or hire external mediators on an as-needed basis. In spite of these variations, there are a number of common elements that characterize the mediation of workplace conflicts and harassment complaints that set this field of practice apart from mediation in other arenas; the process outlined will focus on these commonalties.

Dynamics such as power imbalances, the presence of intense conflict, and the fear of retaliation endemic to workplace harassment complaints require a number of modifications to the structured "settlement-driven" model of mediation. The traditional structured mediation approach involves a neutral third party who assists people in conflict to negotiate an acceptable settlement of contested issues. The mediator does not render a decision but facilitates a process whereby disputants can express their concerns, articulate the issues that need to be addressed, offer proposals for resolving the issues, evaluate the various proposals, and accept those that meet their common and exclusive interests. In cases of workplace harassment, however, while it is often important for both the complainant and respondent to exchange information, share differing perspectives, and mend their relationship, marked power imbalances usually exist, and the complainant feels threatened or intimidated by the respondent to the point where specialized mediation procedures are necessary.

Caucusing, which involves holding private meetings with each employee before and during the mediation, is required for several reasons. Prior to determining whether a case is appropriate for mediation, the mediator must assess each employee's willingness and ability to negotiate. In caucus, the mediator can assist the complainant to develop an impact statement and can educate the respondent regarding harassment issues. Later in the process, private meetings may be preferred for dealing with high levels of emotion or integrating unexpected information. One employee may be having difficulty articulating a proposal; in a caucus, the mediator is in a better position to coach that employee on how to present the proposal.

Shuttle mediation is sometimes used in workplace harassment mediation. The mediator meets the complainant and respondent separately throughout the mediation process, working toward developing a draft settlement agreement that each party can refine. The main disadvantage of shuttle mediation is that employees are not able to communicate directly with each other. Although this model may be preferred by some employees, it also signals that the complainant and respondent are unable or unwilling to deal with one another in a productive or reasonable manner. If there is little need for an ongoing working relationship, this approach can work well, as it serves to resolve the issues without requiring further contact; if an ongoing working relationship will be required, the mediator should work toward preparing the parties for face-to-face discussion of the issues. In most cases, the complainant and respondent will need to continue working together.

Finally, the organization may elect to use either an internal or external mediator, or a combination of the two. Several factors will guide an organization in this regard. Internal mediators are often less expensive, and the mediator's familiarity with the organization's purpose, policies, norms, and culture may serve to expedite the process. On the other hand, an external mediator may be viewed as more neutral and impartial, and less apt to focus on how the organization has historically resolved similar problems. In the presence of an external mediator, disputants are less likely to debate the specifics of personnel policy applications and may be more willing to engage in an open discussion of several creative solutions to the issues.

The mediator who is familiar with relevant employment legislation and precedent-setting decisions will be better equipped to assist all parties in understanding their rights and responsibilities, while enabling them to seek solutions that meet and protect their interests. The mediator who is familiar with both internal and external policies and regulations will be more effective in assisting the parties in developing settlement agreements that are compatible with existing organizational policy and legislative intent regarding workplace harassment.

The Mediation Process

Initial Contact with the Parties. It is important to initiate the workplace mediation process as soon as possible after a harassment complaint is received and the suitability of the case for mediation has been initially determined. A complaint may be brought to the attention of the human resource specialist within the organization who, depending on the organization's policy, then contacts the manager of the department, shop steward, ombudsperson's office, equal employment opportunity or diversity specialist, or organizational development specialist to notify them of the problem, and solicit their expertise in an effort to resolve it. The number of people contacted in this regard before the respondent is notified should normally be kept to a minimum for confidentiality reasons. Conflicts involving sexual harassment, hostile behavior, and threats of violence need immediate attention; delays may cause problems with confidentiality, and the situation may continue to escalate. The workplace harassment mediation process ideally takes place within the context of a clear organizational policy that prohibits harassment, including sexual harassment, physical violence, and other forms of hostility. Only those directly involved in the alleged harassment situation are directly involved in the mediation, and it is understood that there will be organizational follow-up to ensure that the situation is resolved.

The mediator then contacts the complainant and respondent. At this stage, in meeting with each of the parties in caucus, the mediator should clarify his or her role and mediation ground rules, including confidentiality, listen to each party's perspective, and work toward establishing trust and rapport. The goals at this stage are to begin to assess the situation, develop potential mediation strategies, educate the parties about the process, and build a foundation of trust. Toward these aims, the mediator may pose questions such as: What is the problem you are experiencing? What is this conflict really about? How long has it been going on? Have there been any changes over time? What prompted you to bring this forward at this time? Are there power issues involved? What impact is this having on you? What impact is this having on others you work with? What risks are there in proceeding and not proceeding? Who else knows about the conflict? Who knows about your taking this forward? What, if anything, has been done to deal with the conflict? What would you need to resolve this conflict? The emphasis at this stage is on exploring and understanding the context within which the conflict is occurring and the options that may be available to assist with resolution (Burdine, 1996).

Premediation Preparation. In structuring an effective harassment mediation process, attention should be given to establishing specific procedures and guidelines that will promote openness and safety in mediation. Guidelines are needed that clarify the scope of confidentiality in order to encourage the disclosure of information, which is essential to the resolution of the issues. It is critical to specify that threats, demands, and other forms of intimidation will not be tolerated within the mediation process and will be treated as forms of harassment.

Additional ground rules for mediation may be developed by the employees themselves. This is particularly useful for parties who have dealt unsuccessfully with one another in the past; they are the "experts" on what needs to be limited, changed, or tolerated in order for assisted negotiations to have a chance of success.

During this stage, the mediator further clarifies each party's interests; assists each party to assess his or her sources of power; helps each party create or fine tune options for resolution; designs a process that speaks to each party's specific needs, concerns, and styles of negotiation; provides information to each party about the process; and schedules the mediation if the parties are ready to mediate. These tasks are accomplished with each party individually.

Joint Meeting. Only after they are fully prepared for the mediation process, the complainant and respondent are brought together for the joint meeting. The mediator begins the session by reviewing the parameters of confidentiality, clarifying his or her role, and suggesting an agenda for the meeting. The mediator's role is to manage the process and ensure a respectful climate by facilitating communication and understanding, helping to clarify misunderstandings by posing useful questions, and drawing out options for resolution to the conflict from each of the parties.

The mediator works toward "reasonable outcomes," which can be defined by the parties in several ways. In almost every case of workplace harassment mediation, employees will want practical agreements that resolve specific issues. These agreements might involve a written apology, a reallocation of duties, which serves to separate the disputing parties, a change of supervisors, a transfer, specific disciplinary action, or recommended policy revisions. In addition, salvaging or strengthening the relationship between the employees may be a primary goal, and clarifying intentions and circumstances surrounding the incident(s) may be one of the most important outcomes of harassment mediation.

In some circumstances, the very notion of trying to reach a specific, permanent solution may cause an employee to resist any forward movement due to a sense of loss of control or a feeling of being trapped. On the other hand, mediation that remains deliberately vague when employees are anxious to pin things down serves little purpose and may increase the parties' sense of frustration. Depending on the complexity of the issues and the relationship history of the parties, solutions may need to be proposed on a trial, temporary, or incremental basis. The parties may need the opportunity to test their agreements, further examining their perceptions and stereotypes, or changing certain aspects of their behavior.

Follow-up. Prior to ending the mediation, a follow-up plan will need to be developed and included as part of the agreement. It addresses the following questions: Who will monitor both positive and negative changes in the workplace? What will the parties need in order to return to a "normal" work environment? What do others need to know, if anything, in order to bring closure to this conflict? What is the time frame for implementing the agreement? What resources are available if the resolution breaks down? What ongoing contact, if any, should the mediator have with each party? What reports and statistical information are needed to close the file (Burdine, 1996)? Agreements may or may not be put in writing, depending on the preferences of the parties, requirements of the situation, and policy of the organization. Above all, the parties should not feel "abandoned" at the conclusion of the mediation process. A plan for reintegration and monitoring is essential for the success of the mediated agreement.

Alternatives to Mediation

When a harassment complaint is referred to mediation, the mediator's first responsibility is to determine whether the case is or is not appropriate for mediation, that is, whether more formal mechanisms for dealing with the situation are warranted. An alternative process may be recommended by the mediator in the following circumstances: the complainant cannot or will not negotiate with the respondent due to fear for his or her own safety or fear of other forms of retaliation; the complainant is unable to articulate the impact of the respondent's behavior, or blames him- or herself for the harassment; the respondent denies that there is a problem and does not view the complainant as credible or worthy of respect; the respondent is abusive toward the complainant, or the harassment continues after an agreement to mediate; or the respondent has a history of harassing behavior. In these cases, the mediator may recommend to the parties and appropriate organizational representatives that other procedures be initiated, such as commencing a formal investigation, pursuing a formal grievance process through the union contract, filing a formal complaint with a regulatory agency, or filing criminal charges.

The mediation of workplace conflicts and harassment complaints is best seen as an adjunct to institutional and legal means of dealing with workplace harassment. An effective workplace mediation program should, above all, preserve and strengthen existing workplace harassment policies and state and federal legislation focused on the prevention of harassment in the workplace.

References

Burdine, M. 1996. *Mediating Workplace Conflicts and Harassment Complaints*. Vancouver: Justice Institute of British Columbia Centre for Conflict Resolution Training.

DeLeon, L. 1994. Using Mediation to Resolve Personnel Desputes in a State Bureaucracy. *Negotiation Journal* 10(1): 69–86.

Fisher, A. B. 1993. Sexual Harassment: What to Do. *Fortune Magazine* 128(4): 84–88.

Skratek, S. 1990. Grievance Mediation: Does It Really Work? *Negotiation Journal* 6(3): 269–80.
Stamato, L. 1992. Sexual Harassment in the Workplace. *Mediation Quarterly* 10(2): 167–72.

16

CRIMINAL JUSTICE

Victim-Offender Mediation in Criminal Conflict: Toward Restorative Justice

by Mark S. Umbreit

Linda and Bob Jackson's house was broken into while they were away visiting friends in another city. The frustration, anger, and growing sense of vulnerability they felt far exceeded the loss of their TV set and stereo. Allan, the young person who committed this crime, was caught and entered a plea of guilty. When the Jacksons were invited to participate in a program that allowed them to meet their offender, they were eager to get answers to questions such as, "Why us? Were you watching our movements?" The mediation session allowed them to get answers to these and other questions, to let Allan know how personally violated they felt, and to negotiate a plan for Allan to pay them back. While nervous at first, Allan felt better after the mediation. Everyone treated him with respect, even though he had committed a crime, and he was able to make amends to the Jacksons. Linda and Bob felt less vulnerable, were able to sleep better, and received payment for their losses. All parties were able to put this event behind them.

Crime victims are nearly always placed in a passive position by the criminal justice system, often not even receiving basic assistance or information, and are often left feeling powerless and vulnerable. Some feel twice victimized, first by the offender and then by an uncaring criminal justice system that does not have time for them. Offenders are rarely able to understand or to be confronted with the human dimension of their criminal behavior, the fact that victims are real people, not just objects to be abused. Offenders have many rationalizations for their criminal behavior. Thus, it is not unusual for anger, frustration, and conflict to increase for both the victim and offender as they move through the criminal justice process.

The consequences of the criminal justice system are felt by both victims and offenders. There is another core link between them: the victim has suffered painful physical and emotional consequences because of the action of the offender, and the offender has often suffered the legal consequences and personal pain of that action (Gustafson & Smidstra, 1989). Although their lives become intertwined in this way, they live in isolation, and the consequences of the crime and subsequent legal processes remain.

Instead of continuing the depersonalization of both victims and offenders in the criminal and juvenile justice systems, the victim-offender mediation process draws upon some rather "old-fashioned" principles that recognize that crime is fundamentally directed against people and not just against the state. Rather than placing the victim in a passive role and reinforcing an adversarial dynamic, which often results in little emotional closure for the victim and little, if any, direct accountability by the offender to the person they have wronged, victim-offender mediation facilitates an active and personal process of conflict resolution. In doing so, it represents a unique process within the larger criminal justice system, one that attempts to address the interests of both victims and offenders.

The development of victim-offender mediation has occurred within the larger framework of restorative justice theory, a paradigm adhering to a radically different vision of justice. Rather than the state being viewed as the primary victim in criminal acts and placing victims and offenders in passive roles, as is the case in the prevailing retributive justice paradigm, restorative justice recognizes crime as first and foremost being directed against individual people. It assumes that those most affected by crime should have the opportunity to become actively involved in resolving the conflict. Restoration of losses, allowing offenders to take direct responsibility for their actions, and assisting victims in their journey of moving beyond their frequent sense of vulnerability by means of achieving some closure stand in sharp contrast to focusing on past criminal behavior through ever-increasing levels of punishment (Umbreit, 1995b, 1994a, 1991a; Wright, 1991; Zehr, 1990).

The distinction between the dominant paradigm of retributive justice and the emergent paradigm of restorative justice has been developed by Zehr (1990). Whereas retributive justice focuses on punishment, the restorative paradigm emphasizes accountability, healing, and closure (figure 16.1).

During the past decade, an increasing number of social workers, human service professionals, and volunteers have become actively involved in victim offender mediation programs. Through serving as paid and volunteer mediators, board members, program developers, consultants, and/or trainers, they are making an important contribution to the field of restorative justice and mediation of criminal conflicts. Social workers and human service professionals have a rich history in juvenile and criminal justice and have been at the fore-

Figure 16.1   Paradigms of Justice

Restorative	Retributive
1. Crime defined as violation of the state.	1. Crime defined as violation of one person by another.
2. Focus on establishing blame and guilt, past orientation (Did he/she do it?).	2. Focus on problem solving, liabilities and obligations, future (What should be done?).
3. Adversarial relationship and process are normative.	3. Dialogue and negotiation are normative.
4. Imposition of pain to punish and deter/prevent future crime.	4. Restitution as a means of restoring both parties; goal of reconciliation/ restoration.
5. Justice defined by intent and process: right rules.	5. Justice defined as right relationships; judged by outcome.
6. Interpersonal, conflictual nature of crime obscured, repressed; conflict seen as individual against the state.	6. Crime recognized as interpersonal conflict; value of conflict is recognized.
7. One social injury replaced by another.	7. Focus on repair of social injury.
8. Community on the sidelines, represented abstractly by the state.	8. Community as facilitator in the restorative process.
9. Encouragement of competitive, individualistic values.	9. Encouragement of mutuality.
10. Action directed from state to offender: • victim ignored • offender passive.	10. Victim and offender's roles recognized in problem/solution: • victim rights/needs recognized • offender encouraged to take responsibility.
11. Offender accountability defined as taking punishment.	11. Offender accountability defined as understanding impact of action and helping decide how to make things right.
12. Offense defined in purely legal terms, devoid of moral, social, economic, and political dimensions.	12. Offense understood in whole context— moral, social, economic, and political.
13. "Debt" owed to state and society in the abstract.	13. Debt/liability to victim recognized.
14. Response focused on offender's past behavior.	14. Response focused on harmful consequences of offender's behavior.
15. Stigma of crime unremovable.	15. Stigma of crime removable through restorative action.
16. No encouragement for repentance and forgiveness.	16. Possibilities for repentance and forgiveness.
17. Dependence upon proxy professionals.	17. Direct involvement by participants.

Source: Adapted from Zehr, 1990.

front of mediation initiatives in this field of practice, from minor property offenses and nonviolent assaults to serious and violent crime.

The concept of crime victims sitting face to face with their offenders is difficult for many public officials and citizens to imagine. People who are unfamiliar with the process of victim offender mediation are frequently skeptical. They assume that victims are angry and want more severe punishment of offenders. Why would a victim want to meet the criminal? What's in it for the victim? Why would any offender ever be willing to meet his or her victim? What is there to mediate or negotiate anyway?

Despite these concerns, in a growing number of communities throughout North America, increasing numbers of crime victims are meeting with their offenders in the presence of a trained mediator. People who have been victimized have the opportunity to tell the offenders how the crime affected them. They can get answers to lingering questions such as "Why me?" and "Were you watching my movements?" Those who have committed certain types of criminal offenses are able to tell their story, portray a more human dimension to their character, own up to their behavior, and make amends. Together, both parties have the opportunity to negotiate a mutually agreeable restitution plan for compensating the victim.

There were only a handful of programs providing victim offender mediation and reconciliation services in the late 1970s. Today there are approximately 175 victim offender mediation programs in the United States and nearly thirty in Canada (Fagan & Gehm, 1993; Hughes & Schneider, 1989). Most are operated by private nonprofit correctional agencies working closely with the local courts. Some are sponsored directly by probation departments or even the state department of corrections, as in Oklahoma. Nearly all of these programs work with nonviolent property offenses and minor assaults, with some programs processing a small number of more violent offenses. An even larger number of programs exist in Europe where the field began developing in the mid 1980s, largely based upon the Victim Offender Reconciliation Program (VORP) model in the United States and Canada. Program development in Europe is currently growing more rapidly than in North America (Umbreit, 1991b). There now exists a network of 20 programs in England, 293 in Germany, 40 in France, 8 in Belgium, 54 in Norway, and 130 in Finland (Umbreit, 1995c). Austria recently adopted a federal policy to promote the use of victim offender mediation for young offenders on a national basis. The field of victim offender mediation is thus no longer simply an experiment. Rather, it is an emerging field of alternative dispute resolution that continues to grow, yet is little understood by many.

There are two distinct traditions from which the victim offender movement has developed in the United States. Particularly during the mid to late 1970s, there appears to have been little awareness or information sharing between these two sources of experimentation with the concept of mediating victim offender conflict.

The field of victim offender mediation in the United States is often associated with the development in 1978 of the first VORP in Elkhart, Indiana (Umbreit, 1985; Zehr, 1980). This VORP was a joint effort of the Mennonite Central Committee and the PACT (Prisoner and Community Together) organization. It was modeled after the initial VORP in Kitchener, Ontario, which began in 1974. To this day, the VORP tradition remains the most clearly articulated and documented expression of victim offender mediation and has greatly influenced the larger field, particularly private community based agencies, including some church-related organizations.

There has been another tradition, however, that actually predates the VORP movement and has been located in public criminal justice agencies, primarily probation departments. Efforts to experiment with bringing crime victims and their young offenders face-to-face can be traced back to the mid 1960s when a small number of probation departments began to see the value of such a confrontation. A total of thirty-four programs involving victim offender mediation were started between 1965 and 1979 (Hughes & Schneider, 1989). If one looks for the language of mediation in these programs, little will be found. But the actual process employed during these early years, while certainly not fitting a technical definition of mediation, clearly approximates what we now understand to be victim-offender mediation.

Another example of an early program is the Minnesota Restitution Center established in 1970 in Minneapolis by the Minnesota Department of Corrections (Hudson & Galaway, 1974). This was a program in which adult property offenders who were diverted from prison and placed in a residential center would meet with their victims to determine restitution plans. While this nationally recognized program model did not frame its activities as "mediation," the actual process they used had many parallels to what we now would call victim-offender mediation.

Research, Debates, and Trends

A small but growing amount of research in the field of victim-offender mediation has provided increasing insight into how the process works and the impact it is having on its participants and the larger justice system. The most essential findings that have emerged are as follows:

1. Victims of property crime have been found to be quite willing to participate in a mediation session with their offender when given the opportunity (Coates & Gehm, 1989; Gehm, 1990; Galaway, 1988; Marshall & Merry, 1990; Umbreit, 1985, 1989a, 1991a, 1992a).
2. Mediation is perceived to be voluntary by the vast majority of victims and juvenile offenders who have participated in it (Umbreit, 1993a, 1994b).

3. Victim-offender mediation results in high levels of client satisfaction and perceptions of fairness for both victims and offenders (Coates & Gehm, 1989; Dignan, 1990; Marshall & Merry, 1990; Umbreit, 1988, 1991a, 1991b, 1993b, 1994a, 1995a, 1995b; Umbreit & Coates, 1992, 1993).

4. While the possibility of receiving restitution appears to motivate victims to enter the mediation process, following their participation they report that meeting the offender and being able to talk about what happened was more satisfying than receiving restitution (Coates & Gehm, 1989; Umbreit, 1988, 1991a, 1994a, 1995c).

5. Offenders involved in mediation programs, while anxious about a confrontation with their victim, report that meeting the victim and being able to talk about what happened was the most satisfying aspect of the program (Coates & Gehm, 1989; Umbreit, 1991a, 1994a).

6. The victim-offender mediation process has the effect of humanizing the justice system response to crime for both victims and juvenile offenders (Coates & Gehm, 1989; Marshall & Merry, 1990; Umbreit, 1991a, 1994a, 1995a, 1995b; Umbreit & Coates, 1993).

7. Victim offender mediation has made a significant contribution to reducing fear and anxiety among victims of juvenile crime (Umbreit, 1991a, 1994a, 1994b).

8. Juvenile offenders seem to not perceive victim offender mediation to be a significantly less demanding response to their criminal behavior than other options available to the court. The use of mediation is consistent with the concern to hold young offenders accountable for their criminal behavior (Umbreit, 1994a).

9. From 40% to 60% of cases referred to programs result in a face-to-face mediation session (Coates & Gehm, 1989; Galaway, 1988, 1989; Gehm, 1990; Marshall & Merry, 1990; Umbreit, 1988, 1989a, 1991a; Wright & Galaway, 1989).

10. Restitution agreements that are perceived as fair to both parties are negotiated in nine out of ten cases that enter mediation (Coates & Gehm, 1989; Galaway, 1988, 1989; Gehm, 1990; Umbreit, 1986a, 1988, 1991a, 1994a).

11. A number of programs report successful completion of restitution agreements in the range of 79% to 98% (Coates & Gehm, 1989; Galaway, 1988, 1989; Gehm, 1990; Umbreit, 1986b, 1988, 1991a, 1994a).

12. Considerably fewer and less serious additional crimes are committed within a one-year period by juvenile offenders in victim offender mediation programs when compared to similar offenders who did not participate in mediation (Umbreit, 1993b, 1994a, 1994b; Umbreit & Coates, 1993). Although this finding was based on a limited sample, it is consistent with two British studies (Marshall & Merry, 1990; Dignan, 1990).

13. Victim-offender mediation has a significant impact on the likelihood of offenders successfully completing their restitution obligation to victims when compared to similar offenders who complete their restitution in a court-administered program without mediation (Umbreit, 1993b, 1994a, 1994b; Umbreit and Coates, 1992, 1993).

14. There is some evidence that a larger portion of victims of violent crime than initially believed are interested in confronting their offenders in a mediation process (Gustafson & Smidstra, 1989; Umbreit, 1989b, 1995a).

As the field of victim-offender mediation continues to develop in North America and Europe, it faces three major hurdles. Perhaps the greatest danger facing any reform movement such as victim-offender mediation is loss of vision. Programs inevitably become preoccupied with securing more stable funding sources and developing routine day-to-day operating procedures. It becomes easy to lose sight of the underlying values and principles that motivated the individuals who initiated the program and that serve as the foundation for the program's existence. The importance of providing opportunities for addressing the emotional issues surrounding crime and victimization, including the possibility of forgiveness and reconciliation, is a foundational principle of the field. Losing sight of this vision could result in a utilitarian and exclusive focus on restitution determination and payment, allowing little time for sharing facts and feelings related to the crime.

The other hurdles grow out of this loss of vision as programs continue to be preoccupied with becoming accepted into the mainstream of sociolegal services. There can be a tendency to take fewer risks, particularly related to the types of cases being referred to the program. In an eagerness to negotiate new referral arrangements, programs may be too quick to accept those cases that prosecutors' offices deem not to have sufficient evidence or would otherwise ignore. The likelihood of the field becoming increasingly marginalized and not taken seriously by the larger criminal justice system is far greater if victim offender mediation becomes identified with the "easy" cases, those that the system would have done little with in the first place.

An outgrowth of working with primarily "easy" cases is related to a third major hurdle, one that has important public policy implications. The vision of the field is deeply rooted in the mediation process being an alternative to the criminal justice system, including an alternative to incarceration for some offenders (Zehr & Umbreit, 1982). When programs focus upon taking the "easy" cases, many of which would not have even entered the formal criminal justice system, the field of victim offender mediation will have joined the ranks of many other "alternatives" that are associated with wider and stronger nets of social control (Austin & Krisberg, 1981; Dittenhoffer & Ericson, 1983). Despite intentions to the contrary, programs are likely to increase rather than limit state intervention into the lives of individuals who violate the law. For some, greater intervention into the lives of offenders is positive. For many others, however, such increased intervention into the lives of fairly minor first-time offenders is a poor use of the limited resources available to criminal justice systems when such resources are increasingly needed to address more serious crimes.

The Victim-Offender Mediation Process

As the most visible expression of restorative justice theory, the victim-offender mediation process differs markedly across different programs on the basis of referral source, diversion versus post-adjudication referral, use of volunteer mediators, and so on. A basic case management process, however, tends to be present in most of the programs in the United States and Canada (Umbreit, 1988). This process essentially involves four phases: case referral and intake, preparation for mediation, conducting the mediation session, and follow-up.

Nearly all victim-offender mediation and reconciliation programs focus upon providing a conflict resolution process that is perceived as fair by the victim and the offender. The mediator facilitates this process by first allowing time to address informational and emotional needs, followed by a discussion of losses and the possibility of developing a mutually agreeable restitution obligation (which may include money, work for the victim, and work for the victim's choice of a charity).

The process of victim-offender mediation, however, is less concerned with negotiating a settlement between disputants than it is with facilitating a dialogue between a person who has been traumatized and the person responsible for that pain. Through extensive premediation preparation and mediator-assisted dialogue and mutual aid when the parties come together, the mediator taps into the reservoirs of strength in both the victim and offender and facilitates a healing process grounded in the parties' helping each other through responding to important emotional and informational needs.

Victim-offender mediation requires a specialized knowledge base and core skills that are unique to this field of practice. This is especially important for those working with violent crime. The participants have undergone an extremely painful journey, and the process of facilitating a direct and frank dialogue between the parties related to, for example, a murder, the intense grief experienced by family members, and the possibilities for some degree of closure and healing poses numerous challenges. It is essential that the mediator understand the victimization experience and dynamics associated with grief and loss, as well as the effects of post-traumatic stress, and be able to effectively deal with the expression of a range of intense emotions. From the offender's perspective, it is necessary to have a thorough understanding of the criminal justice and corrections system and the offender and prisoner experience, and be able to relate to offenders in a nonjudgmental manner.

The process of mediating a victim-offender conflict begins when a juvenile or adult offender, often convicted of such crimes as theft and burglary, is referred to the program by the court. Most programs accept referrals after a formal admission of guilt has been entered with the court; some programs accept cases that are referred prior to formal admission of guilt as part of a deferred prosecution effort.

During the second, most important phase of the victim-offender mediation process, the mediator meets with the offender and victim separately, before the actual mediation is scheduled. During this individual session or sessions, the mediator listens to the story of each party, explains the program, and encourages participation. Usually mediators meet first with the offender, and then they talk with the victim to determine if he or she is willing to proceed with the mediation process. When granted permission from the offender, the mediator often shares information about the offender with the victim during the preparation meetings; this is often very helpful to victims in deciding whether or not to proceed with mediation.

Program advocates emphasize that victims should not be victimized again by the mediation program, even unintentionally. Many in the field believe that this is the strongest ethical principle of the victim-offender mediation process. They stress that a victim should never be coerced into participating in the mediation and reconciliation process. While coercion is inappropriate, mediators encourage victim participation in the process. Many programs have found that it is the voluntary exercise of choices, including the choice of participation, that leads to victims and offenders feeling empowered. The parties' willingness to participate in mediation is directly related to their feeling completely safe with the process and the mediator.

The preliminary separate meetings with victims and offenders require effective listening and communication skills. Victim participation can be lost at the first phone call. Experienced mediators have found that the initial process of building rapport and trust with the victim and offender, as well as gaining valuable information through the separate meetings, is essential to the quality of the later joint meetings with both individuals.

The victim's participation in mediation must always be entirely voluntary. The victim in particular must be fully ready to undertake the process; this may require a lengthy period of premediation preparation, and in some cases of serious crime and victimization, months and years of work. The offender too must be a suitable candidate for mediation; he or she must take responsibility for his or her actions and must demonstrate some level of empathy for the victim. These are essential conditions for victim-offender mediation; denial of responsibility and lack of demonstrated empathy for the victim are clear signals that mediation is contraindicated.

Offender participation in the mediation process is also voluntary. Actual practice would suggest something quite different. When offenders are ordered by the court, via probation, or are diverted from prosecution if they complete the program, a rather significant amount of state coercion is exercised. Research has also indicated that offenders do not always perceive the process as voluntary. Some programs attempt to temper this by trying to get referrals in the least coercive manner possible and to allow those offenders who are strongly opposed to participating or who are determined to be inappropriate for mediation by the program staff to opt out of the program.

The mediator schedules a face-to-face meeting after the parties have agreed to participate in mediation during the initial separate meetings. The mediation session between the involved parties is conducted during the third phase. This phase requires the completion of six tasks, which are a variation of the stages of the generic mediation model presented in chapter 1. These tasks are:

1. Introductory/opening statement by the mediator.
2. Storytelling by the victim and offender.
3. Clarification of facts and sharing of feelings.
4. Reviewing victim losses and exploring and testing the viability of options for compensation.
5. Developing a written restitution agreement.
6. Closing statement by the mediator.

The meeting would begin with the mediator explaining his or her role, identifying the agenda, and stating any communication ground rules that may be necessary.

A typical mediation session between a crime victim and an offender begins with an opening statement that includes the following:

1. Introduce everyone and arrange seating.
2. Explain your role as a mediator: "I am here to help both of you to talk about what happened and to work out a restitution agreement, if possible. I am not a court official and will not be requiring you to agree to anything, nor will I be taking sides with either of you."
3. Explain ground rules.
4. Identify the agenda; review facts and feelings related to the crime, and begin to discuss loses.
5. Begin the process of negotiating restitution by emphasizing fairness and balance: "Any restitution agreement that is reached must feel fair to both of you."
6. Initiate direct communication between victim and offender: "Mrs. Smith [victim], could you tell John [offender] what happened from your perspective and some of your feelings about the burglary?"

Following the opening statement, each party has some uninterrupted time to tell his or her story, usually beginning with the victim. The first part of the meeting focuses upon a discussion of the facts and feelings related to the crime. Victims are given the rare opportunity to express their feelings directly to the person who violated them, as well as to receive answers to many lingering questions such as, "Why me? How did you get into our house? Were you stalking us and planning on coming back?" Victims are often relieved to see the offender, who usually bears little resemblance to the frightening character they may have visualized.

Offenders are put in the uncomfortable position of having to face the person they violated. They are given the equally rare opportunity to display a more human dimension to their character and to express remorse in a personal fashion. Through open discussion of their feelings, victim and offender have the opportunity to deal with each other as people rather than as stereotypes and objects.

After the victim and offender have discussed the crime and expressed their concerns, the second part of the meeting is initiated. It focuses upon discussion of losses and negotiation of a mutually acceptable restitution agreement as a tangible symbol of conflict resolution and a focal point for accountability. It is important that the mediator in no way imposes a restitution agreement. The restitution agreement is negotiated between the parties, written up by the mediator, and signed at the end of the meeting by the victim, offender, and mediator. Joint victim-offender meetings usually last from one to two hours.

Completion of restitution agreements is monitored during the follow-up phase. A follow-up mediation session may be convened if problems have emerged and the parties are willing to meet again.

The application of mediation techniques in the context of victim-offender conflict involving property crimes and minor assaults is similar to yet different from mediation in other fields of practice. Mediating conflict between crime victims and their offenders is a distinct application of mediation and conflict resolution. Nearly all other applications of mediation are between and among individuals with some type of prior situational or interpersonal relationship (such as landlord/tenant, spousal, and employer/employee). In the context of victim-offender conflict most, but not all, participants in the mediation process are strangers. (An exception is in serious criminal cases, where prior acquaintance or even long-term intimate relationships are normative.) The issues related to the conflict are usually clear: there is a victim and a perpetrator, who has admitted his or her guilt. Determination of guilt is not the focus of the mediation process. The mediation process is a time-limited problem-solving intervention. It promotes a more restorative sense of justice through the sharing of information and the direct negotiation of restitution by the victim and offender themselves.

Power imbalance is of major concern to most victim-offender mediators. Precisely because there is a clear victim and offender, an enormous situational imbalance of power exists. It would be inappropriate to assume that both parties are contributing to the conflict, necessitating the need for strictly neutral terminology in the mediation process. Victim-offender mediation does not involve two "disputants" per se; one of the individuals clearly has been violated. Special attention must be directed toward the victim in order to ensure that he or she is not revictimized by the mediation process. This additional sensitivity to the victim does not have to come at the cost of being insensitive to the offender or violating the process of neutral third-party negotiation assistance. It does mean, however, that victims must have an absolutely voluntary choice about their participation in the program. The time and location of the mediation session must not violate their sense of what is safe, appropriate, and convenient.

Applying the mediation process with strangers may be considered by some to be quite difficult. Experience in the field of victim-offender mediation would suggest the contrary. Far less emotional and historical "baggage" is present. During the mediation process, the prominent dynamic is one of breaking down stereotypes and related fears rather than addressing issues of betrayal and mistrust that are rooted in lengthy prior relationships.

In mediating victim-offender conflict, there is usually a generational imbalance of power. Frequently, the offender is a juvenile or young adult and the victim is an adult or elder (Gehm, 1986; Hughes & Schneider, 1989; Umbreit, 1986b). When the offender is inarticulate, it is important to prepare, even coach, the offender during the prior individual meeting. This type of coaching is more like informal role playing, rather than telling the individual what to say in response to specific questions the victim might ask.

The opportunity to think through some of their questions and express their thoughts in a less threatening situation is important for many offenders. They benefit from preparation and rehearsal for interacting with the victim during the mediation session. This represents one strategy for attempting to balance power in the context of age and communication differences.

It is in the area of political ideology that the concept of victim-offender mediation differs most significantly from more traditional applications of mediation. North Americans have strong feelings about crime and punishment. These feelings often result from the way in which the most atrocious, yet least representative, crimes are highlighted by the media and the political arena. Ours is a punitive society; the United States has now surpassed the former Soviet Union and South Africa in per capita rate of incarceration in the world (Mauer, 1991).

Alternative dispute resolution within the context of civil court conflict may be controversial. It does not, however, confront major ideological barriers related to crime control policy in North American society. The moment mediation enters the criminal justice process, it has stepped over a powerful ideological threshold.

There is growing evidence among both criminal justice officials and the participants themselves that victim-offender mediation can be quite consistent with the community's sense of justice and fairness. Yet there remains strong opposition by many to the notion of the restorative type of justice embodied in the victim-offender mediation process. The more dominant retributive justice paradigm, with its emphasis on severity of punishment and state interests, even at the cost of addressing the interests of the person violated by the offense, is deeply rooted in contemporary culture. This is unlikely to dramatically change in the foreseeable future.

Working with Crimes of Severe Violence

Early in the morning of August of 1983, Stephen Molhan was driving home after a date with his girlfriend. At a stoplight in downtown Providence, R.I., he was approached by a man who had already assaulted two other men in the area. Stephen was shot in the head, robbed, and left to die. Shortly after Stephen's death, his mother, Suzanne Molhan, founded Family and Friends of Murdered Victims in order to offer support to other persons like herself in Rhode Island. Nearly nine years later, Suzanne Molhan confronted her son's killer in a high security prison after ten months of preparation by an experienced mediator. Suzanne Molhan found the victim-offender mediation process to be a pivotal moment in her long journey of grieving and her search for closure. While recognizing that this is not for all victims like herself, Suzanne needed to let the man who killed her son know the devastating effect the crime had on her life and to get answers to many questions.

Suzanne Molhan is one of a small but growing number of victims of extremely violent crime who in their own journey of grieving have found a direct confrontation with the very person who hurt them to be an important step in their healing. They want to express how the crime has affected them. They want to directly confront the source of terror in their lives. They want to be less fearful and more able to let go of the terror they have experienced.

While not usually a replacement for some form of incarceration in severely violent crimes, the process of victim offender mediation and dialogue appears to be effective for some but clearly not all victims of violence. These face-to-face meetings, in the presence of a trained mediator, are only one option that is available to victims; mediators who work with severely violent cases continually emphasize that choice is the key principle, along with providing a safe setting and a highly competent and sensitive mediator with advanced training. Experience with these cases has shown that having a mediator who deeply understands the grieving process, death and dying, and post-traumatic stress is as important as the ability to apply the technical skills of mediation and conflict resolution.

Bringing a victim of violent crime together with the offender and a mediator is done in a relatively small number of cases. It usually requires a lengthy period of preparation for both parties (with multiple separate meetings and phone calls) and coordination of the mediation with other counseling services involving both parties. In the case of Suzanne Molhan, the mediator did not proceed with the premediation process until being assured by Molhan's therapist that mediation would not interfere with the longer term therapeutic process. In fact, it was the therapist who recognized the important role that mediation could play in moving Molhan toward a sense of closure and facilitating her work in therapy.

During the actual mediation session, which lasted approximately two and one-half hours, including a break period, Suzanne's therapist and a chaplain who had been working with the offender were both present in a passive support role. Neither spoke during the mediation session, yet their presence had an important function in the overall process of mediation and healing.

In crimes of severe violence, the process of a mediated dialogue between the victim and offender is grounded in a paradigm of healing rather than problem-solving. There are usually no material issues related to losses that require a traditional problem-solving and negotiation approach to victim-offender mediation, but there is always a tremendous amount of brokenness, pain, and grief. A mediated dialogue between the parties most affected by the crime can allow a safe and potentially healing climate for mutual acknowledgment of the brokenness experienced by the parties. Such acknowledgment, within a process of genuine dialogue, contributes greatly to healing and restoration.

Conclusion

The current level of crime and violence throughout North American society has resulted in a widespread public fear of victimization, a fear that is well out of proportion to the actual risks of being victimized. Understandably, there exists a collective need for more effectively responding to crime and building safer communities. Public fear of crime continues to trigger passionate pleas from many politicians for harsher sentences and greater use of incarceration. Unfortunately, such "quick fixes" have little demonstrated impact on controlling or reducing criminal behavior. Demands for the expensive retributive policies of the past, however, remain potent realities in the national policy debate related to crime and victimization.

Advocates of restorative justice and the practice of victim-offender mediation must effectively address the concerns raised by those who cling to the failed policies of the past. Linkages between enhancing public safety through real, not just symbolic, offender accountability and the philosophy of restorative justice and mediation must increasingly be made explicit. At the same time, however, the limitations of victim-offender mediation must also be made clear. The process is not for everyone; alternatives must be available for those victims who cannot contemplate any form of negotiation with their offender. Mediation is thus presented here as an alternative among or adjunct to a range of options, but one that has far greater potential than has been realized to date.

The traditional retributive criminal justice process places both victims and offenders in passive roles. Crime victims often express a sense of being revictimized by the system that is designed to bring about "justice." They have relatively little input, are frequently provided with little information about the status of the case, and are often ignored by the offender-driven nature of the system. The extent to which victims are needed as evidence, as a "prop" in the adversarial "game" of doing justice, usually determines the amount of attention the crime victim will receive.

While the criminal justice process is clearly driven by a focus on the offender, rarely are offenders confronted with the real human damage they have caused. Rarely are they given an opportunity to make amends in a direct fashion to the victim and victimized community.

Without the presence of victim-offender mediation programs and the restorative justice principles upon which they are based, criminal justice systems in North America will continue to place crime victims in marginal roles, offering them little input to the justice process or actual compensation for their losses, and offenders will continue to be held accountable in indirect and punitive ways.

Victim-offender mediation is not a panacea. It does, however, provide the potential for a number of important benefits. The anger, frustration, and fear of victims can be reduced. Offenders can be held accountable for their behavior and make amends in a direct and personal manner. Victims can receive compensation for their losses. Without undermining the seriousness of their crimes, offenders can be diverted from further court involvement or continued costly incarceration in prison and correctional facilities.

References

Austin, J. & B. Krisberg. 1981. Wider, Stronger, and Different Nets: The Dialectics of Criminal Justice Reform. *Journal of Research in Crime and Delinquency* 18(1): 165–96.

Coates, R. B. & J. Gehm. 1989. An Empirical Assessment. In M. Wright & B. Galaway, eds., *Mediation and Criminal Justice*. London: Sage.

Dignan, J. 1990. *Repairing the Damage*. Sheffield, UK: Centre for Criminological and Legal Research, University of Sheffield.

Dittenhoffer, T. & R. Ericson. 1983. The Victim Offender Reconciliation Program: A Message to Correctional Reformers. *University of Toronto Law Journal* 33(3): 315–47.

Fagan, H. & J. Gehm. 1993. *National Directory of Victim Offender Reconciliation and Mediation Programs*. Valpariaso, IN: PACT Institute of Justice.

Galaway, B. 1988. Crime Victim and Offender Mediation as a Social Work Strategy. *Social Service Review* 62: 668–83.

———. 1989. Informal Justice: Mediation Between Offenders and Victims. In P. A. Albrecht & O. Backes, eds., *Crime Prevention and Intervention: Legal and Ethical Problems*. Berlin: Walter de Gruyter.

Gehm, J. 1986. *Victim Offender Reconciliation and Mediation Program Directory*. Valparaiso, IN: PACT Institute of Justice.

———. 1990. Mediated Victim-Offender Restitution Agreements: An Exploratory Analysis of Factors Related to Victim Participation. In B. Galaway & J. Hudson, eds., *Criminal Justice, Restitution and Reconciliation*. Monsey, NY: Criminal Justice Press.

Gustafson, D. L. & H. Smidstra. 1989. *Victim Offender Reconciliation in Serious Crime: A Report on the Feasibility Study Undertaken for the Ministry of the Solicitor General (Canada)*. Langley, British Columbia: Fraser Region Community Justice Initiatives Association.

Hudson, J. & B. Galaway. 1974. Undoing the Wrong: The Minnesota Restitution Center. *Social Work* 19(3): 313–18.

Hughes, S. P. & A. L. Schneider. 1989. Victim-Offender Mediation: A Survey of Program Characteristics and Perceptions of Effectiveness. *Crime and Delinquency* 35(2): 217–33.

Marshall, T. F. & S. Merry. 1990. *Crime and Accountability*. London: Home Office.

Mauer, M. 1991. *Americans Behind Bars: A Comparison of International Rates of Incarceration*. Washington, DC: The Sentencing Project.

Umbreit, M. S. 1985. Crime and Reconciliation: *Creative Options for Victims and Offenders*. Nashville, TN: Abingdon Press.

———. 1986a. Victim Offender Mediation: A National Survey. *Federal Probation* 50(4): 53–56.

———. 1986b. Victim Offender Mediation and Judicial Leadership. *Judicature* 69: 202–4.

———. 1988. Mediation of Victim Offender Conflict. *Journal of Dispute Resolution* 1988: 85–105.

———. 1989a. Victims Seeking Fairness, Not Revenge: Toward Restorative Justice. *Federal Probation* 53: 52–57.

———. 1989b. Violent Offenders and Their Victims. In Martin Wright and Burt Galaway, eds., *Mediation and Criminal Justice*. London: Sage.

———. 1991a. Minnesota Mediation Center Gets Positive Results. *Corrections Today Journal* (August): 194–97.

———. 1991b. Mediation of Youth Conflict: A Multi-System Perspective. *Child and Adolescent Social Work* 8(2): 141–53.

———. 1993a. Crime Victims and Offenders in Mediation: An Emerging Area of Social Work Practice. *Social Work* 38(1): 69–73.

———. 1993b. Juvenile Offenders Meet Their Victims: The Impact of Mediation in Albuquerque, New Mexico. *Family and Conciliation Courts Review* 31(1): 90–100.

———. 1994a. *Victim Meets Offender: The Impact of Restorative Justice and Mediation*. Monsey, NY: Criminal Justice Press.

————. 1994b. Crime Victims Confront Their Offenders: The Impact of a Minneapolis Mediation Program. *Journal of Research on Social Work Practice* 4(4): 436–47.

————. 1995a. *Mediation of Criminal Conflict: An Assessment of Programs in Four Canadian Provinces.* St. Paul, MN: Center for Restorative Justice and Mediation, University of Minnesota.

————. 1995b. The Development and Impact of Victim-Offender Mediation in the United States. *Mediation Quarterly* 12(3): 263–76.

————. 1995c. *Mediating Interpersonal Conflicts: A Pathway to Peace.* West Concord, MN: CPI Publishing.

Umbreit, M. S. & R. B. Coates. 1992. The Impact of Mediating Victim Offender Conflict: An Analysis of Programs in Three States. *Juvenile & Family Court Journal* 43: 21–28.

————. 1993. Cross-Site Analysis of Victim Offender Mediation in Four States. *Crime and Delinquency* 39(4): 565–85.

Wright, M. 1991. *Justice for Victims and Offenders.* Philadelphia, PA: Open University Press.

Wright, M. & B. Galaway. 1989. *Mediation and Criminal Justice.* London: Sage.

Zehr, H. 1980. *Mediating the Victim-Offender Conflict.* Akron, PA: Mennonite Central Committee.

————. 1990. *Changing Lenses, A New Focus for Crime and Justice.* Scottsdale, PA: Herald Press.

Zehr, H. & M. Umbreit. 1982. Victim Offender Reconciliation: An Incarceration Substitute? *Federal Probation* 46(4): 63–68.

17

SOCIAL POLICY

Mediation and Dispute Resolution in the Field of Social Policy

by Bernard Mayer

One of the fastest growing and most productive applications of mediation and related conflict resolution approaches is in the area of public policy development. The emphasis that policymakers place on achieving broad-scale consensus in the development of social policies and the increasing demand of the public to have a meaningful say in policy-making have encouraged the use of mediation in this arena, particularly in the implementation of potentially divisive policy directives.

Despite social work's systemic orientation and the importance of achieving broad social consensus on major policy initiatives, social policy mediation has lagged behind other areas; the most widespread use of policy mediation has been in the environmental and economic development fields. However, there have been some significant emerging applications of policy mediation in areas of concern to social workers and other human service professionals, and these are increasing in their use.

This chapter examines different types of policy mediation, the forces promoting the use of mediation in social policy, the process of social policy mediation, and applications of mediation to social policy issues. It concludes with a discussion of salient questions, concerns, and prospects for the future of mediation in this field of practice.

Theory, Debates, and Trends

Policy mediation involves the use of a third party neutral to bring together different interest groups in order to make consensus recommendations or decisions about policy issues. Such mediation may occur as part of the effort to formulate policy, implement policy, or resolve disputes that arise about policies already in place (Laue, 1988). Usually, the agencies involved in developing or implementing policy act as either conveners of the process or as parties to the mediation. Facilitated policy dialogues can occur at the local, regional, state/provincial, national, or international levels. There are many different types of policy mediation, and they can be categorized along a number of continua as shown in the following sections.

Dialogue or Negotiation

Some policy forums emphasize communication, dialogue, defining areas of agreement, looking for overarching policy principles, framing the issues in dispute in constructive ways, presenting disputes in terms of the underlying interests of the parties, and outlining policy options. These fora, however, may not have identified the achievement of a negotiated policy recommendation or decision as their stated purpose.

An example of such a forum is the Alaska Wolf Summit, which occurred over a four-day period. This forum brought together about four hundred invited participants and fifteen hundred observers to examine complex issues involving wolf control in that state. The forum occurred following a governmental decision to eliminate a large number of wolves to enhance Alaskan moose and caribou herds. Animal rights and environmental activists objected to the policy, and a boycott was organized, resulting in the governor of Alaska suspending the policy directive and convening the summit. Given that the forum included participants with widely differing values, perspectives, and interests, and that the issues involved were (and continue to be) highly complex and contentious, the forum was not designed to achieve substantive consensus. Nonetheless, an open dialogue among diverse groups enabled the development of a number of overarching principles that provided a foundation for future collaboration.

Other policy fora are convened with the specific purpose of achieving a negotiated settlement on policy issues. Usually these involve smaller numbers of participants and a longer period of time to work through the issues involved. A key part of instituting such a process involves the formation of a negotiation table that represents a broad range of interests and has credibility with the different parties involved.

Advisory or Authoritative Process

Most social policy mediations are advisory in nature, because the authority to set social policy is vested in legislative, executive, or judicial bodies. Typically, a convenor charged with formulating or implementing policy (such as a federal agency, state/provincial public housing authority, or city council) brings together a group of citizens to make recommendations about a policy issue. These recommendations are then forwarded to the appropriate decision-making entity that is not legally bound to follow the decision.

There are, however, an increasing number of dialogue fora that have been delegated some authority to make decisions on policy issues. The most common form is the negotiated rule-making process, or "reg-neg." In the United States, the Environmental Protection Agency (EPA) has used this process extensively, although it was first used on a national level by the Federal Aviation Administration to revise policies concerning rest periods for pilots (Singer, 1994). This process has been institutionalized through the Federal Advisory Committee Act (U.S.). Once a regulatory negotiation group is convened in accordance with procedures specified in this act, the convening agency agrees to utilize the agreement reached as the basis for the proposed rule; this rule is then published in the *Federal Register* and is subject to the standard input and revision process. In a "reg-neg," the responsible agency is a party to the negotiation, so its agreement must be obtained if consensus is to be achieved. Rather than taking away the agency's power, this process redirects it into a new, more collaborative forum.

While advisory groups have long been used by policy-making organizations, a rule-making forum can be distinguished by its specific charge (to negotiate a rule), the use of a consensus decision-making process facilitated by a third party neutral, and the agency's commitment to adhere to the outcome (Haygood, 1988).

While the distinction between advisory and authoritative is crucial, the difference is not always clear in practice. The presence of formal authority is often less important to the power of a group's recommendations than is the credible participation of the different interest groups involved. If a consensus recommendation on a controversial issue is achieved by a group representing the major interests (not just "special interests" but those reflective of broad public concerns), then it is difficult for policymakers with formal power to ignore or overturn the results, although this does occasionally occur.

Formal or Informal Process

Policy mediation processes can be formal and structured, with clearly identified goals, procedures, ground rules, time lines, and structures, or they can be informal and open-ended. The more informal processes are in many respects elaborated public input fora conducted by a facilitator and designed to encourage both dialogue and consensus building among different interests. Formal policy mediations usually involve a more articulated purpose of reaching resolution among designated interest groups about clearly defined issues.

Ongoing or Ad Hoc Meetings

Some policy mediations involve long-term ongoing discussions within a defined group that has permanent or long-term standing. For example, a citizen's advisory board to a government agency that is engaged in controversial decisions (such as military base closures, siting of public housing, and child welfare policy development) may well be involved in extended mediation of difficult policy questions. On the other hand, a group might be brought together for a single meeting or a short series of meetings. If, for example, a social agency wants to work with neighborhood groups on policies that should be used in deciding where to locate group homes for disabled youth in the community, it may plan a one-time gathering or a short series of meetings. Typically, however, policy mediations occur over a period of several months with a group that has been established specifically for the purpose of addressing the issues under discussion.

Closed or Open Process

Policy mediations are often carried out under "sunshine" laws or regulations, requiring that meetings be open and announced to the general public. This is particularly likely if the discussions involve policymakers or others who have a formal role to play in the policy formulation process and a public participation component is necessary. Some policy mediations are designed to be open to all participants who choose to come; others involve a set table of invited participants who negotiate with observers present. There are, however, situations in which policy mediations can occur in a closed and confidential setting. If there are no governing "sunshine" laws, no formal decision-makers, or if the process does not involve government officials, such meetings can be closed. Occasionally, if the issues are sensitive, policy mediation fora are specifically designed to be confidential. On the other hand, if the process is open, it often becomes very important to agree on ground rules for press coverage and statements, and for public participation in the process.

Preventive or Dispute Resolution Orientation

Many policy mediations are preventive in nature, designed to resolve issues that could erupt into serious conflict or to arrive at agreements to forestall subsequent challenges. The growth in the use of regulatory negotiation procedures by the EPA was motivated by the number of court challenges to regulations. In the early 1980s, over 80 percent of the regulations promulgated by the EPA were challenged in court (Haygood, 1988; Singer, 1994). Regulatory negotiations were instituted in an effort to ameliorate this problem. The U.S. Departments of Energy and Defense have initiated a number of citizen participation fora to arrive at policy recommendations concerning the handling of economic, environmental, public health, and land use issues arising from the closure of military bases and nuclear weapons installations.

Other policy mediations occur after conflicts about proposed or existing policies have erupted. In the late 1980s, a policy mediation process was initiated in Denver to make recommendations concerning the distribution of public housing throughout the community after a number of angry public confrontations between neighborhood activists and city officials. The Alaska Wolf Summit referred to previously was called after a boycott had been initiated and considerable media attention generated.

Mixed Processes

Policy mediations tend to be complex procedures that often involve a mixture of different types of processes. For example, some policy mediations may involve a closed table with a clearly defined purpose in addition to a series of open, less structured public meetings. Others may start with open, unstructured, and ad hoc groups of individuals who are concerned about a policy issue and develop into a clearly defined mediation process among a set group of stakeholders.

In most policy mediation, process design is as important as the actual facilitation of the negotiation sessions. Designing a process that has credibility among various interest groups, addresses complex issues in effective ways, allows for the achievement of maximum consensus among different parties, and reflects the political, cultural, and logistical realities of the particular setting is crucial to the success of mediation in the policy arena.

Forces Impelling Policy Mediation

The dramatic increase in the use of mediation in the public policy arena is part of a much larger social process that in many ways is redefining the meaning of democracy. There are several aspects of this process. One involves the trend towards "flattening" and decentralizing decision making. Political processes are still essential to broker different public interests in the policy-making process, but citizens are demanding and obtaining a more direct role in the brokering process. This is also reflected in the trends toward "participatory management," "flat organizational structures," and "self-guided work teams" in organizational settings, in "site-based management" in schools, and in many other facets of the field of alternative dispute resolution. There is also a growth in the sense of "procedural entitlement" characteristic of Western democracies (Mayer et al., 1995), whereby citizens expect the right to a fair process in which their concerns will be heard, accounted for, responded to, and reflected in the public decision-making process. The foundation of democracy is a contract between citizens and government that allows for difficult and even unpopular decisions to be made, based on the fundamental belief that the process of choosing decision-makers and considering decisions has been fair, open, and reasonably evenhanded. The public is demanding an ever-greater degree of openness and involvement in decision-making at all levels and a higher level of accountability of public officials. This has required the development of new fora and avenues for involving citizens in the public policy formulation process.

Another factor impelling policy mediation relates to the perception of an increasing distance between citizens and policymakers. Legislative and administrative bodies appear to be far removed and less accessible and responsive to common citizens. At the same time, policy-making itself has become more complex; more frequently, policy decisions seem to be distributive in nature, involving difficult choices about how limited resources are going to be allocated and competing interests balanced.

Because of the increasing distance and perceived alienation of citizens from the policy-making process, the growing competition among different groups for limited resources, and the rising litigiousness in society, the judiciary has become increasingly involved in the policy-making process. This has resulted in many of the same problems that have led to the use of mediation in other arenas. The transaction costs of adversarial processes are great, decisional flexibility is reduced, and the personal commitment to the outcome achieved is so diminished that even forcefully imposed decisions face enormous implementation obstacles.

These trends have led both policymakers and interest group advocates to look for policy-making processes that are more efficient, collaborative, and inclusive. Mediated consensus-building fora are an attractive alternative to consider under these circumstances. Finally, the growth of mediation in other fields of practice has also contributed to its use in policy formulation.

The Mediation Process

Bradley (1988) identifies common principles that promote collaborative problem-solving processes: the representation of all affected parties; the involvement of the parties in agenda setting; a problem-solving orientation; a transparent process, with an educational emphasis; the use of fact-finding techniques; a consensus-based decision-making model; a focus on implementation; and the use of a neutral process guide. Carpenter and Kennedy (1988) similarly identify principles for effective conflict management of public disputes: attention to procedures; strategic planning; a focus on positive working relationships; searching for a constructive problem definition; involvement of the parties in process design; an interest-based approach to problem-solving; flexibility; preventative planning; and a commitment to "doing no harm."

Beyond such broad principles, the actual process of policy mediation can vary tremendously. There are so many different arenas, players, goals, and contexts for policy mediation that it is crucial that each mediation be tailored to the particular situation. Generally speaking, however, there are several stages or tasks common to most policy mediations; these are detailed in the following sections.

Process Initiation

Before a mediation process begins, the policy issue must be mature and significant enough to warrant the use of a collaborative problem-solving process of some kind. Sometimes, as with many regulatory negotiations, legislation or administrative policy establishes time frames and guidelines for formulating and implementing regulations. Alternatively, a particular incident or site-specific conflict related to a larger policy issue creates the momentum for a policy negotiation. Occasionally, a particular interest group organizes enough pressure on a policy-making entity to force a public process. Policymakers are often aware that a policy-setting process will be particularly contentious and wish to take preventative action. Before policy mediation processes begin, there needs to be a realization that a collaborative problem-solving or negotiation process is desirable. Usually, a governmental official or agency will act as the "convenor" of such a process; the convenor is the authority that initiates the process and contracts with the mediator/facilitator.

Mediators are sometimes selected by a competitive process. Occasionally, a mediator is chosen without such a process due to time pressure, mediator availability, acceptability to parties, expertise, or institutional location. The process of the selection of a third party and the perceived appropriateness and credibility of that party are critical to the outcome of the process. Sometimes, a mediator will act as the facilitator of the convening process, but once they are gathered, the parties will choose a different third party to assist in the ongoing negotiations.

Part of the process initiation stage involves a clarification of the convenor's expectations of the mediator and the mediation process. A lack of clarity about the purpose of the process or the role of the mediator can be a major obstacle to success. For example, if there is confusion as to whether the mediator is being asked to design the process or just conduct it, how participants will be selected, or how much resources can be devoted to the process, then conflicting expectations that can undermine the process will quickly develop.

Situation Assessment, Process Design and Convening

These are sometimes separate processes but are typically intertwined. It is important that a situation assessment phase occur in any policy negotiation.

This involves identifying the key interest groups and the central "players" in these groups, the major issues in dispute, the data necessary to consider these issues, and the forces promoting or inhibiting a problem-solving process. It is important to assess the commitment of the different parties to a problem-solving process, their key interests, and the political or personal dynamics that are at play. Since policy negotiations are resource-intense procedures, it is also critical to consider whether there is enough support, adequate resources, and sufficient time for such a process to have a likelihood of success.

Process design is an ongoing task that should involve all of the participants. In most large-scale processes, a process design group of some form is created with representation from a range of participants to plan the overall process, provide feedback to the mediator, and review the progress of the negotiations. The involvement of different interest groups in the design and ongoing revision of the process is key to the success of policy negotiations. If the process is viewed by participants as having been imposed on them by the mediator or convenor, then it may become a target for resistance, especially when negotiations begin to stall.

Some of the design questions that usually need to be answered include:

- How many participants should be at the negotiating table, how should they be chosen, and who should they be?
- How should other interested parties be involved at meetings? How can representatives of organizations or groups keep their constituents informed and supportive of developments at the table?
- What ground rules should be adopted, and how should they be negotiated?
- What committee structure should there be? What is the role of the mediator in committees?
- Should policymakers or government employees be part of the negotiation process?
- How can necessary information be efficiently and credibly collected and presented in a constructive manner?
- How can key concerns and issues be identified and brought to the negotiating table in an efficient and collaborative manner?
- What consensus-building procedures should be used?
- How often and where should meetings be held, and what overall schedule should be proposed for the entire process?
- How can meetings be designed and conducted to be efficient, inclusive, and productive?

Convening is sometimes a formal requirement with clear components, as in many regulatory negotiations. This can involve a contracted stage in the process within which the mediator assesses the situation, proposes a process, identifies the key parties, builds a proposed negotiating table, gains commitment from the proposed participants to take part in the negotiations, and drafts a convening document summarizing the scope and intended process of the negotiations. At other times, "convening" is used more informally to suggest the process by which the decision to begin a policy dialogue is implemented. A dilemma that mediators often face during this phase of the process is how to build a negotiating group that includes a balance of the different interests involved, but is not so unwieldy as to make open and honest dialogue impossible. Often it is necessary to create a fairly large plenary group and to use a committee structure to carry out much of the work.

Opening the Negotiation Process

After the convening stage is completed, the beginning of the actual negotiation process occurs. Usually this involves a review and refinement of the stated purpose of the negotiations, the ground rules, the process design, the role of the mediator, and the makeup of the table. Some testing on the part of the participants of the process parameters, the commitment of the policymakers to utilize the outcomes, and the neutrality and effectiveness of the mediator is common. It is critical that the mediator not move through this process too quickly. Without buy-in from the participants in response to purpose, process, membership, and choice of mediator, progress will not occur. It is also important at this stage to engage in some group-building processes, although it is important to do this within the norms and culture of the participants.

Issue and Interest Scoping

Scoping the issues to be resolved and the interests of the different parties concerning these issues is usually the first stage of the negotiation process. With multiple parties, this can be cumbersome, and it is helpful to utilize efficient brainstorming techniques. Often, the result of the initial scoping effort is a large and unwieldy list of issues and interests. It is sometimes useful for the mediators, ideally in consultation with a group of the participants, to summarize and categorize the results of the initial scoping in a more useful form. The primary goal of this stage is a productive framing of the issues; this helps participants view the task as a mutual problem-solving effort and to recognize the essential interests of other parties as legitimate concerns that must be addressed for a constructive solution to be found.

Information Processing

Identifying the information needed to constructively discuss the issues and developing procedures for obtaining and presenting this information are key aspects of policy negotiations. The issues are typically very complex, and frequently there is no mutually acceptable source of information. Debates about the accuracy of information, the credibility of a source of information, and the correct interpretation of information often become a surrogate for an open confrontation about the competing values or interests of the participants. The stated need for more information can mask a desire to slow down a process or to avoid a painful choice among alternatives. In the end, most policy decisions have to be made in the absence of complete, credible, or clear information, but it is critical that sufficient information be gathered and discussed to allow for the formation and evaluation of options.

Option Generation and Evaluation

There is a great range of creative procedures for generating and evaluating options in a policy negotiation process. Crafting options that address multiple interests and that can be considered in depth in a large group takes considerable skill on the part of the mediator. The use of single text negotiating documents, subgroups, hi-tech graphic devices, neutral substantive experts, caucuses, agency experts, and brainstorming techniques are all common elements of this stage. Occasionally, it is helpful to gather small groups of participants from opposing points of view and ask each as a team to develop several options to present to the larger group. The process of option generation is one of the most interesting, challenging, and enjoyable aspects of policy negotiations.

Consensus Building

Building consensus is a fundamental component of the policy mediation process and involves identifying the most essential concerns of the parties and crafting options that allow these to be met. It is usually an iterative process that involves successive attempts at formulating proposals that parties can live with and considering a variety of policy "trade-offs." Often, the key to consensus building is helping the participants to identify their most important interests and to consider their needs and evaluate alternatives in light of the interests of the other parties at the table. While consensus is sometimes achieved only when the participants begin to work on the fine details of a written policy proposal, consensus building occurs throughout the policy negotiation process, from the convening and design phase to the final negotiation. The more the group process is seen to be productive and the participants have come to view issues in dispute as mutual problems to be solved, the more likely that consensus building will proceed smoothly.

It is not unusual for a public policy process involving many groups not to reach total consensus on all of the issues among all of the parties. Sometimes there are areas of complete consensus, partial consensus, and disagreement. Occasionally, there are some participants who choose to stand aside and propose their own policy alternatives, allowing the rest of the group to achieve consensus. This is not necessarily a sign that the process has failed. Consensus is sometimes possible only at levels of generality that are of little use, whereas a well-framed and respectful discussion of areas of agreement and disagreement can often be of considerable use to policymakers.

Public Involvement and Ratification

Policy mediation is seldom carried out in a vacuum. Participants usually represent a variety of formal or informal groups, although how this is done may vary tremendously. Occasionally, a mediator has to deal with participants who have moved much further than their constituents toward a consensus position and who may as a result have lost their credibility with the people they represent. It is important, therefore, to consider how to arrange for participants to report back to their organizations and for public input. This can be an ongoing effort, or it can occur at a stage of the negotiation when tentative agreements are being considered.

It is advisable to keep the final policy decision-makers, whether they are elected officials, appointed commissions, or government agents, apprised of the policy recommendations being considered. The feedback from these groups, as well as from members of the public, is often critical to crafting a recommendation that will ultimately be adopted.

Closing

As in other types of mediation, there is a stage in public policy mediation that involves final bargaining, trade-offs, and commitment to a written agreement. This is a point in the process when participants must directly examine the consequences of the agreements they have made and when they often experience "buyer's remorse." It is also a time when people try to gain last-minute concessions and when the level of conflict can suddenly increase. If the process has been perceived as fair and balanced, however, and the key interests of the participants have been addressed, the last minute doubts and final bargaining will not usually prevent a successful conclusion to the mediation. The act of formally endorsing the agreement and concluding the mediation process is important, as policy negotiations usually end not with the actual adoption or implementation of a policy but with a recommendation made to appropriate government agencies or legislative groups. It is important to be clear when the work of the policy negotiating group is really completed. At times, a back-and-forth process of revisions in response to the concerns of policymakers is incorporated into the negotiating process, but this is relatively rare. By formalizing the closing, not only do participants commit themselves to supporting the outcome but clarity that policy-making has proceeded to the next stage is achieved. Usually, some form of ceremony to present recommendations to the decision-makers is included in the process. This could involve a presentation of the report to a governmental authority or a reception to recognize and thank the participants in the process.

Follow Through

The final stage is one of monitoring the recommendations and communicating with policymakers as they consider them. This is not part of the mediation process per se, but it is critical to the final outcome. Often, the policy negotiation process has provided the participants with a more sophisticated and broader view of the issues than has been provided the policymakers themselves, and it is important that an effective communication procedure be developed between the negotiators and the policymakers, whether they are an administrative or legislative body.

Case Study

In the city of Boulder, Colorado, a sales tax was due to be discontinued, or "sunsetted," at the beginning of 1992. Early in 1991, two rival groups began collecting signatures on a petition asking that the tax be extended and that it be used to fund specific needs. One group requested that the monies generated be used for sports and recreational facilities; the other asked for human service programs. Since both groups had the signatures necessary to get their initiative on the ballot, the prospect of rival proposals, each which alone would have a difficult time obtaining passage, seemed very likely. The two groups met and, with the assistance of a mediator, were able to agree on a joint ballot initiative. Members of the city council urged the defeat of the initiative, insisting that there were other potential uses for this money and promising a citizen input procedure to consider what should be done after the expiration of the sales tax. They pointed out that there was a full year left before the tax would expire, and there would be plenty of time to consider this issue. The initiative went to the voters in 1991 and was narrowly defeated, partly because of a promise on the part of city council to institute a careful review of this issue with public participation.

Shortly after the election, the city manager approached the mediator who had worked with the competing groups and asked him to facilitate a public input process not just on the issue of the expiring sales tax but on the overall question of how to finance currently unmet municipal needs. As a result, the Municipal Finance Strategy Committee (MFSC) was formed to evaluate unmet needs and to consider how these might be financed. The city manager's office selected twenty-two committee members representing a spectrum of community groups with an interest in city financing. These included representatives of the two initial petitioning groups, the business community, and neighborhood organizations, other concerned citizens, representatives of other potential fund recipients, and representatives of various ethnic communities. The charge to the group was to identify the unmet needs of the community, to consider potential new funding sources, and to make recommendations about how to utilize these sources. It was clear from the outset that one potential source of funding was the expiring sales tax, which could only be continued by a ballot initiative; however, it was important to the city that this not be the sole focus of the group's deliberations.

The MFSC itself organized into three subgroups: a steering committee to oversee the overall process, a data analysis group, and a community outreach group. The latter organized a series of community focus group meetings, public input meetings, and a survey of the community and community organizations. At the same time, the data analysis group was investigating the potential revenues from different sources of income and was beginning to consider alternatives to propose to the group as a whole. The group in its entirety was also meeting to consider the financial information supplied by the city, to begin to identify the key interests in the community, and to select principles that the group as a whole could use in making its decisions. Periodically during this process, two spokespersons from the committee spoke to the work of the MFSC to the city council and local press.

The outcome of this process, which lasted about eight months, was a set of recommendations on how to generate additional revenue and where this revenue should be spent; a proposal to reinstitute the sales tax, with a specified fund allocation formula; and an agreement on the specific wording of the ballot initiative. Rather than the different interests competing with each other for limited funds, a joint proposal was developed that was supported by the human services, environmental, recreation, arts, and business communities. Several members of city council preferred a ballot initiative that would give the council more flexibility in how to spend the money, but during the public participation component of two successive city council meetings there was considerable support expressed for the MFSC proposal. As a result, the council put two initiatives on the ballot, one asking the citizens whether they wanted the tax reinstituted and the other whether they were in support of the allocation formula and procedures. Defeat of either of these proposals would have meant a rejection of substantial aspects of the MFSC's recommendations, but both were decisively approved by voters.

This mediated dialogue demonstrated the power of citizen input procedures that have community credibility, representation of widespread interest groups, and effective consensus building and conflict resolution mechanisms. Despite the fact that the MFSC had no formal power or legal standing, its recommendations were adopted over the opposition of some influential elected officials. This process also demonstrates how varied citizen input procedures often are. This was in part a policy negotiation, a dialogue about community values, a mediation of some specific disputes between different interest groups concerning a particular sales tax, and a sophisticated community input process. It involved issues of great concern to human service advocates, and it identified many policy principles regarding the responsibility of the local community for meeting human service needs. At times the process was tedious, anxiety provoking, and discouraging; in the final outcome, however, the participants felt empowered, successful, optimistic, and effective. They overwhelmingly expressed the feeling that the mediation (or facilitated negotiation) format was essential to the success of their efforts.

Applications of Mediation to the Social Policy Arena

In a sense, any policy-oriented mediation process almost by definition involves issues of social policy. The distinction between economic, environmental, community planning, and social policy is misleading. As the example demonstrates, policy decisions often involve choices about how to spend limited resources and, therefore, have serious consequences for social services. If social workers take too narrow a view of which areas of policy formation are relevant to them, they will fail to participate in some significant discussions.

There are, of course, applications of policy mediation to areas more traditionally of concern to social workers. Social policy and human services in general operate in areas that are typically characterized by unresolved public value conflicts. The role of government in protecting children, providing a "social safety net," promoting the needs of families, providing for the elderly, and dealing with mental health issues is subject to constantly changing public beliefs. Public ambivalence about these issues is one reason they provide such easy fodder for politicians who want to appeal to a sense of alienation and frustration, and to find easy scapegoats. This suggests the importance of bringing together different interests in fora that encourage dialogue and creative problem-solving. In an era of diminishing resources and rapidly evolving public values about social policy and human services, we can expect to see an increase in the use of mediated policy dialogue formats. Some specific areas in which mediation has or might be used to formulate public policy follows.

Resource Allocation Policies. There have been a number of interesting policy dialogues, similar in some respects to the MFSC process outlined earlier, in which decisions about how to allocate limited resources among competing social or human service programs have been made. A good example of this involved a process called a "Negotiated Investment Strategy," used in Connecticut, Mississippi, Michigan, and elsewhere to resolve policy disputes in allocating Federal Social Service Block Grants (Moore, 1988). This involved the formation of a group of representatives of public and private human service programs to negotiate an allocation formula for Block Grants. Participants were divided into different interest sectors, and a considerable amount of "in-team" negotiations occurred within each subgroup. The overall process was mediated and the results became the basis for the distribution of the Block Grant funds.

Public Welfare. The debate in the United States about various proposals for the reform of the social welfare system, particularly Aid for Families with Dependent Children, was carried out primarily on the basis of values and politics. A national policy dialogue driven primarily by consideration of impact and interests would, of course, be desirable and enlightening. A "welfare summit" with bipartisan sponsorship could lead to a more modulated attempt to look at problems in the welfare system and to propose reforms that would both encourage independence and provide economic protection to children and families. Whether there is the leadership necessary to convene such a national forum or not, any move to devolve welfare policy-making and financing to the state level will pose new opportunities for regional and local decision-making about how to allocate welfare funds wisely.

Child Welfare. Child welfare systems in most parts of the world are overstressed and underserviced. In North America, the foster care system is experiencing severe pressures, and many of the proposed changes in child welfare will stress it further. The appropriate balance between efforts to maintain children in their families, provide foster family care, or utilize group care options is and will be subject to considerable controversy on national, regional, and local levels. Policies governing adoptions, which involve striving toward a balance between the interests of birth parents, adoptive parents, and children, are undergoing a period of rapid change. Mediation has been used successfully to deal with this on a case-specific level (Mayer, 1985), but there is a need for a policy dialogue among advocates of each of these groups as well. The current debate about "repressed memory syndrome" and "false memory syndrome" has the potential of undercutting a growing public awareness of the seriousness of child sexual abuse issues. A constructive forum for bringing together the different interests involved in these issues would be valuable.

Facility Siting. Siting facilities for human services often runs against the "NIMBY" ("Not In My Backyard") phenomenon. Every neighborhood seems to feel that the correct location of homes for children, the mentally ill, or the developmentally disabled is elsewhere. Mediation has often been used to deal with conflicts concerning the location of specific facilities, but it has also been successfully employed to develop policies governing how to locate or disperse facilities in a more general sense.

HIV Prevention Planning. Perhaps no recent public health issue has tapped into the value conflicts in our society as deeply as the controversy about how to combat AIDS/HIV. In 1994, the Colorado Department of Health, in consultation with the Centers for Disease Control, convened a mediated planning group to develop a statewide plan for preventing the spread of the HIV. This process involved over one hundred stakeholders, including people who had tested positive for HIV, relatives of HIV-positive persons, gay activists, representatives of a variety of ethnic groups, evangelical Christians, public health officials, social workers, and others. The process lasted about six months and achieved consensus on a statewide HIV prevention plan.

Questions, Concerns, and Prospects

The use of mediated processes to deal with social policy issues is clearly on the rise and is likely to become an increasingly important part of policy development processes. In the future, social workers will be more likely to participate in such fora, both as participants and as mediators. There are many questions and concerns, however, that need to be addressed if these procedures are to be optimally effective:

- As such processes are time- and resource-intensive, how will they be funded? It is important that enough funding and staffing be made available to ensure that these procedures can be conducted with the skill and depth necessary to consider the complex aspects of major policy questions.
- How can we guarantee that poorly organized or stressed groups are adequately represented in these processes and that important legal and institutional safeguards are not sacrificed in the name of consensus building? In the environmental arena, it is an ongoing struggle to ensure that environmental interests are provided the funding they need to participate in policy fora. Similarly, advocates for children or the poor are often underfunded and in a position of having to allocate their limited resources very carefully. Furthermore, it is important that the trend toward collaborative problem-solving fora not be seen as a substitute for necessary political and legal advocacy.
- Who are the appropriate conveners for social policy fora, and how can they be encouraged to use these processes? The success of public policy mediation is in no small part related to the vision, leadership, and credibility of the convening individual and organization. There are a number of people and institutions who have played this role in the environmental arena, including the Institute for Water Policy of the U.S. Army Corps of Engineers and the U.S. Environmental Protection Agency. There was a long period of planning, training, and piloting procedures

before these groups were ready to undertake these processes on a large scale. To date, there has been no similar consistent leadership in the social policy arena.

- How can social workers and related professionals be better trained to understand these processes and take part as participants and mediators? Schools of social work are just beginning to institute mediation training as an integral part of the social work curriculum. Seldom, if ever, is social policy mediation included as part of the teaching of social work methods or the social policy development process.
- How can we continue to develop, test, evaluate, and institutionalize new methods of social policy mediation? What has occurred so far has been fairly experimental, dispersed, and unevaluated; there is a great need to develop the technology of social policy mediation in a more disciplined and sophisticated manner.

These questions are indicative of the problems facing the implementation of social policy mediation, but they are also signs of its growth, importance, and relevance. The concerns we have to face relate more to *how* to implement this process on a large scale than to *whether* to utilize it. A review of the literature about mediation of policy disputes in 1988 turned up no references specifically dealing with mediation in the social policy arena (Laue and Potapchuk, 1988). That is not the case today and will be less so in the future. This is a growing area of practice for mediators and social workers, and one that is exciting, challenging, and potentially highly productive.

References

Bingham, G. 1986. *Resolving Environmental Disputes: A Decade of Experience*. Washington DC: Conservation Foundation.

Borow, L. S., & M. Wheeler. 1984. *Environmental Dispute Resolution*. New York: Plenum Press.

Bradley, R. H. 1988. Managing Major Metropolitan Areas: Applying Collaborative Planning and Negotiating Techniques. *Mediation Quarterly* No. 20: 45–56.

Carpenter, S. L., & W. J. D. Kennedy. 1988. *Managing Public Disputes*. San Francisco: Jossey-Bass.

Ehrmann, J. R., & M. T. Lesnick. 1988. The Policy Dialogue: Applying Mediation to the Policy-Making Process. *Mediation Quarterly* No. 20: 93–99.

Haygood, L. V. 1988. Negotiated Rule Making: Challenge for Mediators and Participants. *Mediation Quarterly* No. 20: 77–91.

Kunde, J. E., & J. E. Rudd. The Role of Citizens Groups in Policy Conflicts. *Mediation Quarterly* No. 20: 33–44.

Laue, J. H. 1988. Editors Notes. *Mediation Quarterly* No. 20: 1–4.

Laue, J. H. & W. Potapchuk. 1988. Conflict Resolution and Public Disputes: Bibliography and Resources. *Mediation Quarterly* No. 20: 113–18.

Laue, J. H., S. Burde, W. Potapchuk, & M. Salkoff. 1988. Getting to the Table: Three Paths. *Mediation Quarterly* No. 20: 7–21.

Mayer, B. 1985. Conflict Resolution in Child Protection and Adoption. *Mediation Quarterly* No. 7: 69–82.

Mayer, B., S. Wildau & R. Valchev. 1995. Promoting Multi-Cultural Consensus-Building in Bulgaria. *Cultural Survival* 19(3): 64–68.

Moore, C. M. 1988. Negotiated Investment Strategy. *Journal of Dispute Resolution* (1): 143–62.

Singer, L. R. 1994. *Settling Disputes*. 2d ed. Boulder, CO: Westview.

Stamato, L., & S. Jaffe. 1991. Mediation and Public Policies: Variations on a Consensus Theme. *Mediation Quarterly* 9(2): 165–78.

18

INTERCULTURAL DISPUTES

Mediation, Conflict Resolution, and Multicultural Reality: Culturally Competent Practice

by Michelle LeBaron

The picture of intergroup relations in the United States and Canada can be painted in two radically different ways. Is it the melting pot about to boil over, fueled by the somnambulism of the majority, or is it a salad bowl of complex and sometimes conflicted diversity, but one where people are more or less satisfied with their access to the services available? This sharp divergence arises along the fault lines of North American society: lines of socioeconomic class, ethnocultural identity, gender, and cultural difference. Those with privilege, members of one or more dominant groups, tend to perceive fewer problems and lower-intensity conflict; those without privilege are more likely to see conditions as incendiary or deeply troubled.

The topic of community dispute resolution in multicultural Canada and the United States must therefore include a discussion of power, socioeconomic status, and in-group/out-group relations. Advancing panaceas of harmonious collectivities brought about through the universal application of consensus-based conflict resolution does everyone a disservice. Such a discussion raises expectations that cannot be met, and worse, it ignores the disparities that have contributed materially to conflict in the past and therefore does nothing to address sources of ongoing conflict.

The importance of taking status and power variables into account can be illustrated by an investigation of the use of the term *multicultural*. This term at first glance seems to refer to the peaceful and productive coexistence of the many peoples who find themselves together in North America. In practice, multicultural is a label too often used to describe visible minority groups or those who are different. Anglo Canadians, for example, use it to describe others, whether recent immigrants or visible minority group members whose families have lived in Canada for generations. Multicultural thus becomes a boundary between those who are part of the dominant culture and those who are not—between those who have immigrant ancestors and those who do not. It is a way of signaling power distributions in society, a way of generalizing about multiple groups with significant diversity within and among them.

The issue of intergroup relations must not be posed as one of bilateral or trilateral struggle along power, status, or socioeconomic lines alone. Research in both Canada and the United States shows that the fastest growing minority groups harbor strong negative prejudices toward each other. The findings of the Multiculturalism and Dispute Resolution Project ("Multiculturalism Project") conducted at the University of Victoria from 1991 to 1995 parallel this quote from the National Conference of Christians and Jews 1994 report, *Taking America's Pulse:*

> Indeed, despite their shared sense of victimization by whites, the truth is that minorities are more likely than whites to agree to negative stereotypes about other minority groups (including Jews, Muslims and Catholics). It appears as if the more diversity and burgeoning minority groups there are . . . the more prejudices we must overcome. (P. 5)

The Multiculturalism Project findings include evidence of negative stereotypes and significant intergroup conflict among members of several different groups in British Columbia. The issues may crystallize around many foci, including resource distribution (such as the fishing disputes that have arisen between members of the Vietnamese community and Anglos on Vancouver Island); access to services and opportunities (such as the generalized perception reported by some Anglo Canadians that "immigrants take our jobs"); communication in work places and communities; and resentment concerning economic disparities.

The problems that intergroup prejudices among minority groups engender are quite different from those experienced by minority group members at the hands of the majority. Ethnocultural minority groups generally do not wield the reigns of power and thus cannot create and maintain unequal power structures to support their dominance and enforce their differential lenses. At the same time, both minority-minority and minority-majority conflict are important as contributors to a more volatile environment with high levels of unresolved social conflict. This social conflict needs to be addressed through a multipronged approach. Such an approach may include conflict resolution and mediation, but these alone are not sufficient.

A great deal of work is needed both to dismantle the institutionalized nature of discrimination and to eradicate the negative perceptions and assumptions of different ethnocultural groups toward each other. This work needs to be informed by an understanding and awareness of current research and theory about intergroup relations and conflict resolution. The perspectives of both academicians and practitioners in ongoing dialogue are important to the development and critical evaluation of conflict resolution processes to be used in diverse communities.

The Multiculturalism Project included several recommendations directed at ameliorating and preventing intergroup conflict in British Columbia. One of the most frequently made suggestions was the need for education. Education, according to key informants and research participants, is necessary to raise the awareness of the general public about the positive contributions made by immigrants and members of visible minority groups. Educational resources are also important for individuals in transition into Canadian society both to help improve vital skills in English and to provide parenting skills in a culturally sensitive environment. It is also important to train helping professionals including social workers, psychologists, lawyers, facilitators, and mediators in intercultural communication skills.

There was consensus that conflict resolution services need to be provided in partnership with existing community structures and agencies. Services involving members of immigrant groups in helping roles have more credibility and increased community access and sensitivity. Such working partnerships can also facilitate the development of culturally appropriate dispute resolution services for families. This would be especially helpful in addressing the large number of intergenerational conflicts reported. It was emphasized that services should be provided in several languages to optimize accessibility. Issues of accreditation and qualification of a diverse group of experts were also deemed important in fields such as mental health, public health, law, and education. Trusted community members can provide culturally sensitive services and referrals informed by training in conflict resolution.

Conflict and Culture

Family and community mediation and conflict resolution programs have been established across North America, and many of these have struggled to incorporate cultural sensitivity in their practice and to recruit a diverse group of intervenors and clients. The question, Why aren't they here? belies its answer: the initial question, What can we build together in community? was not asked. Consequently, conflict resolution centers have not accrued a laudable record in addressing intercultural conflict.

One of the least attended to and least understood kinds of conflict, according to the Multiculturalism Project, was conflict between individuals from ethnocultural minority groups and representatives of institutions. Institutions in this case referred to a whole gamut of organizations, from banks, schools, and government departments at the municipal, provincial, and federal level to the police and quasi-governmental bodies like the Insurance Corporation of British Columbia and the Workers Compensation Board. This kind of conflict was particularly troublesome because it was not easily dealt with through any community channels for solving problems. It was exacerbated by rumors and accounts of racist treatment of minority group members, leading to a reticence on the part of clients to engage with those holding bureaucratic discretionary power. Conflict between individuals and institutions was complicated further by language accessibility problems and different expectations based on structural and functional differences in government and other organizations between Canada and countries of origin of many immigrants. One of the initiatives of the Multiculturalism Project was the piloting of conflict resolution programs within existing agencies involving staff training and referrals to interculturally skilled intervenors.

This project finding underlines the truism that conflict cannot meaningfully be addressed absent considerations of culture. We are reminded by Merry (1987) that "disputing is cultural behaviour, informed by participants' moral views about how to fight, the meaning participants attach to going to court, social practices that indicate when and how to escalate disputes to a public forum, and participants' notions of rights and entitlements. Parties to a dispute operate within systems of meaning" (p. 2063). It is only through an examination of these systems of meaning that we can begin to draw generalizations about useful approaches to conflict.

This chapter will proceed with the identification of some theoretical frameworks for understanding the cultural lenses through which conflict is perceived. Research from diverse settings across North America, from Albuquerque, New Mexico, to Vancouver, British Columbia, will be discussed as it raises questions about the cultural biases in mediation and points the way to the development of appropriate approaches. Finally, a broad perspective on designing interventions for intercultural intergroup conflict will be presented.

Theory, Debates, and Trends

The process of mediation in community settings has been touted as a way to involve people at grassroots levels and to empower citizens from all walks of life to settle their own disputes cooperatively. As is clear from the foregoing discussion, the process of mediation cannot be the only focus in a discussion of approaches to conflict within the context of multicultural reality. Where issues have structural roots, solutions more amenable to changing structure are required. Where lines of socioeconomic class are crossed, there is some evidence that those with lower status prefer adjudicative settings to consensual ones (Merry, 1993). Reasons for this include distrust of alternative systems; beliefs about fairness in the courts; faith in the impartiality of judges; and desire for formality and certainty. Where parties are from different ethnocultural groups, there is evidence of significant disadvantage in outcomes experienced by minorities in mediation (Rack, 1994), leading to questions of "fitness" of mediation across settings and issues. Mediation may be resisted by members of ethnocultural minority groups out of a desire not to "air dirty laundry" with those outside the group. Mediation is useful only to the extent it is transferable across cultural boundaries and it is seen as one of a constellation of approaches to addressing intergroup conflict.

Relationship between Conflict and Culture

To assess the transferability of mediation across cultural boundaries, it is helpful first of all to consider recent work linking the broad areas of culture and conflict. Culture, broadly defined, is much more than ethnocultural difference. Cultural differences flow from age, gender, socioeconomic status, national origin, recency of immigration, education, sexual orientation, and disability. While this chapter will focus primarily on those differences arising from race, ethnicity, and gender, it is important to keep this diversity of sources in mind.

It is difficult to discuss these dimensions of conflict, because it is undesirable to stereotype all women or members of a specific ethnocultural group in the name of promoting intercultural understanding. Racial, ethnic, and gender divisions all exist in a social milieu and must be understood in context. Only when they are understood in context can we see our collective responsibility for changing those conditions that disadvantage members of certain groups over privileged others in society. Similarly, only when conflict is understood as interrelated with culture in all of its complexity can it be addressed usefully. Every dimension of conflict is touched by culture, including:

- *What constitutes a conflict.* How do the parties view conflict? What are the roots and purposes of conflicts? Are conflicts disagreements, serious questions of principles, different preferences, grave events that seldom occur, or expected events that happen frequently? Who names the conflict? Should a conflict be acknowledged overtly or not?
- *The identity of the parties.* Are the individuals directly involved the parties, or are members of extended families and/or communities also

parties? Do the people in conflict see themselves as individuals or as members of a group? Who should not be surprised? Who may be affected by the outcome of the process? Who are the gatekeepers of the community who may need to be involved in access to the parties and/or implementation of any solution?

- *Whether and how the conflict should be approached.* Do parties have different approaches to identifying and articulating issues? Do parties have a different idea about whether to surface disagreement and how to deal with disagreement once it has been surfaced? Do they have different comfort levels with confrontation and frank conversation? Do they have different values regarding the expression of conflict and emotions; values and thoughts regarding responsibility, honesty, truth, compromise and negotiation, forgiveness and revenge, roles, hierarchy, and authority? Do their boundaries between private and public clash or match? What are the parties' expectations of protocol?

- *Which process is most appropriate for intervention.* Are the parties comfortable assuming responsibility for the outcome? Do parties' cultural expectations include neutrality or partiality? What are the time frames involved in the situation? How formal or informal must a process be to meet parties' needs? Will parties be comfortable meeting face to face? Will parties be comfortable with the ground rules for mediation? Which process design and forum will accommodate all who need to have a voice in the outcome?

- *What constitutes resolution.* How do the parties define fairness, equality, and equity? How do they define closure or ambiguity? What are their expectations regarding the form of an agreement? Would the parties be happy with an apology, an agreement, a promise to avoid similar situations in the future? Is there scope for addressing issues beyond those in which parties are directly interested?

These factors become more salient as the cultural differences between parties increase. Awareness of these variables can be daunting. Even for intervenors equipped with substantial training in conflict resolution, responding to and accommodating cultural differences is challenging. Part of the reason for this is the difficulty inherent in gathering information about culture and conflict. Asking people about their conflicts can be as personal as inquiring about their sexual behavior, as conflicts are embedded in an individual's ideas about right relations among people and how differences relating to identity and values should be handled.

An illustration of the difficulty of gathering accurate conflict-related information comes from the Multiculturalism and Dispute Resolution Project. Participants from five ethnocultural groups were asked to describe their experiences with conflict. After some thought, an elderly Chinese gentleman, who had emigrated to Canada after World War II, disclosed that he had not experienced any conflicts in the past forty-odd years. He chose to see his world through a prism of harmony ("what has worked well or at least acceptably") rather than from the perspective of parceling it up into conflicts. Conflict avoidance or denial seems to be a phenomenon that is pancultural, and the act of surfacing conflict is often fraught with tension and the negative emotions that accompanied the original events.

The context in which conflict takes place is essential to consider, and individual preferences and differences must always be taken into account when intervening in or assessing conflict. Gadlin (1994) cautions that

> Any effort to describe and take into account cultural differences in dispute resolution, or in any other endeavour for that matter, necessarily risks compartmentalizing the phenomenon of racial and gender conflict and separating the psychological dynamics from their social contexts, which actually heightens discrimination. (P. 38)

In addition, emphasizing differences between groups may overlook commonalties that individuals within them share, such as preferences for making decisions in a particular way or a preference for introversion that both parties can recognize, understand, and respect in the other. Instruments like the Myers Briggs Type Indicator or the Enneagram of Personality are being increasingly used to help people build bridges across cultural divides by emphasizing similarities across perceived categories of difference.

Individual behavior cannot be predicted based solely on cultural background or affiliation. However, an understanding of cultural patterns is useful in asking the right questions when involved in intergroup conflict. Three frameworks that are helpful in demystifying cultural differences are:

- individualist versus collectivist societies
- traditional versus modern societies
- high versus low context societies

I will discuss each of these briefly for its explanatory value in understanding intergroup conflict.

Individualist and Collectivist Cultural Perspectives

The individualist/collectivist dimension has been described by Triandis, Brislin, and Hui (1988). Individualists' values tend toward freedom, honesty, social recognition, achievement, self-reliance, comfort, hedonism, and equity. Collectivists' values tend toward harmony, face-saving, filial piety, modesty, moderation, thrift, equality of rewards, and fulfillment of others' needs. Individualists, who tend to take relationships more casually, may be experienced as distancing by collectivists who take the obligations of being in community more seriously. These, like any generalizations, should be applied with caution. As Triandis, Bontempo, Asai, Villareal, and Lucca (1988: 333) write: "One may be a collectivist in relation to one ingroup but not in relation to other outgroups." For example, it is generally thought that collectivists behave toward their friends and co-workers with more intimacy and toward outgroups with less intimacy than do individualists. Thus, the collectivist's behavior may be interpreted as "cliquish" or aloof.

People in every culture have both collectivist and individualist tendencies, but those from Western cultures tend to be more individualistic and those from Eastern and Southern cultures more collectivist. It has been argued that women are more collectivist in orientation than men (Tannen, 1990). In this argument, women's stories tend to revolve around the norms of community and joint action by groups of people; men are more likely to tell stories that center on themselves and the theme of contest.

The implications of this distinction for culturally related conflict are many. Individuals with different orientations on the collectivist/individualist continuum may have difficulty communicating, and these difficulties may manifest in attributing bad faith to each other. Conflicts can escalate beyond the triggering incidents when the individuals involved ascribe bad motives to each other, and power dynamics only exacerbate this phenomenon.

Individuals from collectivist cultures tend to expect vertical hierarchies and function well within them. Many dominant culture Americans carry individualist assumptions, including the primacy of horizontal relationships; that is, they expect equality and acknowledgment, while collectivists may be more comfortable with wider and more pronounced power differentials.

Individualistic and collective values need not form coherent syndromes in polar opposition. There is much still to be understood about how they interact, and conducting research that can take the complexity into account is challenging. Gire and Carment (1992) examined this dimension as it relates to procedural preferences for conflict resolution. They studied whether a preference for the harmony-enhancing procedures of mediation and negotiation would be stronger in collectivist cultures than individualist cultures, by administering an individualism-collectivism scale to a sample of university students from Canada and Nigeria. Previous research that established a stronger preference for such processes in collectivist cultures had been done almost exclusively with Asian subjects representing the collectivist perspective. Gire and Carment wondered whether other factors unique to Asian culture may have accounted for this finding.

Their results contradicted previous research: Both Canadians and Nigerians preferred harmony-enhancing procedures (negotiation and mediation) over those likely to escalate the conflict, such as making threats. Previous research had been interpreted to establish a preference for negotiation and mediation for those from collectivist societies. In this study, Nigerian students showed an almost equal preference for both negotiation and arbitration, while Canadians had a stronger preference for negotiation. Women tended to prefer negotiation more than men, and men indicated that they would use threats more often than women did.

This study supports the application of the individualism/collectivism continuum in a considered and analytical way. No group is merely one way or the other. Within groups, there are extensive differences, and a given group may be collectivist with respect to some issues and groups and not to others.

While Gire and Carment's research is helpful, it contains no explanation of the ethnocultural backgrounds of the Canadian subjects, raising questions about the homogeneity of the sample and the generalizability of their results. Further, findings such as Canadians perceiving negotiation to be a fairer process than Nigerians beg questions of cultural experiences and associations with negotiation and other processes. How do the customs, values, and power relations of Nigerian culture affect the way negotiation is perceived and conducted? How is this different in Canada? Is this finding generalizable to various regions of Canada? How are processes like mediation and arbitration understood by Nigerian and Canadian subjects? These kinds of questions are important to ask in assessing the implications of research on culture and conflict.

Traditional and Modern Cultural Perspectives

Another way of understanding cultural dynamics is through the distinction between traditional and modern societies as described by Lederach (1987). He describes the modern society as having the following characteristics: autonomous/individualistic; impersonal/professional; rational/formal; technical/specialized; achievement/accomplishment-oriented. Traditional cultures, according to Lederach, tend to feature: family/group dependence; personal/relational priorities; affective/assumed interactions; an informal/holistic approach; ascriptive/personal networks.

The differences between traditional and modern cultural perspectives may manifest themselves in conflicts over task orientation versus emphasis on process and the development of relationships. One party may be most interested in "getting the job done" and may be perceived by a more traditionally focused person as impersonal and overly concerned with achievement and accomplishment. Traditionalists may seem too concerned with relational priorities and too informal to the individual from a more "modern" cultural context.

High versus Low Context Cultural Perspectives

Another epistemological tool that may provide helpful clues for analyzing conflict and designing appropriate conflict resolution processes is suggested by Hall (1976), who profiles "low context" and "high context" cultures. Low context cultures generally refer to groups characterized by individualism, overt communication, and heterogeneity. Communication in low-context cultures tends to focus more on the written/spoken word and takes the message at face value.

High-context cultures feature collective identity-focus, covert communication and homogeneity. In high-context cultures, communication tends to be associative. This means that more attention is paid to the context of communication, including behavior and environment, the relationship between the messenger and receiver, the messenger's family history, and so on. This approach prevails in Asian countries including Japan, China, and Korea, as well as Latin American and African countries. The implications of this cultural divide for conflict resolution practices are far-reaching. A well-intentioned intervenor without these understandings who attempts to intervene in an intercultural conflict will encounter initial reticence, and ultimately ineffectiveness, that she or he may not understand.

Synthesis

Clusters of cultural characteristics emerge among the frameworks identified earlier. On one side is a cluster that includes individualistic, "modern," and low context. On the other side is a cluster that includes collectivistic, "traditional," and high context. It is important to recognize that the respective frameworks are not opposites but orthogonal. These constructs reflect patterns of information processing and evaluating events in the social environment that distinguish broadly different cultures. Care must be taken when interpreting the meaning of specific themes in the context of dichotomies in the meaning between cultures. As Triandis, Bontempo, Villareal, Asai, and Lucca (1988) reflect on individualist versus collectivist cultures:

> Several themes, such as self-reliance, achievement, hedonism, competition, and interdependence, change their meaning in the context of the two cultures. Self-reliance for the individualistic culture implies freedom to do one's own thing and also competition with others. Self-reliance for the collectivist cultures implies not being a burden on the ingroup, and competition is not related to it. Competition in collectivist cultures is among ingroups, not among individuals. (P. 335)

In order to use and apply the cultural constructs identified above for conflict resolution, one must acquire an in-depth understanding of cultural differences which recognizes the complexity and interrelationships between a complex set of themes and variables. This includes not only the differences identified in the three frameworks but also individual differences and contextual circumstances. For example, an immigrant from a "traditional" culture may be expected to behave according to "traditional" values. However, that individual may have been educated in and/or lived for some time in a "modern" culture and have adopted many "modern" values and behaviors.

Processes for Conflict Intervention

Mediation

Mediation is a process that tends to be characterized by overt communication, structured confrontation, and intervention by a "neutral" third party with no decision-making power. A quick glance at these descriptors will make the cultural indebtedness of the model clear: the values and approaches to communication that are embedded in it are reflective of the individualistic, low-context, "modern" society. For this reason, this discussion will aim to divine appropriate means for "intervention" rather than an adaptation of "mediation," with all of the cultural baggage associated with that term.

Experience bears out the cultural limitations of the mediation model. Many family and community mediation programs across the United States and Canada have reported difficulty attracting and engaging members of ethnocultural minority groups as intervenors, staff people, and parties. Even in programs targeted for a particular minority group, the use of services has been minimal (Roberts, 1992). More troublesome are the results of studies of compulsory mediation programs in the United States where Hispanic parties were financially disadvantaged compared to white counterparts, except in cases where both co-mediators were Hispanic (Rack, 1994). It is not surprising that structural biases long understood to operate in the justice system would be reproduced in a court-attached mediation program, though many advocates for mediation had touted it as a more client-centered alternative, with at least the potential for enhancing justice for all.

Benvenisti (1986) has lamented the assumption that prescribed processes with easy steps can heal long-standing conflicts. He writes of his exasperation with conflict "resolvers . . . who believe that communal conflicts are like a chessboard where one can think up the best arrangement of chess pieces and move them all at once" (p. 118). At the same time, well-established means for resolving conflicts, intact in indigenous settings, are often fragmented or severely strained in Canada and the United States.

It is not possible, nor even always desirable, to reconstruct culture-specific models. The village *punchayat* system from India, for example, involves male elders hearing all sides and pronouncing a course of action to be followed. South Asian women living in Canada were quite clear in advising the Multiculturalism Project that they had no wish to encounter such a system in their adopted home. At the same time, the impossibility and undesirability of recreating culture-specific models in the image of predecessors should not lend itself to the wholesale adoption of a dominant culture approach. The dominant culture approach is privileged through its adoption by professional groups and those with voice by virtue of race and social class. As Avruch (1992) reminds us:

> The politics of personhood establishes the hegemony of one conception . . . over others. As the proper and acceptable negotiator is evaluated, so too is the process of negotiation. This means that the white theory of negotiation is not simply one theory among a number of alternatives; it becomes a theory for negotiation in general. The discourse of such a theory, which, conceptually speaking, is but one folk model among many, gets reified and elevated to the status of, if not science, then an expert system. (P. 5)

To truly respond to a multicultural community, we must move away from assuming there is only one viable dispute resolution system. This involves challenging the orthodoxy of particular approaches. For example, dominant culture models stress the decoupling of emotions from substance in negotiation or conflict resolution. It is thought that separating them can lead to wiser solutions crafted from rationality, logic, and calmness. In a related strategy, Fisher and Ury (1991) admonish negotiators to "separate the people from the problem." However, while this dualism is treated as a universal principle, evidence exists that this is far from true. For example, Kochman (1981) tells us that American blacks view the "white" idea that they should leave their emotions at the door as devious, a product of a political rather than a reasonable requirement. Relationship, identity, and behavior are not viewed as divisible in collective cultural contexts.

Another example of a nearly unquestioned precept in training is mediator or intervenor neutrality. The existence and desirability of neutrality has been questioned fundamentally in the writing of Cobb and Rifkin (1991), Nader (1992), and others. Many cultural contexts would reject a so-called neutral outsider in favor of a partial insider, one who knows the history and embeddedness of the conflict and the parties.

Conflict theory and practice carry particular assumptions about how people think, behave, and change. If these assumptions are unchallenged, mediators and conflict intervenors will find themselves working with a group of people who share similar ideas and will lament their lack of diverse clients. Embracing mediation without a critical look at research and theoretical underpinnings may cause intervenors to miss some of the following:

- The importance and legitimacy of preserving harmony
- The importance of face saving
- The value of being other than confrontative or forthright

- The systemic roots of conflict and the need for systemic change
- The significance of time stretching far into the past and the future
- The usefulness of time in easing conflict
- An inclusive definition of parties (including extended family, for example)
- The importance of healing
- The significance of the differences between high- and low-context cultures
- The significance of the differences between individualist and collectivist cultures
- The importance of symbolism and ritual
- Visual and nonverbal cues
- The importance of involving "elders," gatekeepers, and "wise ones" in conflict resolution processes
- The legitimacy of advice giving in some cultural contexts
- The honor attached to indirectness and subtlety in various cultural contexts
- The lack of power experienced by members of some groups over a long period of time, such that techniques to "balance power" may be insufficient
- Varying needs for formality or informality
- The meaning of a contract or written agreement; this is considered evidence of bad faith in some cultural contexts and a necessity in others
- Different communication norms and styles in different cultural frameworks

Mediators who recognize the cultural dimensions of their processes will gather information on these dimensions as they consult with parties prior to intervention. Rejecting the notion that one formula is applied to every conflict without adjustment, they will work to include parties in designing a process that fits the cultural common sense of the parties. This will result in higher levels of commitment and procedural satisfaction by all involved.

Elicitive/Educational Approach

There are many examples of cultural-fit problems if the dominant culture mediation model is viewed as a standard from which other processes deviate. An approach alternately called "elicitive" and "educational" begins at a different place. This approach focuses on gathering information from the parties to the conflict about processes that make sense in their cultural context. Parties are invited to consider the setting or forum, appropriate procedures, forms of contact or communication to be used, kinds of outcomes that are desirable, and the roles for outsiders or intervenors in the process. The elicitive process is important because it allows for the emergence of a fit between parties, process, and intervenor.

Lederach (1992), one of the originators of this approach, describes his experience with the difficulties inherent in playing an intervenor role in an unfamiliar cultural context:

> The few accounts I have read of . . . intercultural mediations have tended to present their interventions as the work of competent "anthropologist-politicians" who deftly make their way through the cultural meaning and mazes, understanding what is going on, and press forth to reach agreement. Quite frankly, I felt more like a bull in a china shop. A sensitive bull perhaps but nonetheless a bull who with each step ran the risk of crashing through a delicately arranged social structure. The reason, I think, is clear. The understandings, the process, and the expectations for dealing with conflicts were based on the people's implicit knowledge that they assumed operative but which I had not fully accumulated. (P. 183)

When an elicitive approach is used, it acknowledges the cultural gulfs among the parties and allows for the development of a process that will fit the cultural context, the type of dispute, and the needs of the parties in dispute. In this way, the intervention becomes an education for all involved not only about the conflict but also about the cultural lenses and expectations of selves and others.

The continuum of elicitive to prescriptive has many variations within it. In a multiparty, multicultural conflict, using an elicitive approach to design a process is challenging indeed. At the same time, innovative work in the public policy domain, another forum where issues are complex, highly contentious, and culture-related, shows clearly the benefits of involving all parties in process design and joint training at an early stage (CORE, 1995). Commitment to the process is greater, parties feel loyalty to intervenors they have selected, and the invitation to go back and revise that which "we got wrong" is always open to the codesigner parties.

The degree to which an elicitive approach will be used will vary with the context, the needs of parties, and the exigencies of a situation. True elicitation, it must be pointed out, involves a willingness to offer fundamentally different services than those that may be contemplated as part of dominant culture mediation. For example, in the cases processed in the South Asian Dispute Resolution Initiative it was found that parties relied on their own cultural understandings and expected an arbitrative model (Roberts, 1992). They expressed disappointment that the mediator would not provide guidance after hearing everyone's side, despite extensive explanations of mediator neutrality before the process. It was a cultural expectation that a third party be willing to share his or her "expert" opinion regarding an appropriate outcome, and the lack of fulfillment of this expectation led to disappointment in the process.

An elicitive or educational approach relies on several assumptions. Some of these may differ from those in the dominant culture "expert" system that informs practice in conflict resolution. These assumptions are:

- System functioning is an ongoing evolutionary process that is established, not reflected, in interaction. This conception carries with it the seeds of change: since interactions are constantly being invented, they can be invented in new ways if there is motivation and tools to do so.
- Social interaction is viewed as a process that furnishes resources for making choices, not as a process that produces mechanisms for ensuring cultural uniformity. This recognizes the significance of individual differences within cultural difference. It also regards social processes as positive venues with resources for choice, an empowering idea for a group that is playing a role in designing its own process.
- Classical determinism is rejected; the method is prospective rather than retrospective. This is useful because it does not see people in community as governed by an unalterable set of needs that must be satisfied before change can occur. It upholds the perspective of the individual and the group as able to make choices that are meaningful to them as individuals and as a community.
- Situational and cultural relativism are valued. The rejection of one "right way" to resolve conflict is consistent with evolving processes from particular groups according to needs and the context.
- The human being is viewed as fundamentally a communicator. Using intercultural communication theory, the adept intercultural intervenor will recognize and understand different communication patterns and find ways to bridge these within the group. The attention of the group can be drawn to this process, thus fulfilling the educational potential of conflict resolution.
- Human beings are seen as consciously rationalizing, not consciously rational. They are seen as needing acknowledgment of pain they have experienced before being able to move forward in a process of reconciliation.

If the burden of finding a rational explanation for intergroup behavior is lifted, the focus can be on understanding how choices have been rationalized, an easier place from which to craft an intervention. Understanding the way actions have been experienced and justified may lead to insight about how a group may move forward. When a group has chosen behavior out of a desire to retaliate and there is a pattern of escalation of the conflict with pain and damage on each side, the intervenor should consider addressing the group and individual needs for forgiveness and reconciliation before thinking about instrumental ways to address the issues in dispute (Hare, 1985).

In an elicitive/educational approach, an intervenor seeks to spark creative interaction and respectful engagement while bringing his or her experience of conflict analysis and resolution to the disposal of the parties. The process is thus an interactive exchange where information is shared, ideas are floated, cultural differences are recognized, and a process that includes input from everyone emerges. The soundness of this approach is commensurate with its acceptance by the parties. The needs and expectations of the parties, such as the intervenor bringing her or his expertise to the table, should not be ignored. An intervenor has technical expertise and intuitive resources born of experience, and both of these may be invaluable to the parties in dispute. An intervenor may draw on technical experience to present a "bare bones" template where some of the essential ingredients of a dispute resolution process are presented and the forms possible for their accomplishment offered. Then the intervenor may play the role of facilitator in guiding the process design discussion and offering insight along the way.

The components of this template would include the headings addressed earlier, including:

- Exploring the existence of a conflict and conflict issues
- Naming the conflict and conflict issues
- The identity of the parties and those who should be involved or included but not necessarily at the table (considering organizing sectors for purposes of communication and input)
- The role and necessity of advocates
- Lines of authority and representation from different parties at comparable levels
- The degree of formality/informality of the process
- The degree of confrontation appropriate given the needs, comfort, and preferred communication styles of all parties
- Preliminary steps that need to be taken to build confidence, guarantee safety (physical or emotional), and set a positive tone for discussions (such as joint training or the development of a framework for reconciliation)
- How technical information will be obtained and validated for use in the process
- What role an intervenor might most helpfully play (considering issues of neutrality, function and role, decision-making authority regarding procedure and substance, intervenor identity, and affiliation)
- Intervenor qualifications regarding substantive and procedural expertise; experience level; credibility with parties
- Whether language barriers exist and, if so, how they are to be addressed
- How time will be structured and monitored
- Procedural ground rules to govern the process, including the process by which decisions will be made
- The meaning of consensus if decisions are being made this way
- Needs and expectations for formality of outcome
- Precedents for process used in similar situations

Generally, conflict resolution processes are framed as including a set number of stages that are not necessarily linear. Once an intervenor has used the template as a guide for gathering information, he or she may facilitate process design. The process designer will have to weigh the increased commitment of parties involved in this phase against the possible negative effects of requesting party involvement when doing so violates cultural norms, roles, and expectations. The following process framework may be used as a guide.

Assessment. Information gathering is critical in determining the appropriateness of a range of fora, the menu of possible processes, the history of the conflict, relevant cultural frames of reference, and the "ripeness" of the conflict. It is important also to canvass matters that must be addressed prior to convening a process in order for parties to fully participate. The decision not to proceed at a particular point must be an acceptable outcome. Some conflicts are generative and important to pursue in public or judicial fora for their precedential or justice values. It is during assessment that the elements of a process that make cultural common sense to the parties are elicited. This process is not over in the assessment phase but is ongoing throughout the intervention in revolving feedback loops.

Convening. The parties meet, whether face to face or separately, with the intervention and/or training teams. At this time, the structure of a process is agreed to, including the role and identity of parties, the role and function of the intervenor, procedural guidelines, forum, timing, and general objectives.

Issues. The parties create a substantive agenda and monitor their chosen process for addressing the issues. This process is not purely involved with substance. An issue may involve how differences will be dealt with in the future, primarily a matter of designing a process.

Developing Stories. The parties develop a shared information bank of technical and substantive information relevant to the conflict in a way that fits their cultural needs and expectations. They are encouraged to develop empathy for each other through the hearing and sharing of stories, acknowledging the experience of the other, joining in training and ongoing process discussions with the other, engaging in experiences designed to make the erroneous preconceptions of the other clear, and sharing personal experiences.

Completing. The parties formalize, celebrate, ritualize, and bring closure to the process. This may include a discussion of follow up, next steps, monitoring, dissemination, ratification, and other relevant issues.

This framework is deliberately cast broadly and is meant to be flexible and changeable according to needs and context. It is useful for considering intervention, but it can also be used in structuring demonstrations for conflict resolution training.

Training Applications of Intercultural Conflict Resolution

An illustration of the potency of using a demonstration with this process framework as a reference comes from a training conducted with a multicultural group of intervenors as part of the Multiculturalism Project. South Asian participants demonstrated their approach to resolving an intergenerational conflict. They showed an informal, multi-staged conversation that took place over time, using indirect communication, persuasion, and friendly monitoring. One of the concerns expressed by those who had been trained in a dominant culture mediation approach was that they perceived the process to "drift off" without achieving sufficient closure. There followed an intriguing discussion in which the South Asians explained that it would have been disrespectful within the cultural context to "push" or formalize the tacit agreements between the parties. The need for resolution was addressed through the establishment of a long-term relationship in which follow-up would be assured. Specific or formalized closure would rob the parties of necessary face saving and involve the imposition of a dominant culture conception of the way a conflict is finished.

This example illustrates the importance and utility of individuals from different cultural groups showing their processes to each other and reflecting on the cultural assumptions contained in them. To state that groups have different communication patterns and expectations is far less powerful than to see it, have the opportunity to question how and why and in which circumstances it applies, and consider the implications of the exercise for process design. This experience was a powerful reminder that much conflict resolution training fails to reach beyond the communication skills of the dominant culture to intercultural and other skills necessary to resolve conflict effectively in a multicultural context.

Conflict resolution training in general should be evaluated in three respects: for what is emphasized and how these choices are culturally influenced and biased; for what essential skills are missing that are important for intercultural conflict resolution; and for the inclusion of diverse views and critical analyses of skills and approaches for transferability across cultures.

Conflict resolution training is characterized in the dominant culture model by an emphasis on communication skills and limited self-reflection. This emphasis is constructive insofar as it provides participants with skills in active listening, reframing, restating, rephrasing, summarizing, and strategic questioning. The use of conflict management style inventories is also helpful in assisting participants to become aware of their repertoire of strategies. One such inventory, the Thomas-Kilmann Conflict Mode Instrument (1974), includes two dimensions of conflict-handling behavior: assertiveness and cooperativeness. From an intercultural perspective, however, conflict-related behavior has many more than two dimensions, and these dimensions manifest very differently across cultural contexts. Avoiding, for example, may be seen as unassertive and uncooperative in the dominant culture context in Canada. In collectivist cultures, such as that of the Japanese, avoidance may be seen as cooperative. Assertiveness is not valued as an individual behavior in the same way in collectivist cultures, where it can be viewed as belligerent or overly forceful.

Intercultural skills are frequently neglected in conflict resolution training or given a discreet module. The latter approach communicates that culture is a subject area to consider rather than a lens through which all experience must be evaluated. To enhance intercultural competence, a number of training dimensions are critical to include: relevant culture-specific norms and behaviors, cultural patterns of communication (verbal and nonverbal) of specific groups, development of empathy and trust building, nonverbal communication cues across cultures, cultural assessment tools, and information about how and when to use cultural informants. In general, more information on processes that have worked successfully in specific types of conflicts or settings, tools for encouraging ongoing monitoring or feedback, processes for cultivating synergy and creativity, and exploration of the dynamics of teams and group behavior are helpful.

Conclusion

Conflict resolution as a field can trace its origins to reformers with ideals of increased access to justice and empowerment. In the last decade, the field has expanded rapidly and has come to serve many ends, including cost-effectiveness and efficiency. Our challenge now is to continue these economies without losing sight of our ideals. There is considerable pressure within the field today to standardize processes, training, and qualifications for mediators and conflict-resolution practitioners. Failing to respond to multicultural realities in the systems and the processes we design will lead us to recreate the very structures for which we sought to provide alternatives. We are challenged to develop structures, processes, and trainings that incorporate cultural realities and feature flexibility to realize the goals of social justice and meaningful access to dispute resolution.

References

Avruch, K. 1992. Introduction: Culture and Conflict Resolution. In K. Avruch, P. W. Black, & J. A. Scimecca, eds., *Conflict Resolution: Cross-Cultural Perspectives.* Westport, CT: Greenwood.

Benvenisti, M. 1986. *Conflicts and Contradictions.* New York: Villard Books/Random House. Cited in K. Avruch. 1992. Introduction: Culture and Conflict Resolution. In K. Avruch, P. W. Black, & J. A. Scimecca, eds., *Conflict Resolution: Cross-Cultural Perspectives.* Westport, CT: Greenwood.

Cobb, S., & J. Rifkin. 1991. Practice and Paradox: Deconstructing Neutrality in Mediation. *Law and Social Inquiry* 16: 35-62.

Commission on Resources and Environment (CORE). 1995. *The Provincial Land Use Strategy.* Vol. 4, *Dispute Resolution.* Victoria, BC: CORE.

Duryea, M. L., & B. Grundison. 1993. *Conflict and Culture: Research in Five Communities in Vancouver, British Columbia.* Victoria, BC: University of Victoria Institute of Dispute Resolution, Multiculturalism and Dispute Resolution Project.

Fisher, R., & W. Ury., with B. Patton, ed. 1991. *Getting to Yes.* 2d ed. New York: Penguin.

Gadlin, H. 1994. Conflict Resolution, Cultural Differences, and the Culture of Racism. *Negotiation Journal* 10(1): 33–47.

Gire, J. T., & D. W. Carment. 1992. Dealing with Disputes: The Influence of Individualism-Collectivism. *Journal of Social Psychology* 133(1): 81–95.

Hall, E. T. 1976. *Beyond Culture.* Garden City, NY: Anchor Press.

Hare, A. P. 1985. *Social Interaction as Drama: Applications from Conflict Resolution.* Beverly Hills, CA: Sage.

James, L., & G. Cormick. 1978. The Ethics of Intervention in Community Disputes. In G. Bermant, H. C. Kelman, & D. P. Warwick, eds., *The Ethics of Social Intervention.* Washington, DC: Halstead Press.

Kochman, T. 1981. *Black and White Styles in Conflict.* Chicago: University of Chicago Press.

Lederach, J. P. 1987. Cultural Assumptions of the North American Model of Mediation: From a Latin American Perspective. *Conflict Resolution Notes* 4(3): 23–25.

———. 1992. Beyond Prescription: New Lenses for Conflict Resolution Across Cultures. Waterloo, Ontario: Institute of Peace and Conflict Studies, Conrad, Grebel College.

Merry, S. E. 1987. *PCR Occasional Paper Series: 1987-2: Cultural Aspects of Disputing.* Honolulu: University of Hawaii of Manoa, Program on Conflict Resolution.

Merry, S. E. 1993. *Getting Justice and Getting Even.* Beverly Hills, CA: Sage.

Myers, I., & M. H. McCaulley. 1985. *A Guide to the Development and Use of the Myers-Briggs Type Indicator.* 2d ed. Palo Alto, CA: Consulting Psychologists Press.

Nader, L. 1992. Harmony Models and the Construction of Law. In K. Avruch, P. W. Black, & J. A. Scimecca, eds. *Conflict Resolution: Cross-Cultural Perspectives.* Westport, CN: Greenwood.

Palmer, H. 1988. *The Enneagram: Understanding Yourself and the Others in Your Life.* San Francisco: HarperCollins.

Rack, C. 1994. The Reproduction of Inequality: The Story of Minority Respondents at the Metro Court. Paper presented at Western Social Science Association 36th Annual Conference, Albuquerque, NM, April 20–23.

Roberts, T. 1992. *Evaluation of the Small Claims Mediation Projects of Westcoast Mediation Services and the Conflict Resolution Centre*. Victoria, BC: University of Victoria Institute for Dispute Resolution.

Taking America's Pulse: A Summary Report of The National Conference Survey on Inter-group Relations. 1994. New York: National Conference of Christians and Jews.

Tannen, D. 1990. *You Just Don't Understand: Women and Men in Conversation*. New York: Ballantine.

Thomas, K. W. & R. H. Kilmann. 1974. *Thomas-Kilmann Conflict Mode Instrument*. Tuxedo, NY: Xicom.

Triandis, H. C., R. Bontempo, M. Villareal, M. Asai, & N. Lucca. 1988. Individualism and Collectivism: Cross-Cultural Perspectives on Self-Ingroup Relationships. *Journal of Personality and Social Psychology* 54(2): 323–38.

Triandis, H. C., R. Brislin, & C. H. Hui. 1988. Cross-Cultural Training across the Individualism-Collectivism Divide. *International Journal of Intercultural Relations* 12: 269–89.

APPENDIX
Standards of Practice for Social Work Mediators

Introduction

Social workers sit at the center of many social conflicts. In their role as facilitator of person-to-person, person-to-group, person-to-institution, and institution-to-institution interactions, social workers face the issue of conflict resolution as a normal part of their professional activities. The role of social worker in these conflicts has been variously described as advocate, negotiator, and mediator.

Increasingly, social workers and other professionals have chosen or been asked to play the formal role of mediator, that is, a neutral third party who helps people or groups in conflict arrive at mutually acceptable solutions. Social workers mediate issues such as divorce and postdivorce disputes, parent-child conflicts, child welfare issues, and disagreements concerning care of the elderly. In addition, they mediate neighborhood disputes, community conflicts, and personnel issues. As the use of mediators in a variety of circumstances has increased, a concomitant development has taken place regarding the conceptual framework and skills set within which mediators function. Mediation increasingly is viewed as a powerful intervention tool distinct from—albeit informed by—other approaches to client services.

These developments have led the National Association of Social Workers (NASW) to develop and adopt a set of standards that are intended to guide the practice of social workers who function as neutral third parties. These standards were developed to complement the NASW *Code of Ethics* and to be consistent with the standards of major mediation organizations.

Considered desirable for all social work mediators, these standards are designed to do the following:

Reprinted with permission of NASW Press. Copyright 1991, National Association of Social Workers.

- promote the practice of social work mediation.
- provide direction and professional support to social work mediators.
- inform consumers, employers, and referral sources by providing them with a set of expectations for social worker mediators.

Definition of Mediation

Mediation is an approach to conflict resolution in which a mutually acceptable, impartial third party helps the participants negotiate a consensual and informed settlement. In mediation, decision making rests with the parties. Reducing the obstacles on communication, maximizing the exploration of alternatives, and addressing the needs of those who are involved or affected by the issues under discussion are among the mediator's responsibilities.[1]

The mediator is responsible to the system of people or groups involved in a decision-making process. The mediator must provide this system with the structure and tools to make mutually acceptable decisions under difficult circumstances. In this sense, the mediator's role is to empower the system so that it does not have to resort to outside parties, such as the courts or arbitrators, to make the decision.

Principles Guiding Practice Standards for Social Work Mediators

The following principles govern the practice standards for social work mediators:

- Mediation is a method of social work practice.[2]
- The mediator is responsible to the system of parties involved in the dispute or decision-making process, rather than to any single party or client.
- These standards are to be interpreted within the ethical base and values explicated in the NASW *Code of Ethics*.
- Mediators should be familiar with and trained in the theory and practice of mediation. In addition to social work education, the social work mediator needs specific training and practice experience in mediation and conflict resolution.
- Social work mediators should be accountable, both to the client and to colleagues, for the professional and ethical application of their skills and service delivery.

1. Adapted from the *Model Standards of Practice for Family and Divorce Mediators* (Madison, Wisconsin: Association of Family Conciliation Courts, 1984).
2. Method is used to identify specific types of intervention. See Robert L. Barker, The Social Work Dictionary, 2nd ed. (Silver Spring, MD: NASW Press, 1991), p. 144, the term "methods in social work."

- Because mediation is a growing and developing field, these standards should be reviewed regularly to incorporate new developments in the theory and practice of mediation.

Standards for the Practice of Mediation by Social Workers

Standard 1: Social work mediators shall function within the ethics and stated standards and accountability procedures of the social work profession.

Interpretation: All social workers have a fourfold responsibility: to clients, to the profession, to self, and to society. Social work mediators should identify themselves as members of the social work profession. NASW members shall be familiar with and adhere to the NASW *Code of Ethics* and shall cooperate fully and in a timely fashion with the adjudication procedures of the committee of inquiry, peer review, and appropriate state regulatory boards. They should be aware of and adhere to relevant stated professional standards for social work practices.

Standard 2: Social work mediators should remain impartial and neutral toward all parties and issues in a dispute.

Interpretation: Social work mediators should enter into a dispute as a mediator only when they can maintain a stance of impartiality and neutrality. They should inform all involved parties of any development or circumstances that might contribute to the actuality or appearance of bias or favoritism, or that might interfere in any way with their impartial and neutral role. Impartiality refers to the mediator's attitudes toward the issue and people involved. An impartial mediator acts without bias in word and action and is committed to helping all parties rather than to advocating for any single person.

Neutrality relates to the mediator's relationship to the parties and the issues involved. A mediator should have no relationship with parties or vested interests in the substantive outcome that might interfere or appear to interfere with the ability to function in a fair, unbiased, and impartial manner. Any such relationship must be disclosed to the parties before the start of mediation or as soon as knowledge of such a relationship occurs. If any of the parties or the mediator feels that such a relationship has a potential to bias the mediator's performance, the mediator should disqualify himself or herself from acting as a neutral third party.

It is important that the mediator continue to maintain a neutral stance after the mediation is completed to avoid casting doubt on the legitimacy of the mediation that occurred and to ensure continued availability for future interventions as appropriate.

Standard 3: The social work mediator shall not reveal to outside parties any information received during the mediation process.

Interpretation: As with the success of other social work methods, the success of mediation depends largely on the confidentiality of the process. The mediator should not reveal to other parties any information received during private sessions or caucuses without the express permission of the parties from whom the mediator received the information.

Clients and mediators must be aware that there are legal and ethical circumstances in which confidentiality cannot be maintained. These circumstances include but are not limited to the legally mandated requirement to report suspicion of child abuse or a suspicion of bodily harm or violence to another person. Mediators should be aware of any legal or statutory limits placed on mediation in the jurisdiction in which they practice. Exceptions to confidentiality and any other exceptions that may arise because of the circumstances, legal framework, or institutional structure within which mediation occurs should be disclosed to the parties before or during their initial meeting with the mediator.

The mediator should inform the parties of the possibility that the mediator might be compelled to testify in court or in other ways reveal information gathered during the mediation process. Confidentiality applies to the mediator and the mediator's records.

Standard 4: Social work mediators shall assess each conflict and shall proceed only in those circumstances in which mediation is an appropriate procedure.

Interpretation: Mediation is not appropriate for all types of conflict. Mediators should assess whether each party has the capacity to engage in mediation and has the support necessary to be an effective participant. They should inform parties about alternative dispute resolution processes that are available to them and discuss the appropriateness of mediation at the beginning of the intervention.

If mediation is to be effective, parties at a minimum must have the ability to negotiate for themselves, to assess the information relevant to the case, and to understand the implications of the various agreements being considered. Furthermore, the mediation process should address a potential imbalance of power that might exist between the parties. In those situations in which legal advice or other expert consultation is necessary or would serve parties better, the mediator should make the appropriate referrals. The rule of mediator should not be confused with that of an attorney, psychotherapist, or evaluator, even if the mediator also has expertise in one or more of those areas.

Standard 5: The social work mediator shall seek at all times to promote cooperation, to prevent the use of coercive tactics, to foster good-faith bargaining efforts, and to ensure that all agreements are arrived at on a voluntary and informed basis.

Interpretation: Good-faith negotiation means that the parties are making an honest (even if uncertain) attempt to arrive at an agreement, that they are not using the process for destructive purposes, that they are sharing relevant information in a frank and truthful manner, and that they are not using coercive or dishonest bargaining tactics. Although it is not always possible to ensure that all parties are negotiating in good faith, it is the mediator's responsibility to promote and expect good-faith behavior. The mediator should not allow coercive or bad-faith tactics to continue during the mediation process. If the mediator is aware that these tactics are being used and cannot stop their use, the mediation process should be discontinued.

Standard 6: The social work mediator shall recommend termination of the process when it appears that it is no longer in the interest of the parties to continue it.

Interpretation: Mediation should not be used to prolong a dispute unnecessarily or to prevent the use of a more appropriate conflict resolution procedure. Occasionally, it is in the interest of one party to prevent an agreement from being reached. At other times parties are simply unable to agree, and they reach an impasse. The mediator should not continue with the mediation if these situations occur. The mediator should, however, exert every effort to promote the successful conclusion of mediation and should not abandon the effort prematurely.

Standard 7: The social work mediator is responsible for helping the parties arrive at a clearly stated, mutually understood, and mutually acceptable agreement.

Interpretation: It is the mediator's responsibility to conduct the mediation process, not to promote any particular substantive outcome. Frequently, the solution that the mediator believes best meets the interests of the parties is not the one that parties select. The mediator's role is to conduct a fair process, not to promote a particular outcome. The mediator should try to ensure that the agreement, whether partial or full, reflects a fair and good-faith negotiation effort. If the mediator feels that the agreement is illegal, grossly unfair to a participating or unrepresented party, the result of bad-faith bargaining, or based on inaccurate information, the mediator has the obligation to make this known to the parties involved and to try to correct the problem. When parties agree to an unconscionable outcome, an illegal agreement, or one based on dishonesty or misrepresentation, mediators should disassociate themselves from the agreement in accordance with standards of confidentiality.

Standard 8: The social work mediator shall develop an unbiased written agreement that specifies the issues resolved during the course of mediation.

Interpretation: The written agreements should, to the extent possible, be in the language of the parties themselves, and should be clearly understood by them. The actual determination of whether an agreement is legally binding constitutes a legal judgment. However, it is important for parties to know that any agreement may be legally binding and should not be finalized without the appropriate legal advice.

Standard 9: Social work mediators shall have training in both the procedural and substantive aspects of mediation.

Interpretation: Social workers should mediate disputes only in those areas for which they are qualified by training or experience. If they have no substantive knowledge in a particular area, they should obtain it, work with a qualified co-mediator, have appropriate consultation, or refer the dispute elsewhere. Mediators should obtain formal training in the mediation process, and beginning mediators should work under a qualified supervisor. Formal training is currently available through professional seminars and workshops and university based programs. The standards for training obtained by social work mediators should be in keeping with those currently accepted by the leading professional organizations of mediators in the area in which the social worker is functioning. Social work mediators should upgrade their skills and knowledge in the field of conflict resolution through continuing education programs and participation in relevant professional conferences and seminars.

Occasionally, mediators will be asked to mediate a dispute in which they do not have substantive expertise. If a mediator skilled in that specialty is not available, the mediator either should work with a co-mediator or consultant who is familiar with the substantive area or take the time to become familiar enough with the area to be able to help parties explore their interests and options in an informed manner.

Standard 10: A social work mediator shall have a clearly defined and equitable fee structure.

Interpretation: The fee structure should be presented to all parties at the outset of the mediation. Fees should reflect standards of impartiality and neutrality. All compensation mediators receive for their services should be known to all involved parties, and mediators should accept no side payments or fees based on the outcome of the mediation process.

If at all possible, either a neutral party or agency should cover the cost of mediation or the cost should be split equitably (although not necessarily equally) among the parties. If one party is supposed to pay the entire fee, this should be known and agreed to by all parties at the outset. Under no circumstances should the fee structure give the mediator a vested interest in a particular outcome. Fees should therefore not be contingent on the nature of the agreement or even on the achievement of an agreement.

Standard 11: The mediator shall not use any information obtained during the mediation process for personal benefit or for the benefit of any group or organization with which the mediator is associated.

Interpretation: Mediators are often given access to information that could be used for personal or organizational benefit. It is inappropriate for the mediator to compromise the mediation process by using this information outside the mediation process.

Standard 12: Social work mediators shall be prepared to work collaboratively as appropriate with other professionals and in conformance to the philosophy of social work and mediation.

Interpretation: The mediator should not separately mediate any dispute that already is being mediated. If another mediator has been involved in the case, the mediator should ascertain that this relationship has been terminated before agreeing to become involved.

In cases in which a co-mediation procedure is being used, all the mediators involved should keep each other informed about activities and developments relevant to the case, and the clients should know at the outset that this information sharing will occur. Co-mediators should handle any disagreements they may have in a collaborative manner.

Mediators should respect the involvement of legal, mental health, social services, and other professionals involved in the dispute or with the parties and should work with them in a cooperative and respectful manner.

ABOUT THE
CONTRIBUTORS

Allan Edward Barsky, Ph.D., is assistant professor in the Faculty of Social Work at the University of Calgary and a director of The Network. He has a combined educational background in social work and law, and experience in mediating family, community, and cross-cultural disputes.

Emily M. Brown, M.S.W., is a family mediator, therapist, and trainer, and director of the Key Bridge Therapy and Mediation Center in Arlington, Virginia. She was a founding board member of the Academy of Family Mediators and the first chair of the Academy's Education Committee. She is on the Editorial Board of *Mediation Quarterly,* has written numerous articles on mediation and the emotional process of divorce, and is the author of *Patterns of Infidelity and Their Treatment.*

Jeanne A. Clement, Ed.D., is associate professor in nursing and psychiatry in the College of Nursing at Ohio State University. A fellow of the American Academy of Nursing, she is certified as a specialist in adult psychiatric–mental health nursing. Her areas of interest include practice with persons with serious mental disabilities and their families, mediation, and health care policy. She teaches mediation to graduate students in nursing, psychology, and law and has published in the areas of family practice, dual diagnoses, and mental health mediation. She is co-founder and member of the advisory board of PEERS Unlimited, a consumer owned and operated peer support service.

Enid Opal Cox, D.S.W., is professor of social work and director of the Institute of Gerontology at the University of Denver. Dr. Cox is co-author of *Empowerment-Oriented Practice with the Elderly* with Dr. Ruth Parsons, has research, practice, and teaching experience related to elderly care receiving, caregiving, older workers, and ethnic minority elders, and has several publications in these areas. She also has teaching and research interests in social welfare policy, the history of social welfare, and indirect practice interventions with special emphasis on empowerment-oriented approaches.

Jeanne Etter, Ph.D., is director of Teamwork for Children in Eugene, Oregon. She has published widely in the areas of adoption and permanency planning, and has specialized in adoption mediation in her practice during the past ten years.

Lois Gold, M.S.W., is a family mediator and therapist in private practice in Portland, Oregon, and provides training and consultation in mediation and dispute resolution to schools, the business sector, and government agencies. She is a past president of the Academy of Family Mediators and has been an adjunct faculty member of the Graduate School of Social Work at Portland State University. She is the author of *Between Love and Hate: A Guide to Civilized Divorce.*

Lynn Carp Jacob, M.S.W., has been mediating since 1982. She served on the board of the Academy of Family Mediators from 1990–1996 and was the 1994–1995 president of the Academy. From 1987–1990, she was president of the Mediation Council of Illinois. She is on the faculty of the Chicago Center for Family Health where she teaches an internship on mediation. She has a private practice in both mediation and family therapy, and has written several articles on mediating postdecree cases, boundaries between mediation and therapy, and potential ethical dilemmas, as well as a chapter on facilitating healthy divorce processes in the *Clinical Handbook of Couple Therapy,* edited by Neil Jacobson and Alan Gurman, with Froma Walsh and Virginia Simons.

Harry Kaminsky, M.S.W., is a regional vice-president of the American Arbitration Association. Mr. Kaminsky co-developed and implemented the Community Mediation Program for the City of Phoenix and was its founding director from 1986 to 1992. He has also practiced as a family mediator and a dispute resolution systems design consultant and trainer. He has been a faculty associate at the Arizona State University School of Social Work since 1987, where he teaches graduate-level courses in dispute resolution.

Nancy M. Kaplan, M.S.W., is director of Conflict Resolution Unlimited in Bellevue, Washington, where she has been developing and establishing student mediation programs in elementary, middle, and high schools. She is a former board member of the Academy of Family Mediators.

Edward Kruk, Ph.D., is associate professor in the School of Social Work, University of British Columbia. His research has focused on divorce, remarriage, and family mediation, including noncustodial fathers' disengagement from their children's lives subsequent to divorce, the impact of divorce on the grandparent-grandchild relationship, and the working methods of family mediators. He has worked in the fields of family therapy (Catholic Family Services, Calgary), health care (Royal Hospital for Sick Children, Edinburgh), school social work (Metro Separate School Board, Toronto), and child welfare (Metro and Catholic Children's Aid Societies, Toronto), and is currently practicing in Vancouver as a family mediator. He is author of *Divorce and Disengagement: Patterns of Fatherhood Within and Beyond Marriage* and has published extensively in social work, conflict resolution, family therapy, and gender studies journals.

Michelle LeBaron, LL.B., M.A., is associate professor of conflict analysis and resolution at George Mason University. She has degrees in both law and counseling psychology, and has taught at the university and college level for twenty years. She was the director of the Multiculturalism and Dispute Resolution Project at the University of Victoria, British Columbia, from 1990 to

1992, and has designed training and interventions in intercultural, environmental and public policy, family, commercial, and workplace conflicts. Her research includes multiculturalism, gender, leadership, and spirituality as these relate to conflict resolution.

Peter R. Maida, Ph.D., J.D., is the director of mediation services and training at the Key Bridge Therapy and Mediation Center and one of the directors of the Key Bridge Foundation for Education and Research in Arlington, Virginia. He was on faculty at the University of Maryland for twenty-three years and has had a private mediation practice for fifteen years. Having served on several journal editorial boards and published extensively in the field, Dr. Maida was editor of the *Mediation Quarterly* from 1989 to 1995. He is a member of the Academy of Family Mediators, Association of Family and Conciliation Courts, National Association for Community Mediation, and Society of Professionals in Dispute Resolution. He is currently training mediators in a nationwide project funded by the U.S. Department of Justice to mediate ADA complaints.

Judy Mares-Dixon, M.A., is program manager with CDR Associates in Boulder, Colorado. She has an extensive background in resolving equal employment opportunity and other employee relations disputes, and race relations and civil rights disputes. She has designed conflict resolution systems for large employers and conducts training programs in dispute systems design for CDR Associates. She is the former director of the City of Boulder Division of Human Rights and Community Mediation Services (1988–1992); program manager for the Colorado Department of Social Services (1986–1988); and director of the Boulder County Center for People with Disabilities (1977–1986). She has applied alternative dispute resolution procedures in the private, nonprofit, and public sectors at the local, state, and federal levels, and facilitated strategic planning sessions in both the public and private sectors.

Freda Betz Martin, M.S.W., is a medical social worker at Burnaby Hospital, an acute and extended care facility in Vancouver, British Columbia. Her research has focused on the interdisciplinary division of labor in health care settings and the delivery of clinical services by hospital social workers.

Bernard Mayer, Ph.D., is a partner with CDR Associates in Boulder, Colorado. He has worked as a mediator and trainer in conflict resolution for sixteen years, having designed and implemented conflict resolution programs in child protection, mental health, and intercultural disputes. He was responsible for drafting the National Association of Social Workers Standards of Practice for Social Work Mediators.

Jennifer O'Callaghan, M.S.W., is a medical social worker at the University of British Columbia site of the Vancouver Hospital working in the area of acute and extended care. She has over ten years' experience working in health care institutions, primarily in the fields of geriatrics and family practice.

Ruth J. Parsons, Ph.D., is a professor in the University of Denver Graduate School of Social Work. Her teaching and research interests are in the areas of generalist social work practice, social work with groups, the mediation role in social work, and social work practice with the elderly. Her practice experience includes direct practice, integrated practice, and program administration and planning with children, families, and the elderly. She has published in the fields of aging, mediation, caregiving, empowerment, and integrated practice. Dr. Parsons is co-author of *The Integration of Social Work Practice* with Professor James Jorgensen and Dr. Santos Hernandez, *Empowerment-Oriented Social Work Practice with the Elderly* with Dr. Enid Opal Cox, and *Empowerment-Oriented Practice: A Source Book* with Dr. Enid Opal Cox and Dr. Lorraine Gutierrez.

Andrew I. Schwebel, Ph.D., was professor in the Department of Psychology at Ohio State University. He taught mediation to graduate students in psychology, nursing, and law, and his research interests included community psychology, focusing on the role of universities in assisting in the planning, delivery, and evaluation of human services, and mediation in the mental health field. He authored numerous books, monographs, and journal articles on psychology and mental disability, divorce, and mental health mediation, and psychological principles of horticultural therapy. He was also a member of the advisory board of PEERS Unlimited. Dr. Schwebel died shortly after completing the mental health chapter for this book with Jeanne Clement, with whom he had an eight-year history of collaboration. He will be sorely missed by his colleagues.

Mark S. Umbreit, Ph.D., is director of the Center for Restorative Justice and Mediation, and associate professor in the School of Social Work at the University of Minnesota. Dr. Umbreit serves as a program consultant and mediation trainer for the U.S. Department of Justice and is a practicing mediator. He is author of *Victim Meets Offender: The Impact of Restorative Justice and Mediation* (1994) and *Mediating Interpersonal Conflicts: A Pathway to Peace* (1995), as well as numerous journal articles and research reports.

Ann Yellott, Ph.D., has over twenty years' experience in facilitating collaborative group processes, developing and managing community-based social service agencies, and teaching courses in communication, crisis intervention, mediation, negotiation, and consensus building. She was director of the Community Mediation Program of Our Town Family Center in Tucson for six years and started her own dispute resolution business in 1991. She has served on the Arizona Commission on the Courts, was named to the Supreme Court's Advisory Committee on Alternative Dispute Resolution, and has served as president of the Arizona Dispute Resolution Association. She is currently a faculty member at both the University of Phoenix and the Desert Institute of Healing Arts.